Predestination, Grace, and Free Will

Predestination
Grace, and Free Will

✝

by Dom M. John Farrelly, O.S.B.
ST. ANSELM'S ABBEY, *Washington, D.C.*

THE NEWMAN PRESS · WESTMINSTER, MARYLAND
1964

Preface

THE PURPOSE of this study is to examine the harmony that exists between the primacy of God and the freedom of man in the movement of man toward his eternal fulfillment in the present supernatural order. God's primacy in this mystery is exercised through predestination and grace, and man's freedom through the acts of his free will; the central object of this study, then, is the harmony that exists between God's predestination and grace on the one hand and man's free will acts on the other. Though the grounds for the Church's teaching concerning the *fact* of this harmony will be evident, and the objections raised against this fact answered, our central interest here is in the examination of the *nature* of this harmony. How is it that God's primacy in the supernatural and natural orders and his perfections of being, intellect, will, providence, and causality that constitute his absolute primacy leave man completely free in the actions by which he determines and moves himself to his own perfection? And how is it that man's freedom to determine himself to act or not, to choose to perform one act rather than another, to submit himself to God's primacy in his free acts or to refuse such submission leaves him completely subject to this primacy of God?

After clarifying the nature of the problem by contrasting the main explanations currently given by Catholic theologians (namely, those of Banez, Molina, and the schools associated with them), the sources of the difficulties inherent in these theories and of the differences between them will be identified. These basic matters must be examined in an attempt to gain further understanding of the mystery. Then, the teaching of Scripture and tradition concerning these central questions will be studied, and the conclusions reached will be related to the Thomist and the Molinist theories. After this, the mystery that is expressed in Scripture and tradition will be studied through an analysis of the naturally knowable realities involved, made in accord with the philosophical principles of St. Thomas. This choice of his philosophy is based on a personal conviction of its validity after many years of study devoted to it; the justification, however, of this conviction as it refers to the basic elements of his thought will be found, not here, but in St. Thomas himself and in the many excellent modern works devoted to him. Within the limits of this work it is adequate to presuppose this as a common philosophical background, since those who do not share it with us can examine its validity in other works, and the main proponents of the philosophically different explanations of this mystery among Catholics are united in their acceptance of the basic elements found in St. Thomas' philosophy. In this part the first question will concern God's causality of the created act and specifically of man's individual free act and the succession of free acts by which he moves himself toward his fulfillment. The second question will concern the relationship of God's will, knowledge, and providence respectively to the free acts of the rational creature. We shall make clear in these successive stages the light these natural truths cast on the supernatural mystery.

It may seem fruitless to attempt a new study of this mystery that has for so long been involved in controversy. However, a re-examination of this matter seems to be justified. Theologians generally find both the Thomist and the Molinist explanations of the mystery quite unsatisfactory in some aspects, and each side defends its explanation as a whole only as the most coherent theory presently available. Moreover, the advances made in theology during the last half century give much new evidence relevant to the mystery and the controversy that surrounds it. In the field of biblical studies great advances have been made in the understanding of scriptural doctrine and of the method most appropriate for discovering it; and some of this directly affects the texts that Banez, Molina, and their followers used to sustain their particular explanations of the harmony between God's primacy and man's freedom. In the field of the history of doctrine such a vast amount

vi

of work has been done in the analysis of the teaching of Fathers, theologians, councils, and of other ecclesiastical documents; and the fruits of this work have been so presented that it is now possible to make a more adequate estimate of the teaching of tradition on this subject. And finally, recent studies on the theology and philosophy of St. Thomas give us a grasp of his teaching in general that helps us to gain a more objective understanding of his thought on a particular problem and a better criterion by which to judge later interpretations of his thought. Hence, the dissatisfaction with the explanations of this mystery currently given and the relevance to this subject of recent theological advances give solid grounds for hope that a re-examination of the matter will be both timely and fruitful.

That renewed study of this mystery is also imperative seems evident from various considerations. In the first place, the rejection of God manifested by Communism in the East and by the various forms and degrees of secularism in the West is motivated in great part by the conviction that God is such an obstacle to man's true fulfillment and freedom that he and his law must be rejected if man is to gain his human goal. Men of this conviction look to the initiative of human strength and prudence unlimited by the norms of an objective moral law for the solution of the problems of society. A true understanding of the relation between God's initiative and man's freedom will show how erroneous, misleading, and ultimately futile such an outlook is. Hence, study of this mystery is necessary to reawaken in men a realization of their need to draw strength from God and to seek the solution of individual and social problems through cooperation with the guidance of God's providence manifested in the objective moral order he has established. In the second place, the doctrinal source of the sixteenth-century Protestant revolt from the Church was Luther's understanding of the relation of grace (and thus predestination) to free will. Further study of this subject will serve the cause of the ecumenical movement by clarifying somewhat the doctrine of revelation on a matter that has been an important source of division between the Church and Protestants. Thirdly, one of the great needs of our time is the increase of spiritual vigor and proper direction in the lives and activities of those who, as members of the Church, possess, in a privileged way, truth. To bring this about in his own day, St. Paul (as will be evident later) taught Christians how God's predestination and grace were related to their free will. So in our day this doctrine should be studied to strengthen the bases of true Christian hope and to promote an understanding, on the model of God's providential activity with men, of the true purpose of Christian activity. It is the relevance of this subject to these present individual and social needs that makes a re-examination of it timely and imperative.

Study of this matter has led me to certain opinions that differ from explanations currently given by Catholic theologians, and hence it is fitting and necessary that these opinions and the reasons for them be presented clearly and fully so that their truth or error may be immediately evident to theologians. These opinions I present as tentative and submit to the judgment of theologians, and I shall be the first to modify or change them on the submission of proof to the contrary. In my study and teaching of this matter, however, I have become increasingly persuaded of the correctness of the explanation given here. This, of course, in no way implies a desire to attempt to impose it upon others. In a matter that is freely discussed I have a right only to present all the evidence for a view that seems correct to me. In a question of this importance it does not seem right to weaken the presentation of this evidence out of a false sensitivity to the feelings of others that may, after all, not be involved. Modern historical method forces us at times to attach names to theories from which we differ, a practice not common to the theologians of the Middle Ages, it seems; but arguments directed to a theory are in no way directed to the name to which it is attached.

I originally wrote this work under the title *Predestination and Grace: A Re-examination in the Light of Modern Biblical and Philosophical Developments*, in partial fulfillment of the requirements for a doctorate in theology at the Catholic University of America. Only very minor changes have been made. The bibliography has been omitted since the material relevant to this subject is vast and in large part of minor value, and the references found in footnotes are adequate as initial guides to further study. I owe much to my major professor, the Rev. Eugene M. Burke, C.S.P., for directing this study, and to the Rev. Eamon R. Carroll, O. Carm., and the Rev. John J. Shinners for reading and correcting the manuscript. I also am indebted to Dr. Thomas Prufer of The Catholic University of America for reading the book and making some valuable suggestions concerning the philosophical analysis involved. And above all, I am deeply indebted to the Right Rev. Dom H. Alban Boultwood, O.S.B., Abbot of St. Anselm's Abbey, for the opportunity to engage in higher studies, and his support over the years that led to this work's completion.

Contents

Predestination, Grace, and Free Will

Principal Abbreviations

CG   Aquinas, St. Thomas, *Summae contra gentiles libri quattuor*, Rome, 1927.

D   Denzinger, H., and others, *Enchridion symbolorum*, 29 ed., Freiburg i Br., 1953.

DAFC   *Dictionnaire d'apologétique de la foi catholique.*

DBS   *Dictionnaire de la bible. Supplément.*

DTC   *Dictionnaire de théologie catholique.*

In Sent.   *Commentaria in libros IV sententiarum Petri Lombardi*, by various authors.

In ST   *Commentaria in Summam theologicam S. Thomae Aquinatis*, by various authors.

MG   Migne, J. P., *Patrologia graeca.*

ML   Migne, J. P., *Patrologia latina.*

Sent.   Peter the Lombard, *Libri IV sententiarum*, 2 vols., Quaracchi, 1916.

ST   Aquinas, St. Thomas, *Summa theologia*, 6 vols., Rome, 1927–8.

xiv

CHAPTER ONE

The Problematic

NOW WE *know that for those who love God all things work together unto good, for those who, according to his purpose, are saints through his call. For those whom he has foreknown he has also predestined to become conformed to the image of his Son, that he should be the firstborn among many brethren. And those whom he has predestined, them he has also called; and those whom he has called, them he has also justified, and those whom he has justified, them he has also glorified.*[1]

By these words St. Paul unveiled to the Christians of Rome the mystery of God's predestination of the elect to their eternal glory, a mystery so central to Christian life and yet so obscure that it has never ceased to grip men's minds and hearts or to impel them to seek a deeper understanding of its meaning. For one who accepts the implications of the Christian message, there is no difficulty in realizing the necessity of this predestination. The fact that God does predestine men to eternal beatitude is in accord with other revealed and naturally known truths. In the Bible, God's care to give to creatures what they need is a frequently recurring theme. And by reason we can know that all the perfections or accomplishments that creatures have, they have from God who, acting through his intelligence and will, is the source of all good. The creature's perfection is not simply or primarily the being and powers which it gains with its existence; it is even more properly its achievement of the purpose or end that perfects its being and

[1] Rom. 8:28–30. Unless otherwise noted, the New Testament is quoted according to the Confraternity of Christian Doctrine translation (Paterson, 1941).

1

powers. And as God is the source of its initial being, so too he is all the more the cause of its perfection. This activity of God in directing a creature to its perfection leads us to assert within God an eternal intention and plan ordering the creature to its fulfillment. And this is called *providence* through analogy with man's prudence by which he orders to a goal himself or others over whom he has authority.

Among creatures in the actual order of divine providence, man (and what is said of man is true too of the angels in this matter) is in a special condition in relation to his perfection. For God has, in his divine plan and in the created perfection he confers to bring it about, set for the rational creature an end that wholly transcends the creature's powers to gain for himself in the natural order of things. He has raised the creature to a share in the perfection proper to himself and thus to a fulfillment not owed to or attainable by any creature as such. The implications of this for our purpose may be clarified by an image St. Thomas uses.[2] An arrow can impose upon itself neither the direction nor the impulse necessary to reach its target, and thus can reach it only if sent by one who has this directive and impelling power in himself. Likewise, since the eternal beatitude of the rational creatures is beyond powers native to him, he can reach it only if God directs and moves him to it. The eternal plan in the mind of God directing the elect to this goal is an aspect of God's providence, but it is called more specifically *predestination*. Predestination, therefore, indicates the will and plan in the mind of God that orders his activity in bringing the rational creature to the goal of eternal life. And those who are thus brought to eternal life are called predestined.

Since predestination itself is an eternal plan, it is wholly within the divine mind; its fulfillment in the creature is through God's governance, and more specifically his governance in the supernatural order. The means by which he brings about his eternal purpose are both external and internal to the predestined subject. For example, those that are at least partially external are Christ, his salvific work of teaching and redeeming man, and the continuation of this work through the Church, the ministers of his word and redemptive activity, the sacraments and other elements of God's supernatural governance common to all. Among these

---

[2] See *Summa theologica* (Rome, 1927), 1.23.1.

2

external means are also those that are special to each individual, such as an experience, an example, an enlightening word that turns his mind and heart toward God. The means interior to man by which the divine intention is effected is grace through which man receives God's movement and direction to eternal life. There is habitual grace that raises man's being and powers to an enduring ability to elicit acts proportioned to eternal life; and there are the graces called actual which, through illumination of the intellect and inspiration of the will, bring man to elicit particular acts that move him to his eternal goal.

But this rational creature who is the subject of God's predestination and governance is a free agent. He decides his own values, chooses his own goals, guides his own conduct, and imposes a direction upon his own activity. God, who has given to him this nature, does not act contrary to it in the supernatural order. From what has already been said, it is true that the rational creature is the passive recipient of predestination and the means that bring it about. But he is not only passive; he is active, for he is free, and that is to be self-moving and self-determining. Hence God fulfills his purpose in bringing man to his eternal beatitude, not by suppressing his activity, but by gaining his cooperation through grace to perform the acts necessary to fulfill the divine purpose with him. It is within the context of these certainties that difficulties arise in the explanation of the mystery of predestination for the Catholic theologian. They center around the relation between predestination and grace on the one hand and the free response of man or refusal of that response on the other. These difficulties reach the very core of the Christian life, for they concern the most intimate relation between man's personal freedom and God as affecting that freedom. These difficulties are profoundly intellectual and they are profoundly personal, for on the answer given to them depends man's guidance of his relation to God working within him. Perhaps the best way to see what problems are involved (as a preparation for our own search for some understanding of the mystery) is to outline the main explanations of the mystery currently given by theologians.

These explanations were substantially formulated in the sixteenth century, and they in turn developed from previous attempts to explain, attack, or defend the mystery of predestination and grace. The Greek Fathers of the Church defended man's freedom before God's choice against the determinism of the gnostics, while St. Augustine preserved the gratuity of predestination against the self-sufficiency of the Pelagians. The Gottschalk affair in the Middle Ages gave the Church an opportunity to deny in the mystery any implications of injustice on God's part toward the damned or of a predestination to sin. The great thirteenth-century theologians, in general, tried to integrate the teachings of the Greek Fathers and of Augustine in their vision of this mystery. But after their time there were many narrower interpretations of the mystery, some tending toward a form of Pelagianism that was prophetic of the Renaissance humanism and others presenting a rigid deterministic predestinationism. While the latter explanation of the mystery was commonly accepted by the Protestants, the Church in the Council of Trent reiterated the traditional doctrine of God's merciful initiative and man's perfect freedom in the order of salvation.

It was in this sixteenth century, when there was a dichotomy in Christendom between a radical supernaturalism and a radical naturalism, that there emerged the two prominent and clearly distinct Catholic interpretations of the mystery of predestination. As was true of the great defenders of the faith in previous ages, each of these schools was an attempt to preserve the doctrine from contemporary errors threatening its purity. Dominic Banez, the principal spokesman for the school since called Thomist or Banezian, in explaining the doctrine of predestination was particularly careful to defend it against Pelagian interpretations. Louis Molina, on the other hand, the foremost exponent of the doctrine of the opposed school that has since borne his name, stated explicitly that he was harmonizing the doctrine of predestination, grace, God's foreknowledge, providence, and reprobation with the truth of human freedom denied by the Protestants. Thus, though both of these theologians drew on the same heritage of Scripture and tradition and even presented their doctrine in the form of commentaries on the same questions in the *Summa theologica* of St. Thomas,[3] their interpretations of the doctrine are quite different in detail and in spirit.

[3] Dominic Banez, *Scholastica commentaria in primam partem Summae theologicae s. Thomae Aquinatis* 1 (Madrid, 1934). Louis Molina, *Liberi*

4

1. *The Answer of Banez*

The complementary truths that form for Banez the foundation for any adequate explanation of the revealed mystery of God's plan and causality that lead man to his eternal beatitude are the complete primacy of God as first cause and the complete dependence of the creature upon God in its action. God is the source of all the perfection of the creature. He gives to the creature, not only the power of acting which it then puts into effect, but also the act itself of the creature. Its action is a passage from potency to act, and it is thus a gain of being, of goodness, and of perfection. Since its act is an act of potency and every created perfection is a participation of the perfection of God, the creature's act itself is a participation in the act of God through God's causality. What is true of the creature as such does not cease to be true when the creature considered is man, for this is a metaphysical truth that depends upon the nature of the creature as creature and God as God. Nor does it cease to be true when the relation considered between God and man is the supernatural relation in which God elicits a specific free supernatural act or gives to man the gift of eternal life. Any theory attempting to explain predestination and grace that is inconsistent with this cannot be true. The same must be said of any theory that detracts from divine omnipotence. Scripture, St. Augustine, St. Thomas, and the Church frequently teach that if God wants something to occur, no creature can prevent it from occurring. Once more this is a truth that does not lose its force when the creature considered is man with his free will, or man acting freely in the supernatural order. If God wants a man to be saved, or if he wants him to perform a good act, it would detract from the divine power to say that he was prevented by man from fulfilling his will. God would not be omnipotent if he could not gain the created will's consent, for there would be something he could not do.

This, of course, is not to say that God's action or will destroys the contingency of the acts of contingent created causes. God's

---

arbitrii cum gratiae donis, divina praescientia, providentia, praedestinatione, et reprobatione concordia (ed. Rabeneck; Madrid, 1953).

perfection does not militate against the perfection of his creature, nor does his causality diminish the causality of his creature. In fact, God has willed that some acts of creatures take place contingently, and hence he has fitted contingent created causes for these effects, as he has willed that other acts take place necessarily and hence has fitted necessary created causes for them. Properly speaking, however, a created effect is called necessary or contingent with reference to its immediate cause, not to the will and providence of God, since "every effect in its relation to God takes place infallibly nor can it be prevented."[4] God does not, as some think, act in a necessary way with creatures of necessary action and in a contingent manner with free creatures; his action cannot be impeded even when it reaches free causes. "He reaches all things strongly and sweetly, therefore, insofar as he most efficaciously performs what he wills, not destroying the condition of secondary causes."[5] God's will is so powerful that it causes not only the act of the creature, but even the manner of its act. So he causes not only the act of man's free will, but the very freedom of this act. Hence, the act is free with reference to the human will; but with reference to God, it is necessary on the supposition that God wills it. This necessity is called a *necessity of consequence* to indicate that *if* God wills it, it will take place. God causes the act to be elicited in a free manner; so there is not a *consequent necessity* in the act, or the necessity there is in creatures without free will.

In terms of these basic truths we can explain the mystery of God's relation to the free will of man to some extent. The mystery does not cease to exist; but since we are approaching it from certain truths, we can know that the mystery that remains results from the transcendence of the truth and not from the error of our principles. We shall examine the relationship between God and the free creature first in the order of intention, i.e., God's eternal will, knowledge, and plan for the creature, and then in the order of the relation of grace to the free will act.

[4] In *ST*, 1.19.8, p. 430. For Banez's explanation of the harmony between God's will, knowledge, providence, predestination, and free will, see his commentaries on the appropriate questions in the first part of the *Summa*, namely, QQ. 19 (especially articles 6, 8), 14 (especially 13), 22 (especially 1), and 23 (especially 2, 3, 5).
[5] *Ibid.*

6

It follows from what we have said of the divine causality that, as St. Thomas expressed it, "the will of God is the cause of goodness in things. And hence from this fact are some things better, that God desires for them a greater good; so it follows that he loves more those things that are better."[6] Goodness is a perfection of being which has as its first cause the free will of God. So a difference among creatures in the goodness that they possess must be reduced ultimately to God's will as first cause. If one is more perfect than another, it is because God has freely willed a greater good for it. And this continues to be true in the supernatural order. Indeed, it is true by still another title in this order because of the gratuity of the order of grace, the gratuity then of the term of grace (which is eternal glory), the means to this (which itself is grace and particularly the grace of perseverance), and the divine intention granting this to an individual (which is the divine choice). The total gratuity of God's gift is frequently expressed by St. Paul, for example in the ninth chapter of *Romans*, where he proves this gratuity from God's choice of Jacob over Esau before they had done any good or evil, a choice God made *that according to choice the purpose of God might stand, not from works but from him who calls*. This is the explanation of God's statement through the prophet Malachias quoted there by St. Paul: *Jacob I have loved, but Esau I have hated.*[7] This doctrine on the gratuity of eternal life is also constantly defended by St. Augustine, whose works on grace are frequently quoted by Banez in support of his views. Corresponding somewhat to the different effects of God's love for the predestined, Banez states that one can imagine in the simple unity of God various acts.

> The acts which we can imagine being in the divine mind both with reference to all and those proper to the predestined are these. God knew all possible men, among whom he loved certain ones with reference to natural existence, and these he willed to create. Among these he loved some still further for the supernatural end. This

---

[6] *ST*, 1.20.4.

[7] In *ST*, 1.23.5, p. 523, where Banez quotes Rom. 9:11 in the Vulgate, "ut secundum electionem propositum Dei maneret non ex operibus, sed ex vocante dictum est ei. . . . Jacob dilexi, Esau autem odio habui." Throughout his commentary on this article, he uses various texts in Rom. 9 to prove the gratuity of predestination. Also he uses 2 Cor. 3:5; John 15:5; Eph. 1:4–5; Rom. 8:28.

divine love is called choice insofar as he separated these for himself from among others whom he willed to create. And finally he predestined these chosen ones; that is, he foresaw and ordained that through definite supernatural means, they would effectively arrive at their supernatural end.[8]

What is true of the gift of eternal life is true too of the gift of each grace. If two men experience the same temptation and one overcomes, it is due to grace and not to his own will that the one is better than the other.

This doctrine concerning God's will as the source of all good of the creature is confirmed by St. Thomas' doctrine of the divine knowledge of created things and specifically of the free future act of the creature. Banez vigorously rejects Molina's doctrine of God's knowledge as false to the principles of St. Thomas as well as to the principles of sound philosophy. St. Thomas rejected any explanation of God's knowledge of the creature and its acts that would put within God's intellect a passive determination brought about by the creature. And he taught that divine knowledge was, like that of the artist with reference to his work, a causative knowledge. In the first place, God knows his own essence perfectly and in it sees all the possible ways in which he can be imitated by creatures. Besides seeing all possibles, God sees too all things in his divine essence that he will actually effect in time. As the artist knows what color and shape his work will take because he decides it, so too God knows all creatures and their acts because by his own divine will he determines efficaciously what they will be. It is, then, the decree of the divine will that is the medium of God's knowledge of what the creature will do. This is not to be understood in the sense Molina asserts it, for he holds that between his knowledge of the possibles and his knowledge of what the free will of the creature will actually do, God has a knowledge of what the will would do given any arrangement of circumstances. In this explanation, Banez holds, God's knowledge is not causative; and the act of the divine will does not intrinsically cause the created free act, but is restricted to the determination of the circumstances and graces that will surround the created will. Such a divine will is not effective of itself over the created will, but simply over the choice of circumstances, and this is to withdraw

[8] In ST 1.23.2, p. 480.

8

the highest acts of the creature from the intrinsic causality of God. Banez holds, on the other hand, that God decrees what the created will actually will do, and this decree is intrinsically efficacious of itself in bringing about the intrinsic determination of the will in accord with its nature. It is in virtue of such decrees that God has infallibly certain knowledge of all future free acts of creatures.

It is true that St. Thomas taught that God sees the free acts of the creatures through their presence to his eternal knowledge, but he did not mean by this to contradict what he had taught previously on the causative character of divine knowledge. His purpose was simply to show that the divine knowledge was intuitive as well as causative. And "even if God did not know contingent futures as present in his eternity but only in their causes, his knowledge would be certain and infallible . . . for knowledge that is through determined and complete causes is certain and infallible."[9] It is true also that St. Thomas taught that the free future acts of creatures could not be known with certainty in their causes. Here, however, he was referring to causes of the free act insofar as they were indetermined and impedible, and this is true only of created causes. Since God knows free acts insofar as their immediate causes are subject to the determination of the divine will and knowledge, he does know them in their causes, not merely as contingent, but as determined and efficaciously bringing about the act. Hence, for God, knowledge of free acts in the cause which is his own divine decree is infallibly certain knowledge.[10]

As the passage quoted above on the divine acts concerning the predestined shows, Banez's doctrine on predestination itself is wholly contained in the principles on the gratuity of the gift of eternal life, the divine will as the first and efficacious cause of this gift, and the divine knowledge as causative and as depending upon the intrinsically effective decree of the divine will. Providence and predestination are acts of the divine intellect and will, and thus an explanation of the latter is an explanation of the former. In general God's providence, or the plan pre-existing in the divine mind ordering creatures to their end, must have the efficacy of the divine will and knowledge as its own properties. Providence itself, then, presupposes God's effective will of the

9 In *ST*, 1.14.13, p. 352.
10 See *ibid.*, p. 351.

9

end, and it includes means that are not only apt but infallibly effective in bringing the creature to its perfection. Otherwise it would be imperfect and applied to the creature in vain.[11] Predestination, which is God's providence over the elect, presupposes God's will of the term of beatitude for the predestined subject; and of its nature it consists in a "plan pre-existing in the divine mind about the efficacious means to achieve the end."[12] The supernatural means by which the end is gained for the adult are the supernatural acts he performs; but since they are means to the end, "good works are not foreseen as preceding predestination but as infallibly following it,"[13] for it is characteristic of prudence to determine the means only after the end has been determined.

But so far this leaves untouched the problem of how there can be in God a truly universal salvific will asserted by St. Paul who taught that God *wishes all men to be saved and to come to the knowledge of the truth*.[14] It also does not explain how the divine will and intellect are related to the evil of sin and of man's loss of eternal beatitude. In short, what is the lot of those for whom there does not exist an eternal divine decree of predestination or of determination to a supernaturally or naturally good act? Here Banez admits there is mystery, but it is a mystery made, not by man's theory, but by God's revelation.

Some light is cast upon this mystery through the distinction drawn by St. Thomas in dependence upon St. John Damascene between God's antecedent and consequent will. Antecedent to his consideration of all the particular circumstances, God wills that all men be saved; but consequent upon such consideration, he wills to reprobate some men. In other words, he does not choose them for eternal life. Scripture itself teaches this, as the statement Paul quotes from Malachias indicates in its context in the ninth chapter of *Romans: Jacob I have loved, but Esau I have hated*.[15] Statements from Augustine and St. Thomas prove that this reprobation is a part of God's providence in the supernatural order. God, who could save each man if he willed, actually permits some

---

[11] See In *ST*, 1.22.1., p. 468.
[12] In *ST*, 1.23.2., p. 481.
[13] In *ST*, 1.23.5., p. 523.
[14] I Tim. 2:4.
[15] Rom. 9:13. He also quotes 1 Cor. 9:27; 2 Cor. 13:5; 2 Tim. 2:20; Matt. 7:23.

10

men to fall into sin. This permission, or the lack of decision on God's part to determine the creature to do good, is infallibly followed by sin or defection.[16] And God's knowledge of the evil men do has certainty from this divine permission. "Hence, from the fact that God knows that his own will has not determined the created will to act well in the matter of temperance, for example, he knows evidently that the created will will sin and fail in the matter of this virtue."[17] We shall see below that Banez asserts that in the order of God's governance, the first and adequate cause for God's denial of efficacious help for the performance of a particular good act is the fault of the created free will. But ultimately, as there is not a cause of predestination in the predestined, so too there is not a cause in the reprobate for God's first permission that they sin. Banez notes with reference to the fallen angels: "However there is no need that they previously sin for this that God by his consequent will desire to permit some of them to defect from their ultimate end. . . ."[18] St. Paul has defended this action of God from the accusations of men in his famous ninth chapter of *Romans,* and he has also indicated the ultimate reason for this reprobation. The particular consideration because of which God allows an individual to be reprobated is the good of the universe as a whole, the manifestation of divine justice in punishing sins and of God's mercy in saving the predestined.[19] This does not mean that God decrees to punish man before he foresees his sins or that he predestines man to sin; it simply means that God previous to the foreseen sins permits the creature to fall, and after the creature's foreseen demerits lasting until the end of his life he punishes him. So the punishment comes after the foreseen sin,

[16] See In *ST,* 1.14.13., p. 353. For a modern expression of this, see R. Garrigou-Lagrange, *The One God* (tr. by B. Rose, St. Louis, 1946), p. 687: "But sin follows inevitably the divine permission to sin which, as was stated, implies that one is not maintained by God in the performance of good."

[17] *Loc. cit. ST,* 1.14.13., p. 353.

[18] In *ST,* 119.6., p. 422. Though Thomists generally agree that there exists an antecedent negative reprobation for those individuals who are not predestined, there are several different explanations among them as to the nature of this reprobation. Some have described it as an exclusion from eternal glory as from an unowed benefit, but most understand it to be a permission to sin which will merit the exclusion from heaven. See R. Garrigou-Lagrange, "Prédestination," *DTC,* 12.2 (1935), 2986.

[19] See In *ST,* 1.22.1., p. 469. See also Rom. 9:22–24.

11

but the leaving of the sinner to his own weakness that results in sin precedes the foreseen sin and is ordained by God to the end that he may manifest his justice.[20]

Since by his consequent will (i.e., consequent upon God's knowledge, not of the individual's sins, but of the purpose of the universe as a whole) God permits some to be reprobated, his universal salvific will is really God's antecedent will. While Banez holds that it can safely be held that this will exists formally in God, "it seems much more probable that the will that is signified by this name *velleity* does not formally exist in God; but it is enough that such an antecedent will be said to be eminently in God."[21] What God actually wills he fulfills; but since he does not actually fulfill his antecedent will, it is better that this not be said to exist formally in God. On the other hand, the disposition to save all men was in Christ who died for all and in the prayers of the saints. Since what exists in the creature pre-exists in God, its cause, this universal salvific will should be said to exist eminently in God, as in the one who caused the disposition in Christ and the saints. From this salvific will, God gives sufficient graces to all moral adults and commands them to do nothing impossible.[22]

We are now in a position to explain to some extent the way in which the divine plan and intention is executed in eliciting through grace the good acts of the free will. Following the order Banez used in a special treatise he wrote on this subject,[23] we shall show the nature of man's free will as it is relevant to the question, the nature of the aid by which God brings about the good act of man, and thus the harmony between grace and free will.

Banez begins by quoting Molina's statement that "that agent is

[20] See *ibid.*

[21] In *ST*, 1.19.6., p. 421. This both as a doctrine and as an interpretation of St. Thomas is rejected by all Thomists now. Basing themselves on the statement of St. Thomas in *De Veritate*, 23.3, "voluntas de Deo proprie dicitur, et haec est voluntas beneplaciti, quae per antecedentem et consequentem distinguitur," they hold that a universal salvific will is formally in God. See R. Garrigou-Lagrange, *The One God*, pp. 535–8.

[22] In *ST*, 1.23.3., p. 495. Banez holds: "Possibile est secundum legem ordinariam quemlibet hominem dum est in hac vita, salvari."

[23] Banez, "Tractatus de vera et legitima concordia liberi arbitrii creati cum auxiliis gratiae Dei efficaciter moventis humanam voluntatem," in *Comentarios inéditos a la prima secundae de santo Tomás*, 3 (ed. V. B. de Heredia, Madrid, 1948), 351–420.

called free which, once everything necessary for acting has been granted, is able to act or not to act, or to do one thing in such a way that it could also do the opposite."[24] The main criticism against this definition is that Molina understands by "everything necessary for acting" not only what is required before the free act takes place, but also what is required in the moment of acting. And he asserts that even in this moment the will is able to act or not to act. The difficulty with this is that the will's act is a passage from potency to act and thus is dependent upon the actuation by God. Hence "our free will, when it passes from not deliberating to deliberating and freely determines itself to act, is nevertheless by a priority of nature determined by the divine will."[25] When it determines itself to act, therefore, it cannot do otherwise, given this actuation (i.e., *in sensu composito*), though it could do otherwise, given the condition it was not thus determining itself (i.e., *in sensu diviso*). For example, when I am sitting, I cannot stand while I retain my sitting position, though I can if I relinquish this position. This kind of inability to do otherwise is not contrary to the freedom of the will; only the inability to act otherwise *in sensu diviso* would be contrary to freedom. But Molina asserts the first sort of freedom and thus is mistaken.

Because Banez denied that freedom consisted in the indifference ascribed to it by Molina, he was accused of teaching that the will's indifference consisted formally in something passive, namely, its receptivity to different actuations. This, he says, misrepresents his view. He holds, in the first place, that if freedom is understood to include both God's creative act and the rational creature's free act, it demands an indifference that is negative and active. By negative, he means that the will is not of its nature determined to the act and that the object, in itself and in the intellectual knowledge by which it is presented to the will, does not have a necessary relation to the happiness of the one who chooses and thus does not necessitate his act. By active, he means that it is in the power of the will to perform the act or not. Indifference in the free

---

[24] *Ibid.*, 1, c. 1, n. 1, pp. 353–4. ". . . illud agens liberum dicitur quod, positis omnibus requisitis ad agendum, potest agere et non agere, aut ita agere unum ut contrarium etiam agere possit." This is found in Molina, *Concordia*, q. 14, a. 13, d. 2, n. 3, p. 14.

[25] Banez, *op. cit.*, n. 6, p. 358.

will of the creature is not purely active; since the created will is potential, before it actively chooses it must be reduced to act. Thus it has a passive indifference or receptivity to different actuations, but "the power of free choice and the use of that power, no matter what created free will it is, does not consist formally in its being actuated or in the potentiality of that power. Indeed the faculty is truly active and its use is action."[26] Having by a priority of nature been actuated, the will actively acts; and it is in this that the indifference that constitutes its freedom properly consists. In this act the will is choosing an object that does not necessitate it and thus it is able to act or not, to do one thing or another, but this must be understood *in sensu diviso* and not *in sensu composito.* Given the fact that it has been reduced to act, the will cannot do otherwise; but this is not contrary to freedom. Christ was not able to do otherwise than obey his Father once he received his command, but that did not diminish the freedom of his sacrifice. The act is called free not from the will's ability to act otherwise in Molina's sense, but "from the power and kind of power from which it proceeds; namely, from the power of intellect and will which of themselves are indifferently related to both objects, either by a negative indifference or by a privative and passive one."[27]

With reference to the aid God gives to the will that is the source of its act, Banez rejects Molina's doctrine of God as a partial cause of the effect with the will, and he shows that God is the total first cause who moves the will itself from potency to act by a physical created causality that both moves and determines the will and does so by a natural antecedence to the act of the created will. This antecedent movement is not simply the moral movement of the object upon the will, as Suarez believed, but a physical movement, since the effect is itself a physical act of the will.[28] If asked

[26] *Ibid.*, c. 2, n. 6, p. 367. The doctrine of modern Thomists continues to be the same as Banez's. See R. Garrigou-Lagrange, "Prédestination," 2968–73.

[27] Banez, *op. cit.*, c. 3, n. 3, p. 370.

[28] Cf. *ibid.*, In ST 1-2, 109.1.n.2, p. 22. Similiter etiam causis liberis operantibus suos effectus liberos, apponit Deus suam motionem physicam et moralem, qua suaviter movet et determinat liberum arbitrium ad bene et libere agendum; ita ut bonus ipse usus liberi arbitrii sit effectus infallibilis decreti voluntatis absolutae Dei, ac proinde divini auxilii quo Deus intime movet voluntatem ad recte agendum . . . quae quidem motio praemotio dicitur secundum divinae providentiae rationem, non secundum necessi-

more specifically what this passive premotion is, Banez answers: "I indeed confess that I do not understand what that divine pre-motion is, if it is considered passively, other than the very power of the intellect placed in completed act by the author of nature, who works in all things according to the plan of his providence."[29]

The aid that moves the will in the supernatural order is grace that is called actual since it causes a particular act. Different forms of this grace are indicated by Scripture. There is the grace that anticipates our supernatural actions (called prevenient) and that by which we actually perform the good act (called helping or assisting). There is also the grace that is *sufficient* to bring about the good work and that which is *efficacious* or effective in bringing about the good work. Augustine indicated this difference often as, for example, when he taught that the ability to persevere was given to Adam, but not actual perseverance in original innocence. It is also shown from Scripture that while all are redeemed by Christ (and thus receive sufficient aid to reach heaven), this redemption is not applied to all in an efficacious way to bring them to heaven, but only to the predestined. Of these Christ said: *No one shall seize them from my hand.*[30]

---

tatem naturae, qualis est motio corporis caelestis in haec inferiora. And in the same place, "Deus enim applicat nostram voluntatem ad actionem bonam et consensum liberum applicatione reali seu physica, ut ipse dicit, et non solum applicat ut causa moralis proponendo objectum sub ratione appetibilis." The expression *praedeterminatio physica* was used for the first time in the *Apologia fratrum praedicatorum* composed by Banez, Peter Herera, and Alvarez and sent to Pope Clement VIII with the dossier of the Grand Inquisitor of Spain on the controversy about 1599. See E. Van-steenberghe, "Molinisme," *DTC*, 10.2 (1929), 2157.

[29] Banez, "Tractatus," 2, c. 2, n. 2, p. 384. It seems that the physical causality that reduces the will from potency to act is not exercised through the object of the will in Banez's opinion, as the quotations in the previous note show. Cajetan (In *ST*, 1.80.2, n. 6.) holds that while the object pre-sented to the will specifies the will, it is not the cause of the exercise of the will. This is the appetite itself. Garrigou-Lagrange (*art. cit.*, 2983) rejects the Augustinian explanation of grace as a *delectatio victrix* because this "n'étant qu'une motion morale, par manière d'attrait objectif, et non pas une motion physique, 'ab intus quoad exercitium,' ne saurait être in-trinsèquement et infailliblement efficace." Grace moves the will to act "par une 'motion qui applique notre volonté à poser vitalement et librement son acte (I^a, Q. cv, a. 4 et 5),' et qui, pour cette raison, par opposition à la motion morale, est dite *prémotion physique*. Les Thomistes ajoutent même: cette motion est prédéterminante, en tant qu'elle assure infailliblement l'exécution du decret éternel prédéterminant." *Ibid.*, 2984.

[30] Banez, "Tractatus," 2, c. 3, n. 6, p. 392. In addition to John 10:28,

It is true that every grace given by God is effective of some result, whether this is simply the semi-deliberate attraction of the will to a good act or the deliberate free act itself. But the problem is whether the former, which is sufficient grace with reference to the latter, is really the same as the grace that actually elicits the deliberate act (as Molina and Suarez teach) or is really distinct from it. Banez holds that it must be really distinct. If after receiving an initial prevenient grace that attracts the will to a good act, the will could of itself reduce itself from potency to act and actually respond with no further need to be moved to act by God, then it would be man who would be the source of the act itself, while grace would give no more than the power to act. The actual passage to act would be due to man and not to the grace of God, a doctrine contrary to Scripture, Augustine, and the prayers of the Church. Hence there must be another grace by which God actually moves the will to act; in other words, efficacious grace is really distinct from sufficient grace.

The fact that this is the true concord between God's action and the free created will is seen from the principles that are its source, and from the inconclusiveness of the arguments brought against it. One of the objections against it is that sufficient grace is not really sufficient if there is always the need for efficacious grace. But we can say that it really does accomplish something necessary for the act, namely, to put the power in first act or to prepare it proximately for the deliberate act of will. To the objection that in this theory man is excused from sin and incapable of virtue since God determines not to give some men efficacious grace, we can advance several considerations. For sin to be possible, all that is needed is that the good act that would avoid it be possible, and this is always true because man does have sufficient grace. To the statement that God will not give efficacious grace and thus is the cause of sin, Banez answers that ". . . if this is understood to be without foreknowledge of the future resistance of the free will, I

---

he also uses Rom. 9:12–16 (*ibid.*, c. 4, n. 3, p. 400) to show the efficacy of predestination. The existence of efficacious grace is also shown by Esth. 13:9 ("Non est qui possit resistere voluntati tuae."); Ps. 134:6; Rom. 9:19; *ibid.*, n. 5, p. 404. On the other hand, the existence of graces that are resisted by man are shown by Job. 9:4; Ps. 75.8; 16:8; Acts 7:51; I Tim. 2:4; Matt. 23:37, *et al.*

deny the antecedent."[31] When a cause is the total cause of a specific effect in every way, then the denial of that cause is the cause of the lack of that effect. But both God and free will are the cause of the good act, so the negation of the effect does not have as its cause the negation of the first cause; it can have as its cause the negation of the second cause. So the deficiency of free will can be the source of the sin. In fact, if the sin is looked upon as a privation of morally right action, it has as its cause the deficient free will. Only if it is looked upon as a pure negation of being, "I concede that of that negation of being the cause is purely the negation of effective help, that God was not held to give. He preferred to permit the sin, and this not always as a punishment of another sin."[32] "Still the first and adequate cause of the denial of help, considered as an execution [of God's providence] in time, is the free will that has of itself the power to desire to defect and to disobey the command of God, with God's permission. . . ."[33] Hence there is a harmony between God's grace and free will.

With the rather small changes indicated above, the doctrine of Banez has remained the doctrine of Thomists generally down to the present. In the present century particularly, however, there have been some attempts by those who claim to be Thomists to explain the problem of moral evil more adequately than it is felt Banez has done. For example, Guillermin in a series of articles[34]

[31] *Ibid.*, c. 4, n. 2, p. 398.

[32] *Ibid.*, p. 399.

[33] *Ibid.*, p. 400. This doctrine of the antecedence of man's bad will to God's permission in the order of God's governance is at times said to have originated with Thomists later than Banez. But Banez holds it and quotes *ST*, 1–2, 112.3 ad 2 to prove it.

This doctrine is still held by Thomists generally as is seen in the most profuse modern defender of the system, Garrigou-Lagrange. Of the sin of man God has an eternal decree, "positif et effectif quant à l'entité physique du péché, et permissif quant à la déficience." "Prémotion," *DTC*, 13.1 (1939), 72. But "Dieu ne détermine jamais à l'acte material du péché que si la créature s'est déjà déterminée à ce qu'il y a de formel dans le péché." *Dieu, son existence et sa nature* (Paris, 1950), p. 700. And finally, "God, to the extent that it lies with him, is prepared to give efficacious grace to all who have sufficient grace, and does not deny it to any man except through his own fault, at least by a priority of nature, if not antecedent in time." *Grace* (St. Louis, 1952), p. 220.

[34] H. Guillermin, "De la grâce sufficante," *Revue Thomiste*, 9 (1901), 505–19; 10 (1902), 47–76, 377–404, 653–74; 11 (1903), 20–31.

developed once more the doctrine of J. Gonzalez de Albeda that sufficient grace does more than simply place the will in first act. It also gives "an impulse to second act, although it does not remove the impediments to this act and, in fact, is resisted; thus it is a physical premotion, even a predetermination, but impedible, not infallible."[35] Marin-Sola goes further and holds that sufficient grace gives in addition to an infallible beginning of the virtuous act an impulse to second act that can itself often result in second act if it is not resisted.[36] F. Muniz, O.P., distinguishes a "double action or divine movement: one unimpedible, irresistible, absolutely efficacious; and the other impedible, resistible, and frustrable."[37] He holds that "final perseverance is an effect elicited by predestination which can only be caused by an infallibly efficacious grace."[38] But he also teaches that "the efficacious election for glory and the consequent predestination are after the foreseen merits that come about through premoving and predetermining grace which is conferred by the general providence of the supernatural order. It is, nevertheless, totally gratuitous."[39] Maritain,

---

[35] The summary given of this doctrine by R. Garrigou-Lagrange in *Grace*, p. 230. See concerning Gonzalez de Albeda in H. Lange, *De Gratia* (Freiburg i Br. 1929), p. 482.

[36] See F. Marin-Sola, "El sistema tomista sobre la moción divina," *Ciencia Tomista*, 32 (1925), 5-54 (esp. 28-32). He gave his answers to objections raised in "Respuesta a algunas objeciones acerca del sistema tomista sobre la moción divina," *Cien. Tom.*, 33 (1926), 5-74, and in "Nuevas observaciones acerca del sistema tomista sobre la moción divina," *ibid.*, pp. 321-97. See for a favorable judgment on this, G. Bavaud, "La doctrine du P. Marin-Sola sur la grâce est-elle une concession au Molinisme?" *Revue Thomiste*, 58 (1958), 473-83. The author concludes by stating: "Le refus de la grâce de la persévérance finale, Dieu le décide seulement après la prevision de multiples resistances? A notre avis, rien n'empêche un thomiste de defendre cette position."

[37] Francisco Muniz, "Apendice II," in *Suma Teologica de Santo Tomás de Aquino*, 1 (Madrid 1947), 1008. De donde se infiere que, en conformidad con el doble género de decretos existentes en Dios, es preciso admitir una doble acción o moción divina: una inimpedible, irresistible, absolutamente eficaz, y otra impedible, resistible y frustrable.

[38] *Ibid.*, p. 1034. . . . la perseverancia final es efecto elicito de la predestinación, que sólo puede ser causada por la gracia infaliblemente eficaz.

[39] *Ibid.*, pp. 1029-30. Le eleccion eficaz a la gloria y la consiguiente predestinación son *post praevisa merita facta ex gratia praemovente et praedeterminante collata per providentiam generalem ordinis supernaturalis*, y, sin embargo, es totalmente gratuita.

18

too, in an effort to show more clearly than Thomism does the initiative of the creature in evil, explains grace as susceptible to rejection on the part of man.[40]

But Thomists generally would feel that these attempts leave many problems without having the coherence of the Thomist explanation. One criticism that even admits difficulties with the traditional theory is given by M.-J. Nicolas, who admits: "The whole problem then lies in this point of the relation between the divine permission and the evil initiative, the failure of the creature. I see the two ways that are open to explain this, and each of them seems impossible to follow to the end."[41] If the ultimate priority belongs to the creature, then how does God know this evil initiative? This would make God passive before creatures. If, on the other hand, God knows our failure in his permission, there is a necessary connection between that permission and our failure. If this is so, how can God be absolved from responsibility for man's sin? He suggests that the difficulty lies in attempting to gain too profound an understanding of the mystery.

2. The Answer of Molina

Molina's explanation of the revealed mystery of the relation of the rational creature to God in the supernatural order differs so strikingly from that of Banez which we have just examined that one finds it difficult at first to believe that both these men were describing the same objective mystery according to the data of sources common to both. It becomes understandable when we recall that, as Banez took as his governing principle the universal causality and the omnipotence of the divine will, Molina began with the fact of man's freedom. His whole book is an attempt to show how grace, God's foreknowledge, will, providence, predesti-

[40] G. Maritain, "L'existant libre et les libres desseins eternels," *Court traité de l'existence et de l'existant* (Paris, 1947), pp. 141–95.

[41] M. J. Nicholas, "Simple réflexions sur la doctrine thomiste de la grâce," *Revue thomiste*, 58 (1958), 649. Others criticize these new theories without showing uncertainty concerning the adequacy of the Thomist explanation. See Garrigou-Lagrange, *op. cit.*, p. 231; and J. H. Nicholas, O. P., "La permission du péché," *Revue thomiste*, 60 (1960), 5–37, 185–206, 509–46. A recent Thomist critique of Suarez is found in T. Mullaney, O. P., *Suarez on Human Freedom* (Baltimore, 1950).

nation, and reprobation are in harmony with the freedom of the creature's will. In this explanation, as can be seen in the very structure of his book, his theory of the creature's freedom and the manner in which God cooperates with it is the determining factor. This prepares the way for his analysis of God's knowledge; and, once he has done this, he finds no great difficulty in showing that God's will, providence, predestination, and reprobation are in accord with the exigencies of the creature's freedom. It should be borne in mind that much of the force of Molina's proofs of his distinctive interpretation comes from the critique he makes at each stage of explanations given by others of the same doctrines, including always the teaching we find expressed in Banez. Their weaknesses are in large part Molina's strength.

Man's freedom is a freedom from extrinsic and intrinsic determination and is defined as follows: "That agent is said to be free which, once everything necessary for acting is given, is able to act and not to act or to do one thing in such a way that it could also do the contrary."[42] The implications of this definition become clear through Molina's doctrine on the concurrence of God with the free acts of the creature. He rejects a theory that would deny secondary causality to creatures as well as a theory that would reduce concurrence to God's creation and conservation of the creature's power to act. After describing St. Thomas' explanation that God moves the creature to act through applying the creature's power to act as the carpenter applies the saw to cut, Molina states: "I frankly confess that it is very hard for me to understand this movement and application which St. Thomas demands in secondary causes."[43] For Molina, God's concurrence is neither antecedent to the creature's act nor bearing upon the creature's potency; rather it is simultaneous causation of the act with the creature, both God and the creature being partial as causes (though the totality of the effect is due to God) forming one in-

[42] Molina, *Concordia*, q. 14, a. 13, d. 2, n. 3, p. 14. For the quotation, see above, footnote 24. For an analysis of Molina's thought on this whole matter, see E. Vansteenberghe, "Molinisme," 2101–41, 2145–53.

[43] Molina, *op. cit.*, Q. 14, a. 13, d. 26, n. 2, p. 165. Later in this same passage (n. 5), Molina states that perhaps St. Thomas has the same opinion as he does, since Cajetan interprets this article in the sense Molina takes. See B. Romeyer, S. J., "Libre arbitre et concours selon Molina," *Gregorianum*, 23 (1942), 169–201.

tegral cause, as two men drawing a boat to shore are partial causes
of the same effect. God does not exercise this causality through a
created act that would affect the will, for in that case he would
not be immediately present to the effect of the will. Moreover, if a
created act were necessary to conserve the act of the will in existence, then another created act would be necessary to conserve this
act in existence, and so on to infinity. It is better to say that God
concurs immediately by his own power with the act of the will.
Furthermore this causality by which God concurs with the created
nature or free will is a universal causality or a general indifferent
influence that is determined or specified through the created nature
or the choice of free will. It is in the power of the will to act
or not, to produce this act rather than another, to make one effect
rather than another under the influence of this causality. This
teaching, namely, that God's causality is a general or indifferent
one and that it is determined to one by the creature and specifically by the self-determination of the free will, is looked upon by
many as the key point to the doctrine of Molina and his school.[44]

[44] See Molina, op. cit., nn. 5–15, pp. 165–70. The passages in which he
expresses this central doctrine are as follows: N. 5, p. 165, "Dicendum
itaque est Deum immediate immediatione suppositi concurrere cum causis
secundis ad earum operationes et effectus. . . . Quo fit ut concursus Dei
generalis non sit influxus Dei in causam secundam, quasi illa prius eo mota
agat et producat suum effectum, sed sit influxus immediate cum causa in
illius actionem et effectum." And n. 11, p. 167, "Deus namque generali
concursu influit ut causa universalis influxu quodam indifferenti ad varias
actiones et effectus, determinatur vero ad species actionum et effectuum a
particulari influxu causarum secundarum qui pro diversitate virtutis cuiusque
ad agendum diversus est, aut si causa libera sit, in ipsius potestate est ita in-
fluere ut producatur potius haec actio quam illa, puta velle quam nolle, aut
ambulare quam sedere, et hic effectus potius quam ille, nempe hoc
artefactum potius quam aliud, vel etiam suspendere omnino influxum ne ulla
sit actio." His famous simile asserts that God and the creature cause one
action and effect, "non secus ac, cum duo trahunt navim, totus motus
proficiscitur ab unoquoque trahentium, sed non tamquam a tota causa
motus, . . ." *Ibid.*, n. 15, p. 170. Some of Molina's followers substitute an
indifferent premotion for his simultaneous concurrence, and still hold all
his major doctrines because they hold it is the indifferent character of God's
causality and thus the ability of the creature to determine it that is the key
to Molinism. For example, see Louis Rasolo, S. J., *Le dilemme du concours
divin* (Rome, 1956), p. 44. "Le concours indifférent est bien le clef de
voûte de tout le système." He shows that Bellarmine and Lemos (O. P.)
interpret the doctrine of the Jesuits in this fashion. Rasolo also states (75):
"Le péché est une exclusivité de l'homme. L'homme a donc une causalité

God cooperates with the creature's supernatural acts through prevenient and helping grace, *gratia praeveniens* and *gratia adiuvans*. Prevenient grace is the interior grace that proximately prepares the will for a deliberate, free, supernatural act; and insofar as it is related to this deliberate act, it differs from God's natural concurrence with the creature. For in this respect it is both antecedent to the creature's act and it is an influence upon the will itself. It consists formally in the vital acts of the illumination of the intellect and the inspiration of the will, contrary to what many theologians teach. And it gives to the will fully sufficient aid to elicit a supernatural act, so completely that no further or intrinsically different grace is needed for the will to act. With this grace the will is able to resist or respond; and if it responds, the prevenient grace becomes efficacious grace or a helping grace. This grace forms one integral efficient cause of the supernatural act with the will under the general influence of God's natural simultaneous concurrence. As helping grace it is neither a premotion nor a movement of the will itself. It is a simultaneous principle causing the act's supernaturality, while the will's act, which renders this grace efficacious by giving the necessary condition of its own response, determines this general influence of God and is the source of the freedom of the act.[45]

propre, exclusive. Et ce ne peut être que la détermination de l'acte. Et de fait, c'est la détermination qui rend l'acte bon ou mauvais." See also 53.

[45] See Molina, *op. cit.*, q. 14, a. 13, d. 37, nn. 2–4, pp. 225–6; d. 41, nn. 1–2, pp. 257–8; d. 45, nn. 5, 6, 8, pp. 272–4. See Vansteenberghe, *art. cit.*, 2151. "Le consentement de la volonté à la grâce prévenante ne donne pas à celle-ci l'efficacité, mais réalise une condition sans laquelle ce secours ne sera pas efficace; la volonté coopère avec la grâce, mais elle le fait par sa force naturelle, et si l'acte produit lui doit d'être libre, il doit à la grâce seule d'être surnaturel." While the Molinists in general hold that *gratia praeveniens* consists in the illuminations of the mind and inspirations of the will, some attribute to it only a moral influence upon the deliberate will act, and others, with Molina, attribute to it a physical influence upon the deliberate act to bring about its supernaturality. See S. Gonzalez, "De gratia Christi" in *Sacrae theologiae summa*, 3 (2. ed., Madrid, 1953), 650. This is not to say that the object has a physical causality in bringing about the will act as such. Molinists seem to agree with the Thomists that the object does not reduce the will to act "quoad exercitium," and indeed they seem to go even further and deny it a physical extrinsic formal causality of the specification of the act. Cf. Suarez, *De anima*, liber V, cap. 3, *Opera Omnia*, 3 (Paris, 1856), 758–9. "Potentia appetitiva absque efficientia appetibilis cogniti elicit actum suum." And he argues against any physical efficacy on the part of the final cause in the sense that the object ". . . per se quoque

Once this doctrine on the nature of freedom and of God's concurrence has been clarified, Molina explains God's knowledge of contingent futures. He examines and rejects as inadequate some theories proposed by his precedessors. St. Thomas teaches that all things are present to God in the eternity of his knowledge as the points on a circumference of a circle are equally present to the center. And thus God can know all free future acts without destroying their freedom. This is an inadequate explanation since God knows not only what will exist but, as statements from Scripture prove, what would exist given all hypothetical circumstances. For this and other reasons, "God does not need their existence in his eternity to know them with certainty."[46] He also rejects the view forwarded by Scotus and attributed by some of St. Thomas that God knows what the free creature will do through intrinsically and infallibly efficacious decrees of the divine will. This is contrary to the freedom of the will and the manner of God's cooperation with it.[47]

The true solution is based on the fact that God knows what the free will of any possible creature would do given any possible circumstances, and on the manner in which God has this knowledge. Molina distinguishes a threefold knowledge in God. First, there is God's *natural* knowledge, that by which he knows his own essence perfectly and all things possible to him either immediately or mediately through the natural or free possible creatures. Secondly, there is God's *free* knowledge that occurs after the free decision of the divine will determining what definite circumstances (among all the possible ones) will surround each creature, and that is the

---

ad substantiam ipsam actus concurrat." He gives as one of his arguments, ". . . cum enim appetitus ex se habeat sufficientem inclinationem ad objectum, ex se est sufficiens elicere proprium actum: superflue ergo fingitur efficientia in objecto. Deinde induci videtur quippiam impossibile: cum enim appetitio sit vitalis elici aliter non potest quam a potentia cuius est actus. . . ." See also P. Dumont, S. J., *Liberté humaine et concours divin d'après Suarez* (Paris, 1936).

[46] Molina, *op. cit.*, Q. 14, a. 13, d. 49, n. 11, p. 311. Molina proves that God has certain knowledge of conditional free futures, i.e., the object of *scientia media*, from Christ's statement (Matt. 11:21) concerning the penance Tyre and Sidon would have done if his miracles had been performed in them, as well as from some other passages in Scripture, 1 Kings 23:10–12; Wis. 4:11, 14. See *ibid.*, n. 9, p. 310.

[47] See *ibid.*, d. 50, pp. 317–26.

23

means whereby he knows the absolute future, either natural or contingent. Thirdly, there is *scientia media,* a knowledge of what each free created will would do, given each one of the infinite variety of circumstances and graces with which God could surround it. This knowledge is not God's free knowledge since it precedes it in the order of nature and has a different object. Nor is it God's natural knowledge which is a necessary knowledge, for if the free creature would determine itself differently, which it truly can, God's *scientia media* would have a different object. The medium by which God knows what the free will would do, given all different possible circumstances, is his perfect comprehension of his own essence, of the natures of his effects, and thus of what each free will would choose given any circumstances.[48] This knowledge is not drawn from creatures since it is gained through God's perfect knowledge of his own creative essence.

This explanation of God's causality and knowledge is determinative for Molina's defense of the freedom of the created will before God's will, providence, predestination, and reprobation. This will be clear as we recall Molina's doctrine on these further points. The will of God which is part of providence, predestination, and reprobation and which follows *scientia media* does not determine first the end of the creature absolutely and then the means absolutely effective in realizing this end, but simply chooses to realize certain circumstances and graces that do in fact lead to the end. God by his antecedent and conditional will wants all rational creatures to be saved. This will of God is not always fulfilled, but his absolute will is always fulfilled whether for the good in that they achieve their destiny, or for the evil who escape from God's saving will only to fall under his will to punish sin-

---

[48] See *ibid.,* d. 52, esp. nn. 9, 10, pp. 339–40; Vansteenberghe, *art. cit.,* 2118–20 and 2168–9 where the different opinions of the Molinists on the medium of God's *scientia media* are presented. Some agree with Molina's explanation, but others criticize it and hold the opinion that Molina described and rejected in the second edition of his work. That is, for any future possible act of will there are at least two alternatives. One of them, the one the free will would choose, is eternally true; and God knows what the will would do in any circumstances through knowing this objective truth. Some followers of Molina, while they accept *scientia media,* refuse to attempt any explanation of the medium by which God has such knowledge. Vansteenberghe quotes Perrone (2169) as stating that "il convient de renoncer totalement à un problème si obscur, dont aucun essai de solution n'échappe aux difficultés."

24

ners. The sin of man is in no way willed by God, but simply permitted.[49]

Providence, to which all creatures are subject, is an act of the divine intellect to which an act of the divine will is joined ordering creatures toward their end. Contrary to what some theologians teach, providence does not necessitate an actual achievement of the end by the creature, for it can be conditional on the free will of the creature. It presupposes the knowledge of what the creature would do in any circumstances, and the will of God choosing a set of circumstances that do in fact order each rational creature toward its end. According to how God foresees that the creature would act in these chosen circumstances, it reaches or does not reach the appointed end of eternal beatitude, is predestined, or ends by being reprobated. But this does not detract from the certainty of divine providence, which God has through his *scientia media* and free knowledge, nor does it mean that those who do not reach heaven escape from God's providence.[50] In other words, God's providence is infallible because, before he gives any specific grace, he knows what the result will be in the free will of the creature. This knowledge comes not from the intrinsic efficacy of this grace or God's decree, as Banez teaches. It comes from the fact that God's will to give it follows *scientia media* in which God knows how the will would respond to it. In this sense, every grace with which man cooperates is efficacious antecedent to the will's actual consent.

Predestination, then, which is God's providence toward the rational creatures who reach eternal beatitude, can be defined as follows: "Predestination is the plan in God of the order or means by which he foresees that the rational creature will be led to eternal life with the intention of executing that order."[51] (When we do not further qualify predestination as that to grace, we mean by it predestination to glory.) Hence, it is basically an act of the divine intellect to which an act of the divine will is added. This act of the divine will follows upon the knowledge of what

[49] See Vansteenberghe, *art. cit.*, 2120.

[50] See Molina, *op. cit.*, q. 22, a. 1, d. 2, esp. nn. 6, 16, pp. 434, 438.

[51] *Ibid.*, Q. 23, a. 1 and 2, d. 1, n. 8, p. 455. See Vansteenberghe, *art. cit.*, 2122-3. See also J. Rabeneck, "Docuitne Molina praedestinationem hominum ad gloriam fieri 'ante' vel 'post' eorum praevisa merita?" *Miscellanea Comillas*, 18 (1952), 11–26.

the will would do, and it first of all bears upon the means or the realization of successive circumstances in the life of the rational creature. It does not first of all bear upon the end; in other words, election to glory does not precede God's choice of the means. So the order of the divine intention concerning the predestined follows the order of the execution of this intention; that is, the intention to predestine to glory succeeds the intention to actualize circumstances that are the means in which God by his free knowledge foresees that the creature will merit eternal beatitude. Predestination in this proper sense is *post praevisa merita*.[52] But why does God choose these particular means for this particular creature when he knows an infinite number of circumstances that would not result in beatitude for it? Predestination in this improper sense of the choice of the circumstances that as a matter of fact lead to beatitude has no cause other than the divine good pleasure. That God chooses this set of circumstances among all he sees by *scientia media* is not due to his knowledge of the creature's conditional merits or its conditional good use of free will before or after grace; and predestination in this sense is after knowledge of the creature's conditional merits, but *not because of* such knowledge. But the fact that God's choice of these conditions becomes predestination for these particular adults rather than for others has as its *reason* what the free will of those adults would actually do, given those circumstances and helps. And in this sense there is a reason for predestination in the good use of free will on the part of the creature.[53]

[52] See Molina, *op. cit.*, d. 2, nn. 8–9, pp. 458–9. See Vansteenberghe, *art. cit.*, 2169–70 for a comparison of the Congruists with Molina on this point. Also see I. M. Dalmau, "De Deo uno et trino" in *Sacrae theologiae summa*, 2 (Madrid, 1952), 195–8. The Congruists, of whom the greatest are Bellarmine and Suarez, hold that God fixes the end before he chooses the means and thus that predestination to heaven is anterior to God's foreknowledge of the creature's merits. Reprobation is antecedent to foreknowledge of demerits. Molinism becomes for the Congruists a means whereby God can fulfill his purpose without acting upon free will in a way that would, in their opinion, detract from its freedom.

[53] See Molina, *op. cit.*, q. 23, a. 4 and 5, disp. 1, memb. ult., n. 10, pp. 585–6. See Vansteenberghe, *art. cit.*, 2129, where it is shown that Molina taught that though God was not bound by what he foresaw of man's conditional merits through his *scientia media*, he did frequently take it into account; he somewhat modified this doctrine in the second edition of the *Concordia*. See *ibid.*, 2153. Note here that all who accept *scientia media* hold that the grace given to man which is followed by

This allows Molina to teach also that reprobation is only *post praevisa demerita*. St. Paul, he admits, seems to teach that men are reprobated without the cause of their reprobation being in them. This is the way many interpret his account of Esau in the ninth chapter of *Romans*. But the proper understanding of this depends upon the proper understanding of God's knowledge. Concerning the reprobate, there are three acts of the divine will, all of which presuppose God's foreknowledge of what the free creature would do given different circumstances. The first act is God's permission to sin which consists in his choice of those circumstances and graces which give wholly adequate means to avoid sin, but in which God knows that the creature will sin. There is no reason in the creature why God chooses these particular circumstances. But the fact that these circumstances result in sin is wholly due to the creature's misuse of God's fully adequate help. The second act is that of hardening the sinner, and it consists in God's choice of means of conversion which are adequate, but which God foresees will result in a greater hardness of the sinner and final impenitence. Only in the third act does God exclude the sinner from heaven and condemn him to hell. Hence, God does not choose first to damn a person and then the appropriate means to bring this about efficaciously. The third and the second act are posterior to God's

man's consent was *in actu primo*, or before man's consent, infallibly certain to gain that consent, for God knew that it would have such an effect and he chose to give this particular grace. This prevenient grace is, in this theory, extrinsically efficacious, for it depends upon God's *scientia media*, and is not intrinsically efficacious, as the Thomists teach. Does this antecedently infallibly effective grace result from a divine will to give a greater benefit than another grace which God knows would be adequate, but would not be accepted by the created will? It is clear that Suarez and the Congruists teach that it does result from such a divine will, for they teach that God wants with an absolute will that a man perform a particular good act and then gives the means or grace that will infallibly effect this. Moreover, the Superior General of the Jesuits, Aquaviva, in 1613 ordered all Jesuits to hold that efficacious grace was efficacious *in actu primo*, not only in fact, but from the intention of God, who gave it for the very purpose that it would infallibly gain man's acceptance. There is some doubt about Molina's opinion on this matter. The Thomists generally say that he would answer the question in the negative. Molina's followers generally answer the question in the affirmative and hold that Molina does the same. Some texts of Molina suggest that their interpretation is correct. Cf. Molina, *op. cit.*, q. 19, a. 6, disp. 2, n. 2. pp. 420–1. See also q. 23, a. 4 and 5, disp. 3, n. 15, p. 597. And see H. Quillet, "Congruisme," *DTC*, 3.1 (1923), 1120–38.

foreknowledge of actual sin, and hence both are chastisements justly merited by the sinner. It is only the third act that, strictly speaking, is reprobation, and for this there is always a cause in the creature, namely, his foreseen sins and final impenitence.[54] But if reprobation is taken as including the permission to sin, then the integral effect of reprobation has no cause but only a condition in the creature. However, its certainty depends not upon a divine decree but upon divine foreknowledge and ultimately the choice of the human will.

3. *The Basic Problem*

There have been still other attempts advanced by Catholic theologians since the sixteenth century to explain the mystery of predestination and grace in their relation to free will. While the analysis of these would show even more graphically the difficulty men have experienced in understanding this mystery, it would not add greatly to the clarification of the problem itself. These theories do not on the central issues differ from the positions of the schools we have already investigated, and hence in great part they labor under the same difficulties. Some Scotists and the Augustinians generally teach with the Banezian school that at least fallen man is predestined to eternal glory antecedent to God's foreknowledge of his merits, while the Sorbonne or Syncretist school generally agrees with the Molinists in teaching that this predestination is only after man's foreseen merits.[55] The former, for the most part, teach that the grace that elicits man's good acts is antecedently, infallibly, and intrinsically efficacious in bringing about this effect. However, they reject the Banezian *praemotio physica praedeterminans* in explaining this, and they substitute for it either a codetermining movement or a movement through the attraction of the good.[56] St. Alphonsus Ligouri, who is considered a Syncretist,

[54] See Molina, *op. cit.*, q. 23, a. 4 and 5, disp. 4, esp. nn. 4-21, pp. 599-606.

[55] For an account of these theories and a bibliography relating to them, see H. Lange, *De gratia,* pp. 481-94.

[56] The Augustinians, such as Berti and Bellelli, are generally considered to have taught a moral predetermination. But just recently Winfried Bocxe, O.S.A., in his book, *Introduction to the Teaching of the Italian Augustinians of the 18th Century on the Nature of Actual Grace* (Heverlé-Louvain,

held that for easy acts of virtue antecedent grace was not infallibly efficacious, and for difficult acts it was. But in general these schools have not been able to answer the problems which their borrowings from the Thomist or the Molinist schools give them. In adopting intrinsically efficacious grace and antecedent pre-destination from the former, they have the Thomist's difficulty in explaining free will; and in adopting the contrary elements from Molina, they have difficulty in showing how God has infallible knowledge of man's free future acts.

It is really in these basic differences between the major systems that problems for the human spirit are raised, and the fact of having unanswered problems is common to both of these schools. If we study the Thomist explanation of this mystery, we can see that predestination is the cause of the creature's salvation through the circumstances of the individual's life, and particularly the interior grace that brings about his free acts which merit heaven. As a cause it precedes in some way its effect. But what then becomes of human freedom under such a divine intention and the means by which it is effected? If it is held that the grace which interiorly moves man's will is predetermining, does the reality of freedom remain? Or if one holds that only the circumstances of man's life are determined without his inner freedom being touched (the Congruist doctrine), the question remains whether this is in accord with divine causality and whether this is not still a determinism incompatible with freedom. What, too, of those who do not reach heaven? This shattering evil inevitably follows if a person is reprobated; but if he is reprobated before a foreknowledge of his sins, how is the creature responsible for the lack of God's pre-destinating intention in his regard? And if he is not responsible,

---

1958), has presented texts to show that they agreed with the Thomists in teaching a physical predetermination, while they differed in other matters such as their denial of such a grace to the state of innocence. The different interpretations of the Augustinians would seem to be due to the fact that Berti and other Augustinians considered grace as an illumination of the intellect to be what is called a moral premovement. Since for them efficacious grace is a love (*delectatio victrix*) inspired in the will by God, they said that the grace that moved the will is a physical premovement or predetermination and not simply a moral premovement. For the Thomists and Suarezians, however, the attraction of the good, or *delectatio victrix*, is a moral movement, and not a physical movement. See J. L. Berti, *Opus de theologicis disciplinis* (Venice, 1760), lib. 14, c. 7 and 9, pp. 38 and 46 (quoted in Bocxe, *op. cit.*, pp. 36-7).

does it not seem that the creature is subject to a grave injustice? Salvation is a gift, one may say, and so too is predestination, its cause. But is this answer adequate, given the present condition of mankind where for the moral adult the inevitable alternative to heaven is the pain of hell? How too is this compatible with the revealed truth that God *wishes all men to be saved and to come to the knowledge of the truth?*[57]

If one would seek to escape the difficulties to which this explanation of the mystery gives rise by denying with Molina that predestination is really antecedent to foreknowledge of the creature's meritorious acts, or that the grace that elicits man's good acts is intrinsically efficacious, one falls into other difficulties. For example, why, then, is it called *pre*destination? More importantly, if it is consequent upon man's acts or the foreknowledge of them, it can scarcely be the cause of his achievement of the end; so that such an immense good seems to be withdrawn from the first causality of God's will and divine plan. Similar difficulties seem to attend the related theory of God's causation of man's acts. Does man perform supernatural acts (or natural acts, for that matter) through the addition of his human power to God's power, or through the addition of his determination to God's general influence? Does not this seem to ascribe something divine to human freedom—and something creaturely to divine knowledge, power, and mercy?

If the only difficulties to which the attempts to explain this mystery gave rise were speculative ones, perhaps one could resign himself to accepting the matter as it stands. But these perplexities touch very intimately the sources of Christian life and activity, as is immediately apparent in the understanding of their relation to the theological virtue of hope. Hope is a desire for eternal happiness based on a reliance upon God's merciful intention to use his power to help one to this goal, and upon the effectiveness of this help that God gives. Such an intention with the consequent aid is intimately related to predestination and its effect in the temporal order. So the conduct of the Christian's life is absolutely dependent upon what this predestination is, and it can be profoundly affected by his concept of it. I say it *can* be, since it is also possible that there be a dissociation between one's Christian life in practice and

[57] I Tim. 2:4.

the explanation one gives of the divine mystery on which that life is based. This can be harmful enough since it can lead to an undervaluing of the intellectual grasp of the faith, or to a guidance of one's life by some means other than an objective understanding of one's faith. But if there is a close association between the Christian's thought and life, an inadequate explanation of predestination results in an inadequate Christian life. For example, if one lives by the conviction that predestination is anterior to any knowledge God has of one's good or evil acts, an injunction to work out one's salvation in fear and trembling seems inappropriate,[58] for it seems that if one has been predestined, one's salvation is certain; and if one has not, it is impossible. If one is simply uncertain whether such a divine intention exists or not, it seems that the foundations of hope and thus of a vigorous Christian life are to that extent weakened. If, on the other hand, one accepts the statement that predestination is consequent upon God's foreknowledge of a life lived in fidelity to him and that this grace is rendered efficacious by man's response, then man seems cast back upon himself and his own resources. He seems to have less reason to rely completely on God, for here he is certain that God has not already predestined him. He knows that God waits to see what the outcome of his life will be before predestinating him, and what the outcome of his response will be before his grace can be called truly efficacious.

It is true that such difficulties can attend the mystery of predestination. Man can by misunderstanding this mystery form for himself a more or less distorted notion of God and his relation to the creature, and therefore commit himself to presumption, despair, negligence, or an unchristian self-confidence. But St. Paul presented the doctrine of predestination to the Christians of Rome as a motive of hope. Hence, a true understanding of it should lead to a strengthening of the motives of true hope and of the vigor of the Christian life, because it will lead to a more adequate understanding of the objective relation between God and the creature in the work of salvation.

To prepare the way for such understanding, I feel it important to compare briefly the analyses given by the Thomists and the

---

[58] See Phil. 2:13.

Molinists of the harmony between God's initiative and man's freedom in the order of grace to see where they agree with one another and at what point they begin to differ. They agree in accepting the revealed truth that affirms both sides of this seeming antinomy and the harmony that exists between them. And they agree in attempting to explain the relation between God's initiative and man's freedom in a way that does justice to both. They attempt to develop their explanation in accord with the teaching of Scripture and tradition, and thus conformity with these norms of revelation is the measure of the adequacy of their explanations. The Thomists and the Molinists present their explanations within the framework of the development of philosophy in the Middle Ages, a development that added new tools and new difficulties to this perennial problem. It added new tools because it gave deeper knowledge than that previously possessed of such elements of the mystery as causality and freedom; it added new difficulties because such progress demanded that the revealed mystery be harmonized with natural truths not previously known, and there was disagreement among theologians in their philosophical explanations of these natural truths. In their explanation of the revealed mystery or of texts from Scripture and tradition referring to this mystery, the theologians of both schools seemed to give a primary influence to their philosophical theories. Some of their exegesis that would not be accepted by theologians today was due simply to an inadequacy in the understanding of particular passages of Scripture. But some of it was also due to an undue influence of their philosophical principles inclining them to give to texts more specific meanings than they actually had or meanings contrary to the larger context in which the passage was found.

In their explanations of the harmony between God's act and the free creature's act in the supernatural order, the Thomists took as their starting point the uncontested truth that God was the origin of all good that is found in the creature, whether this good is that of the supernatural or of the natural order; and they were convinced that an explanation of the mystery that was in accord with this primary truth would be in accord with the exigencies of created freedom. The Molinists took as their point of departure the revealed and defined dogma that man's will is free in such a way, under the initiative of God exercised through grace, that it can either accept or reject grace; and they were convinced that nothing could be true of God's perfections and activity that would be contradictory to this.

Approaches to the same mystery from different starting points may result in different emphases, but it is not necessary that they result in mutually contradictory explanations of the same mystery. However, there are elements on which they agree in their understanding of God's initiative and man's freedom that of their very nature give rise to a dilemma that seems to lead to the basic differences between their explanations. As the mystery refers to the divine initative, both Thomists and Molinists understand by predestination an *absolute* divine intention that an individual free creature gain heaven in such a way that once he is predestined it is impossible for him to fail to reach heaven.[59] This conviction is based upon statements of Scripture and tradition. For example, Christ says of those who are his sheep that *they shall never perish, neither shall anyone snatch them out of my hand . . . no one is able to snatch anything out of the hand of my Father.*[60] St. Paul teaches that God makes all things contribute to the welfare of those whom he has called *according to his purpose;* and he proves this by showing that those whom he has foreknown and predestined, he has also called, justified, and glorified.[61] In the ninth chapter of Romans, St. Paul illustrates this truth by his account of God's choice of Jacob and his rejection of Esau. Moreover, there are many texts among the Fathers and later theologians which interpret Scripture's doctrine on predestination as an absolute divine intention. Given this premise, in accord with their differing points of departure, the Thomists teach that predestination is antecedent to God's foreknowledge of man's merits and the Molinists that it is subsequent to it.

As the divine initiative refers to the order of God's governance of man in time and his use of grace to elicit salutary acts from man's free will, there is between the Thomists and the Molinists an initial difference. The Thomists hold that the goodness of man's

[59] See above, pp. 9–10, 25–26.

[60] John 10:28–29. Other passages attribute man's perseverance in good emphatically to God (e.g., Phil. 1:6; 1 Peter 5:10) or warn Christians to ask God for this gift (the Our Father). An opportune death is God's gift (e.g., Wis. 4:11).

[61] See Rom. 8:28–30 above, on page 1.

act is due to God and his initiative as first cause. If two men are faced with the same temptation and one overcomes it, his superiority to the other man is due to grace and not to himself in any way that would nourish pride. Thus he is better than the other because he has received a greater grace from God that came from a greater divine love for him, a love that gave him not only sufficient power to perform the good act but the performance of the act itself. In other words, it is God who distinguished him from the other through giving him a prevenient grace which was greater than that given to the other and which, antecedent to the man's response, was efficacious or infallibly certain to gain his free response. Molina began with the fact of man's freedom and taught that grace is a power to perform a good act which man chooses either to use or to reject, and so the reason for the difference between the two men before the same temptation was the good choice of one and the sinful choice of the other. This position was attacked by the Thomists as giving man initiative in his good acts and making him the source of his being better than another. The Molinists answered (and some say that this is the position of Molina himself) that such was not their view. They acknowledged that God's greater love was the reason for the better position of the one man over that of the other, and thus they taught that the prevenient grace given to the one was greater than that given to the other. But they explained this in the only way that seemed to them consistent with freedom, namely, by Molina's explanation of God's causality of the created free act and of God's *scientia media*. Hence they taught that God knew what the created will would do given any circumstances and then chose to give the man he loved more a grace that he knew would gain his consent. So both sides hold that the good acts of man (in either the supernatural or the natural order) are due to a divine intention and a divine help that, antecedent to the actual response of the created will, are infallibly efficacious. This agreement was expressed during the *Congregationes de Auxiliis* held in Rome between 1597 and 1607 that investigated this controversy between the Dominicans and the Jesuits. The theologians representing both sides of the controversy agreed on a set of propositions that described the nature of efficacious grace, the last two of which stated that: "We hold that this movement is a real and antecedent application of the will, moving

34

and inclining the will to some determined act. When the help of prevenient efficacious grace is given, the man is infallibly converted."[62] Their disagreement was centered on the nature of this efficacious grace.

They find evidence for this doctrine of God as the cause of the distinction of the good man from the evil and the source of his good acts in the teaching of Scripture and tradition that God can move the created will as he desires, that he causes the good act itself of the free creature, and that man has nothing in his good actions of which to be proud. To cite a few representative passages, Ezechiel attributes to God the effective change of the human heart when he recounts God's promise of purification of his people: *I will give them a new heart and will put a new spirit within them: I will remove the stony heart from their bodies, and replace it with a natural heart, so that they will live according to my statutes, and observe and carry out my ordinance, . .* [63] In the book of Esther, Mordecai addresses his prayer to God for *there is no one who can resist you, who are the Lord;* and in answer to the prayers of his servants, *God changed the king's spirit to mildness.*[64] St. Paul taught that man's good works were so much the effect of God's grace that man was left with no motive of false pride: *For who singles thee out? Or what hast thou that thou hast not received?*[65] Tradition also seems to give evidence for this position. The official statements of the Church against the Pelagians and the Semi-pelagians show that the initiative in man's salutary acts is in God's love and his grace, and that this grace gives not only the power to perform the good act but the actual act itself. Such was the doctrine of St. Augustine and of later theologians

[62] See Vansteenberghe, *art. cit.*, 2157. The texts and arguments commonly used to defend this are most copiously and persuasively advanced by Lange, *op. cit.*, pp. 424–43.

[63] Ezech. 11:19–20. Unless otherwise noted, the Old Testament is quoted according to The Holy Bible: vol. 1 Genesis to Ruth; vol. 3 Job to Sirach; vol. 4 The Prophetic Books (ed. Confraternity of Christian Doctrine, Paterson, New Jersey, 1952–61). For O. T. books not contained in this version, our quotations are taken from *The Complete Bible: An American Translation* (Chicago, 1939).

[64] Esth. 13:11; 15:8 (verse 11 in Vulgate).

[65] 1 Cor. 4:7. Christ too teaches that it is God who differentiates the elect from those who are not chosen: *For many are called, but few are chosen.* Matt. 22:14. See above, footnote 30, for graces that are not accepted by men.

35

also. And it seems to be demanded by other truths such as the gratuity of grace, the infallible efficacy of divine providence, the eternal infallible divine knowledge of the future free acts of rational creatures,[66] and thus by philosophical principles as well as by the teaching of Scripture and tradition.

As the theologians of both camps agree on these aspects of divine initiative with reference to man's free acts in the order of grace and of nature, they also agree to some extent in their philosophical account of the manner in which the will is reduced to act. For example, both sides deny to the object of the will a physical causality in eliciting the act of the will.[67] The causality of the object with reference to the act of the will is a moral causality. The causality in no way detracts from the freedom of the will's act, but it is not the manner in which the will is actually moved to act, since the will's act is a physical reality and must be due to a physical and not simply to a moral cause. Moreover, the object of the will in this life is a mixture of good and evil, and thus when it is presented to the will, it is not antecedently efficacious in gaining its consent. Since God moves the will to act in accord with its nature and his efficacious grace is antecedently effective, it does not operate through the object of the will. God reduces the will to act not through its object, but through what we may call the order of efficiency rather than the order of finality. The dispute between the Thomists and Molinists is whether the will is reduced to act by a divine premoving, predetermining causality or by a divine concurrence in this order of efficient causality. Their difference here is related to the difference of their starting points, the Thomists holding that the former is a necessary conclusion of God's first causality and the Molinists that the latter is a necessary conclusion from the will's freedom.

It seems, then, that there are points on which the Thomists and the Molinists agree that are the roots of a dilemma that in turn is the source of their differences. It is very necessary, then, to examine these points of agreement to see whether in fact they are imposed upon us as the teaching of revelation or of reason. Since

[66] Both Banez and Molina hold that God's foreknowledge of the free act of the rational creature is not dependent upon the presence of this act to God by reason of his eternity. See above, pp. 9 and 23.

[67] See above, footnotes 28, 29, and 45.

the mystery that we are studying is a supernatural mystery, the controlling and primary source of understanding will be Scripture and tradition. Reason, as all theologians agree, has a very real but subordinate function in the explanation of a supernatural mystery. It must bring itself into accord with revelation; and if revelation seems to teach something contrary to a philosophical principle, this principle must be re-examined to see whether it in fact is completely true. Reason's function is to show that the supernatural mystery is not contrary to truths naturally known and to help explain it analogically through realities that are naturally known. The supernatural mystery of the harmony of God's initiative and man's freedom in the order of grace does involve natural truths that are to some extent subject to philosophical investigation. For example, predestination is an act of divine providence and thus of God's will and intellect. God's causality through grace of man's salutary acts is a causality of a created free human act. And thus the study of these natural realities is necessary for an adequate explanation of the mystery.

Hence in this study we shall try to explain in some degree the mystery of God's primacy and man's freedom in the order of grace according to the evidence of Scripture, tradition, and philosophical principles, always giving to Scripture and tradition the controlling influence. We are not primarily interested in refuting what seems to us inadequate in the theories of the Thomists and the Molinists, although in our own explanation we must take into consideration what they teach; and when we differ from them in the interpretation of Scripture, tradition, and philosophy, we must give the reasons for our difference.

CHAPTER TWO

Scripture: Examination of Old and New Testaments Viewed Particularly Through St. Paul

IN THIS chapter we shall examine the teaching of Scripture concerning the harmony between the divine salvific intention and grace on the one hand and the freedom of man on the other, both the man who achieves eternal salvation or a particular good act to which God calls him and the man who fails to achieve eternal salvation or to perform a good act commanded by God. We are examining this harmony as it actually exists in the present and normal order of divine providence, not as it could perhaps exist in another order or now exists in a unique case. And we ask whether the divine intention directing to heaven one who will in fact reach it is both antecedent to and contingent upon his free response in such a way that the individual could reject it and fail to reach heaven. We ask also whether the one who fails to gain heaven does so fail, although there was antecedent to his personal and unrepented sins a divine intention that he too gain heaven. Furthermore, we ask whether man can resist the prevenient grace that will in fact gain his consent, so that prevenient grace for those who reject it and for those who accept it is, as antecedent to their free choice, normally frustrable (i.e., can be, in the full sense of the word, frustrated or resisted). And we ask finally whether, in the case of one who actually performs the good act to which God draws him through grace, the free act itself and not only the power to perform it is the effect of grace. The scriptural answer to

38

these questions determines whether or not one must accept the dilemma which the Thomists and the Molinists face, and hence a study of the scriptural doctrine concerning them is determinative of the rest of our study. We shall examine this doctrine, not through answering each question successively, but through presenting the teaching the Old and the New Testaments concerning God's relation to those he is said to choose and to those he is said to reject.

1. *The Old Testament*

The response of the Old Testament to this question is limited, since throughout most of it there is absent a clear notion of a personal eternal beatitude and hence of God's intention and the means he takes to lead the individual to that fulfillment. The destination to which God was leading his chosen ones was described in largely temporal and social terms. But in this there was implicit and progressively more explicit the goal of personal happiness in a future life with God for God's chosen ones. And in any case, St. Paul saw in God's dealings with the Israelites of the Old Testament a type of his activity in bringing the Christian of later times to his eternal fulfillment.[1] So an investigation of God's activity in the Old Testament with men who are said to be somehow chosen or somehow rejected is relevant to our question. For the most part, in the Old Testament this activity of God with men is described in its obvious effects, and not in the ultimate terms of God's eternal intention and man's freedom. But even as such it contains teaching on God's providential design and man's freedom. As some divine attributes in the natural order can be known from the visible created effects of God, so something of the divine providential intention is seen in the actual effects of God's governance of men, particularly when these effects are presented by Scripture for the purpose of informing men of these divine intentions. Hence in the Old Testament we shall examine some representative incidents that indicate God's relation to those he is said to love in a special way, or choose, and to those he is said to reject.

[1] See 1 Cor. 10:1-11. Note that we will not attempt to show the stages in the gradual development of the Old Testament doctrine we are studying. That can be found in part in F. Dreyfus, "Le thème de l'heritage dans l'Ancien Testament," *Rev. des sciences phil. et théol.*, 42 (1958), 3-49.

Even in the account of the creation of the world and of God's relation to the first parents, we see the main elements of the response to our question. In the account of creation nothing other than God is indicated as the ultimate reason for God's activity. The different parts of the world with their goodness are seen to result from God's free, sovereign, and creative will. With this same free initiative he created man and set him to dwell in Eden, where God walked in friendship and intimacy with him. Adam was given an enduring life and a harmony with God, within himself, with his wife, and with the rest of the world over which he was given dominion. But the continuance of this state was made dependent upon his obedience to God's command. Because he rejected God's order, he was thrown out of the garden and stripped of the privileges he had enjoyed there. But even in this condition of estrangement from his maker, and before he had done anything to reverse it, God promised him victory over the evil one who had drawn him into opposition to God, and in this victory a return to friendship with God.[2]

The intention of the author of Genesis was to show men religious truths relevant to their own experience, and thus the elements of God's relation to Adam not indicated as proper to man's condition as innocent remain true in his relation to Adam's descendants.[3] So in the teaching of these first chapters of Genesis, we see that all man's goods come from God's free gift not elicited by a previous good in man. Man's present goods come from God's past gifts; and his future goods, to which he looks forward, come from God's past promises, the endurance and the fulfillment of which for individual men are wholly conditioned upon man's not rejecting God's commands. Even one so loved by God as Adam had it in his power to reject God's commands and thus his gifts; the same is true of the later chosen ones of God.

God's relation to Abraham, the father and example of all believers,[4] bears this out. Nothing is written to indicate that Abraham had made himself particularly worthy of God's gift at the time of his first call by God. Yet at this very first call, God made to him a

---

[2] See Gen. 1–3. It seems at least that the later Old Testament saw this victory promised in Gen. 3:15.

[3] See A.-M. Dubarle, *Le Péché originel dans l'écriture* (Paris, 1958), pp. 46 f.

[4] See Rom. 4:1–25.

40

promise that included implicitly all later gifts Abraham was to receive from him: *In you shall all the nations of the earth be blessed.*[5] The final purpose of God with Abraham was promised him before he had done anything good, but it was a promise the fulfillment of which was contingent upon Abraham's faith in God and his consequent submission to God's call. Abraham could have refused this belief and obedience; there is no contrary indication by Scripture, so the account of Abraham's call must be taken to mean that it was in reality conditioned upon his response and that he could in reality have refused that response. Later it is said that *Abram believed the Lord, who credited the act to him as justice.*[6] Abraham's faith and obedience were followed by the covenant in which God gave him absolute assurance that his previous promise would be fulfilled, and a sacrificial rite which ratified his un-conditioned promise of its fulfillment.[7] The history of Abraham shows more clearly perhaps than any other section of the Old Testament that those who gain their eternal fulfillment are antici-pated by a divine intention giving this fulfillment to them, an intention the realization of which is initially conditioned upon man's free response and frustrable by man's rejection, and that is unconditioned and absolute only after man's fidelity has been proved.

The antecedent, gratuitous, and conditioned character of God's intention for those whom he loves is seen also in his governance of the people of Israel. They were told: *It was not because you are the largest of all nations that the Lord set his heart on you and chose you, for you are really the smallest of nations. It was because the Lord loved you and because of his fidelity to the oath he had sworn to your fathers, . . .*[8] God freely chose them from all the nations of the earth because of his own love, and he struck an alliance with them in which he gave himself to them as their

[5] Gen. 12:3.

[6] Gen. 15:6. See Gal. 3:6; Rom. 4:3, 9, 22.

[7] Gen. 15:9-20. See Dreyfus, *art. cit.*, 25. See Gen. 22:16-18. Note that the promise is that his offspring shall have the land of Canaan and that all nations shall be blessed in Abraham, not necessarily a confirmation in personal justice till death. It may have also meant the latter. Some saints have been confirmed in justice at a particular stage in their lives while yet on earth, but the text does not demand this meaning in God's promise to Abraham or to his descendants, Isaac and Jacob.

[8] Deut. 7:7-8.

41

God: *I will take you as my own people, and you shall have me as your God.*[9] He extended to them the promises he had given to Abraham. They were to be the instruments through which all the nations of the earth would be blessed; they were to have the promised kingdom, God's special concern and aid, and all the benefits, both temporal and spiritual, which would result from that. But this promise, which even at the time of God's choice of this people was so extensive that it would be developed not through addition but merely through explication of what it already contained, was given in the form of an alliance or covenant; and insofar as it referred to any individual or group among them, its fulfillment was made conditional upon their fidelity to God. *I set before you here, this day, a blessing and a curse: a blessing for obeying the commandments of the Lord, your God, which I enjoin on you today; a curse if you do not obey the commandments. . . .*[10] The people freely gave their consent to this alliance.

God, for his part, was faithful to the covenant: *What more was there to do for my vineyard that I had not done?*[11] However, the history of God's chosen people who had been anticipated with such special love showed not the faithfulness of their father Abraham, but frequently recurring infidelities to the covenant. Again and again they disobeyed the commands of God and turned aside to false gods or to practices God had forbidden. Through the prophet, God says of his people: *I said, Here I am! Here I am! to a nation that did not call upon my name. I have stretched out my hands all the day to a rebellious people, . . .*[12] God's people dis-

---

[9] Ex. 6:7.

[10] Deut. 11:26-8. See also Ex. 19:5-8, and P. van Imschoot, *Théologie de l'Ancien Testament* I (Tournai, 1953), 246: See also Dreyfus, *art. cit.*, 27-8, 37-8, 40-42, and Pierre Biard, *La puissance de Dieu* (Paris, 1960), Ch. 1, "La puissance de Dieu révélée dans l'histoire d'Israel," 27-54. And see W. Eichrodt, *Theology of the Old Testament,* 1 (trans. by J. A. Baker, London, 1961), 36-45. The conditional character of God's desire of salvation for the individual seems implied (in view of the New Testament) by the Old Testament doctrine on the Book of Life (a register of the community), for everyone whose name is found written in it will be saved (Dan. 12:1; Is. 4:3; Mal. 3:16), while sinners have their names removed from it (Ex. 32:32-3; Ps. 69:29).

[11] Is. 5:4. See Biard, *op. cit.*, 84, 91-94, on God's fidelity to the promises he made and the indomitable power with which he realizes his promises for those who are faithful to him.

[12] Is. 65:1-2. See Rom. 10:21.

obeyed him: *So he turned on them like an enemy, and fought against them.*[13] He delivered his chosen people into the hands of their enemies because of his wrath, provoked by their sins. And yet his chastisements were paternal acts of mercy by which he tried to purify them, to make them expiate their sins, to realize their need of God, and to return to him.[14] The chosen people who continue in infidelity fall under the wrath of God, but they shall not frustrate the divine purpose. For the prophets see that God will save a remnant and will send his spirit within them so that they will walk in God's ways and obey his commands.[15] Could there be a stronger proof that the love God has for his chosen ones does not make it impossible for them in this life to refuse submission to him and suffer his ultimate abandonment?

If it is in this manner that God treated those whom he chose from all nations on the earth, how did he act toward those whom he turned against or did not choose, such as Esau, Pharaoh with his Egyptians, and the Canaanites dispossessed by the Israelites? He said: *I loved Jacob, but hated Esau.*[16] Concerning Pharaoh, he told Moses: *I will make him obstinate, however, so that he will not let the people go.*[17] He commanded the Israelites to destroy the Canaanite nations in the promised land and to show them no mercy.[18] If God's dealings with Israel show an antecedent choice of them, do not these acts show an antecedent rejection?

To this we must say, first of all, that the unique gift which God gave to Israel, namely, to make it the nation that was to be the

---

[13] Is. 63:10.

[14] See Wis. 11:9-10; 12:22. The persevering love Yahweh bore his unfaithful spouse, Israel, is movingly portrayed by Osee, c. 2.

[15] See Is. 10:22 f. and Rom. 9:27-8. See F. Dreyfus, "La doctrine du Reste d'Israel chez le prophète Isaie," *Rev. des sciences phil. et théol.*, 39 (1955), 361-86. See also Jer. 31:33-4; Ezech. 11:18-20; and above, p. 35, for the use made of the latter text to prove the infallible efficacy of grace as antecedent. On texts such as this see I. de la Potterie, "L'impeccabilité du chrétienne d'après 1 Joh., 3, 6-9," *L'Evangile de Jean, études et problèmes* (Bruges, 1958), pp. 161-77.

[16] Mal. 1:3.

[17] Ex. 4:21. See also Ex. 7:3.

[18] See Deut. 7:1-11, 16; Nm. 21:1-3; Jos. 6-7; 1 Sm. 15. For an explanation of God's seeming injustice in the Old Testament, see van Imschoot, *op. cit.*, 70-80; Paul Heinisch, *Theology of the Old Testament* (trans. by W. Heidt, Collegeville, 1950), 76-80; and A. Descamps, "Justice et justification. 1. L'Ancien Testament," *Suppl. du dict. de la Bible*, 4 (1949), 1458; and Eichrodt, *op. cit.*, 258-69, 139-41.

channel of God's blessings to the rest of the earth, was, as we have seen, a special and singular gift which God could confer upon the people of his will without thereby being unjust to other nations. God spoke of himself to Moses as *I who show favors to whom I will, I who grant mercy to whom I will.*[19] But one cannot identify the gift God gave to the Israelites with salvation to the extent that other nations, by not receiving this gift, were denied eternal salvation. Melchisedech, Job, and the people of Nineveh to whom Jonah is said to have preached were not Israelites, and yet they were the objects of God's mercy and were pleasing to God. So the fact that Esau did not receive the promise given to Abraham in no way means that he was denied eternal salvation. Before the birth of Esau and Jacob, the Lord had stated simply that *the elder shall serve the younger.*[20] God, who had promised Abraham that in his offspring all nations would be blessed, was free to choose among his offspring the one who would receive the promise. This choice of the younger Jacob simply illustrates the freedom of God's choice. The statement of the prophet Malachias centuries later (quoted above) refers not to Esau personally but to the people who came from him, the Edomites; moreover, it expresses not God's antecedent denial of eternal salvation to this people, but the rigor with which he punished their sins compared with the mercy he showed to the Israelites after their offenses. It is true that God is said to harden Pharaoh's heart, but this results from the Jewish tendency to pass up secondary causes and reduce all events to the causality to God. In other passages, Pharaoh is simply said to have become stubborn.[21] Neither were the Canaanites punished without previous guilt on their part, for they had been idolaters and had committed many grave crimes.[22] In fact, the Book of Wisdom, in a passage that is reflected in the famous ninth chapter of Romans, presented God's dealings with Pharaoh and the Canaanites as an example of God's mercy.[23] They had committed abominable sins of all sorts, and so God could in all justice have used his infinite power to destroy them immediately. As a matter of fact, he sent

[19] Ex. 33:19. See Rom. 9:15.
[20] Gen. 25:23. See Rom. 9:6–13.
[21] See Ex. 8:11, 28; 9:35.
[22] See Gen. 15:16; Lev. 18:25–8.
[23] See Wis. 11:2–12:27; Rom. 9:22–4. Compare Rom. 9:20–1 with Wis. 15:7.

minor punishments to these people in the beginning and only gradually more rigorous ones: *you rebuke offenders little by little, warn them, and remind them of the sins they are committing, that they may abandon their wickedness and believe in you, O Lord!*[24] God did this, not from any weakness or from his lack of understanding of the measure of men's guilt or of the evil of their hearts. Rather, *you have mercy on all, because you can do all things; and you overlook the sins of men that they may repent. For you love all things that are and loathe nothing that you have made; . . .*[25] God put off the full punishment of the Egyptians so that they could have time to repent and turn in belief to God; but since they contemned God's initial punishments, they hardened their hearts and brought upon themselves the ultimate calamity.[26] They refused to glorify God through submitting themselves to him, but their resistance did not prevent God from fulfilling his purposes in freeing the Israelites. In fact, God used the very resistance he had tried in his mercy to overcome to manifest his power over the opposition of men, his wrath toward sin, and his mercy toward the chosen people whom he saved in the midst of such obstacles.

What conclusion can be drawn from this doctrine of the Old Testament other than the fact that God leaves those whom he chooses for eternal salvation free to resist him, and that his lack of choice of men for eternal salvation is only after man's continued resistance to him? It is true that God is all powerful and no one can resist his will, but in the actual order of his providence God does not exercise this omnipotence by making infallibly certain the fulfillment of his antecedent intention for those individuals he loves, or by antecedently reprobating those who lose eternal life. He shows his omnipotence in overcoming all obstacles placed in the way of his chosen ones who do not reject him, in punishing those who resist his merciful designs, and in turning their very resistance to further his own purposes of mercy toward his chosen ones. The book of Ecclesiasticus makes clear this respect or tolerance of man's freedom that is a part of God's plan: *Say not: "It was God's doing that I fell away"; for what he hates he does not*

[24] Wis. 12:2. See Biard, *op. cit.*, 95–100.

[25] Wis. 11:23–4.

[26] See Wis. 12:26–7; 19:4–5. Cf. J. Weber, in "Le livre de la Sagesse," in *La Sainte Bible*, ed. by L. Pirot, 6 (Paris, 1946), 524.

45

do . . . When God, in the beginning, created man, he made him subject to his own free choice . . . Before man are life and death, whichever he chooses shall be given him.[27]

2. The New Testament: The Gospels

The indications of the divine providential plan which we find in the Old Testament are more clearly expressed in the New Testament with reference to the eternal destiny of the individual. It is expressed by the Synoptics in relation to their doctrine of the kingdom of God. It is those who enter the kingdom of God who are the privileged ones among men.[28] For it is of such absolute value that a man will sell all that he has to purchase it, like a treasure in a field or a pearl of great price. It is the reward promised to those who fulfill the beatitudes.[29] This kingdom has an external character, for Christ appoints ministers of his kingdom which he calls his Church, and he gives to these ministers the administration of spiritual goods, of baptism, the Eucharist, and the forgiveness of sins. Being external and temporal, it thus has a history during which it will grow, as the mustard seed, which is the smallest of seeds, grows to be the largest of herbs.[30] While the kingdom is external and temporal, entrance into it assures eternal life, for it gives salvation; it is the ultimate gift that the judge at the end of the world will give the good; it is the joy of God himself; and Christ

[27] Ecclus. 15:11, 14, 17. Hence the texts that express God's *power* to move the will as he desires (see above p. 35) do not prove that as a matter of fact God makes use of antecedently infallibly effective decrees and graces to move men's wills in the present order. The doctrine of the Old Testament seems to us to be contrary to a normal use of such decrees and graces by God to move free will to good. The Old Testament evidence of such decrees seems to be restricted to acts of creatures inferior to man (see Gen. 41:32), and to events which God will bring about either with the cooperation of men or over their opposition (e.g., liberation of Israelites from Egypt and the fulfillment of his promise to Abraham).

[28] For an analysis of the doctrine of grace in the Synoptics in relation to the kingdom of God, see P. Bonnetain, "Grâce," *Supplément du dictionnaire de la Bible*, 3 (1938), 950–73. See also J. Bonsirven, *Le règne de Dieu* (Aubier, 1957); and A. Feuillet, "Le Régne de Dieu, la personne de Jesus d'après les Evangiles synoptiques," in *Introduction à la Bible.* ed. A. Robert and A. Feuillet, 2 (Tournai, 1959), 771–818.

[29] See Matt. 13:44–6; 5:3, 10.

[30] See Matt. 10:1–4; 28:19–20; Luke 22:19; Matt. 16:18–19; 13:31–2.

says to the ministers of this kingdom: *Rejoice in this, that your names are written in heaven.*[31] Hence in the Synoptics generally there is no sharp distinction between the kingdom in its temporal phase, and the kingdom as union with God in heaven. Entrance into the former is spoken of as entrance into the latter.

This entrance into the kingdom is received by man simply as a gift from God: *Whoever does not accept the kingdom of God as a little child will not enter into it.*[32] Men cannot gain it of themselves, for with reference to this gift they are like captives to be liberated, debtors who are insolvent, blind who are given sight, and the dead who are raised to life.[33] It comes to men wholly because, as Christ said to the Apostles: *It has pleased the Father to give you the kingdom.*[34] God brings men into it with the loving solicitude of the father in the parable of the prodigal son,[35] and Christ, God's agent in establishing this kingdom, says that *I have come to call not the just but sinners.*[36]

But God, who in his own free initiative gives man the kingdom and in that gift eternal happiness with himself in heaven, makes its eternal fulfillment conditioned upon man's response. It is only those who have treated men in need as Christ himself, those who have accepted Christ's words in faith and who have had a filial confidence in him that will enter heaven.[37] Does this mean that those whom God with a special love brings into his kingdom in its earthly stage can, but in fact will not, defect, because they are sustained by God's infallible decree? Or does it mean that God's antecedent choice of them for eternal life does not take away from them the power to defect and lose this gift? The latter seems more in accord with the Synoptics, for while they state strongly that the gift of the kingdom is the gift of heaven, they teach too that the kingdom of God in its earthly stage is like a field that holds both wheat and chaff, a net with good and bad fish. At the end of the world God will gather to himself the wheat and the good fish,

[31] Luke 10:20. See also Matt. 19:25; 25:34, 21, 23.
[32] Mark 10:15.
[33] See Luke 4:18 ff.; Matt. 18:23 ff.; Luke 15:14; 15:24–32.
[34] Luke 12:32.
[35] See Luke 15:11–32.
[36] Matt. 9:13.
[37] See Matt. 25:32; Mark 1:15; Matt. 6:25–34; and J. Bonsirven, *Théologie du Nouveau Testament* (Paris, 1951), pp. 131–3, 149–59.

while rejecting the rest.[38] What truth can harmonize these various statements concerning the kingdom other than the fact that while entrance into the kingdom on earth contains God's promise of eternal life, the fulfillment of this promise is simply conditioned on man's subjective response? If he denies his submission, the promise will not be fulfilled.

What then of those who have not been brought into the kingdom of God? Does this mean that God has antecedently rejected them by the fact that he has freely chosen others for his kingdom? Mystery remains after giving the Synoptics' answer to this, but it is clear that Christ meant to exclude no one from his kingdom. He sent the messengers of the gospel into the world to make disciples of all nations.[39] And he affirms in the parable of the lost sheep: *Even so, it is not the will of your Father in heaven that a single one of these little ones should perish.*[40] The parable of the wedding feast in which the men who, because of their preoccupation with their own pursuits, rejected the invitation and were therefore destroyed, indicates that it is only man's antecedent bad will that is the cause of his consequent rejection by God.[41] The opposite teaching, namely, that there is in God an intention not to sustain man in doing good before the individual's resistance to God, seems wholly alien to God's mercy shown in Christ who wept over Jerusalem

[38] See Matt. 13:24–30, 36–43, 47–50. The phrase at the end of the parable of the great supper in Luke, *make them come in,* has been interpreted as an absolute divine decree. But this interpretation is now rejected. See L. Marchal, "Evangile selon s. Luc," in *La Sainte Bible,* ed. by L. Pirot, 10 (2. ed., Paris, 1950), 184–5; M.-J. Lagrange, *Evangile selon s. Luc* (8. ed., Paris, 1948), pp. 402–8. Neither does the text quoted above from Luke concerning the names written in heaven refer to such a decree, since these words of Christ seem to have included Judas. Moreover they refer to the doctrine of the Book of Life which in the Old Testament indicates a conditional assurance of God's friendship (see above, footnote 10). The one phrase that may indicate an absolute divine decree of a free created act in the Synoptics is contained in Christ's prayer that Peter's *faith* not defect (see Luke 21:31–2), and that he confirm his brethren in the faith. This was essential for the Church Christ founded and was fulfilled without the preservation of Peter himself from grave sin.

[39] See Matt. 28:19.

[40] Matt. 18:14.

[41] See Matt. 22:1–14. On the text, *For many are called, but few are chosen* (Matt. 22:14), that concludes this parable, see M.-J. Lagrange in *Evangile selon s. Matthieu* (8. ed., Paris, 1948), p. 425. See also E. Sutcliffe, "Many are called but few are chosen," *The Irish Theological Quarterly,* 28 (1961), 126–31.

48

and lamented: *How often would I have gathered thy children together, as a hen gathers her young under her wings, but thou wouldst not! Behold your house is left to you desolate.*[42]

The doctrine of St. John concerning God's relation to man in bringing him to his eternal beatitude is the same as that of the Synoptics, but it gives evidence of a deeper penetration into the designs of God and the nature of the gift he offers. St. John sums up his message in the words: *God so loved the world that he gave his only begotten Son, that those who believe in him may not perish, but may have life everlasting.*[43] Only God's love freely given is the source of this gift of life everlasting. It cannot be won by acts that owe their initiative to man. *No one can come to me unless the Father who sent me draw him. . . .*[44] Man can do nothing of himself; in this order of things, his acts depend upon Christ, as the life and fruitfulness of the branches depend upon the life of the vine that courses through them.[45] This life that God gives is such that, as Christ says, *he who hears my word, and believes him who sent me, has life everlasting.*[46] The Jews to whom Christ spoke thought that the good man would gain everlasting life after he departed this temporal life, but Christ taught them that the one who believed in his words already had this everlasting life even in this world. What they thought man entered into after this life, Christ said man entered into when he believed. It is immediately apparent from his words that the one who believes has the heavenly fulfillment of this eternal life already begun, not in its ultimate stage of growth, but in God's assurance and in its seed that is already in the believer. Christ said of those who believed in him: *My sheep hear my voice, and I know them and they follow me. And I give them everlasting life; and they shall never perish, neither shall anyone snatch them out of my hand. What my Father*

[42] Matt. 23:37–8. The problem raised by the obduracy of the Jews we will treat particularly in our account of Paul's teaching. On the synoptic teaching in this matter, see J. Gnilka, *Die Verstockung Israels: Isaias 6:9–10 in der Theologie der Synoptiker* (Munich, 1961).

[43] John 3:15. See 1 John 4:10.

[44] John 6:44. Cf. F. M. Braun in "Evangile selon s. Jean," in *La Sainte Bible* ed. by L. Pirot, 10 (3. ed., Paris, 1950), 363.

[45] See John 15:1–11.

[46] John 5:24. See also 6:54; 11:25–6; and M.-J. Lagrange, *Evangile selon s. Jean* (8. ed., Paris, 1948), CLXV-VI.

has given me is greater than all; and no one is able to snatch anything out of the hand of my Father.[47]

The achievement of this fulfillment in the next life, however, is dependent upon the dispositions and acts of the believers in Christ. There is needed not only the initial faith, rebirth, trust, love of God, and the obedience to God's commands that flows from these inner dispositions. There is also needed a perseverance in this till death. As St. John teaches: *If that abides in you which you have heard from the beginning, you also will abide in the Son and in the Father. And this is the promise that he has given us, the life everlasting.*[48] How is this statement to be harmonized with those we have just quoted that affirm that the believer already has eternal life and shall never perish? Does it mean that in the choice for heaven of the believers antecedent to their merits, God has an absolute intention to see that man does fulfill the conditions required? Or does it mean that man in this life really retains the ability to defect and thus lose eternal life, so that God's choice and grace as antecedent are objectively effective insofar as they depend on God, but are still frustrable by man's resistance? It can only mean the latter, since the assurance that they already have eternal life is given to all who believe and give themselves to Christ. And yet Christ knew that some of these would not reach heaven. Only if Christ's assurance of heaven to all those who followed him was both objectively absolute and yet conditioned on the subjective response of man, can the various elements of St. John's teaching be harmonized. It would be incompatible with elements of that teaching to say that God has toward some who now have that life an intention antecedent to their resistance not to sustain them in fidelity to himself. And with other elements of John's teaching it is impossible to harmonize an absolute and unconditional infallibility of God's antecedent intention to bring those chosen ones to eternal life.

But is God's choice limited? What of those who do not receive

---

[47] John 10:27-9. See also John 6:37-9, and the commentaries of Lagrange, *op. cit.*, pp. 179-81, and of Braun, *op. cit.*, pp. 363-5, upon it. They reject deductions of predestination and reprobation in the ordinary sense from this text.

[48] 1 John 2:24-5. For a study of St. John's teaching that the Christian is impeccable and that this is conditioned on his fidelity, e.g., in 1 Joh. 3:6-9, see de la Potterie, *art. cit.*

the gift of faith in Christ through which eternal life is gained? If God's gift is wholly free, do men lack that gift because God has not given it? Some passages in St. John seem to suggest this. *But I have told you that you have seen me and you do not believe. . . . No one can come to me unless the Father who sent me draw him.*[49] And on another occasion Christ tells the Jews: *But you do not believe because you are not of my sheep.*[50] And finally John, reflecting on the disbelief of the Jews, says: *This is why they could not believe, because Isaias said again, "He has blinded their eyes, and hardened their hearts; lest they see with their eyes, and understand with their minds, and be converted, and I heal them."*[51]

Although these passages have been used in the past as evidence of God's antecedent reprobation, no exegete would do so today because of the context, both remote and immediate, in which they are found. St. John's teaching on the universality of Christ's saving mission is too clear. His death *is a propitiation for our sins, not for ours only but also for those of the whole world.*[52] Christ's whole public ministry was an attempt to bring the Jews to belief in his mission, but he told them: *And you have not his [the Father's] word abiding in you, since you do not believe him whom he has sent. . . . you are not willing to come to me that you may have life.*[53] This unwillingness of the Jews to believe, to submit themselves to Christ in the concrete historical context in which he presented himself to them, was the reason for their lack of belief indicated in the passages cited above.[54] John's quotation from Isaias is an answer to the scandal that may arise in the hearts of some from the seeming frustration of Christ's mission by the Jews' unbelief, a frustration that seems to reflect upon the divine omnipotence. His Hebraic expression does not mean that God's hardening of the Jews' hearts was the cause of their disbelief; Christ, like Isaias, was sent for the very purpose that they may believe. But it does show that those who rejected Christ did not escape the

[49] John 6:36, 44.
[50] John 10:26.
[51] John 12:39–40. The text quoted is Is. 6:9.
[52] 1 John 2:2. See also John 1:9, 12; Apoc. 3:20.
[53] John 5:38, 40. See Stephen's rebuke to the Jews, Acts 7:51.
[54] Cf. Braun, *op. cit.*, p. 399, for comments on John 10:26. See also A. Charue, *L'incrédulité des Juifs dans le Nouveau Testament* (Paris, 1929), on this whole matter.

51

sovereignty of God since, because of their bad dispositions, the mission of mercy through the fact of its rejection resulted in a greater blindness and hardening of their hearts, and God used their very rejection to bring about his designs.[55]

3. St. Paul

It is above all in the epistles of St. Paul and more specifically in Romans 8:28–30 and 9:6–24 that there has been found the doctrine of God's predestination and reprobation. Hence it is of the greatest importance to investigate these passages to see whether in fact they teach that the predestination of the individual is absolute or conditioned, and whether they teach antecedent or consequent reprobation. Moreover, they must be interpreted in the context of the purpose of St. Paul in the whole epistle and in each particular section, and in view of St. Paul's personal method of developing his theme. It is due to the lack of such an approach that the most varied interpretations have been given to these key passages.

An outline of the dogmatic section of this epistle will give us the context of these passages and also St. Paul's doctrine on the wrath of God.[56] The purpose of the epistle's doctrinal part (c. 1–11) is expressed by St. Paul as follows: *For I am not ashamed of the gospel, for it is the power of God unto salvation to everyone who believes, to Jew first and then to Greek. For in it the justice of God is revealed, from faith unto faith, as it is written, "He who is just lives by faith."*[57] The mystery of Christ and of his redemptive activity is the way in which God exercises his power to save all who believe, both Jew and Greek. St. Paul proceeds to show that outside of this dispensation, all men are subject to the *wrath of God* (1:18–3:20). This wrath of God is the complement of his justice, for as the latter in the biblical sense means primarily God's

[55] See Braun, *op. cit.*, pp. 415–16, for an excellent commentary on John 12:37–43.

[56] For analyses of the organization of the epistle that are somewhat different from one another but, for our purpose, not significantly so, see A. Viard, "Epître aux Romains," in *La Sainte Bible*, ed. by L. Pirot, 11.2 (Paris, 1951), 10–20, and S. Lyonnet, *Les épîtres de s. Paul aux Galates, aux Romains*, a fascicle of *La Sainte Bible . . . de Jérusalem* (2. ed., Paris, 1959), pp. 66–70.

[57] Rom. 1:16–17.

action in the world to save men, so the former indicates the anger with which God responds to the sins of men. In continuity with the Old Testament and the Gospels, St. Paul's teaching is wholly incompatible with a wrath of God that is antecedent to the sins of the men against whom it is directed. For Paul, God's wrath is wholly subsequent to man's sin. The first sentence of this section makes this clear: *For the wrath of God is revealed from heaven against all ungodliness and wickedness. . . .*[58] This wrath will be manifested particularly on the day of judgment, but it is also partially exercised during history in God's allowance of the sins of men to bear their natural fruit of spiritual blindness, hardness of heart, and disorders external to man. This period too is one of God's patience by which he attempts to draw men to repentance. *Or dost thou despise the riches of his goodness and patience and long-suffering? Dost thou not know that the goodness of God is meant to lead thee to repentance?*[59] It is really superfluous to recall that the purpose of God's patience with men is their conversion; but we are forced to express it, since some have thought that God was patient out of a prior intention that these men should multiply their sins and thus give God a chance to exercise his wrath.

The salvific justice of God is revealed through Christ's passion that merits justice for all men, since they are all sinners and thus subject to the wrath of God, and that is appropriated by man through faith, a faith which, like that of Abraham, removes the basis for human pride (3:21–4:25). The justification effected through this instrument assures eternal salvation to all Christians (c. 5–11). The death of Christ and the superabundant grace he has gained for us assure us of this (5:1–21). The union with Christ that effects this justification is a definitive break with sin (c. 6) and a liberation from the old law that could never save (c. 7). The law of the Christians is the Spirit, and those who walk by the Spirit rather than by the flesh will not be condemned, but saved! (8:1–13). All those whom the Spirit animates are sons of God. *But if we are sons, we are heirs also: heirs indeed of God and joint heirs with Christ, provided, however, we suffer with him that we may also be glorified with him.*[60] Thus, St. Paul teaches, we who

[58] Rom. 1:18. See Lyonnet, *op. cit.*, pp. 57–8.
[59] Rom. 2:4.
[60] Rom. 8:17.

are animated by the Spirit from whom comes charity are destined for glory. There is a witness of this in the aspiration of material creation for the glorification of the sons of God, and in Christian experience in which we hope for glory with a hope given us by the Holy Spirit (8:18–27). We know too that God's purpose is to bring to glory those who love him (8:28–30); and if God is for us, nothing can defeat us (8:31–38). To the objection that some may forward, namely, that God's promise failed the chosen people of the old dispensation, the next three chapters (c. 9–11) are the answer.

These chapters we shall examine later, but now within the context, in the eighth chapter, of the assurance St. Paul gives of their eternal salvation to the Christians of Rome animated by the Spirit, we shall examine St. Paul's explicit teaching on predestination:

> And we know that God cooperates in all things for the good of those who love him, of those whom he has called according to his purpose. (v. 28)
> For those whom he has foreknown, he has also predestined to become conformed to the image of his Son, that he may be the first-born of many brethren. (v. 29)
> And those whom he has predestined, he has also called; those whom he has called, he has also justified; and those whom he has justified, he has also glorified. (v. 30)[61]

The interpretation of this passage is made difficult by the large number of controverted questions that surround it. On some of these questions, such as what the subject of the dependent clause in v. 28 is, we need not delay, since their solution does not affect the meaning of the passage. In answer to the other questions, we must keep in mind that in the context of this passage St. Paul is presenting to the Christians of Rome different reasons that show them the certainty of their eternal salvation. In fact, this particular text is the culminating argument for the certainty of their salvation. And within this text, vv. 29, 30 are offered by St. Paul as a proof of v. 28, namely, that God does work in all things for the

---

[61] Rom. 8:28–30 (author's translation). A. Merk, *Novum Testamentum Graece et Latine* (6. ed., Rome, 1948). See M. Black, "The Interpretation of Romans viii: 28," *Neotestamentica et patristica* (Leiden, 1962), pp. 166–72. He shows that there is less difficulty in supposing τὸ πνεῦμα as the subject of συνεργεῖ in v. 28. This word may be understood from v. 26 or as the original reading for πάντα.

welfare of those who love him, those who are called according to his purpose.

St. Paul introduces the fact that God has predestined those whom he has foreknown to prove the foregoing verse. All agree that the word for predestined (προώρισεν) adds something to foreknowledge, namely, an act of the divine will, which, as the aorist in the context indicates, has already carried its object to the purpose indicated, namely, *the image of his Son*. Some understand by this *image* that which the Christian has through grace.[62] But the context, in which Paul is assuring Christians of the certainty of their salvation, seems incompatible with such a restriction of its meaning. Such a restricted meaning would not prove Paul's point. Hence it must refer mainly to conformity with Christ in his glory, the interpretation given to it by the majority of modern exegetes.[63] This interpretation is corroborated by the next section of the passage, where Paul indicates the acts through which God gains the end to which he has predestined man. Those whom he has predestined, God has called, justified, and glorified. This verse expresses the order of execution of the divine act of predestination affirmed in the previous verse. Moreover, these acts that are the successive acts through which the term of predestination is gained, namely, eternal glory, are by their position shown to be the effects of God's predestination. They are also expressed in the aorist which, in the context, affirms that they in some way have already come about.

Granted, then, that Paul is here teaching a predestination to eternal glory, who are the objects of such a divine decree? Since vv. 29 and 30 that express this predestination are a proof of the assertion in the preceding verse, where it is stated that God makes all things cooperate for those who love him, for those whom he has called according to his purpose, the answer to this question depends upon who are called according to the purpose indicated.

---

[62] See F. Prat, *The Theology of St. Paul* (trans. from 11th ed. by J. L. Stoddard, Newman, Md.), I, 244–5. Note that even he, while holding that grace is the direct object of predestination, holds that Paul considers eternal glory as the natural development of grace.

[63] See Ceuppens, *Theologia biblica*, 1 (2. ed., Rome, 1949), 272–3 where he refers to a good number of modern exegetes who hold the same view. He also shows that almost all modern exegetes see in ἐδόξασεν heavenly glory even more directly than grace.

The Greek Fathers interpreted this purpose as man's and not God's purpose. Thus they taught that God called man according to his good intentions which God foreknew antecedent to man's predestination.[64] Modern exegetes, as well as the Latin Fathers, understand this purpose to be God's purpose, not man's, in accord with the other uses of the word by St. Paul and his intent in the present passage to show the Christians their motives for hope, based on God's firm purpose of making all things cooperate for their good.[65] St. Augustine distinguished in St. Paul those called according to God's purpose and those simply called, a distinction he modeled upon the distinction in the parable of the king's marriage feast between the chosen and the called. So he held that God has predestined only that select group of Christians that was called according to his purpose, not the other Christians who have been simply called. Exegetes in general reject this distinction in St. Paul for, as they point out, the words *called* and *chosen* do not have the difference of meaning for him that they have in St. Matthew. For Paul, the *called* are those who now stand in the faith and are on the way to eternal salvation.[66]

Who then are they who are called according to God's *purpose?* Thomists and Molinists generally seem to agree with Prat's interpretation of this word in St. Paul when it is used of God: "From all that precedes, it results that πρόθεσις designates in St. Paul *an eternal act of the consequent and absolute divine will referring to a particular benefit,* for example, to an efficacious call."[67] Accord-

---

[64] For the texts of the Eastern Fathers on this passage, see Prat, *op. cit.,* pp. 443–8. Origen and Cyril of Alexandria interpreted the purpose as both God's and man's, but their interpretation of the passage was substantially the same as that of the other Greek Fathers.

[65] See Ceuppens, *op. cit.,* pp. 265–76, for his treatment of the whole passage, and more specifically pp. 266–7.

[66] For St. Augustine's interpretation, see Ceuppens, *loc. cit.,* and Prat, *op. cit.,* pp. 450–54. For Paul's different use of the words involved from that of Matthew, see *ibid.,* pp. 436–7. See above, footnote 41.

[67] *Ibid.,* p. 435. For the identification of this word in St. Paul with an absolute, unconditional decree of God in either the Thomist or Molinist sense, see also, for example, F.C.-R. Billuart, *Summa Sancti Thomae hodiernis academiarum moribus accomodata,* 1 (Artois, 1867), 381; H. Lange, *De gratia,* p. 431; Garrigou-Lagrange, *The One God,* p. 662; Ciappi, *La predestinazione* (Rome, 1954), p. 25; A. Medebielle, "Epitre aux Ephésiens," in *La Sainte Bible,* ed. by L. Pirot, 12 (Paris, 1951), 33; Ceuppens, *op. cit.,* p. 263; perhaps M.-J. Lagrange, *Epître aux Romains* (Paris, 1950), p. 214 (who simply quotes Prat without comment); and

ing to this interpretation those are called according to God's purpose who have been called by an absolute divine decree or will. And since those who are mentioned as predestined are called according to God's purpose, they are ordered to the term of predestination by such an absolute divine decree. Hence, if the *image of his Son* and glory in this passage refer to the state of grace, St. Paul is teaching the Christians of Rome that they have been justified because of such an absolute divine decree. And if these terms refer, as we have shown to be the case, to man's eternal salvation, St. Paul is teaching that those whom God has predestined reach heaven owing to an absolute divine decree. Who, then, we may ask, has St. Paul said are predestined by God? This depends, most authors would say, upon the meaning of God's foreknowledge (προέγνω) mentioned in v. 29. Some, following the general teaching of the Greek Fathers, understand it to mean a speculative knowledge by which God has a vision of the good men do. These whom God has foreknown in this way, he then predestines.[68] Others however reject his interpretation. They point out that the Greek Fathers' interpretation of God's foreknowledge here in this sense depended upon their understanding of the purpose in the previous verse as referring to man's dispositions; since that is not now an acceptable interpretation, one cannot hold that the foreknowledge mentioned in the passage is a speculative knowledge of man's merits that precedes predestination. Moreover, when the biblical expression *to know* has God as its subject and men chosen by him as its object, it means not a merely speculative knowledge but a loving, practical, approving knowledge distinguishing one person from another.[69] Because of this Thomists have appealed to this passage to prove their concept of God's causative knowledge and their doctrine of predestination antecedent to God's foreknowledge of man's merits. To this, however, we must say that the scriptural understanding of God's knowledge as choice does not imply an *unconditioned* choice of a man and thus does not sustain the Thomistic understanding of God's causative knowledge. For

---

J. Huby, *Epître aux Romains* (nouvelle édition par S. Lyonnet, Paris, 1957), p. 309, footnote 2.

[68] See Prat, *op. cit.*, pp. 240–6, and A. D'Ales, "Prédestination," *DAFC*, 4 (1922), 201 f.

[69] See, for example, Amos 3:2; Ps. 1:6; Matt. 7:23; Gal. 4:9; etc. See also Lagrange, *op. cit.*, pp. 215–16, and Ceuppens, *op. cit.*, pp. 269–71.

these reasons, neither the Molinist nor the Thomistic theory of predestination seems to be sustained by this passage. Moreover, according to the interpretation of both of these theories, St. Paul would be asserting that God has predestined only some of the Christians at Rome. And this could scarcely be a motive of hope for all of them, or assure all of them of the certainty of eternal salvation. Hence, Huby follows Lagrange in presenting another interpretation: "In this passage . . . St. Paul takes a social viewpoint. He considers not the faithful individually but the assembly of Christians, 'the new community of the children of God destined for glory,' let us say the Church."[70] In other words, St. Paul is not stating that God has predestined any individual to heaven; he is simply saying that he has predestined the Church to glory. This interpretation, however, does not fit into the purpose St. Paul had here. He was proving to the Christian at Rome the certainty of their personal salvation, and such an assertion about the Church would be irrelevant. Moreover, all the words Paul uses in the context and text refer to Christians and not to the Church (e.g., *those who love God*), so the predestination must also refer to them.

These difficulties of interpretation come from the assumption by the authors that for St. Paul, God's purpose and his predestination are not conditional but infallibly efficacious, either intrinsically (Thomists) or extrinsically (Molinists). If this is so, Paul cannot be telling the Christians at Rome that all of them have been predestined, because all exegetes admit that the fact of being justified does not of itself preclude the possibility of defection and reprobation. But the question is: does God's purpose and predestination in St. Paul's meaning preclude the possibility of man's resistance and reprobation? Or is it objectively efficacious insofar as it concerns God's will and grace, but subjectively conditioned on man's response? It is clear that the word πρόθεσις means a "plan, purpose, resolve, will"[71] in the places where St. Paul applies it to God, but not that it is efficacious in the sense of the scholastics where it refers to a particular act dependent on the free will of the creature. They argue that St. Paul was speaking to men who had in fact

---

[70] Huby, *op. cit.*, p. 305. See also Lagrange, *op. cit.*, p. 217.

[71] W. Bauer, *A Greek-English Lexicon of the New Testament* (trans. by Arndt and Gingrich, Chicago, 1957) p. 713. St. Paul applies the word to God in Rom. 8:28; 9:11; Eph. 1:11; 3:11; 2 Tim. 1:9.

been converted to Christianity, and he said they were called according to God's purpose. So God's purpose in calling them was effective or efficacious. I grant this, but that in no way proves that it was antecedently effective in the sense of the scholastics, since God's purpose may well have been completely conditioned upon man's lack of resistance, of which man was fully capable when he was given the prevenient grace of faith. Moreover, the argument, such as it is, is based on the interpretation of v. 28 as referring to God's purpose as restricted to man's justification, or as not including his achievement of his eternal glory. This, however, is not tenable. The following verses prove that God works for the welfare of those whom he has called according to his purpose precisely by showing that God has predestined them to heaven, has already called, justified, and glorified them. From the relation between these verses and v. 28, it seems that God's predestination is contained within his purpose. Hence, the purpose indicated refers to the eternal salvation, and not only to the justification that has already been realized by the Christian.[72]

So if we approach the text with complete objectivity, we must conclude, it seems to us, that St. Paul is asserting that God has predestined to eternal glory all those who love him; i.e., all the justified, all those who have been united with Christ in the Church, in short, all the Christians to whom he is writing and whom he supposes to be animated by the Spirit. The difficulty standing in the way of this interpretation, the only one that is in accord with the context, has been the conception of predestination as infallibly efficacious and not conditioned. If such is the case, Paul cannot be telling all Christians that they are predestined. Hence the varied attempts at other interpretations, none of which is satisfactory. The one satisfactory interpretation is that based on accepting the predestination taught by St. Paul as one whose fulfillment is conditioned and frustrable. That this is St. Paul's meaning will be apparent from our examination of the following chapters; but before we approach that, it is well to examine briefly

[72] See William Sanday and A. Headlam, *A Critical and Exegetical Commentary on the Epistle to the Romans* (7. ed., New York, 1902), p. 216, where the purpose is interpreted as "the comprehensive plan or design in accordance with which God directs the destinies of men."

St. Paul's later text on predestination that is parallel to the one we have just studied.

In his introduction to the Epistle to the Ephesians, he praises the benevolence of God (1:3–14), shown in God's eternal plan (vv. 3–6) and in its temporal fulfillment in Christ (vv. 7–10), by which both the Jews and the Gentiles were called (vv. 11–14). He praises the Father for all blessings, and enumerates among them the fact that God has chosen us in Christ before the foundation of the world to be holy in love. Also, *he predestined us to be adopted through Jesus Christ as his sons, according to the purpose of his will, unto the praise of the glory of his grace. . . .*[73] He praises God, too, that this eternal plan has embraced those of the Jews who believed in Christ: *In him, I say, in whom we also have been called by a special choice, having been predestined in the purpose of him who works all things according to the counsel of his will, to contribute to the praise of his glory. . . .*[74]

Some interpreters understand the object of this predestination to be the state of grace, which is expressed by the adoption as sons.[75] We may say that this is an understandable interpretation; it follows their interpretation that St. Paul understood by God's purpose and predestination an absolute, infrustrable decree concerning the human will, for St. Paul could only assert such a decree of some effect of God's purpose that has already taken place, such as the conversion of the Christians at Ephesus. However, the context of these verses seems to militate against the interpretation of this predestination as being directed simply to grace. The gift of grace for St. Paul was the assurance of heaven, for if grace makes us sons, it makes us heirs of heaven, and thus possessors of heaven in hope, and sharers of the Holy Spirit *who is the pledge of our inheritance.*[76] So for St. Paul the fact that God has justified us shows

---

[73] Eph. 1:5–6.
[74] Eph. 1:11–12.
[75] See Medebielle, *op. cit.*, pp. 28–9; Ceuppens, *op. cit.*, p. 257.
[76] Eph. 1:14. A note given by *La Sainte Bible traduite en français sous la direction de l'Ecole Biblique de Jérusalem* (Paris, 1956) on Eph. 1:4 states: "Première bénédiction: l'appel des élus à la vie béatifique, déjà commencée d'ailleurs de façon mystique par l'union des fidèles au Christ glorieux." As the following note shows, Eph. 1:5–6 is understood as parallel to Rom. 8:29 which must be understood of predestination to eternal glory.

us that he has predestined us to heaven. His firm, deliberate purpose is to bring us to heaven.

But many interpreters of this passage would object to such a meaning for God's purpose. Thus Ceuppens comments on Eph. 1:11 that "the purpose or divine decree is efficacious and absolute, because it comes from him who performs all things that he wills and as he wills."[77] Also there is found the word βουλή in this text. Commenting on another passage of St. Paul, Spicq teaches that for St. Paul βούλομαι signifies "a firm will, an absolute order . . . certain divine decrees are absolutely infrustrable."[78] In answer to this, we can say that St. Paul is using strong words to indicate a deliberate, divine decision that firmly intends to bring Christians to heaven. But he does not mean that this divine will for this purpose is infrustrable by the resistance of the human will, or that it leaves no possibility of such resistance, or that such resistance and ultimate reprobation is incompatible with this will of God. The fact that St. Paul says that God has this will for the eternal salvation of all Christians who are in the Spirit, and the larger context in which Paul shows so clearly the possibility of the Christian's defection and reprobation, seem to us to prove this conclusively.[79] From textual arguments we can conclude nothing but the objective firmness and efficacy of God's will to bring all Christians to heaven, together with the subjective ability of Christians to defect and therefore to be reprobated even though God has such a will in their regard.

[77] Ceuppens, *op. cit.*, 263: . . . propositum seu decretum divinum est efficax et absolutum, quia provenit ab illo qui operatur omnia quae vult et sicut vult.

[78] C. Spicq, *Les épîtres pastorales* (Paris 1947) 58, commenting on 1 Tim. 2:4, states: "Mais l'exégète peut noter que θέλω, trés frequent dans saint Paul (plus de 60 fois), désigne souvent le désir du coeur, un sentiment, alors que βούλομαι (cf. II, 8; V, 14) s'emploie d'une volonté arrêtée, d'un ordre absolu . . . certains décrets divins sont absolument infrangibles: . . ."

[79] The texts which Spicq advances as illustrative of the meaning of βούλομαι when applied to the divine will in the New Testament (Luke 10:22; Heb. 6:17; 2 Peter 3:9; 1 Cor. 12:11) are in accord with our interpretation. The text from Hebrews is a good example. This epistle expresses the absoluteness of God's promise to bring the faithful to heaven (6:17, 18) at the same time as it expresses the absoluteness of man's ability to defect from this will (3:12–19; 10:26–31), and thus fail to obtain the promise. If one perseveres, however, there is no question but that he will receive the promise (6:13 ff.).

Other, philosophical difficulties may remain against such a solution. Thus theologians generally apply to God's grace the same kind of efficacy they ascribe to the divine decree. And St. Paul affirms the absolute gratuity, not only of God's choice of man for heaven, but also of the grace that God gives: *I will have mercy on whom I have mercy, and I will show pity to whom I will show pity.*[80] Moreover, St. Paul shows that man so owes his good acts, even the most interior, to God that man has nothing to be proud of in them; for it is not he that distinguishes himself from other men. *For it is God who of his good pleasure works in you both the will and the performance.*[81] If man's work is totally due to God, many argue, man is not adding anything to God's causality to make it effective; it is effective before man's response, either intrinsically or extrinsically effective. Otherwise the gift of grace that a good man accepts would not be a greater gift than the grace that another rejects. And man would, by adding his response to God's call, separate himself from unbelievers; it would not be wholly God's work. Hence, it seems to them, grace and God's decree must be absolutely effective antecedent to man's response. This also flows from the explanation of the certainty of God's knowledge, whether the Thomist or the Molinist explanation is accepted.

To this we can simply say that the thought of St. Paul embraced both aspects which these theologians think are incompatible. It is already clear from the texts we have analyzed, and will be more so below, that he thought the divine decree and hence grace for the Christian were objectively effective on the one hand and subjectively frustrable on the other. St. Paul taught, as we have shown, that God has predestined those whom he united to Christ by justification and that he has already given them the means that will bring them to their eternal fulfillment. Since the essential means to move man to his supernatural fulfillment is interior grace, God has given the grace to the justified to complete what he has begun and bring them to heaven. St. Paul, however, knew that one who was justified could reject God's intention for his salvation, or his predestination. Hence, too, he could reject the prevenient grace that was the effect of this predestination. For St. Paul, then, the gratuity of God's choice and grace, the effective-

---

[80] Rom. 9:15, a quotation from Ex. 33:19. See above, p. 44.
[81] Phil. 2:13. See also 1 Cor. 4:7.

ness of this, and the totality of God's causality of man's meritorious acts are not contradictory to the fact that man can frustrate God's will and his grace in their purpose to bring him to heaven or a particular salutary act. Granted that it is a mystery, granted that it is difficult to harmonize with some accepted philosophical principles, it is still taught by St. Paul.[82] And on this matter there is harmony between Paul's teaching and the teaching of the gospels and of the Old Testament. Since revelation has the primacy in the interpretation of a supernatural mystery, the Christian response can only be one of acceptance. For the present we are examining only the scriptural doctrine of the relation of predestination and grace to man's free will. Later we shall see whether there is in fact the contradiction that appears to exist between philosophical principles and this revealed doctrine.

In his Epistle to the Romans, after teaching the certainty of the salvation of Christians in chapter 8, St. Paul expresses his great sorrow for the condition into which the Jews had fallen. God rejected the Jews to whom he had given such great promises. This fact (besides being related to the central theme of Romans) raises a crucial problem for St. Paul's doctrine concerning the certainty of the salvation of the Christians because of the divine intention in their regard. Was God unfaithful to his promises to the Jews? Or did the Jews frustrate the fulfillment of his plan? If this is the case, if God is either unfaithful or unable to fulfill his plan, then what strength can Christian hope have? Paul's answer is: *It is not that the word of God has failed,*[83] and he develops his answer to the problem through the next three chapters.

This section is relevant to our study of the biblical doctrine on the effectiveness of God's predestination and grace, and on the relation of his rejection or reprobation to man's sins. Chapter 9

[82] For confirmation of our interpretation of predestination in St. Paul as subjectively conditioned as well as objectively effective, see Lyonnet, "Notes au commentaire du Père Huby," in Huby, *op. cit.,* p. 617.

[83] Rom. 9:6. For the history of the interpretations given this chapter, see Sanday and Headlam, *op. cit.,* pp. 269–75. For analyses of the whole section, see commentaries indicated above and particularly Viard, *op. cit.,* pp. 109–33; Lyonnet, "Les épîtres . . ." chapters 9–11, the footnotes; and Lyonnet, "De doctrina praedestinationis et reprobationis in Rom. 9," *Verbum Domini,* 34 (1956), 193–201, 257–71.

in particular has seemed to a great number of exegetes to teach the absolute effectiveness of God's predestination and, even more definitely, an antecedent reprobation. For God is said to have preferred Jacob to Esau before either had done good or evil, and to have hated Esau. He is said to have hardened Pharaoh, to make from the same clay vessels for honorable and dishonorable uses, and to desire to show his wrath and power. To this, all contemporary commentators answer that Paul is directly discussing God's providence toward the Jews and the Gentiles as groups, and not the predestination or reprobation of the individual with reference to eternal salvation. The rejection of the Jews that raises the problem is the rejection of them in the historical mission envisaged for them in the Old Testament as the means through which God would save the world; St. Paul does not affirm that the eternal lot of all of those so rejected is one of damnation. And the individuals he mentions, such as Essau and Pharaoh, are types of the Jews who are rejected, not treated for their own sakes with reference to their eternal lot. This answer, however, to the foregoing interpretation of the passage is not adequate, for the passage has in St. Paul's intention a relation to the predestination of the individual Christian. Their security rests on God's promise of salvation, and God's treatment of the Jews raises the question of how effective God's promise is. Will the Christian be disowned by God, as it seems the Jews have been? Hence the importance of this passage for us, and the limits of our study of it. We simply ask whether God was faithful to his promise, whether he rejected the Jews antecedent to their sins, and whether God's purpose was effective.

In his response to the problem raised, St. Paul answers these three questions in turn. He shows that on God's part there was no infidelity to his promise correctly understood (c. 9); that the Jews were rejected because of and after their refusal to submit themselves to God's way of salvation through belief (c. 10); and that God's purpose to save the world has not been frustrated by their resistance (c. 11). In the interpretation of parts within this passage, it is of primary importance to give to Paul's texts a meaning strictly within the limits of the question he is immediately answering. If one extends their meaning beyond their context, he will attribute to St. Paul doctrines that are contradictory to his teaching in other passages where he *ex professo* treats the subject concerned. It is really for lack of such a recognition of Paul's method of exposition that so many exegetes have found the doctrine of antecedent reprobation in chapter nine.

In this chapter (c. 9) St. Paul shows that God was not at fault in the Jews' rejection. God's promise (vv. 9–13) did not extend to all the offspring of Abraham in the first place. God showed this from the beginning in giving the promise to Isaac rather than to Ismael, to the younger Jacob over the older Esau. Indeed, he chose Jacob over Esau before either was born or did anything good or evil, *that the purpose of God might remain one of choice, not depending on works but upon him who calls.*[84]

But is not this unjust of God? (vv. 14–24) Is it not an arbitrary exercise of his power? No, Paul says, because what God was giving was purely a gift not owed to any man, and he has sovereign freedom to dispose of his gifts as he wills. This is proved both by the case of Moses on whom he had mercy, and by that of Pharaoh in whom he showed his power. *Therefore he has mercy on whom he will, and whom he will, he hardens.*[85] But such an answer seems simply to deepen the mystery, for man depends upon God's gift. If he does not receive it, how can man be blamed? After all, who can resist the will of God? To such a questioning of God's ways, St. Paul quickly points out the inappropriateness of the creature questioning the ways of his maker. Cannot a potter make from the same mass of clay one vessel for an honorable use and another for a common use? Then Paul gives in brief his answer to the question of God's justice and man's responsibility, an answer he will develop through the next two chapters.

> But what if God, wishing to show his wrath and to make known his power, endured with much patience vessels of wrath, ready for destruction, that he might show the riches of his glory upon vessels of mercy, which he has prepared unto glory—even us whom he has called not only among the Jews but also from among the Gentiles?[86]

One can see in this highly compact answer the total initiative of the Jews as the cause through their sins of their rejection, only if

[84] Rom. 9:11. This is the author's translation. For the meaning of God's preference of Jacob and his hate of Esau, see above pp. 43–44.

[85] Rom. 9:18. On Pharaoh, see above, pp. 43–45.

[86] Rom. 9:22–4.

he interprets it in view of Paul's larger thought. Paul multiplies indications of this blameworthiness of the Jews here. The teaching of the passage is clearly reminiscent of the doctrine of the Book of Wisdom on God's punishment of Pharaoh and the Egyptians; and, as we have seen, that explanation locates the total initiative for the evil that resulted in their punishment in the resistance by the Egyptians to God's merciful approaches.[87] He speaks of the rejected Jews as *vessels of wrath;* and we have seen that, for Paul, God's wrath was simply a response to man's sins.[88] He calls them *ready for destruction,* as opposed to the vessels of mercy which are *prepared for glory,* to remove any implication of God's authorship of their sin. And he affirms that God endured them with much patience even when their sin had advanced so far that they were ready for destruction, and we have seen that the purpose of God's patience with sinners is their conversion.[89] In brief, Paul affirms here what he develops in the next chapter, where he asks why the Jews failed to attain the justice that is from faith (10:1–4), and answers that *they have not submitted to the justice of God.*[90] He shows that the Old Testament itself taught that justice comes through faith (5–11). The one who would try to defend the Jews from responsibility for their lack of belief would fail. For the gospel was preached to them; they heard, understood, and refused to believe it (14–21). Their responsibility is beyond question.

From this it is apparent that St. Paul is denying that God induced the Jews to the disbelief that merited for them their rejection. He is teaching that God's will toward their disbelief was simply one of tolerance or permission. And this tolerance is not one implied by the lack of a divine choice of these Jews, who have now been rejected, antecedent to their personal sins of disbelief, or the lack of an antecedent divine intention to sustain them in the practice of what was morally good. It is simply that tolerance or permission implied by the Old Testament doctrine that God's choice of the Jews and the consequent means that he gave them to fulfill the conditions necessary to receive what he had promised them were in the case of any particular individual or group among

[87] See above, pp. 44–45.
[88] See above, p. 53.
[89] See above, *loc. cit.* Another reason for God's patience with the Jews was the conversion of the Gentiles.
[90] Rom. 10:3.

the Jews contingent upon their free fulfillment of his will in faith. God's choice and helps could be rejected by those whom he loved. While his choice and help were objectively effective, they were subjectively frustrable. Since at least part of the reason why St. Paul is in this whole section explaining God's dispensation to the Jews is to show the Christian the confidence that he can have in God's promise, choice, and predestination, this doctrine implies that God will not fail in his promise or intention to bring the justified Christian to his heavenly fulfillment, will not permit him to fail through any lack of a divine intention to sustain him in the practice of the good, but will allow the Christian to reject God's choice and helps by which God directs and moves him to heaven.

It is not sufficient, however, for St. Paul to assert that the Jews were completely responsible for their own rejection. If one simply shows that God is not to blame for their failure, he has not defended God's justice in the biblical sense; i.e., that the actions of God with men are directed toward the end of the salvation of the world.[91] Also to stop there would leave the impression that God's purpose with the Jews has been frustrated. The question remains then: why did God tolerate the Jews' disbelief? In other words, why were those whom he had chosen not helped by God by an aid that was antecedently infallibly effective in gaining their belief? God's toleration of the evil of their resistance was not due to his weakness or inability to use such an antecedently effective means to gain their cooperation with his designs. Therefore there must be some greater good than the concrete value of the Jews' acceptance of Christ that justifies God's tolerance of such an immense evil. In a manner parallel to the Book of Wisdom's explanation of God's wrath, power, and mercy when the Egyptians resisted him, Paul explains, in the text quoted above, why God endured the Jews' resistance to his antecedent desire that they be the instruments of the extension of his kingdom among the Gentiles. Paul answers in effect that God did not need the Jews' acceptance of Christ to fulfill the historic mission he had mercifully given to them, as he had not needed Pharaoh's willing cooperation to free the Jews from Egypt. God is so powerful that he

---

[91] See S. Schmidt, "S. Pauli 'iustitia Dei' notione iustitiae, quae in VT et apud S. Paulum habetur, dilucidata," *Verbum Domini*, 37 (1959), 97–105.

could raise up other agents to fulfill the mission refused by the Jews. In fact, if they resisted him, God would use their very resistance to manifest his transcendence or the fact that he did not need their cooperation, and to fulfill his purpose in a manner that would show his power even more dramatically, as he had in the case of the liberation of the Jews from Egypt over the resistance of Pharaoh. Moreover, even though they resisted, they would manifest the holiness of God, now not by their willing submission to him and their sharing in that holiness, but through their being the objects of God's wrath and thus evidence of the incompatibility of God and sin. Finally, though they did not willingly take the historic mission of being the intermediaries of God's mercy with the Gentiles, God would use their very resistance to further his plans of mercy toward the Gentiles, as he had used Pharaoh's resistance to give greater evidence of his merciful care in liberating the Jews from Egypt. This is developed by Paul in chapter eleven, where he teaches that God's rejection of the Jews is not total because a remnant is saved through God's grace, whereas the others who did not accept this way of God's justice have been blinded (1–10). Moreover, their fall has brought salvation to the Gentiles (11–24), a fact Paul had experienced in his own ministry. The small number of Jews who did become Christians proved to be a real obstacle to the salvation of the Gentiles through the narrow attachment to the old law on the part of so many of them. If all the Jews had become Christians, the Church would have had much more difficulty in freeing itself from the old law and thus in being acceptable to the Gentile converts.[92] God uses the conversion of the Gentiles in turn to stir up in the Jews a desire to join them in the Church. And St. Paul concludes by prophesying that once the Gentiles have been converted, the Jews, too, will enter the Church, and thus God's mercy will be extended to all. *Oh, the depth of the riches of the wisdom and of the knowledge of God! How incomprehensible are his judgments and how unsearchable his ways!* (25–32).[93]

The conclusion, then, of St. Paul's explanation of God's relation to the Jews is that God's choice and the means which he gives to men to respond to that choice are not antecedently infallibly

---

[92] See Viard, *op. cit.*, p. 126.
[93] Rom. 11:33.

efficacious. In fact, Paul makes this point explicitly when he warns the Christians to learn from God's dispensation with the Jews, *his severity toward those who have fallen, but the goodness of God toward thee if thou abidest in his goodness; otherwise thou also wilt be cut off.*[94] God allowed the Jews, whom he had chosen, to resist his mercy and to fall into disbelief; and in spite of his previous love, he was severe with them. So, too, God allows the Christians to refuse to believe; but if they do so refuse, the promises of God will not be fulfilled in them, and they will in their turn experience the severity of God. Thus St. Paul does not defend the power of God by any theory of antecedently infallibly efficacious decrees and grace where it concerns the salvation of the individual. He does so through showing that those who continually resist God fall under his wrath. Nor does he conclude from the gratuity and the antecedence of God's choice and grace the antecedence of his rejection. Though his explanation of the mystery of evil does not explain everything, it is clear that God's rejection of his chosen ones is only consequent upon their refusal to submit to him.

But a question still remains. Granted that God does not reject his chosen ones before their resistance, what is his intention toward those who have not been chosen, those who were neither Jews nor Christians? St. Paul answers this elsewhere by asking Christians to pray for all men. *This is good and agreeable in the sight of God our Savior, who wishes all men to be saved and to come the knowledge of the truth.*[95] What St. Paul states here has been expressed in Christian tradition as the universal salvific will of God. The word Paul uses to express this desire ($\theta\acute{\epsilon}\lambda\omega$) is not as strong as the word he uses to indicate God's intention to bring the Christian to heaven (e.g., $\beta o\acute{v}\lambda o\mu a\iota$), but it does express a real desire on God's part. Some exegetes, such as Augustine who insisted on the infallible efficacy of the divine will, have interpreted this passage in some restricted manner. Thus Augustine in all of his later interpretations of it restricted in some way this divine will to save. It means that God wants to save all those who actually are saved, or men from every nation and walk of life; or it means that he wants his servants on earth to desire and seek

[94] Rom. 11:22.
[95] 1 Tim. 2:3–4. See also above, footnote 78.

the salvation of all.[96] Such interpretations are accepted by no recent exegete,[97] since the whole passage stresses the universality of God's will to save. Christians are urged to pray for *all men;* God is said unequivocally to wish to save *all;* and the reason given to prove this is the fact that Christ gave himself as a ransom for *all.* One reason why St. Paul did not have difficulty in harmonizing this with the fact that not all men were saved was the conditional character of God's call and grace. And this aspect of his teaching was understood by the Greek Fathers. St. John Chrysostom, in commenting on the predestination passage in Ephesians, distinguished two wills or desires in God: "The first will is that those who have sinned shall not perish, the second will that they perish who have lived sinfully."[98] St. John Damascene develops this further:

> It is necessary to realize that God antecedently wishes all to be saved and to partake of his kingdom. For he did not make us to punish us but, since he is good, that we may be sharers of his goodness. However he wishes sinners to be punished since he is just. Therefore the first, antecedent will is called also good pleasure, being from him. But the second, consequent will is also called permission, having its origin from us. . . .[99]

[96] See Augustine, *Epistolae* 217.6, 19 (ML 33.986); *Enchiridion* 103 (ML 40.280); *De Correptione et Gratia* 15.47 (ML 44.945).

[97] See Ceuppens, *op. cit.,* 1.183–5; Spicq, *op. cit.,* pp. 57–9.

[98] Chrysostom, *In epistulam ad Ephesios homiliae* 1.2 (MG 62.13).

[99] John Damascene, *De fide orthodoxa* 2.29 (MG 94.968).

CHAPTER THREE

The Church's Teaching During the Period of the Fathers

IN THE preceding chapter we found that God's predestination and grace in his common providence of the present order are antecedent to man's acts and frustrable by man's will. They are, according to our understanding, not infallibly destined to achieve their result in man's will antecedent to his free response. Moreover, God's intention not to sustain man in the practice of the moral good, and his reprobation, are only consequent upon and because of man's unrepented sins. But Thomists and Molinists both find in the official teaching of the Church and in that of the Fathers and theologians evidence for their own theories and for what they hold in common concerning the efficacy of predestination and grace. Since the interpretation of Scripture must be in accord with tradition, they would for this reason call into question the validity of the interpretation we advanced of revelation as expressed by Scripture. Hence it is necessary to examine tradition in this matter to see whether in fact the analysis of Scripture we have presented is opposed to the teaching of the Church or in accord with it. In our opinion the evidence shows that our interpretation is contrary to no valid theological tradition, but is rather in accord with the Church's teaching. We will find, we think, that the investigation of tradition or of the development of dogma in this matter turns out to be a study of the gradual conquest of the revealed teaching on predestination and grace with which our interpretation of Scripture is in full accord.

The development of the Church's understanding of an element

71

of revelation is seen in the official teaching of the Church and in the witness to that teaching contained in the belief of the faithful. It is the magisterium of the Church that constitutes the official proximate norm of faith and the agent that canonizes, as it were, a new stage of theological understanding of the revealed truth. So the official teaching of the Church has the first place in order of importance in our study of tradition. But a second norm of the Church's teaching is the witness given to Catholic belief in different ages by the faithful. The privileged witnesses of this belief are, of course, the Fathers and the theologians, so we shall investigate their teaching in the different periods of the history of the Church. In this investigation we are interested mainly in their teaching on the central problem under discussion, namely, the efficacy of predestination and grace, and not on the many secondary problems involved or on the various proofs they bring forward to support their views. An examination of the problem from the viewpoint of theological reason in later chapters will be concerned with the philosophical arguments that are advanced, so we need not dwell on them here. Finally, we are interested not in the individual Father or theologian for his own sake but for his function as a witness to the belief of the Church. Since it is the moral unanimity of such witnesses or the special witness of one as receiving general acceptance by the Church that is the basis of their value as norms of faith, we need not delay for long on most individuals. This also allows us to abstract from many historical problems of interpretation that are not essential to our purpose. This chapter will treat, in this restricted way, the development of the doctrine in the East and its development in the West until the II Council of Orange (529). The following chapter will treat its progress since then.

In the examination of the period of the Fathers, historians generally balance the Eastern Fathers, among whom there is a recognized unity of thought on this problem, with the outstanding theologian of the West on the subject of grace and predestination, namely, Augustine. A good indication of the difference of approach that existed between them can be found in their different interpretations of two key texts of St. Paul. The first of these texts states that God cooperates in all things for the good of those *whom he has called according to his purpose.*[1] The Greek Fathers interpreted this *purpose* as man's response to God's grace or, in the case of Origen and Cyril of Alexandria, of God's and man's purposes conjoined. Thus the sense of the passage is that God has called and predestined men to justification according to their cooperation with his grace. For Augustine this *purpose* is God's exclusively, and so he interprets the passage differently. Among those whom God has called, he had called some according to his purpose, and these he has predestined to heaven with an insuperable power. The second text asserts that God *wishes all men to be saved.*[2] The Greek Fathers understood this as indicating a really universal salvific will in God which, through man's rejection of God's grace and light, gave way finally to a second will to punish men who misused their free will. Augustine, on the other hand, in his later writings restricted in various ways the universality of this divine intention to save. Thus the Greek Fathers treated more directly the order of the execution of God's plan than the plan itself and emphasized the universality of his salvific will and its conditioned character. Augustine descended from God's purpose to its infallible fulfillment and hence indicated the limitations of God's saving will. These differences will be borne out by a more detailed account of their teaching.

1. *The Greek Fathers*

The historians who analyze the doctrine of the Greek Fathers on predestination and grace are struck by the unity of doctrine among them on this matter,[3] and this allows us to treat them as a unit, for the most part. There were very real reasons for this continuity of thought, the first of which was the fact that the attacks against which they defended the doctrine denied the freedom of the will and the justice of God. The gnostics, for example, taught that men are divided into different classes by nature, the spiritual who will necessarily be saved, the material who will necessarily be

[1] Rom. 8:28. See above, p. 55 f., for text and various interpretations given it by the Fathers.

[2] 1 Tim. 2:4. See above, p. 69 f., for text and interpretations given it by the Fathers.

[3] See, for example, L. Ciappi, *La predestinazione*, p. 44.

damned, and the psychic who, alone of men, are not necessitated
to one of these, but are free. Marcion, another adversary whom the
Greeks had in mind when they expounded the doctrine of God's
providential dispositions, distinguished the God of the New Testament from that of the Old and held that the latter was unjust and
arbitrary in his treatment of men and not guided by their merits
or demerits in his judgment of them. Celsus, against whom
Origen wrote, held that if God had certain foreknowledge of what
man would do there was no possibility of freedom.[4] Against all of
these the Greeks constantly defended the freedom of the human
will. For instance, Irenaeus wrote:

> But that which he said: "How often have I desired to gather your
> sons and you would not?" demonstrates the ancient law of human
> liberty, because God from the beginning made man free, having
> his own power, as his own life, to accept the will of God freely and
> not as forced by God.[5]

Another element that is common to the Greek Fathers is their
understanding of the Christian life as a participation in the divine
life and hence caused by God. Justification is a new creation that
is as dependent upon God as the first creation. One could not state
more clearly that God is the total first source of man's salvation.
Man receives from God, not only the power to change from evil to
good, but the actual change and every inclination that carries him
progressively nearer to the perfection God wants for him. For
instance, St. John Chrysostom asks: "What do you have which you
have not received but is the effect of your personal power? Absolutely nothing."[6] St. Cyril of Alexandria simply affirms: "Therefore
every inclination which carries us to justice comes from God the
Father."[7] And St. John Damascene states: "God himself is the
beginning and cause of all good."[8] So it is clear that they attribute
to God the whole initiative in the order of salvation and the first

[4] See A. d'Ales, "Prédestination," 204, and H.-D. Simonin, "Prédestination d'après les Pères grecs," *DTC*, 12.2 (1935), 2825.

[5] Irenaeus, *Adversus haereses libri quinque*, 4.37.1 (MG 7.1099). For
a multitude of like texts, see M. J. Rouet de Journel, *Enchiridion patristicum*
(18. ed., Freiburg i Br., 1953), "Index theologicus," n. 221, 301.

[6] *In epistolam primam ad Corinthios*, homilia 12.2 (MG 61.98). The
whole passage ascribes man's faith, virtues, and good deeds to God's grace.

[7] *Explanatio in epistolam ad Romanos*, 8.28 (MG 74.828).

[8] *De fide orthodoxa*, 2.30 (MG 94.972). See too St. Gregory Nazianzen,
Oratio, 37.13 (MG 36.297).

causality of every good act. And yet in spite of these expressions reducing all of man's good actions to God as their cause, expressions which no convinced Pelagian or Semipelagian would admit, there are found at times in the Eastern Fathers statements which Semipelagians could later use to defend their orthodoxy. For instance, St. John Chrysostom says that when we have desired to advance in the ways of the spirit, God increases that desire.[9] This, if taken out of the context of the whole of his thought, would deny that God's grace anticipates all of man's salutary acts as well as causes them. But such statements of the Eastern Fathers are not generally so interpreted. They are directly contrary to other statements of the same Fathers, and so show not a definite Semipelagian doctrine, but that lack of accuracy that is common before a heresy has made the Church aware of a particular difficulty. Moreover, the Greek Fathers did not achieve a perfectly adequate expression of *how* God's initiative in the order of grace and man's free will were harmonized; this is due in part to the lack of the philosophical tools necessary for this. Hence a certain ambivalence or inexactness of expression appears from time to time.

As this implies, the very affirmation both of God as the origin of man's good Christian life and of man's free will leads to further problems for them. If God gives man justice as a new creation and pours into him the good acts and desires that he has, how is it that not all are saved? Moreover, how can man be free if God knows from eternity what man will do? How can God be just if he saves only some men? There is a continuity and a very perceptible development in the answers which the Greek Fathers give to these problems that arise from the doctrine of God's initiative and man's freedom in the order of salvation. They teach in the beginning in a merely practical way and later in a more theoretical and reflective way that as a result of God's gift and man's freedom, man must be prompt to good and thus gain his eternal happiness. As time goes on, they more clearly describe the theoretical bases of such teaching or the nature of God's will that men be saved.

[9] See *In epistolam ad Philippenses*, homilia 8.1 (MG 62.240). For other such texts in the Greek Fathers, see J. Tixeront, *Histoire des dogmes* 2 (2. ed., Paris, 1909), 144–8; Simonin, *art. cit., passim*. On St. John Chrysostom, see A. Kenny, "Was St. John Chrysostom a Semipelagian?" *The Irish Theological Quarterly*, 37 (1960), 16–29.

For example, before Origen, the Pastor of Hermas promises the faithful that if they truly do penance, they shall have their names written in the Book of Life.[10] St. Justin teaches that it is the foreknowledge of God that allows him to reward every man according to his merits. He foresees that certain men who are not yet born will be saved through penitence. And he puts off the punishment of his enemies until the "number of the foreknown" is complete.[11] St. Irenaeus defends the justice of God against Marcion. God gives to all men the power to be good, so if they are not good it is their own fault, and they are judged justly. If, on the other hand, they are good, then they merit a reward, since they could have been evil. The blindness and hardness of Pharaoh is a punishment for such resistance to God. God, who has foreknowledge of all things, is able through the foreknowledge to judge justly.[12] Clement of Alexandria also ascribes the goodness of man to God and imputes the evil of man totally to man; but he is sure that God will triumph over man's evil by making it serve a good purpose. He also speaks of the predestined as "those whom God has predestined, having known from before the beginning of the world that they would be just."[13]

With Origen we come definitely to a profounder treatment of God's beneficent providence in its relation to the free will of man, for he speaks more directly of the order of God's intention and the relation of his foreknowledge to predestination and man's acts. Origen, as we have seen, in commenting on St. Paul interpreted the design or purpose according to which men are called as both God's and men's, for God's purpose, excluding a consideration of men's, does not achieve the effect of salvation. This same explanation governs the relation between God's knowledge and man's actions and salvation. Origen distinguished the scriptural and the common meaning of foreknowledge. If knowledge (or rather foreknowledge) is taken in the common sense, he argues

[10] See *Hermae pastor*, Vis. 1.3.2 and Sim. 2.9 in *Patrum apostolorum opera*, 3 (ed. O. de Gebhardt, A. Harnack, and T. Zahn, Leipzig, 1877), 12–14, 138.

[11] See *Apologia prima pro Christianis* 1.45 (MG 6.396). Also see Simonin, *art. cit.*, pp. 2818–9.

[12] See *Adv. haer.*, 4.29.1-2 (MG 7.1063–4), and Simonin, *art. cit.*, pp. 2819–21.

[13] *Stromata*, 7.17 (MG 9.552).

76

against Celsus, "not for that reason will something occur because God foreknows it will be; but because it will be, God foreknows it."[14] God's foreknowledge in Scripture, however, is not that of a spectator, but an active, loving knowledge, one of approbation. Thus he is said not to know evil, but to know those who are his own.[15] Now the relation of this knowledge to predestination is described by Origen as follows: "If this [predestination] were the principle of all that follows, those who introduce the absurd doctrine concerning nature (i.e., fatalists) would have the better of the argument, but foreknowledge comes before predestination."[16] The evil acts of men are not due to the knowledge of God, but the good acts of men do seem, for Origen, to be due in some limited way to God's knowledge. He says: "Neither our free will without the knowledge of God nor the knowledge of God makes us progress, if we do not cooperate with it in the direction of the good."[17] And further, "Hence the cause of our salvation or perdition does not lie in the foreknowledge of God."[18]

Does Origen's doctrine on the knowledge or foreknowledge of God mean the same as the *scientia media* of the Molinists or the same as the infallibly efficacious divine causative knowledge of the Banezians? Origen's texts indicate that for him God's knowledge differed from both of these later schools. It very definitely differs from that of the Banezians, since Origen held that God's knowledge does not of itself assure the progress of the free created will. He held that God's knowledge and purpose abstracting from that of man were not absolutely efficacious in bringing about the salvation of man. His whole doctrine of the pre-existence of souls and their successive tests until they freely turned themselves to God is an indication that he, in common with previous tradition of the Greek Fathers, held something quite different from Banez's conception of God's causative knowledge that is of itself absolutely efficacious. On the other hand, he does indicate that God's knowl-

---

[14] *Commentaria in epistolam beati Pauli ad Romanos*, 7.8 (MG 14.1126). See Simonin, *art. cit.*, pp. 2122–8.

[15] See *In Rom.*, 7.8 (MG 14.1123).

[16] *In Rom.* 1, preserved in *Philocalia* 25.2 (MG 14.841). Commenting on Rom. 8:28, Origen states that predestination is not the first of God's acts with reference to the predestined.

[17] *De principiis*, 3.1.22 (MG 11.302).

[18] *In Rom.*, 7.8 (MG 14.1126).

edge in scriptural terms is not simply that of a spectator; it is active and loving. And he does indicate that God's knowledge has an influence, if the free created will does not resist, in bringing man to God. So his doctrine cannot be equated with *scientia media*. It follows from this whole context of his doctrine, as well as from his explicit statements, that if predestination is taken in an absolute sense, it is preceded by God's foreknowledge.

The Greek successors of Origen were greatly influenced by him. While avoiding his error, later condemned, of the pre-existence of souls, they generally taught that God's foreknowledge was not the cause (at least wholly) of man's sins or good deeds.[19] They held therefore, in common with the whole of Greek theology, that God's activity for men did not take away the character of its being conditioned on the subjective dispositions of men. Men in the fullest sense of the word could fail God, or rather fail to respond to God's grace. The main advance made by the successors of Origen on this matter was their clarification of the implications of the universality of God's salvific will. We have already shown the main statements on this matter in the commentaries of St. John Chrysostom and St. John Damascene on St. Paul.[20] The first will of God, or his will of good pleasure, is that all men be saved. This is called a 'vehement' will and an 'antecedent' will. God's second will is that men who live sinfully perish. This second will, St. John Damascene says, has its origin, not in God, but in us. Our own moral evils are not willed either by an antecedent or by a consequent will; they are simply permitted.[21]

[19] See Simonin, *art, cit.,* pp. 2828–32. Among those who deny that God's foreknowledge is the complete cause ($\alpha i\tau i\alpha$) of man's acts, he adduces Chrysostom, *De prophetiarum obscuritate,* 1.4 (MG 56.171); Theodoret of Cyrrhus, *Interpretatio epistolae ad Romanos,* 8.30 (MG 82.141–4); and John Damascene, *Dialogus contra Manichaeos,* 79 (MG 94.1577).

[20] See above, p. 70.

[21] See *De fide orth.,* 2.29 (MG 94.968). A study of this doctrine of the Greeks on predestination and grace as it appears in their commentaries on St. Paul's epistle to the Romans and the contrast of their doctrine with that of Augustine is found in an author sympathetic to Augustine, K. H. Schelkle, "Erwählung und Freiheit im Römerbrief nach der Auslegung der Väter," *Theolog. Quartalschr.,* 131 (1951), 17–31, 189–207. A study of later Byzantine teaching relevant to this matter is found in H. Beck, *Vorsehung und Vorherbsetimmung in der theologischen Literatur der Byzantiner* in *Orientalia Christiana Analecta.* 114 (Rome, 1937).

We may say, therefore, in conclusion, that in their desire to defend the justice of God and the freedom of the will, the Greek Fathers taught with St. Paul the conditional character of predestination and grace as well as the universality of God's salvific will. They did not teach with the same firmness and consistency St. Paul's doctrine on the objective efficacy of predestination and grace with its implications. They did not teach without ambivalence that God has so predestined the one united to Christ to heaven that he is, as it were, already there. Nor did they teach with this firmness the fact that God's grace anticipates and causes each act of man that is profitable for salvation. These aspects of St. Paul's doctrine, as St. Augustine will find, are difficult to combine. And so it is understandable that the Greek Fathers, who were never so preoccupied with heresies on grace as the Latins, would not express these aspects of Paul's doctrine constantly with the clarity we would like. But it remains to ask what theological value the doctrine of the Greek Fathers has with reference to predestination. Some say that they considered the problem only concretely, and hence their doctrine does not have great value in relation to God's providential intention of predestination and reprobation. We may answer that they began with concrete discussions on God's actual governance of men, but this very governance is a positive indication of God's intention. If this is not used to understand what God's providential plan is, what can be used? Moreover, as time went on, they spoke more directly of the order of intention to save and reprobate in God. Others say that the Greeks' doctrine is not of great value since it was constructed for apologetic and pastoral purposes, but in answer to this we need only recall that St. Paul's doctrine on predestination was constructed for a like pastoral purpose and does not by that lose any of its value.

2. *Augustine*

Since the Latin Fathers previous to St. Augustine teach essentially the same as the Greek Fathers,[22] we may turn immediately

[22] See A. D'Ales, *art. cit.*, p. 205; Ciappi, *op. cit.*, pp. 65-9; Simonin on Jerome's acceptance of Origen's doctrine on free will and God's foreknowledge, *art. cit.*, pp. 2828-9.

to the study of the doctrine of Augustine and the councils of the Church in the West concerned with Pelagianism and Semipelagianism. We shall in no way attempt to give an exhaustive analysis of this teaching, but we shall try to see what Augustine and the councils added to our understanding of the revealed mystery. And we shall try also to show what limitations remained in the teaching of St. Augustine that provoked later controversy and development of the Church's understanding of the dogma. Since it was particularly in view of Pelagianism that Augustine developed his doctrine on grace and predestination, we shall give in this section a brief analysis of the relevant Pelagian doctrine and an account of Augustine's doctrine referring to the gratuity and efficacy of predestination and grace. Then, in the next section, we shall show in the context of the controversies on grace that lasted until the II Council of Orange the Church's approbation of Augustine's doctrine on grace.

Pelagius was a monk from Britain who was deeply influenced by the spirit of Stoicism and was particularly concerned to defend against the Manichees the reality of free will in man.[23] His basic tenet on the relation between the free creature and God is such a definition of freedom that it rejects any intrinsic dependence upon God and his causality. He wrote that "it is not free will if it needs the help of God."[24] Julian of Eclanum wrote in the same vein: "Freedom of choice, by which man is emancipated from God, consists in the possibility of accepting sin or abstaining from it";[25] and Celestius wrote that "the will is destroyed which needs the help of another."[26] This doctrine of self-sufficiency that makes God's interior activity in the will of man contrary to his freedom is both a philosophical and a theological error. It resulted logically for Pelagius and his associates in a denial of the necessity of grace for salvation even in the order of fallen nature, or rather, since he did

[23] For an account of his doctrine and its history, see H. Rondet, S. J., *Gratia Christi* (Paris, 1948), pp. 112–121; G. de Plinval, *Pélage, ses écrits, sa vie, et sa doctrine* (Lausanne, 1943).

[24] This text is found in St. Augustine, *De gestis Pelagii*, 42 (ML 44.345).

[25] St. Augustine, *Opus imperfectum contra Julianum*, 1.78 (ML 45.1102).

[26] This sentence is found in St. Jerome, *Epist.*, 133 (ML 22.1154); and if it is not a direct quotation from Celestius, it does at least represent his doctrine. See Rondet, *op. cit.*, p. 114, where these quotations are found.

not recognize an original sin inherited by all men, for the descendants of Adam. He admitted under pressure the existence of grace in secondary senses; for instance, he called free will itself a grace since all creation is a gratuitous gift. He called revelation a gift or grace, or the moral law, the example of Christ, or the remission of sins. Finally, he admits a grace of interior illumination (but does so in an equivocal way so that it is not certain that this means more than external revelation) and that grace may facilitate the exercise of liberty.[27] But his doctrine is contradictory to an interior grace moving the will to the meritorious acts of the Christian life. The initiation, growth, and fulfillment of the Christian life for Pelagius are due to man's efforts based on the intrinsic power of free will. He explains St. Paul's doctrine of God's choice and predestination in harmony with his doctrine of man's self-salvation. God's choice is caused by the future foreseen merits of the person chosen, for otherwise it would be arbitrary and would show partiality. Predestination is the same as foreknowledge for God. Those whom he foreknows will believe he calls and in the process places no constraint upon them.[28]

In Augustine's doctrine on grace and predestination, there is a real development, but one that in the main took place before the outbreak of the Pelagian controversy. In a commentary on some passages of the Epistle to the Romans written between 393 and 396, St. Augustine explained through God's foreknowledge the statement of St. Paul: *Jacob I have loved but Esau I have hated.*[29] For Augustine this passage refers to the eternal salvation of Jacob and the eternal perdition of Esau. How is it that God has treated equals differently? God has foreknown what their future merits would be and treated them accordingly. These foreknown merits are not the merits of works, since these come to man through grace of the Holy Spirit, but the merit of faith which is in the power of the human will to give to God's call. This doctrine, which he repudiated later when he learned that faith too is a gift of God, has

[27] See *ibid.*, pp. 118-121.

[28] See de Plinval, *op. cit.*, pp. 152-3, where texts are cited from Pelagius.

[29] Rom. 9:11-13. For St. Augustine's early explanation of this passage, see *Expositio quarumdam propositionum Epist. ad Romanos*, 60-64 (ML 35.2078-80).

Pelagian overtones. But Augustine corrected himself before the Pelagian controversy, when he was commenting on this same ninth chapter of Romans in giving an answer to questions which Simplicianus, the successor of St. Ambrose in Milan, had sent him.[30] His later writings during the period of his controversy with the Pelagians (412–421), and particularly his letter to Sixtus,[31] gave rise to some misunderstandings. This letter was read in a monastery at Hadrumetum and stirred up controversy and division among the monks there. There was recurrence to Augustine to settle the matter, and there followed two more works from his pen, *De gratia et libero arbitrio*[32] and *De correptione et gratis*,[33] both written about 426 or 427. While the last of these books brought peace to the monastery, it aroused a reaction in Gaul, particularly among the monks of Marseilles and the surrounding areas. Two laymen, Hilary and Prosper, informed Augustine of the difficulties these men had with his doctrine, and asked him to write an answer to the problems they raised. The result of this request was Augustine's *De praedestinatione*[34] and *De dono perseverantiae*,[35] written in 428 or 429, a year or so before his death.

With such a wealth of material, it is still difficult to reach an accurate, organic understanding of Augustine's thought on predestination and grace together with the basic reasons that moulded his teaching. At times, interpreters of his thought who were themselves convinced of the truth of a particular theory of predestination have returned to Augustine for confirmation of their own views. By imposing upon him an organization of principles akin to their own and selecting many passages from his different books, they found the support for which they looked. But by im-

[30] *De diversis quaestionibus ad Simplicianum libri duo,* liber 1, q. 2 (ML 40.110–128). This will be referred to according to the Maurist edition of Augustine's *Opera,* 6 (Paris, 1685), 88–104. For references to most of the recent interpretations of Augustine's doctrine on predestination, see the article (written after my study of Augustine was completed, but not affecting it) by A. Trape, "A proposito di predestinazione: S. Agostino ed i suoi critici moderni," in *Divinitas* 7 (1963), 243–84.

[31] *Epist.,* 194 (ML 33.874–91).

[32] ML 44.880–912.

[33] ML 44.915–946.

[34] ML 44.959–992.

[35] ML 45.993–1034. These two originally formed one work.

posing upon him an organic unity of thought that comes from a later system, one exposes onself to the danger of misinterpreting him. It would be better if we could see exactly how the problem posed itself to Augustine, the deepest principles of his solution, and the secondary matters he looked upon as flowing from these central principles. This actually is possible by an examination of his *De diversis quaestionibus ad Simplicianum,* Book 1, q. 2. This work, written in 397, was the first indication of a change in his views on faith as a gift and the consequences of this. It was written before the polemic with Pelagius, and hence has an order and calmness about it lacking in some of his later works. And thirty years after writing this work, he refers to it with approbation. He says that in it he strove to defend freedom of choice, but the grace of God prevailed and he realized the truth of Paul's statement: *For who singles thee out? Or what hast thou that thou hast not received?*[36] He says that his understanding of the gratuity of grace shown in that work was revealed to him by God.[37] He answers those who accuse him of disquieting Christians through his definition of predestination against the Pelagians by showing that he had reached his views against the Pelagians in this work to Simlicianus long before the hersey arose.[38] He asks these men to investigate this writing and see "whether I have not there sufficiently argued that even the beginning of faith is God's gift; and whether from what is there said it does not by consequence result, although it is not expressed, that even perseverance to the end is not given, except by him who has predestinated us to his kingdom and glory."[39] If Augustine looks back at the end of his life to this work with predilection and finds in it the principle from which his later teachings on the subject of grace and predestination flow, we will with the least chance of error gain an objective understanding of his doctrine by a close study of the pertinent section of this work.

In this section Augustine responds to a question that asks no less than an explanation of what Paul meant in the ninth chapter of Romans by his teaching on God's choice of Jacob and rejection

[36] I Cor. 3:7. See Augustine, *Retractationes,* 2.1 (ML 32.629).
[37] See *De praedest. sanct.,* 4.8 (ML 44.966).
[38] See *De dono persev.,* 20.52 (ML 45.1026).
[39] *Ibid.,* 21.55 (ML 45.1027).

of Esau and what follows. St. Augustine begins his answer by stating that the intention of Paul in the whole epistle was to show

> that no one should be proud of his works . . . that works do not precede grace but follow; so that no one should think that he received grace because he worked well, but rather that he could not work well unless through faith he had received grace. . . . There come about certain beginnings of faith, like to conceptions; however there is need not only of being conceived but of being born to reach eternal life. But none of these occur without the grace of the mercy of God. . . .[40]

In the ninth chapter Paul proves this complete gratuity of grace by the case of the twin children of Isaac and Rebecca. God told Rebecca before they were born or had done anything either good or evil that the elder would serve the younger to show that the gift of God depends not on their works but on God who calls. St. Paul said this occurred *so that the purpose of God might remain according to choice.*[41] But Augustine asks how this can be just or how there can be a choice when there is no difference between the two. What is the basis for God's statement through the prophet: *Jacob I have loved, but Esau I have hated?*[42] There seems to be no basis for a choice of Jacob, and the rejection of Esau seems unjust. It is clear from Augustine's use of these words that he sees in the choice of Jacob the fact that he is assured heaven and in the rejection of Esau his eternal damnation. Moreover, he takes Jacob as a type of the saved and Esau of the damned so one can appreciate the problem that he faced in explaining the passage. The reason for the choice of one over the other is not a difference of nature, for Paul was careful to show their equality in nature. Was it because God foreknew the future faith of Jacob not yet born that he loved and chose him? If this were so, how could the case Paul took prove what he states it proves, namely, that God chose when neither had done anything good or evil to show that the choice did not come from works?[43]

If it is not from works or faith or nature, whence is the choice (*electio*, the word Augustine uses throughout this section)? A choice presupposes a difference among those things from which one

---

[40] *Ad Simp.* 1, 2, 2 (M 88–9).
[41] Rom. 9:11.
[42] Rom. 9:13.
[43] See Augustine, *op. cit.,* 1, 2, 5 (M 91).

is chosen, and Paul states that there was a choice of Jacob before he or Esau was born or acted. What is the basis for this? The answer is that God's purpose does not come from his choice as though there was a difference among men that led to God's choice and his purpose. Rather, "since the purpose of God remains to justify those who believe, he therefore finds the works which he now chooses for the kingdom of heaven."[44] There is, then, first God's purpose and as a result man's good works and God's choice of the person for eternal salvation. Augustine, probably because of the distinction between the called and the chosen in the parable of the guests invited to the feast when it is said that *many are called but few are chosen*,[45] says that this temporal choice (by which he means a choice for heaven) presupposes justification.[46] Therefore the choice of God comes as an effect of his purpose and not vice versa; the preference for Jacob here was due to the liberality of God's gifts and not to Jacob's works or his faith.

But Augustine adds the question that is always returning in this work. What, then, of Esau, of whom it is written that *Esau I have hated?* By what evils did he merit this? If he hated him because of his foreknowledge of his sins, then he loved Jacob because of his future merits and God's grace would come from men's works.[47] If it is not due to God's foreknowledge of his sins, then was Esau an object of hatred before he was born? The Apostle realized the problems that would arise in the human mind before this enigma and so he added: *Is there injustice with God? By no means! For he says to Moses, 'I will have mercy on whom I have mercy, and I will show pity to whom I will show pity.'*[48] But the question continues to recur. Why was this mercy withdrawn from Esau before he was born? "Is it perhaps because he refused (to believe)?"[49] But this would involve the conclusion that Jacob believed because he willed it, and thus faith would not be God's gift, and Jacob would have something that had not been given to him.[50] Or is it

---

[44] *Ibid.*, 6 (M 92).
[45] Matt. 22:14. See above, p. 56.
[46] Aug., *loc. cit.*
[47] See *Ibid.*, 8 (M 92).
[48] Rom. 9:14–5.
[49] Aug., *op. cit.*, 10 (M 93).
[50] See *ibid.*

85

because, while no one can believe unless he is called, even though he is called he need not believe? That is, God gives us the power to act, but the act is up to us? But Augustine adds, how then can it be true that it is not of man's running or willing but of the mercy of God? For if to God's call man adds his completion, "there is therefore need of willing and running."[51] Moreover, Esau was not yet born, so he could not refuse this grace or mercy. And if one said it was through God's foreknowledge of Esau's bad will, then he would have to say that his choice of Jacob was through fore-knowledge of his good will, and thus choice would come from the works of man. "Why then was he rejected when still in the womb? We return to those difficulties, so troublesome not simply because of their obscurity but also because of our frequent repetition."[52]

This leads Augustine to consider the effectiveness of God's mercy and call. If the words of the Apostle are closely considered, it is clear that he does not mean by God's mercy simply the help of God offered to us to get to heaven. Rather he means what he stated elsewhere: *For it is God who of his good pleasure works in you both the will and the performance.*[53] So God effects the good will itself in man. If Paul meant only that the will of man by itself was not sufficient without the mercy of God, he could also say: "Therefore it is not due to God having mercy but to man willing, because the mercy of God alone does not suffice unless the consent of our will is added."[54] Augustine cannot see how one can say: "God has mercy in vain unless we will. For if God has mercy, we also will."[55] But if God's call is effective of man's good will, how is it that not all who are called follow God? If it is because man, once called, can refuse to give his consent, then the Christian life is due not to God's mercy, but to man's willing and running. Is it perhaps that a man who, being called one way would not respond, if called another way will respond? Augustine accepts this view, for it is in accord with the omnipotence of God and the effectiveness of his mercy when he wishes to give it; "for God has mercy on none in vain; the one on whom he has mercy he

[51] *Ibid.*, 10 (M 94).
[52] *Ibid.*
[53] Phil. 2:13.
[54] Aug., *op. cit.*, 12 (M 94).
[55] *Ibid.*

calls in such a way as he knows is fitting for him, so that he will not reject him who calls."[56]

But again, this does not solve the problem of Esau. Still Augustine returns to this obstinate difficulty and asks why he was not called in such a way that he would want to obey. God was powerful enough to call him in a way in which he could respond, so the reason was not in the weakness of God. Augustine finally answers this question by quoting God's statement to Pharaoh which is cited by Paul: *For this purpose I have raised thee up that I may show in thee my power, and that my name may be proclaimed in all the earth.*[57] And Paul adds to prove, according to Augustine's interpretation, that it is not of man's running, but God's mercy, that: *Therefore he has mercy on whom he will, and whom he will he hardens.*[58] This hardening is interpreted by Augustine as God's refusal of mercy and not an impulsion to sin.[59] "But if this comes about with no distinction of merits, who will not burst forth into that cry which the Apostle presented to himself: *You say to me then 'Why then does he find fault? For who can resist his will?'*"[60] Augustine admits the question as it stands, namely, that God chooses one for eternal salvation with no regard for his merits and rejects another from this or withdraws his mercy from him with no difference of merits, and that this is the general law of divine providence. He obviously feels the difficulty, but, granting this mystery, he says that we must with the Apostle hold that there is no injustice in God. How is it that this is not a case of injustice? That can be seen from the practice of justice among men, for justice in human affairs is a share in God's own justice. In human affairs, no one can be accused of injustice who either demands what is his due or forgives what is owing to him. "Therefore all men are . . . in a way one mass of sin, owing punishment to the transcendent, divine justice, and whether that is exacted or forgiven, there is no injustice."[61] It is this truth that compels Paul to

[56] *Ibid.*, 13 (M 95).
[57] Rom. 9:17.
[58] Rom. 9:18.
[59] See Aug., *op. cit.*, 15 (M 96).
[60] *Ibid.*
[61] *Ibid.*, 16 (M 97); Cf. also 19 (M 100); 18 (M 99).

From this it can be seen that Augustine justified God's plan of predestination and reprobation primarily by the fact of original sin and therefore that his doctrine on this matter presupposes original sin. In this sense

ask men who they are to answer God. Does clay say to the potter, "Why have you made me?" Doesn't the potter have the right to make of the same mass of clay some vessels for honorable uses and others for dishonorable uses? Thus Augustine interprets Paul's simile as a metaphor referring to all the offspring of Adam as one mass of clay from which God at will makes some vessels of mercy and others 'vessels of perdition.'[62]

This doctrine of the Apostle is not contrary to the statement in the Book of Wisdom that God hates nothing that he has made, for God does not hate Esau as a man nor does he hate him insofar as he ordains Esau's sin to gain the salvation of others. He hates the sin of Esau or Esau the sinner. The reason for his action with reference to Esau, i.e., God's rejection of him before he had done anything good or evil (and not because of his foreknowledge of Esau's future sins) and thus making of him a vessel of perdition, is shown by the Apostle who recalls God's words to Pharaoh: *For this purpose I have raised thee up that I may show in thee my power, and that my name may be proclaimed in all the earth.*[63] God endures those who are ready for perdition "that he may destroy them in an orderly manner, and use them as instruments for the salvation of others on whom he has mercy."[64] They serve this purpose by showing God's justice and power and thus causing others to fear and also by showing the measure of mercy God has in saving others from the same mass of sinners.

The purpose of the Apostle in all of this was to show man that he should not glory in himself, but in God. "The free choice of the

---

his doctrine is infralapsarian and can only be understood if this perspective is taken into account. This perspective has been given its full value in two studies: O. Rottmanner, "L'Augustinisme," *Melanges science relig.*, 6 (1949), 28–48 (a translation from the German of a work that appeared originally in 1892 and provoked much controversy); A.-M. Jacquin, "La prédestination d'après saint Augustin," *Miscellanea Agostiniana,* 2 (Rome, 1931), 853–78. E. Portalié's analysis of Augustine's thought on this subject in "Augustin," *DTC* 1.2 (1923), 2375–2408, is criticized by Jacquin (862, note 2). Banez's and Molina's doctrine on predestination and grace extend likewise to the angels; and so neither can claim Augustine's authority (except by a deduction of questionable validity), since he justified antecedent reprobation by the fact of the fall.

[62] Aug., *op. cit.,* 18 (M 99). Augustine refers to *Ecclesiasticus.* 33:10 ff. to sustain this interpretation of St. Paul.

[63] Rom. 9:17.

[64] Aug., *op. cit.,* 18 (M 99).

will is of great value; indeed it is, but in those who are sold under sin, of what worth is it?"[65] The flesh desires against the spirit so that we do not that which we will. We are commanded to live rightly, but we cannot do this unless we are called, i.e., unless our mind is touched by the evidence for faith and by love of what we attain through faith.

> Therefore when those things delight us by which we advance towards God, this is inspired and granted by the grace of God; it is not bought by our desire and industry or the merits of our works, for that there be a desire of our will, that there be the industry of our effort, that there be works burning with charity, he gives, he grants. . . . Therefore what else is shown to us save that to seek, to ask, and to knock he has given who commands that we do these things.[66]

The source of Augustine's later thought is, as he himself stated thirty years later, clear from this section of his work in reply to the questions of Simplicianus. For him the purpose of St. Paul in the ninth chapter of Romans was to show that grace and eternal life are given to men through no merits of their own, but through God's mercy alone. Paul uses the case of Jacob and Esau to prove this gratuity of grace, and he means by God's choice of the one and the rejection of the other eternal salvation and eternal damnation. Jacob was chosen for eternal life according to God's effective purpose before he did anything good and without reference to his future acts. From this Augustine concludes, as indeed the Apostle states, that Esau was, before he had done anything evil and without reference to his future acts, not chosen to be saved from eternal damnation. To state otherwise would jeopardize the gratuity of the grace given to Jacob. From the fact that eternal salvation is not from man's will and running, but from God's mercy, Augustine deduces his conclusion that God's mercy effectively brings about man's change of heart and is frustrated by no one. But the question of the justice of God's treatment of Esau remains. The ultimate reason why justice remains in God's withdrawing mercy from him previous to any evil he did is the fact of original sin, which makes all men debtors of God. The reason why God rejects and makes vessels of perdition is for the manifestation

---

[65] *Ibid.*, 21 (M 102).
[66] *Ibid.*

of his power to punish sinners and the mercy he has given the just in making them just. As one can see, this does contain in germ Augustine's later doctrine on the gratuity and necessity of grace, predestination, the insuperable efficacy of God's predestination, mercy, will, and grace to save those he has chosen, the nature of perseverance, the restricted character of God's salvific will, and the lot of the condemned.

There is no need to show the development of Augustine's thought in his later writings on the subject of the necessity and the gratuity of grace for salvation. His doctrine on this will be seen in the statement we shall bring forward from the councils of the Church, and the very fact of his influence upon the Church's teaching gives eloquent witness to the pre-eminent and enduring importance he has had in the elucidation of the mystery of grace. But it is worthwhile to show what conclusions Augustine draws from this gratuity in his doctrine on the efficacy of God's will and grace for those who reach heaven, and what consequences he draws from this for those who do not reach heaven.

The offspring of Adam who reach heaven through grace have nothing of their own to offer whereby they will merit the grace and the term of grace as a reward of their efforts. So, as Paul's doctrine with reference to Jacob shows, they achieve it through God's predestination or eternal plan and its effects. "Thus they have been chosen before the creation of the world by that predestination in which God has foreknown his own future deeds; they have been chosen from the world by that call by which God fulfills what he has predestined."[67] This predestination of the saints is nothing other than "the foreknowledge and preparation of the benefits by which they are most certainly liberated whoever are

[67] *De praed. sanct.*, 17.34 (ML 44.986).

Rondet, in *Gratia Christi*, p. 141, says that Augustine's doctrine of predestination must be interpreted by his doctrine of the relation of eternity to time. The implications he draws from this seem to be that God does not predestine to heaven antecedent to his knowledge of what the free creature would do. However in his work to Simplicianus, Augustine taught an absolute choice for heaven that was causally (if not temporally) antecedent to the acts of the free creature (who was a descendant of Adam). His teaching on Esau's reprobation and Jacob's predestination as well as his later teaching on the limited salvific will all demand this interpretation.

liberated."[68] Since God has predestined man, he, of course, foreknows his activity by which he makes them holy, and thus foreknowledge and predestination are so closely united in God that Augustine could say, "to have predestined is to have foreknown what he himself would do."[69]

As the above quotations already show, God's predestination of a man to his eternal salvation is *infallibly efficacious* in achieving its effect. "If anyone of these perish, God is deceived; but none of them do perish, because God is not deceived."[70] No one can frustrate the mercy of God or resist the will of God.

> It is then not to be doubted that human wills cannot resist the will of God . . . so as to prevent his doing what he wills since he does even concerning the very wills of men what he wills when he wills . . . without doubt having the most omnipotent power of inclining the hearts of men whither it should please him.[71]

The fulfillment of the divine purpose is not subject to doubt, for those whom God chooses from the descendants of Adam will with

[68] *De dono persev.*, 14.35 (ML 44.1014).

[69] *Ibid.*, 18.47 (ML 45.1023). See also *De praed. sanct.*, 19.38 (ML 44.988).

Portalié, in *art. cit.*, p. 2402, holds that Augustine attributed to God a *scientia media*. J. Saint-Martin, in "Prédestination, S. Augustin," *DTC* 12.2 (1935), col. 2850–52, tends to see in the kind of knowledge Augustine attributes to God a causative knowledge that follows an infallibly and intrinsically efficacious divine decree. As a matter of fact, Augustine does not seem to have realized the metaphysical problems about divine knowledge that his theory raised; his description of God's knowledge seems at times to be like that of the Thomists, at times like that of the Molinists, and at times like neither. For fallen man the divine knowledge of predestination does seem to follow an absolute divine decree not influenced by man's works. In his use of his knowledge, God can convert whomever he chooses because he knows the circumstances and graces that will bring about the conversion (see above, note 56 and passage from which this was drawn). Adam's grace (*adiutorium sine quo*) seems to imply that in his case God's knowledge of his sin was not certain antecedent to Adam's actual sin. Also when Augustine speaks of how God causes the free will act through grace (see above, notes 56, 66, and the passages referred to), he differs from both schools. While they explain God's causality in the order of efficiency and say that the final cause has no more than moral influence in eliciting the act of the will, Augustine seems to ascribe to the end or final cause a physical influence in eliciting the will's act.

[70] *De cor. et grat.*, 7.14 (ML 44.924). Augustine is referring to the predestined and foreknown of Rom. 8:28.

[71] *Ibid.*, 14.45 (ML 44.943).

certainty hear the gospel, believe it, and persevere in love until the end of their life or return to this after a lapse from grace. The call given to them is different from that given to those who will not accept, or having accepted, not persevere; that given to the elect is what the Apostle describes as a call according to God's plan or purpose.[72] Of course, these do respond to God's call and do good, but it is God who prepares their will to respond and makes them will good: "It is certain that we act when we act, but he brings about our act through giving to the will most efficacious powers."[73] This power is the power of grace that gives to the will, not only the strength to act well, but the act itself. For if God gave man weakened by original sin simply the power to do well, he would be overcome by his own weakness and fall away from God. "Therefore there has been aid given to the weakness of the human will so that under divine grace it might act unchangeably and invincibly and, therefore, though weak, would still not fail nor be overcome by any adversity."[74]

The necessity of this kind of grace is supposed by Augustine to come mainly from the weakness caused in the will from original sin.[75] And so while St. Augustine speaks of the grace given to fallen men as an *adiutorium quo*, i.e., an aid that effects man's very act, he calls the grace of Adam (and the angels) an *adiutorium sine quo*, i.e., one by which he had the power to persevere and indeed did what good he did do, but one from which he could also fall away.[76] Augustine was completely confident that such a grace as is given to fallen man is not contrary to his freedom and he wrote a book, *De gratia et libero arbitrio*, in which he proved from Scripture that freedom does remain though God's grace brings about the works of man. Man's weakness in the fallen state demands such a grace, and hence grace through freeing him from

---

[72] See *ibid.*, 7.13–14 (ML 44.924). Augustine is referring to Rom. 8:28.

[73] *De grat. et libero arbit.*, 16.32 (ML 44.900).

[74] *De cor. et grat.*, 12.38 (ML 44.939).

[75] See Rondet, *op. cit.*, p. 161, note 2, where he refers to the canons of the Council of Orange II to sustain his statement, some of these canons being statements from St. Augustine, that the Council held that grace was necessary because of the fall. Augustine goes further than the Council and sees the grace given to fallen man as infallibly efficacious.

[76] See *De cor. et grat.*, 11.31–2 (ML 44.935–6).

92

the flesh and sin is not only not contrary to true freedom, but per-fective of it.[77]

Those of the offspring of Adam, on the other hand, who do not reach heaven were never separated from the mass of sinners by God's predestination and foreknowledge and thus were not called according to his purpose, chosen, or given perseverance to the end.[78] We have seen that in his work to Simplicianus, Augustine taught that God's mercy was not withdrawn from men because of his foreknowledge of their future sins or refusal to believe. He thought this would involve God's choice of Jacob because of his future merits or belief. Also he found it against the nature of God's mercy which gave to fallen men who acted well not only the power to act well but the actual acts. The case of the death of unbaptized infants seems to confirm this view that God withdraws his mercy justly, and not because of man's sins that are foreknown. In his later writings, Augustine at times states simply that he does not know why God has withdrawn his mercy from those who do not persevere until the end;[79] but he also adds in the same book that they are most justly judged since when they die they either lie under the bondage of original sin or have added through their own free will their own sins to this.[80] At times he seems to place the initiative in God for their failure in some duty in this life. For example, he says that these are not called according to God's pur-pose or plan,[81] that it was not given to Tyre and Sidon to be-lieve,[82] and that, if there is not perseverance to the end, persever-ance has not been given.[83] Moreover, in God's salvific plan itself, according to all of Augustine's later attempts to explain Paul's statements concerning this, there is some limitation or restriction.[84]

---

[77] See *ibid.*, 8.17 (ML 44.926).
[78] See *ibid.*, 7.16 (ML 44.925).
[79] See *ibid.*, 8.17 (ML 44.925–6).
[80] See *ibid.*, 13.42 (ML 44.942).
[81] See *ibid.*, 7.14 (ML 44.924).
[82] *De dono persev.*, 14.35 (ML 45.1014).
[83] See *ibid.*, 6.10 (ML 45.999). Also see *Epist.* 217, 6.19 (ML 33.985).
[84] See above, chapter II, note 96, and Jacquin, *art. cit.*, p. 868. Jacquin and some others say that Augustine taught this restriction of God's salvific will because he did not know of the distinction between God's antecedent and consequent will. However, if this distinction is taken in the sense of St. John Damascene, namely, that the factor because of which God reprobates a man in his evil life, this is not Augustine's explanation of reprobation of men in the fallen state,

But if God does not have mercy on all of fallen humanity, he is not unjust; to that Augustine always returns.[85]

Though we see that Augustine's later writings on the subject of predestination and grace do in their central tenets cohere with the doctrine of his work to Simplicianus, there are statements in the other works of Augustine that are difficult to harmonize with this unified thought. Some say that his works directly on grace should be corrected by his other works, sermons, and letters.[86] But it seems a better historical method to use the works in which St. Augustine is *ex professo* concerned with the problems of grace as the central norm of his doctrine.[87] Not all of these are polemical; Augustine himself defended the validity of his doctrine through recalling in the last years of his life that he had developed it in its essence in his work to Simplicianus before the Pelagian heresy erupted. Moreover, even while explaining his doctrine within controversy, he was aware of difficulties that would be raised against it and continued to hold it. For example, in the last of his works on the subject he said the predestination should not be taught to the simple people in all the clarity with which he had expressed it. They are to be encouraged to put their hope in God from whom every good gift comes and particularly the gift of perseverance, and they are to pray for this gift of perseverance hoping that God intends to give it to them since he inspires them to pray for it.[88] But in the same book, speaking not to the people, he said with reference to his explanation of the gift of perseverance and the predestination on which it depends: "This I know that no one can without error dispute against this predestination which we defend according to Holy Scriptures."[89] Since Augustine continued to hold all the elements of his explanation of this mystery, but dissuaded priests from preaching it to the people as it stood, one can scarcely take Augustine's sermons as indications that he did not really hold what he taught in works dedicated specifically to the subject.

How does one explain that Augustine at one time holds that all

[85] See *De cor. et grat.*, 10.28 (ML 44.933).
[86] See Rondet, *op. cit.*, pp. 142–3.
[87] Thus Rottmanner and Jacquin, for instance.
[88] See *De dono persev.*, 22.57–62 (ML 45.1028–31).
[89] *Ibid.*, 19.48 (ML 45.1023).

Adam's offspring who fail to reach heaven have been reprobated by God antecedent to his knowledge of their personal sins and at another time gives practical directions for the Christian life that seem to indicate that all can reach heaven? Some say that there is no contradiction between these elements of his teaching. Be that as it may, the former of these elements is, as we have seen, not sustained by the scriptural passages advanced by Augustine, and Scripture's concrete doctrine on the Christian life supposed an understanding of the divine will for man's salvation that seems different from that of Augustine. So there is opposition between these elements of Augustine if they are judged in the light of revelation. Others say that Augustine's works on grace must be interpreted in the light of his doctrine in other works. But there seems such opposition between them at times that to interpret the one by the other would seem to change the nature of Augustine's explanation of grace. A supposition that Augustine was always completely self-consistent lies behind the desire to interpret his works on grace by his other works. This supposition is not necessarily historically valid. A greater objectivity seems to demand that we accept his works on grace for what they say, and his other works for what they say, and then recognize a certain disunity within his thought on this matter.

This seems understandable to some extent if we distinguish Augustine's faith from his explanation of that faith in the matter of grace. His *faith* was that of the simple people of his day. In his *explanation* or theory of grace, he associated an antecedent reprobation, an absolute antecedent predestination, and an infrustrable grace with St. Paul's doctrine of the efficacy and the gratuity of grace. His explanation of the mystery of grace which he held by faith was not completely free from fault and did not do justice to all the facts of Christian life. This he seems to have recognized to some extent by the fact that some of his teaching in sermons and other works transcended the limitations of his explanation or theory of grace. Moreover, his faith was manifested when he instinctively adopted a somewhat larger view in his writings of the Christian life and faith outside of the context of his explanation or theory of grace. But these other writings of his do not show that he gave up his explanation of grace as a theory. They do show, however, that he did not give up his faith for his theory and that he held the faith of the simple people of his day more deeply than the explanation that he advanced to illuminate that faith.

3. Magisterial Approbation of Augustine

The elements of this doctrine of St. Augustine on grace that were officially approved by the Church will be evident from a study of the Church's definition of the truth against the Pelagians and against those who later came to be known as Semipelagians. The interesting historical details concerning the spread of Pelagianism, the initially uncertain reaction of the Church to it, and its final condemnation must be read elsewhere.[90] This final action took place in the Council of Carthage in 418 which condemned the doctrine of the Pelagians and taught the contrary revealed truth in 8 canons (omitting the later rejected Canon 3) that show clearly the influence of Augustine. Here it was defined that Adam was not created mortal by God, but became mortal through sin (Canon 1); that those born of Adam do inherit original sin and therefore need baptism for its remission (Canon 2); that the grace of God causes not only the remission of sins, but gives aid lest we commit them in the future (Canon 3), not only in the sense that it helps us know the commands of God, but in the sense that it gives us a desire and ability to obey them (Canon 4), which we could not do without grace (Canon 5).[91]

Another aspect of Augustine's teaching on grace, the fact that all of man's acts profitable for eternal salvation (even those in the beginning of faith) are anticipated and caused by grace, was canonized by the Church later, particularly in the Second Council of Orange (529). But the bridge between the Council of Carthage and this later Council was the reaction to what were considered extreme elements of Augustine's thought by influential Christians

[90] See G. de Plinval, "Les luttes pélagiennes," in Histoire de l'Eglise, ed. by A. Fliche and V. Martin, 4 (Paris, 1948), 79–120.

[91] See Denzinger, 101–105. In the following three canons (D 106–8) the doctrine of the sinlessness of the just is rejected. On the original third canon that stated that the unbaptized children who died became sharers of the lot of the devil, see note in D 102 and de Plinval, art. cit., p. 110, note 1; and on Rome's approval of Carthage, see ibid., 109–10. Specifically for its approbation of Canons 3, 4, 5, see D 136–8.

in Gaul, and the resulting controversies. Augustine was informed of the difficulty these men had with his teaching by the letters he received from Prosper of Aquitaine and Hilary about the years 427 and 428.[92] His opponents were found among those influenced by Cassian, whose monastery was near Marseilles, and among the monks of Lerins, such as Honoratus and Vincent of Lerins and the many bishops of Gaul (e.g., Hilary of Arles, Faustus of Riez) who during the fifth century were drawn from this monastery. So before the death of Augustine and throughout the fifth century there was a large group in Gaul that would not accept the whole of his teaching. They accepted the fact of Adam's sin, its transmission to this offspring and thus the weakening of human nature, the need of baptism and of grace for salvation. But they were men involved in the task of stirring up to a full Christian life either monks or the lay-people of Gaul, and they thought elements of Augustine's doctrine were contrary to Christian experience, and an influence that weakened men's desire to practice the virtues. They taught that, at least in the case of many, man took the initiative in seeking God to the extent of beginning to believe in him and that God completes by his grace what they have begun. They held that the power of nature had not been so extinguished by original sin that man could not perform some initial acts preparing himself for God. And they also taught that God desires the salvation of all men and hence does not, antecedent to his foreknowledge of man's sin, determine their reprobation. God's predestination was explained through God's foreknowledge of what man would do through free will and grace and then his decree that those who remained faithful would reach heaven. Thus they denied a predestination to heaven antecedent to man's merits (and based it upon man's acts) and also Augustine's explanation of perseverance. Man has the power to accept or reject grace. When Augustine's disciples brought up the case of unbaptized infants who died and thus did not get to heaven, they answered that God determined their lot by his foreknowledge of what they would have done had they grown up. All this was told to Augustine by Prosper and Hilary in their

---

[92] These letters are marked 225 and 226 among Augustine's letters (ML 33.1002–1012). The following treatment of the dispute from the death of Augustine till the Council of Orange II depends upon G. de Plinval, *art. cit.*, pp. 117–128, and the same author's "L'activité doctrinale dans l'Eglise Gallo-Romaine," *op. cit.*, pp. 397–419, and Rondet, *op. cit.*, pp. 144–161.

letters. An example of such teaching can be taken from the famous thirteenth book of Cassian's *Conferences:*

> So great is the love of the Creator toward his creature that he not only accompanies but even precedes him by his continual providence. . . . When he has seen in us a certain beginning of good will, he immediately illumines it and strengthens and stirs it up to salvation, giving an increase to that which either he planted or he sees has been merited by our effort.[93]

Augustine's own response to this trend, namely, his *De praedestinatione sanctorum* and *De dono perseverantiae*, did not quiet the fears and opposition of these men. After his death the conflict against these teachings was carried on principally by Prosper of Aquitaine, who gained support from Rome.[94] During the period immediately after the death of St. Augustine, Prosper composed works against the opponents of Augustine in Gaul.[95] And he gained a general approval of the life and the work of St. Augustine from Pope Celestine, which did not, however, mention the doctrines of Augustine which were currently disputed.[96] After the death of Cassian in 435 brought a certain peace in Gaul, Prosper went to Rome where he later composed his collection of statements of Augustine that was to exercise an influence on the Council of Orange.[97]

There were three main documents of those combating Pelagianism and Semipelagianism that seem to have come from Roman authors at this time. One of these, the *Hypomnesticon*, is, apart from Augustine's writings, "the most important and complete work which has been elaborated against the heresy" of Pelagian-

[93] Cassian, *Collationes*, 13.8 (ML 49.912–13). Other quotations are given in Rondet, *op. cit.*, pp. 144–5.

[94] The existence of another current of defense of Augustinian teachings that resulted in a predestinationism is disputed among historians. See de Plinval, *art. cit.*, pp. 402–3. Still another current different from both is represented by Fulgentius, who perhaps more closely represented Augustine's thought than Prosper and the trend called a 'mitigated Augustinianism.'

[95] For a chronological list of Prosper's writings, see St. Prosper of Aquitaine, *The Call of All Nations, Ancient Christian Writers* no. 14, trans. and ed. by P. de Letter, S.J. (Westminster, 1952), pp. 164–5, note 52.

[96] See D 128 for an extract from this letter of Celestine to the bishops of Gaul in May 431.

[97] *Liber sententiarum ex S. Augustino* (ML 51.427–96).

ism.[98] It developed the argument from Scriptures and theological reasoning and, though it was inspired by St. Augustine, it was very clear in stating: "Sinners have only been *known* in their sins by foreknowledge before they came into the world and have not been predestined, but punishment was predestined for them in consequence of this foreknowledge."[99] The second document was a collection of statements from the letters of Popes Innocent and Zosimus against Pelagianism and from the 418 Council of Carthage, ending with a summary of the doctrine deeply influenced by Augustine.[100] It anticipates the Council of Orange in teaching a more all pervasive influence of God's grace on the Christian life than the Council of Carthage. It states that God is the author of all works and desires by which, even from the beginning of faith, men tend toward him, and that all of man's merits are anticipated by his grace so that in reality man's merits are God's gifts. This grace of God, by which man begins to desire and to do good, does not destroy man's free will, but frees it through enlightening, justifying, and healing it. It brings it about that men will what God wills and so makes men, not lazy, but cooperators with the grace of God.[101] The document abstains from "the more profound and difficult aspects of the related questions which those who have resisted the heretics have treated more extensively," and it neither contemns them nor approves of them.[102] The third of these documents is the treatise *De vocatione omnium gentium*, written most probably by Prosper about the year 450.[103] Prosper takes it for granted, as proved from St. Paul, that God does desire the salvation of all

[98] *Hypomnesticon* (ML 45.1613–64). This evaluation is from de Plinval, *art. cit.*, p. 124.

[99] *Ibid.*, 6, 6, 8 (ML 45.1662).

[100] *Praeteritorum Sedis Apostolicae episcoporum auctoritates* or *Indiculus,* D 129–42. See de Plinval, *art. cit.*, p. 125. Some attribute this to Leo the Great while still a deacon and others to Prosper of Aquitaine. It was accepted as the genuine doctrine of the Apostolic See in the early sixth century. Rondet, *op. cit.*, pp. 168–71, gives quotations from the sermons and letters of Leo the Great which teach the same doctrine as the *Indiculus,* grace as antecedent to and as causing man's acts profitable for salvation. Leo did not teach Augustine's doctrine of the infallible efficacy of grace or his doctrine on reprobation.

[101] See Canon 9, D 141.

[102] Canon 10, D 142.

[103] *De vocatione omnium gentium* (ML 51.647–722). P. de Letter, in the introduction to his English translation of this, *op. cit.*, pp. 7–9, reviews the history of the question of authorship and the reasons that make

peoples, and his problem is to reconcile this with other truths of grace. If God wishes the salvation of all men, why are not all saved? If it is said that this is due to the free will of man, grace seems to be weakened and to be something merited. If this is not the reason, then why is grace not given to all?[104] His essential answer is that God gives a general grace to all men as a result of his desire that all be saved; but he gives a special grace only to some, and only these are saved.[105] This has left itself open to different interpretations. Some say that Prosper teaches a real universalism of God's will to save; others, that he does not really achieve this; and others, that he does not teach one coherent theory. We may say at least that he recognized the difficulties inherent in Augustine's teaching on the will of God to save and tried to bring his theory on grace into greater harmony with the universality of God's will to save without falling into Semipelagianism. And that indeed is the tendency of these three documents, a modification of Augustine's doctrine, together with a fidelity to his doctrine on the initiative and need of grace for all acts of man profitable for salvation.

The controversy on the subject of grace and predestination had been quiet for some time when it again came alive on the occasion of the error of Lucidus, a priest of the diocese of Riez, who taught that Christ did not die for all men, that some men were from eternity predestined to eternal life while others through the foreknowledge of God were forced inevitably into eternal death. His bishop, Faustus, who was also a former monk of Lerins, had him sign a statement in the Council of Arles in 475 abjuring his errors.[106] And, not content with this, Faustus composed a treatise on grace and free will[107] in which he not only attacked Pelagianism and predestinationism, but proceeded to fall into Semipelagianism through reducing predestination to God's foreknowledge and giving man initiative in the order of salvation. When this came to the knowledge of the African bishops in exile from

---

Prosper's authorship more probable. He characterizes the work as (p. 165) "the fruit and symptom of a partial withdrawal of the Augustinians."

[104] See *De vocat. omn. gent.*, 1, 1 (ML 51. 648–9).

[105] See *ibid.*, 2.25 (ML 51.710–11). For different interpretations of this work, see de Letter, *op. cit.*, p. 166, note 56.

[106] See D 160a, 160b.

[107] *De gratia et libero arbitrio* (ML 58.783–836).

their native land on the island of Sicily, Fulgentius of Ruspe wrote against Faustus and for his part fell into the confusion of St. Augustine on the salvific will of God.[108] The matter was finally brought to a conclusion by one who was both a devoted student of St. Augustine and a former monk of Lerins, St. Cesarius of Arles. This occurred at the II Council of Orange in 529 where there was a condemnation of Semipelagianism and an acceptance of what can be called a moderate Augustinianism.[109]

The doctrine of the II Council of Orange is succinctly stated in the recapitulation after the last canon. It confesses that through original sin, free will has been so weakened "that no one thereafter can either love God as is necessary, or believe in God, or do for God what is good, unless the grace of the divine mercy has anticipated him."[110] By this it rejects the Semipelagians' theory of the goodness of nature left after original sin that would allow some to strive to be good or to believe and thus anticipate the grace of God, or that would make of God's grace simply the accompaniment of man's own efforts. It states, contrary to this, that grace anticipates all acts that are of value for eternal salvation, even those in the beginning of faith, many examples of which are given in the preceding canons. Grace not only anticipates man's good acts; it causes them, and these acts are therefore God's gifts. These two aspects are the essentials which Orange takes from Augustine: all acts profitable to salvation in fallen humanity are *anticipated* by the grace of God and are *caused* by the grace of God.

---

[108] *Contra Faustum* which is lost. *Ad Monimum; liber primus. De duplici praedestinatione Dei, una bonorum ad gloriam, altera malorum ad poenam* (ML 65.153–78), and *De veritate praedestinationis et gratiae Dei* (ML 65.603–71).

[109] See D 174–200 for the canons of this Council and 200a, 200b for the confirmation of the Council by Boniface II. See also G. Fritz, "Orange (II° Concile d')," *DTC* 11.1 (1931), pp. 1087–1103; Rondet, *op. cit.*, pp. 156–61; de Plinval, *art. cit.*, pp. 416–19. There are different theories on the way in which the statements of the Council were constructed. What is certain is that the acts fall into three parts: Canons 1–8 (probably part of the first recension of the acts sent to Rome by Cesarius and returned); Canons 9–25 (number 10 of these coming from Prosper's *Contra Collatorem*, the others from his collection of Augustine's statements, with some changes); and a recapitulation (probably composed by Cesarius).

This doctrine is found in St. Gregory the Great at the end of the sixth century. Cf. *Moral.*, 33.40 (ML 76.699). For other quotations, see Rondet, *op. cit.*, pp. 165–8. He does not teach the infallible efficacy of grace.

[110] D 199.

Then the Council goes on to teach against predestinationism that all the baptized can and ought with the help of Christ to fulfill those things necessary for the salvation of their soul. It anathemizes those who would say that "some are predestined to evil by the divine power."[111]

Now that we have seen what was taught by St. Augustine, by the opponents of Semipelagianism, and particularly by the official acts of the Church, there remains the problem of assessing the scope of the Church's teaching contained here on the subject of grace. All admit, as is clear from the history without further elaboration, that the doctrine of Augustine and of the magisterial statements prove that an interior grace of illumination and inspiration is necessary for salvation. Indeed, such grace anticipates every act profitable for salvation in fallen creatures, and causes every such act. Many theologians, however, go further and use St. Augustine and the magisterial statements against the Semipelagians to prove the *antecedent infallible efficacy* of the grace that gains its effect in the will of man. And they prove also from the doctrine of St. Augustine the infallible efficacy of God's predestination and gift of perseverance antecedent to God's knowledge of what the free will of the creature will actually do, as well as reprobation independent of the actual future sins of the one rejected. Let us examine these claims in turn, with reference first to the *Indiculus* and the II Council of Orange, and then to the teaching of St. Augustine.

Many theologians hold that there is for fallen man a grace which is given to man's will and which is, before the will acts, infrustrable or, in the state of anticipating the will's act, infallibly efficacious. There exists such a grace in the first act of the will; therefore, the second act infallibly follows. This means that God has distinguished this grace in the first act from the one that does not gain its effect, and has by an eternal decree determined that it will gain its effect. They say that it is theologically certain such an antecedently infallibly efficacious grace exists for fallen man. Some say that it is certain that the more difficult acts profitable for salva-

[111] D 200. It is in these last two doctrines above all (as well as in what the Council did *not* associate with the gratuity of grace) that the moderation of the Augustinian theory on grace accepted at Orange is apparent. See Fritz, *art. cit.*, col. 1103.

tion elicited by the human will demand such an antecedently infallible grace. And they say that it is much more consonant with Catholic teaching to hold that all of fallen man's acts profitable for salvation come to be as a result of such a grace. The main and usually the only magisterial statements they call upon to show that this is Catholic teaching are the *Indiculus* and the II Council of Orange. For instance, they cite the statements of the Council that "it is a divine gift when we think rightly and keep our feet from error and injustice; for as often as we do good, God works in us and with us so that we may work."[112] And from the *Indiculus:* "Of all the good desires and acts . . . by which we tend to God from the beginning of faith, we confess that God is the author, and we do not doubt that all the merits of man are anticipated by his grace."[113]

But it does not seem to us that these statements express the antecedent infallible efficacy of God's grace. They do teach that of the works profitable for salvation which man performs God is the author and cause through his grace, or, in other words, the fact that grace causes the second act of the will, the actual desire or act. They also teach that God's grace anticipates man's acts or inspires him to perform the act profitable to salvation. So they teach that man's good acts are caused by God's grace, and they teach the antecedence of God's grace. But they do not teach the efficacy of God's grace in the state of anticipating man's acts, or *qua* antecedent. This is another question which the statements do not bring up, much less solve. To say that grace in first act will infallibly elicit the second act or is infrustrable adds a new doctrine to the statements that grace anticipates man's acts, and that God's grace causes these acts. But those who see in these statements a proof of their doctrine say that if the grace that as a matter of fact does elicit the good response of the will were not infallibly efficacious in first act, there would not be a greater benefit or love given to the one who uses the grace well than to the one who falls into sin. So, too, of two men in the same temptation, one of whom overcomes and the other fails, the one would not be loved more by God and would be the cause of his own better state than the other. Therefore, an antecedently infallible

112 Canon 9, D 182.
113 Cap. 9, D 141.

grace is a necessary conclusion from the teaching of these magisterial acts.

To this we can answer that this is a necessary conclusion only if there is not possible another conclusion from the same statements. And another conclusion is possible. If two men receive grace equally before the same temptation and one fails, it shows that the man who failed did so though he had the same power to overcome and though he was as much loved by God as the other in the state before his sin. Hence, both his freedom and his responsibility are manifest. If the other overcomes the temptation, he does so through God who, as first cause, anticipates his will with a grace that he can resist (as it is in first act) but which as a matter of fact brings about the salutary act of the man. Any positive goodness in man's response, his not resisting and his co-operation with God, is thus caused by God's grace, but without in effect taking away man's ability to resist anticipating grace. So if the will acts, it is through God's causality and the love that is the source of his grace. This is then another conclusion that can be drawn from the statements of the *Indiculus* and of II Council of Orange, and hence the first conclusion is in no way necessary or proved from these statements. As a matter of fact, this alternate conclusion which we have just drawn is more in accord with the conditional character of grace and of predestination that we have seen is taught by Scriptures, whereas the other is based on a doctrine of absolute predestination that does not, in our opinion, have support in Scriptures. And now it is seen that this unconditional grace is not proved by the magisterium, for it is based by its defenders on the doctrine of the Church against the Semipelagians, which teaches such a grace neither directly nor indirectly. We are not saying that God could not give such a grace nor are we denying that God ever gives such a grace. We are simply saying that the teaching of the Church as indicated by these documents does not show that God gives it as a matter of fact and far less that this is the ordinary course of his providential dispositions. The interpretation we have presented of Scripture, then, is not opposed to the official teaching of the Church as expressed by the II Council of Orange.

But what of the teaching of St. Augustine? Do not his teachings contained in his work addressed to Simplicianus and later writings that develop his ideas contained there prove the thesis of antecedently infallible grace, of an absolute predestination and gift of perseverance unconditioned by man's response, and an antecedent reprobation? In answer to this we must remember that Augustine's teaching is of value insofar as it is a witness to the teaching of the Church or insofar as it is proved by the reasons he brings forward. These theories distinctive of him at that time are not a witness to the teaching of the Church. For, as we have seen, in the opposition to the Semipelagians after his death the Church deliberately and consciously abstained from accepting these aspects of his teaching. In fact, the teaching on the universal salvific will of God in Prosper, the teaching that all the baptized can and ought to fulfill with Christ's help the things necessary for salvation, and the condemnation of a predestination to evil in the II Council of Orange mark the Church's resistance to these teachings of Augustine which he deduced from the gratuity of grace as taught by St. Paul. His doctrines on the restricted character of God's salvific will, on the difference between those called 'according to God's purpose' and those not so called, on the antecedent reprobation of Esau and those for whom he is a type were not sustained by the Church. Moreover, the Greek Fathers are in contradiction to this aspect of St. Augustine's teaching, as we have seen. Indeed Augustine himself is opposed to this theory. For in other writings where he is not attempting to construct a coherent theological theory explaining the revealed doctrine of predestination and grace, and in his directions concerning the manner in which this doctrine is to be taught to the people, there are statements incompatible with an antecedent rejection of man and an antecedently infallible predestination and grace. Hence in this, Augustine is not a witness of the Church's teaching. Nor are his conclusions sustained by the arguments he adduces. In the first work in which he defended this view (and which he approved thirty years later), he based his doctrine on the ninth chapter of St. Paul's epistle to the Romans. For him, St. Paul in this chapter was trying to prove the gratuity of grace and used Jacob and Esau as symbols to express and prove this gratuity. For modern biblical scholars and in accord with the interpretation of this passage we presented in the previous chapter, the purpose of St. Paul was to prove that God was not unfaithful to his promises to the Jews. And the chapter does not prove either an antecedent reprobation from eternal salvation or an antecedent absolute predestination. In fact,

as we have shown, Paul teaches elsewhere a conditional predestination and grace, objectively antecedent to man's acts, wholly
gratuitous, and objectively effective, but conditioned on the non-
refusal by man of this gift. This is the normal manner of God's
providence. So Augustine's exegesis is, in our opinion, contrary to
the intention and teaching of St. Paul, and hence is not probative.
And our interpretation of St. Paul is not opposed to the teaching
of the Fathers as this teaching is a witness to the belief of Christians.

However, in the later history of Christian reflection on the
mystery of predestination and grace, many will follow Augustine's
interpretation of St. Paul that attributes to him the doctrine of an
infallibly efficacious antecedent predestination and grace and of
an antecedent reprobation. Some of these later appearances of
St. Augustine's interpretation will be grotesque caricatures of his
thought; and they will not be modified as Augustine's was through
a fuller perspective of Christian teaching and life that corrected
his views in writings where he was not developing a theory of
grace. Others will be much more conscious of God's mercy and in
their very attempt to preserve this mercy will show a repugnance
for this doctrine of antecedent reprobation as unworthy of God.[114]
But insofar as they accept an absolute unconditioned predestination and grace as the normal providence of God and an antecedent
reprobation of the moral adult, they seem to us to labor under the
same basic weakness Augustine's theory did. Such a view rests
upon what seems to us to be an incorrect interpretation of the
admittedly tortuous passages of St. Paul whose doctrine, in fact, is
quite opposed to this. The marvel, from a human point of view, is
not that this doctrine under the influence of St. Augustine has been
so long lived, but rather that the Church in her official teaching
has never accepted the complete doctrine of Augustine on this
subject of grace, a doctrine that through his genius and sanctity
imposed itself so widely in later ages.

114 See, for example, L. Janssens, O.S.B., *Summa Theologica ad modum
commentari in Aquinatis Summam*, 2 (Freiburg i. Br., 1900), 447. After
stating that he is forced to accept an antecedent reprobation as a consequence of the gratuity of grace for fallen man, he adds: "Ceterum
fateor hic agi de re ardua valde, et si a superius exposito dilemmate me
excipere possem, equidem libenter facerem; sed non valeo."

CHAPTER FOUR

The Later Development

I N THIS chapter we shall examine the later development of tradition on the mystery concerning the relation of predestination
and grace to man's freedom. The purpose of this investigation is
to see whether our understanding of Scripture is opposed to or
in accord with the Church's official teaching and theological tradition that is a witness to the belief of the Church.

The most important advance in the later development of the
Church's official teaching is found in the Council of Trent's decree on justification with which, we hope to see, our interpretation
of St. Paul is in full accord. In successive ages theologians bear
witness to the Church's constant acceptance of the seeming antinomies of the mystery, the fact of predestination on the one
hand and the fact of man's freedom and responsibility for sin on
the other. The denial of one or the other of these aspects of the
mystery always indicates the presence of heresy. But we shall
see that each new age has brought forth mutually opposed explanations of the harmony of these seeming antinomies. For some
theologians, God's predestination of man is antecedent to foreknowledge of his merits; and since this predestination is understood to be an absolute divine intention, this seems to others to
restrict the universality of the salvific will and to involve other
difficulties. Hence others hold that God predestines man consequent upon foreknowledge of his merits, but this seems to the
former group inconsistent with the fact that predestination is the
cause of man's merits and is gratuitous. Hence in each age, when
there is an explanation of predestination according to one of these

views, the other view is presented as a corrective; and so the division has prolonged itself.

Because of the evidence we shall present that shows this basic unity of faith and yet this constant diversity of theories to explain it, we think that theological tradition does not compel us to accept either the Thomist or the Molinist explanation in full. Nor do we think that theological tradition compels us to accept the theological affirmations of these schools that are the source of their dilemma. The following pages will show, we think, that theologians do not teach with moral unanimity the antecedent infallible efficacy of grace and, more specifically, of the grace of perseverance. Moreover, though theologians in general have thought that predestination is an absolute divine intention for the salvation of the individual, the fact that some have constantly considered it antecedent and others consequent upon God's foreknowledge of man's merits shows that there is no compelling theological tradition against our understanding that St. Paul teaches God has antecedently, but conditionally, predestined all the justified. In fact, it seems to us that our understanding of St. Paul is more fully in accord with tradition than either the Thomist or Molinist explanation taken singly, since our explanation affirms both the antecedence of predestination and the conditional character of God's intention for the salvation of the individual during his period of trial in this life.

Our study of tradition in the following pages will be limited to important and representative theories proposed in successive ages. We shall try to indicate the basic position of the theologians who advanced these theories; and we shall abstract, for the most part, from secondary problems (such as that of the nature of the preparation for justification) associated with the one we are examining, since theologians could agree on such problems and disagree on the subject we are studying. Though we are directly interested in their witness to the belief of the Church and not in the reasons for which theologians took the positions they did on this matter, we shall at times present those reasons since they make understandable to us the continuing tradition and diversity within it. Our study will survey in succession the periods from the early Middle Ages until 1277, from that time through the early sixteenth century, and from the Council of Trent into the modern period.

1. *The Medieval Period to 1277*

THE EARLY MIDDLE AGES.—While Leo the Great, Gregory the Great, and the official statements of the Church avoided the implications of antecedent reprobation and the antecedent efficacy of grace in Augustine's teachings, others exaggerated them. One of these was Saint Isidore of Seville, the seventh-century glory of the Spanish church, who wrote:

> There is a twofold predestination, either of the elect to eternal rest or of the reprobate to death. Each is carried out by the divine judgment that makes the elect always follow the higher and interior goods, and by deserting the reprobate permits them always to be delighted by the lowest and exterior goods . . . One wishes to be good and cannot; another wishes to be evil and is not permitted to be destroyed.[1]

This doctrine of a necessitation to evil was present in the Spain of the eighth century to the extent that, in a letter to the bishops of Spain, Pope Hadrian I (772–95) condemned it by teaching that "he [God] did not prepare for the wicked their evil wills and evil works, but he prepared for them just and eternal punishments. . . ."[2]

Perhaps this seventh and eighth century recurrence of predestinationism had some influence on the ninth century monk Gottschalk, who drew from Augustine a doctrine of a twofold predestination, the one of the elect to eternal happiness and the other of the reprobate to eternal suffering.[3] His teaching appeared heretical to Hincmar of Reims and Rhabanus Maurus, and they had Gottschalk condemned in 848 and again in 849, and then imprisoned in a monastery. The matter did not rest there, because Hincmar's expression of his own doctrine, which was quite

[1] Isidore, *Sententiarum libri tres*, 2.6 (ML 83.606).

[2] D 300.

[3] For an account of the Gottschalk affair see E. Amann, *L'époque carolingienne* in *Histoire de l'Eglise*, ed. by A. Fliche and V. Martin, 6 (Paris, 1947), 320–44. For the somewhat differing traditions concerning what Gottschalk taught, see B. Lavaud, "La controverse sur la prédestination au IX° siècle," *DTC* 12.2 (1935), 2904–7.

different from that of Augustine, evoked an attack by Ratramnus of Corbie. From this time on, tract followed tract; longer tracts followed shorter tracts. Hincmar was unfortunate enough to gain the help of Scotus Erigena, who depended more upon dialectic than on the Church's teaching in his defense of man's free will, and in his tendency to reduce predestination to God's foreknowledge. Finally Hincmar convoked a council of bishops favorable to himself at Quiersy (853) where his doctrine against Gottschalk and predestinationism was taught. Two years later his opponents (such as Ratramnus, Lupus Servatus, Prudentius, and others), who had dissociated themselves from Gottschalk, convoked a council at Valence. Here they accused their brother bishops of imprudence in their action and error in their teaching; and they condemned the teaching of Scotus, expressing in their turn the orthodox doctrine in more Augustinian terms than their counterparts at Quiersy.[4]

The difference between the councils was a difference of emphasis that, in the background of all the tracts then written, assumed very large proportions. The adherents of the different sides saw themselves as deeply opposed to each other's views. Quiersy taught that there was only one predestination, either of the just to be saved or of the evil to be punished, not to sin. God chooses according to his foreknowledge those whom he predestined through grace to eternal life. God wants all without exception to be saved, and Christ likewise died for all. Valence, on the other hand, admitted a double foreknowledge, one of what the just would do through God's grace, and the other of what the evil would do through their own fault, either that of original sin or their own personal sin. They also affirmed a double predestination. In that of the good for salvation, God's mercy precedes the good merit; in that of the punishment of the evil, the evil merit of man precedes the just judgment of God. They rejected a predestination to evil. Christ died that all *who believe in him* would not perish. Of the regenerated, those who persevere to the end will be saved; but others fail because they did not will to remain faithful.

[4] For the canons of both councils, see D 316–9, 320–5. It seems from a statement of Prudentius that Pope Nicolas I confirmed the decrees of Valence. See Amann, *op. cit.*, pp. 340–1.

The opposition that is apparent here was much more apparent in the voluminous literature of the time. Hincmar, finally appealing to the authority of the Greek Fathers, stressed the foreknowledge of God and the universality of his saving will, but added that, if man is saved, it is God's gift. His opponents, using Augustine as the touchstone of orthodoxy, stressed God's fulfillment of his eternal, immutable designs, but added that, if man is reprobated, it is his own fault. Finally bishops who represented these different views achieved together in the Council of Thuzey in 860 a unity that glossed over some of their differences. This ninth-century controversy was neither the first nor the last example of such varied explanations of the same mystery of predestination and grace.

SOME TWELFTH CENTURY THEOLOGIANS.—When this debate had for long been a thing of the past, the subject of predestination was treated once more, and this time in a masterly way by St. Anselm (1033–1109), who was in this, as in many other matters, the Father of Scholasticism. In a book which he wrote on the fall of the evil angels, he clearly ascribed the perseverance of the good angels to God: "It is clear therefore that as that angel who stood in the truth persevered because he had perseverance, so also he had perseverance because he received it, and he received it because God gave it."[5] This text is used at times to prove that the grace of perseverance is antecedently infallibly efficacious, but the context shows that such was not Anselm's teaching. For he proceeded to show that when the fact that something is given is the cause of its reception by another, the fact of its not being given inevitably results in its not being received. But there can be another reason for its not being received. Although the first gives it, the second does not accept it, either because he cannot or he will not. Such was the case of the evil angels. God gave them initially the ability and the will to persevere, but what God gave them they rejected through their desire for something incompatible with submission to God. Hence the cause of their lack of perseverance was not the lack of God's gift, but their own free refusal of that gift.[6] For Anselm, then, the grace of perseverance for the angels was a frustrable grace, one that could be rejected.

[5] *De casu diaboli*, 2. *Opera omnia*, ed. by F. S. Schmitt, 1 (Seckau, 1938), 235.
[6] See *ibid.* 3, p. 240.

111

His teaching on the relation of predestination and grace to the will of men in the fallen state shows the same attribution of all good to the initiative of God's mercy. In a book dedicated to this subject,[7] he gives many explanations which will later be frequently repeated by the Scholastics. He first defends the harmony that exists between God's foreknowledge and man's free will. He explains that God's knowledge is the cause of good in creatures, but not of evil; that if God foreknows some future act, it will occur; that, however, because of the relation of eternity to time, this does not take away freedom from contingent acts.[8] Secondly, he shows the problem predestination raises for free will, but holds that, through the relation of eternity to time, there is harmony between them. When he treats grace and free will, he is very clear in holding that justice is a gratuitous prevenient gift of God to man. For those who are regenerated through faith, perseverance is completely possible because of the help of God's grace. But can the lack of belief by which one is not regenerated be imputed to man? To this he answers that an inability to act that is caused by sin is to be imputed as long as the sin remains. Man's loss of justice and the inclination to sin he inherits from Adam is to be imputed to him. So the infant's lack of ability to gain the justice that God demands does not excuse him, and the non-baptized's inability to have the understanding that leads to belief does not excuse him, for it too comes from sin.[9] In brief, though Anselm offered many considerations to show the harmony between God's sovereignty and man's free will, he stopped short of denying any divine rejection of the moral adult in the present order antecedent to God's foreknowledge of his individual sins. In this the influence of Augustine is apparent.

In the generation following Anselm, Abelard (c. 1079–1142) and St. Bernard (1091–1153) showed once more the two, now familiar, opposed tendencies in the explanation of the mystery of predestination and grace. Abelard used the expressions of St. Paul to attribute all to grace, but considered reason and free will themselves graces. God gives these both to the elect and to the rep-

[7] See St. Anselm, *De concordia praescientiae et praedestinationis et gratiae dei cum libero arbitrio, Opera omnia,* 2 (Edinburgh, 1946), 243–88.

[8] See *ibid.,* q. 1, "De praescientia et libero arbitrio," pp. 245-60.

[9] See *ibid.* 3.7, pp. 273-4; also 3.3, p. 266.

robate. Moreover, God points out the way to heaven and invites men to himself by exhortations and precepts. Some obey him by living well, while others reject his commands.[10] St. Bernard, on the other hand, expressed himself in words that recall St. Augustine. Speaking of the predestined and of the reprobate, he wrote that "in both cases the sentence of eternity stands fixed, both for those who are saved and for those who perish."[11]

The opinion of Peter the Lombard on this subject is particularly important, since it was his work on which theologians generally commented down to the sixteenth century. It is clear that on the subject of predestination and reprobation he adhered to the teaching of Augustine, whose interpretation of the ninth chapter of Romans and works on grace he frequently quoted. With scholastics generally he taught that God's foreknowledge was not contrary to human freedom and that predestination was infallibly efficacious from eternity, so that it was impossible for one who was predestined to be lost.[12] Again with Augustine and all the great scholastics, he taught that predestination is gratuitous and not merited by man; there is no cause of God's predestination of the elect other than God's mercy. Peter's explanation of this gratuity was essentially the same as that of Augustine, and he interpreted to this effect St. Paul's words: *He has mercy on whom he will, and whom he will he hardens.*[13] Following Augustine, Peter found in this same chapter Paul's teaching on reprobation. If reprobation is considered as God's *eternal lack of a will to have mercy* on a particular individual such as Esau, there is no more cause for that than there is for predestination of the elect. As God does not predestine one because of his knowledge of his future merits, so he does not reprobate another because of his knowledge of his future sins. If, on the other hand, reprobation is considered as the temporal hardening of man's will that occurs through the withdrawal of grace, it is always due to man's sins; but it is too, in

---

[10] See Abelard, *Apologia* in *Opera omnia,* ed. by V. Cousin (Paris, 1859), 2.731–2. Abelard's doctrine on the sufficiency of free will was condemned along with other errors in the Council of Sens in France, held in 1140 or 1141. See D 373.

[11] *Serm. in Ascensione Domini* 2.5 (ML 183.303).

[12] See Peter the Lombard, *Libri quattuor sententiarum,* lib. 1, d. 40, c. 1 (2. ed., Quaracchi, 1916) 250.

[13] Rom. 9:18.

some way, the effect of the eternal reprobation that precedes both it and God's foreknowledge of man's personal sins.[14]

THIRTEENTH CENTURY THEOLOGIANS TILL 1277.—In their teaching on this matter Alexander of Hales, St. Bonaventure, and St. Albert the Great saw in God's foreknowledge of man's merits a *reason*, though not a cause, of predestination. Bonaventure well represented their thought when he taught that there are three elements in both predestination and reprobation. There is the eternal decree (either predestination or reprobation), the acts that occur in time (the predestined is made pleasing to God, and the other is hardened), and the final destiny (glory or damnation). The final destiny in both cases falls under merit, and the eternal decree in neither case is strictly merited, by what the creature will do as foreknown by God. The hardening of one that occurs in time is something that is merited, while the development in grace of the other is partially the effect of merit and partially not.[15] They differed from Peter the Lombard in teaching that, though there is not a *cause* in the acts of man for the eternal decree, there is a *fittingness* in these acts which God takes into account in ordaining one to glory and the other to damnation. For example, St. Bonaventure asked: "Why does he wish to save Peter rather than Judas? I answer: because the former had good merits, and the latter evil."[16] St. Albert and Alexander of Hales held essentially the same

[14] See Peter the Lombard, *op. cit.*, 1.41.1, p. 253–4. In his explanation of St. Paul's statement that God wants all to be saved, Peter is particularly concerned to show that God efficaciously fulfills whatever he wills. Hence he interprets Paul's doctrine in a restricted way. See *ibid.* 1.46, 1 and 2, pp. 278–80. There are a great number of texts in the twelfth century, however, that attempt to harmonize the fact that Christ died for all and yet that not all are saved, by the distinction between sufficient and efficacious help. See A. Landgraf, "Die Unterscheidung zwischen Hinreichen und Zuwendung der Erlösung in der Frühscholastik," *Scholastik*, 9 (1934), 208–28, where a great number of examples of this are given. Most of these texts refer to the redemption as merited by Christ, e.g., Simon of Tournai (p. 215): "Christus redemit omnes quantum ad sufficientem, non quantum ad efficientem."

[15] See Bonaventure, *Commentaria in IV Libros Senteniarum*, lib. 1, d. 41, a. 1, q. 1., *Opera omnia*, 1 (Quaracchi, 1882), 729; Alexander of Hales, *Summa theologica* 1, q. 28, memb. 3, c. 1. Vol. 1 (Quaracchi, 1924), 322; Albert the Great, *Summa theologica* 1, q. 63, memb. 3, 2.1., *Opera omnia*, 31 (Paris, 1895), 648–9.

[16] Bonaventure, *Op. cit.*, lib. 1, d. 41, a. 1, q. 2, p. 733.

doctrine.[17] Accepting predestination as absolute, these theologians taught that God's foreknowledge of man's merits precedes and influences it.

What is the teaching of St. Thomas concerning the mystery we are studying? And by this we are asking, not what his philosophical principles were, for he would be the first to admit that the mystery of predestination is a supernatural mystery and hence to be answered through the doctrine of revelation. He used his philosophy to explain and defend supernatural truths, not to prove them. So the use of such principles in this case was not the determining factor of his doctrine. Later we shall show that they do in fact help us to a deeper understanding of the mystery as expressed by St. Paul, but here we restrict ourselves to an investigation of his understanding of the central points of the revealed mystery of predestination and reprobation and how they are effected.

It is clear that he shared the presupposition of his contemporaries on the absolute character of predestination. He called upon St. Paul's teaching and Augustine's explanation of it to establish this,[18] and he taught that the infallible certainty of predestination is one not simply of knowledge but of God's providential direction of the individual creature to his eternal destiny. It will infallibly bring the individual rational creature to his destiny of eternal beatitude, though without taking away from the creature his free will. How God brings it about infallibly and still in harmony with the exigencies of the creature's free will is understandable if we distinguish the two ways in which a cause produces its effect. At times God's providence uses a single cause to produce an effect. But the term desired can also occur "in another way when from

---

[17] Albert the Great, *ibid.*; Alexander of Hales, *op. cit.*, c. 2, p. 324. We may note also that while these three theologians teach the necessity of grace for perseverance, they do not teach the antecedent infallible efficacy of such grace. See A. Michel, "Persévérance," *DTC* 12.2 (1933), 1273–4.

[18] See *De ver.* 6.3, sed contra 1. In the *corpus* of this article he asserts that he is treating here *only* the certitude of order as distinct from the certitude of knowledge, and he writes: "Sed ordo praedestinationis est certus non solum respectu universalis finis, sed etiam respectu particularis et determinati, quia ille qui est ordinatus per praedestinationem ad salutem, nunquam deficit a consecutione salutis. . . . Unde praeter certitudinem praescientiae ipse ordo praedestinationis habet infallibilem certitudinem; . . ."

the concurrence of many causes that are contingent and able to fail in bringing about their effect the one result is gained. . . ."[19] In this way God prepares graces for the one whom he has predestined, so that if earlier graces fail, the later ones will gain their effect. And thus he will bring the one predestined to his eternal destiny in a way that is both infallible and consistent with freedom. St. Thomas, then, did not hold that every grace that moves the created will is infrustrable, though on the other hand he found no difficulty in harmonizing an infrustrable grace with man's freedom. God's will is so powerful that what God wants to occur will infallibly occur, even though this refers to a single act of the created free will. "If God moves the will to something, it is incompatible with this position that the will be not moved."[20] This is not contrary to man's freedom, for "since the divine will is supremely effective, it follows not only that those things happen that God desires to happen, but also that they occur in the way in which God wishes them to occur. He desires some things to come about necessarily and others contingently. . . ."[21] St. Thomas seems to have taught that at times God uses this power to effect in an infallible way a change in the human heart. Thus in commenting upon Paul's statement that God calls and justifies those whom he predestines, he wrote: "And this call is efficacious in the predestined, because they consent to a call of this kind. . . . Although this justification is frustrated in some because they do not presevere to the end, it is never frustrated in the predestined."[22] He did not teach that all of the good acts of the predestined are anticipated by a grace that is infallibly efficacious as prevenient, but he does seem to have taught that such graces do occur. It is clear that his doctrine on their occurrence is de-

---

[19] *Ibid.:* ". . . alio modo quando ex concursu causarum multarum contingentium, et deficere possibilium, pervenitur ad unum effectum; . . . et hoc modo est in praedestinatione." In his later defense of man's freedom before God's predestination, he was not as specific as this. He simply stated: "Ad hoc etiam consideranda sunt, quae supra dicta sunt, de divina scientia, et divina voluntate, quam contingentiam a rebus non tollunt, liceat certissima, et infallibilia sint."

[20] *ST,* 1–2, 10.4. ad 3. See also *ST,* 1.23.6. *ibid.,* 112.3.

[21] *ST,* 1.19.8. See also *ibid.,* ad 2; 1–2, 10.4 ad 1; *Quodl.* 11.3; 12.3.

[22] *In ep. ad Romanos,* c. 8, lect. 6, in *In omnes s. Pauli apostoli epistolas commentaria* (Turin, 1917), 1.123. See *De malo,* 6.1. ad 3. The grace that brings about actual perseverance seems for St. Thomas to be antecedently infallibly efficacious. See *ST,* 1–2, 109.10.c. and ad 3.

pendent upon his understanding of predestination, in the manner of Augustine, as an infrustrable providential order of God.

The gratuity of this predestination has been defended by St. Thomas in words that have become the classic expression of this aspect of the mystery. After asking whether God has predestined definite men because of his foreknowledge of their merits, he explained that no one would teach that God's foreknowledge of a man's merits is the cause of the *divine act* of will that predestines the man, for such an act has no cause outside of God. But some have held that God has preordained that he would give the effect of predestination to men because of some merits. Origen said that it was given to men because of their merits in a previous life; the Pelagians held that the grace that fulfilled men's salvation was given to those who prepared themselves by their own initiative for it; and still others taught that God determined to give it to those who he foreknew would use grace well. St. Thomas showed that God does give one effect of predestination because of another. He gives grace that man may merit glory, and he gives glory as the final cause of grace. But if one considers the whole process, including the helps God gives and man's response by which the predestined gains heaven, it is all the effect of God's eternal predestination of the individual. The fact that man has the grace that brings him to heaven and the fact that he responds to this grace is all the effect of predestination. Considered as a whole, then, the effect of predestination can have no cause in the acts of men; its cause is the divine goodness as the reason because of which God predestines some, and the source from which this gift comes.[23] This, in view of the fact that predestination is absolute for St. Thomas, implies that in the order of God's providence the final lot of the predestined is absolutely determined causally before and independent of their acts.

If all men who reach heaven do so through an antecedent absolute predestination, those who fail to reach heaven have been reprobated antecedent to foreknowledge of their personal sins. Did St. Thomas teach this? If we look to his commentary on the *Libri quattuor sententiarum,* we find him teaching that the privation of grace is a hardening of man. This privation comes from man's lack of will to receive it and from the fact that God does

[23] See *ST,* 1.23.5.

not infuse it. But the second of these is always on the supposition
of the first, for God does not want this evil except insofar as it is
good. It is not good, simply speaking, that an individual lack
grace, but only if he does not want it or prepares himself negli-
gently for it. In this case, to deny him grace is just, and on this
condition God wants the man not to have it. "It is therefore clear
that of this defect the absolutely first cause is on the part of man
who lacks grace; there is not a cause of this defect on the part of
God except on the supposition of that which is the cause on the
part of man."[24] Also in the same work he uses St. John Damascene's distinction of antecedent and consequent will to explain
God's desire to save all men. Antecedent to his consideration of
all concrete circumstances, God wishes to save all men. But when
all things are considered, it is not good that all men be saved:

> It is not good that the one who is unwilling and resists be saved,
> for it is not just. . . . Hence this man, considered under these
> conditions, God does not wish to save . . . and this is called the
> consequent will, because it presupposes foreknowledge of his acts
> not as a cause of (God's will), but as the reason for the thing willed
> (i.e., his not being saved).[25]

This seems to indicate that St. Thomas taught that God's reprobation is consequent and dependent upon his foreknowledge of
the sins committed by the reprobate. But for several reasons these
texts are not of themselves probative. These texts are not the latest
statements of St. Thomas on the subject; his commentary on St.
Paul's epistles, for example, was written after the first part of the
Summa theologica.[26] Moreover, we have already seen that Peter
the Lombard distinguished the eternal reprobation and the temporal hardening of the sinner. He held that while the latter has as
its reason the sin of the reprobate, the former is not because of
God's foreknowledge of man's sin. Hence, St. Thomas' doctrine
that privation of grace has as its first cause man's bad will does

[24] In 1 *Sent.*, d. 40, q. 4, a. 2. See also *ST*, 1–2, 112.3. ad 2.

[25] In 1 *Sent.*, 46.1.1. See also *ibid.*, 47.1; *De ver.*, 23.2.c. and ad 2;
and *ST*, 1.19.6. ad 1 which more or less clearly indicate man's sins as
the reason for God's consequent will not to save the individual.

[26] See S. Thomas, *Quaestiones disputatae* (9. ed. by R. Spiazzi, Turin,
1953), 1. xvi, where Spiazzi, depending on recent research, shows the
dates for the composition of the *Summa theologica, prima pars* (1266–8),
prima secundae (1269–70), and of the commentaries on Paul's epistles
(1269–73).

118

not as such indicate his doctrine concerning the reason for God's eternal reprobation of man. Finally, even if he taught that God's reprobation is due to man's sins, the question remains whether the sin referred to is the sin of the individual or original sin inherited from Adam by all men in the present order.

In fact, St. Thomas denied that the descendants of Adam are reprobated because of their personal sins. He wrote that "the reason for reprobation in men is original sin, as Augustine says . . . or even this that there is no obligation that grace be given them. I can reasonably desire to deny someone something which is not owed to him."[27] Perhaps he added this alternative to explain the reprobation of those from whom original sin was taken away by baptism. In the same place an objection is raised to his doctrine from St. Anselm's teaching that the reason for the fall of the evil angels was their unwillingness to receive grace. St. Thomas answered that "the foreknowledge of the abuse of grace was not the cause of reprobation in Judas, except perhaps from the part of the effect, although God does not deny grace to any who wish to receive it."[28] Here St. Thomas denied that the eternal reprobation

[27] *De ver.*, 6.3. ad 9: "Ratio autem reprobationis est in hominibus peccatum originale, ut dicit Augustinus, vel (etiam fuit hoc) quod est non habere debitum ad hoc quod eis gratia conferatur. Rationabiliter autem possum velle denegare aliquid alicui quod sibi non debetur." What is contained in parenthesis is the phrasing found in Capreolus' use of this quotation in *Defensiones theologiae divi Thomae Aquinatis. In Sent.* 1, d. 41, q. 1, a. 1, conc. 6. Vol. 2 (Turin, 1900), 500-1. The modern editions the writer has seen have "in futuro per hoc ipsum." See also *ST* 2.2, 2, 5. ad 1. We may note here that in a letter written in 1201 to the Archbishop of Arles, Innocent III taught: "Poena originalis peccati est carentia visionis Dei, actualis vero poena peccati est gehennae perpetuae cruciatus." See D. 410. This indicates an advance over St. Augustine's understanding of the punishment God meted out for original sin; but its implications contrary to Augustine's interpretation of the ninth chapter of Romans on reprobation were not recognized at the time.

[28] *Ibid.*, ad 11: Ad undecimum dicendum, quod praescientia abusus gratiae non fuit causa reprobationis in Iuda, nisi forte ex parte effectus, quamvis Deus nulli volenti accipere gratiam eam deneget; sed hoc ipsum quod est velle accipere gratiam, est nobis ex praedestinatione divina; unde (non) potest esse causa praedestinationis. (Note that while this *non* does not appear in available editions, it is demanded by the context.) St. Thomas does not explicitly state that the fallen angels were reprobated antecedent to God's foreknowledge of their sins, but he does speak of the angels who reached heaven as predestined (*ST*, 1.23.1. ad 3). Since he thought predestination was absolute and antecedent to man's or the rational creature's

119

of the descendants of Adam is due to God's foreknowledge of their personal sins. The effects of reprobation that are the hardening of the sinner in this life and his damnation in the next can be from foreknowledge of the man's personal sin, but not the eternal act of reprobation.

Essentially the same doctrine is found in his commentary on Paul's epistles much later. In his commentary on the ninth chapter of Romans we find the main lines of Augustine's commentary. The love God is said to have for Jacob indicates his eternal predestination, and the hate he is said to have for Esau indicates his eternal reprobation. We have seen that the created effect of eternal reprobation involves sins in this life and punishment in the next. God's foreknowledge of man's sins can be a reason for reprobation from the part of the punishment, for God proposes to punish sinners for the sins that they have from themselves and not from him.[29] But he interpreted St. Paul as follows: "It is said that without preceding merit, God chooses one and reprobates the other."[30] This is not unjust because distributive justice (the only form of justice of which there can be question here) refers to the distribution to men of things that are *due* to them. If a man distributes gifts or forgives injuries, he is not bound by such justice. God is in such a position before all who are descended from Adam, so he has complete freedom to draw some from their condition to eternal glory and to leave others in their misery. God's action toward the latter is not to dispose them to evil, since they have this from original sin itself; he simply permits them to do what they desire, and does this to show his justice and his power over them, as well as his mercy to the saved.[31]

For the sake of brevity we have restricted ourselves to the statements of St. Thomas that reveal most pointedly his answers to the ultimate questions about predestination and reprobation. But we must recognize that he tried to lessen the apparent harsh-

merits, it would follow that those angels who were not predestined were antecedently reprobated.

[29] See *In Rom.* 9, lect. 2, *op. cit.*, p. 133.

[30] *Ibid.*, lect. 3, *op. cit.*, p. 134. It is true that at times St. Thomas states that foreknowledge precedes predestination, but this is foreknowledge of the end, namely, eternal glory for this individual, not of the means. See *In Sent.*, 1.38.1.1. See also *ibid.*, 40.1.2. ad 2. So he does teach that God predestines antecedent to his foreknowledge of man's merits.

[31] See *ibid.*, lect. 3 and 4, *op. cit.*, pp. 134–40.

ness of this doctrine in many ways. For example, he held that Christ's redemption was sufficient for all, though it was efficacious only for the elect.[32] In fact, he so tried to modify some of the implications of his doctrine that, as shown by the texts cited, he at times sacrificed consistency for this purpose. It is clear, though, that he held that absolute predestination was causally antecedent to God's foreknowledge of man's merits, and eternal reprobation was likewise antecedent to man's personal sins. The reason for this teaching was not philosophical. It was the authority of St. Paul as interpreted by Augustine.

2. *From 1277 through the Early Sixteenth Century*

While in the thirteenth century there were relatively different interpretations of the doctrine of predestination and grace within the bounds of orthodoxy, in the sixteenth century there were the radically opposed beliefs of the Protestants and the Rationalists, both of which were heretical, one denying freedom and the other the sovereign providence of God. The cause of the emergence of these later views was the gradual disintegration of the relative unity of religion and life of the thirteenth century, an evolution that manifested itself in many aspects of late medieval life. Among the contributing factors bringing about the radically opposed doctrines of the sixteenth century concerning God's relation to man were the teachings on this subject by the theologians after the period of St. Thomas. A detailed study of these is completely unnecessary to prove the lack of a moral unanimity among these theologians in their explanation; this is immediately evident in the multiplication of theories during that time. But a brief survey

[32] See *In 1 Tim.*, c. 2, lect. 1, *op. cit.*, 2.194. When St. Thomas comments in this same place (193) on Paul's statement that God *wishes all men to be saved* (1 Tim. 2:4), he advances different interpretations. In explaining St. John Damascene's distinction, he indicates that the reason for God's consequent will not to save all is the punishment of sins. But he does not say more definitely whether these are personal sins or original sin. There are many texts we could quote that reject the imputation of sin to God (e.g., *ST*, 2–2, 18.4. ad 3), but this would simply show that St. Thomas did not think antecedent reprobation was incompatible with such a position. Also when he is not dealing immediately with predestination or reprobation, his teaching is more in accord with the common belief of the faithful that has always rejected an antecedent reprobation.

stressing the formative ideas in the works of the theologians most influential on later thought will indicate the continuing inability of theologians to find an adequate explanation based on the presupposition that predestination is absolute rather than conditional according to revelation, the degree to which philosophy determined the explanations given, and some of the sources of Protestant doctrine on the subject.

A TURNING POINT.—Before tracing this development, one does well to recall what seems to be the point of departure in this period of theological decline. During the second half of the thirteenth century, there was growing a heterodox Aristotelianism, the main proponent of which was Siger of Brabant, which accepted Aristotelian doctrines and more specifically Averroistic interpretations of Aristotle, even when they were opposed to Christian beliefs. This group was moving toward a determinism and toward a limitation of the causality, knowledge, and providence of God in the world. In various ways there was a vigorous reaction to this tendency by the main theologians of the day. Moreover, Bishop Etienne Tempier of Paris opposed the tendency by the condemnation of thirteen of its characteristic propositions in 1270. When the movement continued, he went beyond this and in December, 1277, he condemned over 200 propositions that embraced not only Averroes and Avicenna, but also some teachings of St. Thomas which some conservative theologians of the age interpreted as excessive concessions to Greek philosophy. In general, then, this condemnation, which was later substanially reiterated by Archbishop Robert Kilwardby of Canterbury, was a very vigorous and even intemperate reaction to doctrines that denied or seemed to diminish the freedom and omnipotence of God.[33] Its effect on later theology was immense. For the subject which we are studying, it is particularly important to recognize that theologians generally after 1277 reacted against the limitations of God's power and freedom that were associated with the intellectualism of Averroes, Avicenna, and Aristotle.[34]

[33] See E. Gilson, *History of Christian Philosophy in the Middle Ages* (New York, 1955), pp. 402–410.

[34] See *ibid.*, p. 409: "Scotism and Ockhamism are dominated by the desire to insure the freedom of the Christian God with respect to the

The result of such a reaction in the theologians' explanations of the mystery of predestination and grace was a growing emphasis upon the very elements of the current explanation that did not represent the teaching of Scripture, namely, antecedent reprobation, the infallible efficacy of God's predestination and of the grace that effects it, and, in short, the independence of God's saving activity from man's completely free response.

The first theologian to be representative of this tendency and to have an immense influence on later thought was John Duns Scotus. In his commentary on Peter the Lombard's passage on the cause of predestination and of reprobation, Scotus presented St. Thomas' doctrine as found in the *Summa theologica*, the contrary teaching of Henry of Ghent, and his own doctrine which agrees with St. Thomas on the basis of their common interpretation of St. Paul under the influence of Augustine.[35] However, the philosophy whereby Scotus explained this predestination and reprobation differs from that of St. Thomas. While that of St. Thomas is more easily consistent with a conditioned predestination (as we shall see later in this work), that of Scotus seems to make almost inevitable an absolute antecedent predestination. This is particularly evident in Scotus' doctrine of the divine will and intellect. By its knowledge of his divine essence, the divine intellect conceives all possibles. So far, this does not give God knowledge of actual contingent future events. But when the divine will determines interiorly to choose one part of these possibles, it both determines what the extrinsic effect of its causality will be and gives the

---

world of things. Greek necessitarianism is the Carthage they are eager to destroy."

[35] On Scotus' doctrine of predestination and grace, see P. Vignaux, *Justification et prédestination au XIVᵉ siècle. Duns Scot, Pierre d'Auriole, Guillaume d'Occam, Grégoire de Rimini* (Paris, 1934), ch. 1, pp. 8-41. The study that follows on these fourteenth century theologians is almost completely dependent upon this excellent work of Vignaux, and the quotations given from their works are also taken from Vignaux's voluminous quotations, according to the editions he uses. For John Duns Scotus he uses *Opera omnia* (Lyons, 1639), 12 vols., the so-called Wadding edition. (I have checked these quotations according to the *Vives* edition.) For Scotus' presentation of the doctrine of Henry of Ghent, of St. Thomas, and his own essential agreement with the latter, see *Opus oxoniense, In 1 Sent.*, d. 41, q. unica. Scotus applies St. Thomas' opinion to the angels also, *ibid.*, n. 13. There is a recent analysis of Scotus' teaching on predestination in W. Pannenberg, *Die Prädestinationslehre des Duns Skotus im Zusammenhang der scholastischen Lehrentwicklung* (Gottingen, 1954).

intellect the basis for its infallible knowledge of what will actually occur.[36] We should note that this implies that, from the very structure of the divine psychology, it inevitably follows that man's final lot and each free act are predetermined by an intrinsically infallible decree of the divine will. This seems to preclude the possibility of a frustrable predestination and grace that are of themselves objectively effective in the sense of St. Paul. But let us continue our analysis. This act of the divine will determines which of the possible natures will in fact exist, the laws that will consequently govern them, and indeed the acts those natures will elicit; God's action in accord with these laws and natures is called his ordered power (*potentia ordinata*). But God's will could have chosen another order of natures and laws, and thus his power could have acted in ways other than that in accord with present laws. God's absolute power (*potentia absoluta*) is that in accord with all these other possible orders as distinct from the present one, and it is able to do all that is not contrary to the principle of contradiction.[37]

Scotus applies his doctrine of the divine will to explain Paul's doctrine of predestination and reprobation. Creatures are not a necessary object of the divine will. Hence God is completely free in giving them existence and more free, if possible, in giving rational creatures the ultimate good of eternal life. This act of the

---

[36] See Scotus, *Quaestiones Quodlibetales* 14, n. 16: Completo igitur toto ordine motionis necessariae, sequitur motio contingens . . . primo ad intra, quia nisi ipsa voluntas determinatur in se ad volendum alteram partem, nunquam determinabit aliquid ad extra. Primo igitur determinat se ad volendum hoc fore determinate; secundo, ex hoc intellectus videns istam determinationem voluntatis infallibilem, novit hoc esse futurum. It is interesting to note that while Scotus' explanation of God's infallible knowledge of man's free will act in time is essentially the same as that we have found in Banez, his analysis of the nature of the free will act and God's causality of it seems to be substantially the same as that of Molina and Suarez. See, for example, *Ox.*, In 1 *Sent.*, d. 39, q. un., a. 2, n. 22; a. 3, n. 15–17; In 2 *Sent.*, d. 25, q. un., n. 20. In this last text he writes: "Sed rationabile est, quod tam nobilis perfectio animae, cuiusmodi est voluntas, qua anima est in actu primo, possit exire in actum secundum, quo anima formaliter perficitur in actu secundo, nullo alio activo requisito; . . ." See also In 4 *Sent.*, d. 1, q. 1, n. 33. And see E. Gilson, *Jean Duns Scot: introduction à ses positions fondamentales* (Paris, 1952), pp. 354 and 581–93.

[37] See Vignaux, *op. cit.*, pp. 9–11, and Scotus, *Reportatio Parisiensis*, In 4 *Sent.*, d. 1, q. 5, n. 2. See Gilson, *op. cit.*, pp. 285, 308, 611–4 for a correction of false interpretations of Scotus' voluntarism.

divine will choosing an individual rational creature for grace and glory is, properly speaking, predestination.[38] But one who wills both the end and the means in an orderly way first wills the end and then the means that lead to the end. Thus God first wills beatitude for the individual and then, in a way posterior to and because of this, the graces that will effect this purpose. So God knows the person's merits, which are the means by which he gains heaven, in a way consequent upon his knowledge of his predestination to glory.[39] Thus, too, there is no reason in the predestined for his predestination, but there is a reason, Scotus states, for the reprobation of the damned. This can be seen in the logical distinction of moments in the divine will. God first wants rational creatures united with him in glory. He then wills this specifically for Peter, but there is an absence of such a will for Judas. In the second moment, he wills the means whereby the elect will gain beatitude, but there is still no will regarding Judas' last end. Thirdly, he permits sin, that of Adam and all those that follow, and this makes mankind a mass of perdition. He allows this both for Peter and for Judas. In the fourth place, he sees that Peter will be withdrawn from this mass of perdition (because of the previous will in his regard), but that Judas will die in sin. Then and then alone he justly wills to punish and to reprobate Judas.[40] This is in effect a doctrine of reprobation antecedent to man's sins that gives a more explicit explanation than that of St. Thomas and Peter the Lombard for the damnation of the reprobate, since it shows more clearly that the reason the person does not have grace is that there is lacking the will in God to give him the end and hence the means to reach it.

The complete dependence of the creature in the order of grace on God's free liberality appears too in Scotus' *doctrine of divine acceptance*. Peter the Lombard had taught that charity was, not a created habit, but the Holy Spirit in the will of the creature. Scotus taught that grace and charity were one, and that according to God's ordered will charity was a created habit. In accord with God's absolute will, however, a person could be in grace without

---

[38] See Scotus, *Ox.*, In 1 *Sent.*, d. 40, q. u., n. 2.

[39] See Scotus, *ibid.*, In 1 *Sent.*, d. 41, q. u., n. 11.

[40] See *ibid.*, n. 12. This is a supralapsarian view for Scotus, applied to the angels as well as to the descendants of Adam. See *ibid.*, n. 13.

a created habit, for it is not the nature of the created habit that ordains a person to heaven so much as the acceptance by God of his being ordered to heaven. Therefore, of God's absolute will a person could be in a purely natural condition and yet accepted for heaven.[41] In a like way, for a person to merit heaven in the proper sense of the word, two things are involved in the present order. There is the act that comes from charity and there is its acceptance by God as ordered to eternal life. The second is the principal element, for grace is a created habit and thus is not proportioned to eternal life, which is so much greater. Thus God by his absolute power could refuse to give eternal life for an act performed under created grace,[42] as well as give heaven for an act performed without it. In short, all depends on the liberality of God.

In conclusion, we can say that, in our opinion, this doctrine, together with that of St. Thomas, differs from St. Paul's by teaching an absolute antecedent predestination and an antecedent reprobation. Moreover, it seems to make man uncertain of God's objective dispositions toward the just and in effect to limit the universal salvific will of God. But Scotus differed from St. Thomas, as shall be clearer later, in almost proving his theory of this supernatural mystery by philosophical means. What in our opinion is St. Paul's teaching he seems to prove to be impossible by his philosophical doctrine of the divine will as of itself, and without reference to the causally subordinate self-determination of the creature's free will, determining the final lot and each contingent act of the creature. This doctrine of Scotus as well as his doctrine on God's absolute and ordered power and on the divine acceptance was to be quite influential in the later history on the subject we are studying. In fact, what Scotus looked upon largely as a simply possible order—man being ordained to heaven and justified by God's acceptance without an interior created grace—is later taken as an adequate explanation of the present order.

FOURTEENTH AND FIFTEENTH CENTURY THEOLOGIANS.—Even where it did not bring theologians to accept predestination as completely antecedent to man's merits, the philosophical principles

[41] See Vignaux, *op. cit.*, pp. 32–3.
[42] See *ibid.*, pp. 19–21.

Scotus used influenced the state of the question. Peter Auriol (d. 1322) and William of Ockam (d. about 1350) both taught that predestination is consequent upon God's foreknowledge of man's works, but the first rejected and the latter accepted Scotus' doctrine of acceptance.

Peter Auriol insisted that Scotus' doctrine of predestination did not do justice to Paul's teaching that God wants all men to be saved. This teaching applies to Judas as well as to Peter.[43] Auriol taught that the general and universal salvific will of God is specified by the merits of each. One person places obstacles in the way of God's will until death, and he is reprobated; the other does not place obstacles in the way, and he is saved. Thus predestination is an act of the divine will following (from our viewpoint) God's knowledge that the man does not place obstacles to his grace.[44] It is only this that can be the cause of predestination (and even then not a meriting cause) since all positive good use of the will or disposition for grace is the effect of predestination.[45] "A man can, however, from his purely natural powers not place an obstacle because in this there is no positive act but a mere negation."[46] All this explanation is intermixed with a refutation of Scotus' philosophy of acceptance and the substitution in its place of a nominalist philosophy that embraces both God's necessary complaisance in created perfections and his free power. In accord with his principles, Peter explained that if one means by God's absolute power a reference to the *term* of his action, then by this power he can condemn Peter and save Judas, because the commutative justice that, in his opinion, exists between man's merits and eternal life does not bind the power of God.[47]

Ockham attacked Peter's doctrine that God had a necessary complaisance in created goods and particularly in created grace. He defended and went further than Scotus in holding that God was completely free to accept man and his works for eternal life or not according to his absolute power. Indeed he so used his merciless nominalistic logic to attack any intrinsic bond between man's

[43] On Peter Auriol, see *ibid.*, pp. 43–95. See Auriol, *Commentarium in 1 Sententiarum, pars prima* (Rome, 1596), d. 41, a. 1.
[44] See *ibid.*, d. 40, a. 1.
[45] See *ibid.*, d. 41, a. 1.
[46] *Ibid.*
[47] See *ibid.*, d. 44, a. 5.

works in charity and the merit or eternal life that followed, and he so constantly recurred to what God could do by his absolute power that his conception of God's possible orders of providence prevailed over the actual order. In the present order created grace or charity always accompanies the gift of the Spirit,[48] but created charity is neither a necessary nor a sufficient condition of acceptance. God's act of acceptance is the one important element of merit and of man's ordination to eternal life. If man has this, his purely natural acts can be meritorious, or he can be acceptable, though really sinful. Without it, man's acts in charity are not acceptable to God or meritorious of eternal life.[49] God can decree that those who are good on a particular day be saved and that those good on another day be damned;[50] he is not bound by man's works. In the present order there is no cause, strictly speaking, for man's predestination or reprobation, but there is a logical antecedence of man's act to God's. In reprobation, obstinacy in sin is the cause in Ockham's nominalist sense of man's damnation. There are two classes of the predestined. Some, like the Blessed Virgin, are the objects of a special grace that prevents them from sinning; and for the predestination of these, there is no reason in the creature's acts. Others are saved because of their merits; here the foreseen grace or merit is the reason for predestination.[51]

In both of these explanations, God is in large part viewed as somewhat passive before man's acts. Complaisance and acceptance are responses to an act or a value. But these theologians tried to preserve God's transcendence by their doctrine of God's absolute power not bound by the creature's act. Neither of them, however,

[48] On Ockham, see Vignaux, *op. cit.*, pp. 97–140. On this particular point, see 119 and *Guilhelmi de Ockam anglici super quatuor libros sententiarum subtillimae quaestiones earumdemque decisiones* (Lyons, 1495), *In 1 Sent.*, d. 17, q. 1.

[49] See *ibid.* Ockham defended his teaching that natural acts can be meritorious of grace and glory from the accusations of Pelagianism by saying that the Pelagians were wrong in making a necessary connection between natural acts and grace. Ockham avoided this, since he made the connection depend solely on the acceptance of God. See Vignaux, *op. cit.*, p. 127, footnote 1. The nominalism of Ockham had an influence on Luther particularly through the writings of his follower, Gabriel Biel. See C. Ruch, "Biel," *DTC* 2.1 (1932), 816, 824–5. Also see R. H. Fife, *The Revolt of Martin Luther* (New York, 1957), pp. 64, 154 f.

[50] See Vignaux, *op. cit.*, p. 105, and Ockham, *In 1 Sent.*, d. 17, q. 1, P.

[51] See *ibid.*, d. 41, q. 1, G. See Vignaux, *op. cit.*, pp. 134–8.

escaped elements akin to Pelagianism or Semipelagianism. Hence, as though by an historical law, there arose one to describe the relation of God to man in the contrary sense, Thomas Bradwardine (d. 1349). He ascribed his understanding of the true initiative of God's grace to a divinely given comprehension of Paul's statement that *there is question not of him who wills nor of him who runs, but of God showing mercy.*[52] His famous book, *De causa Dei adversus Pelagium et de virtute causarum, ad suos Meritonenses, libri III,* defended the sovereignty of God against those who attributed too much to man's will in the order of salvation. While Bradwardine stated that he found his doctrine in St. Augustine and St. Paul, he proved it largely as a philosophical deduction from the nature of the divine will. And his teaching on the will of God is in great part the working out of implications of Scotus' doctrine on the subject. Hence his doctrine on the supernatural mystery of God's relation to man through grace is proved by natural philosophy and is implicit in his doctrine of God's will.

The existence of every creature and of every creaturely act is reduced to the divine will as its ultimate cause, and thus it is the decree of the divine will determining such existence that is the medium by which the divine intellect knows that any contingent thing will exist. The determination of the divine will is like a mirror in which the divine intellect immediately sees the existence of the contingent being or act. And this divine knowledge is infallible, since "the divine will is universally efficacious, insuperable, and necessary in causing, not impedible or frustrable in any way."[53] This is no less true when it causes the free act of the rational creature than it is in its causality of any other creaturely act. But the efficacy of the divine will does not destroy the true freedom of the creature, since this consists in a freedom from any determination by secondary causes, such as by the planets, fate, or a psychological determinism. Creaturely freedom is consistent with a theological determinism or the irresistible power of God. "It is sufficient to man that he be free with reference to all that is

---

[52] Rom. 9:16. See P. Glorieux, "Thomas Bradwardine," *DTC* 15.1 (1946), 770. See also G. Leff, *Bradwardine and the Pelagians* (Cambridge, 1957), and H. A. Oberman, *Archbishop Thomas Bradwardine: A Fourteenth Century Theologian* (Utrecht, 1957).

[53] See Bradwardine, *De causa Dei adversus Pelagium et de virtute causarum ad suos Mertonenses, libri III* (London, 1618), 1.10, quoted by Glorieux, *art. cit.,* col. 768.

below God, and only a slave of God, a spontaneous not a forced slave."[54] Although the creature's will is necessitated by the divine will, "that is, by a necessity that is naturally preceding"[55] its own act, it remains spontaneous. And this is enough to merit by its good acts and to be responsible for its sinful acts. This doctrine does not make God the author of the evil of sin, since sin has a deficient, not an efficient cause, and since the disorder of sin exists not with reference to the order of the world as a whole (the way in which it comes from God), but with reference to the individual will.[56]

This doctrine of the divine will with its implications of an absolute predestination and reprobation antecedent to man's acts, implications drawn by Thomas Bradwardine himself, influenced Gregory of Rimini (d. 1358), among others.[57] On the one hand, Gregory accepted Ockham's doctrine of God's absolute and ordered power. In the present order a created grace accompanies the Spirit in man's justification, and thus man is just by intrinsic denomination. It would, however, be completely possible according to God's absolute power that he have only the Spirit without the created grace if God accepted this for justification, and in such an order he would be justified by extrinsic denomination.[58] But on the other hand, like Bradwardine, he attacked the Pelagianism of Peter of Auriol and Ockham. His all embracing pessimism concerning the effects of original sin in the present order goes beyond Augustine's. In his doctrine he asserted that he wished only to follow St. Augustine and St. Paul, and he taught that predestination and reprobation are absolute divine acts antecedent to any consideration of man's acts.[59] The influence of Gregory on Luther is apparent in Luther's claim that Gregory's is the one true explanation of St. Augustine and St. Paul among the scholastics.[60]

[54] Bradwardine, *op. cit.* 3.9.

[55] *Ibid.* See Glorieux, *art. cit.*, col. 769–70.

[56] See *ibid.*, where Glorieux also shows that Bradwardine taught such theses as justification by faith alone and a twofold predestination.

[57] See *ibid.*, col. 771. On Gregory of Rimini, see Vignaux, *op. cit.*, pp. 141–75.

[58] See *ibid.*, pp. 142 f., and Gregory, *Lectura in primum et secundum librum sententiarum* (Venice, 1518), *In 1 Sent.*, d. 16, concl. 3, ad 2.

[59] See *ibid.*, *In 1 Sent.*, d. 40 and 41, a. 2.

[60] Vignaux quotes Luther's comment on Gregory's doctrine on grace and free will (from his *Opera*, ed. Weimar, 2.394–5), in *op. cit.*, 2, f. 2.

130

Another theologian deeply influenced by Bradwardine was John Wyclif (d. 1384) who accepted his philosophical determinism and indeed made it even more universal in extending it to include God himself.[61] Some basis of Wyclif's doctrine identifying the Church militant with the congregation of the predestined was found in Bradwardine; but in accord with his teaching on the Bible as the only and adequate source of faith, Wyclif justified the doctrine by appealing to Paul's doctrine on predestination.[62] Of course, Wyclif interpreted St. Paul as teaching an absolute predestination. And from this he deduced the invisible character of the Church and other teachings about the Church. We may note that Wyclif's *Trialogus*, which developed at length the philosophical proofs of determinism, seems to have influenced Luther's *De servo arbitrio*.[63] Wyclif also influenced the doctrine of John Huss (d. 1417), who tried to relate Wyclif's notion of the Church as the *congregatio praedestinatorum* to that of the Church as the *congregatio fidelium*.[64] Many of the doctrines of both were condemned at the Council of Constance. Among the condemned propositions are Wyclif's doctrine that "all things happen of absolute necessity," and Huss' statement that "the foreknown are not parts of the Church," and "taking the Church for the gathering of the predestined, whether they are in grace or not according to present justice, in this way the Church is an article of faith."[65]

Defenders in the later Middle Ages of predestination and reprobation as both antecedent and absolute were not found only

---

[61] Concerning Wyclif, see L. Cristiani, "Wyclif," *DTC* 15.2(1950), 3585–3614. He indicates Bradwardine's influence on him, *ibid.*, 3586. Glorieux shows the same thing in *art. cit.*, col. 772.

[62] See Cristiani, *art. cit.*, col. 3595.

[63] See H. Humbertclaude, *Erasme et Luther, leur polémique sur le libre arbitre* (Paris, 1909), p. 101, f. 1.

[64] See P. de Vooght, "'Universitas praedestinatorum' et 'congregatio fidelium' dans l'ecclésiologie de Jean Huss," *Ephemerides theol. Lovanienses*, 32 (1956), 487–534; and *L'hérésie de Jean Hus* (Naples, 1960).

[65] The errors of Wyclif condemned by Constance are contained in D 581–625; those of Huss in D 627–56.

At this point we may note another pertinent condemnation by the Church in the same century. Peter of Rivo, a teacher at the University of Louvain, taught that statements concerning future contingents are neither true nor false. The implications of this concerning prophesies and hence God's knowledge of free futures are that the prophesied events are, previous to their occurrence, either not true or unimpedible. His propositions to this effect were condemned in 1474. See D 719–723, and Gilson, *History*, p. 802.

among the disciples of Scotus. Capreolus (d. 1444) taught the same doctrine and held that a contingent predestination was impossible for the philosophical reason that it would imply mutability in God.[66] Peter Auriol had objected to the fact that some theologians interpreted St. Paul's image of the potter making different vessels from the same clay according to his will as meaning that God would reprobate men, not for their sins, but according to his pleasure even if there had not been original sin. Against Auriol, Capreolus held that Paul used the image without the presupposition of original sin,[67] and it is just that God so act since grace and glory transcend the limits of nature. Hence Capreolus held a supralapsarian view of antecedent reprobation, and he interpreted St. Thomas as holding the same view.

In the midst of all these theories concerning grace and predestination, the author of the *Imitation of Christ* gave evidence of the belief of the faithful in his concrete directions for the spiritual life. He taught that all of the saints ascribe their holiness to God's prevenient call and grace, that God fulfills all of his promises to the faithful, that he who is anxiously concerned for his perseverance should do now what he would if he knew that he would persevere.[68] This practical doctrine of the spiritual life is in accord with Paul's teaching concerning conditional predestination.

THE EARLY SIXTEENTH CENTURY.—In the sixteenth century there continued to be the division among Catholic theologians in their explanation of the mystery of God's relation to man through predestination and grace. But there was also the much more radical division between those humanists who minimized the providence of God and man's dependence on him on the one hand, and the Protestants who generally taught a predestinationism. The humanists who were guilty of the excess of rationalism in large part found their doctrines in the University of Padua where Aristotle as interpreted by Averroes was a great influence, or in the pre-Christian authors who were the heroes of the day. They found

[66] See Capreolus, *Defensiones, In 1 Sent.*, d. 40, q. 1, a. 3, A, concl. 3., *Opera*, 2.488.
[67] See *ibid.*, a. 2, B, n. 2, p. 504.
[68] See Thomas à Kempis, *De imitatione Christi*, 1.25; 3.35; 3.58. *Opera Omnia*, 2 (Freiburg i. Br., 1904), 52–3, 209–10, 256–61.

132

their impulse to accept such an affirmation of man's freedom from dependence on God in the secularism so prevalent in the day and in their emulation of the glory of the men of ancient Greece and Rome.[69]

The contrary extreme, which was common to the reformers, was represented most strikingly in the life and doctrine of Luther. The pertinent facts of his life are too commonly known to be mentioned here. We should simply recall that Luther was a divided, anxious man in a divided age, a man passionate by nature and without sane guidance in the chaotic thought of his time. It seems that the driving force that progressively held him more and more in its grip during his religious life was an anxious quest for the security that comes from subjective certainty about one's salvation.[70] This had a part in influencing his entrance into the monastery; it had an influence on the way he applied himself to the practices of the religious life and in his quest for a doctrine of God's relation to man. But his quest did not give him the assurance he craved; and in the midst of his life of increasing activity and decreasing inner assurance, he suffered very deep depressions in his consciousness

---

[69] For some indications of this trend see C. Constantin, "Rationalisme," *DTC* 13.2 (1937), 1692 ff.

[70] See E. de Moreau, "Luther et le Luthéranisme," in *La crise religieuse du XVI⁰ siècle,* vol. 16 of *Histoire de l'Eglise,* ed. by A. Fliche and V. Martin (Paris, 1956), 39–40, for an excellent analysis of the psychological reasons that lay behind Luther's evolution after his entrance into the religious life. "Il a peur de Lui, il éprouve des angoisses, des scrupules; il doute de sa prédestination. Les confessions qu'il fait, les pénitences aux quelles il se livre ne lui apportent pas la consolation qu'il y cherche, car il veut se *sentir* débarrassé de ses péchés, se *sentir* en grâce avec Dieu. Il *sent* au contraire en lui la concupiscence et il se croit responsable devant Dieu des mouvements mauvais de son âme. Il se désespère. Enfin il trouve la libération de toutes ses misères lorsqu'il découvre le sens d'un texte de l'épître de saint Paul aux Romains. Dès lors, il n'a plus à se preoccuper de ses péchés. Dieu, par sa miséricorde, ne les lui impute pas parce qu'il a confiance. Plus de grâce sanctifiante et plus de mérites: tout cela devient pour lui inutile, antichrétien" (italics his). For evidence of Luther's anxiety, see also Fife, *op. cit.,* 72, 101, 119f., 224–5, etc. See also L. Cristiani, "Réforme," *DTC* 13.2 (1937), 2055: "Le moteur secret de tout son enseignement c'est le besoin de certitude et de sécurité." In this article 2151–62, it is shown that there is essential agreement among the principal reformers (Luther, Zwingli, Calvin, the 39 Anglican articles) in the denial of free will (at least in the moral order) and the acceptance of an extreme predestinationism.

of his own guilt and inability to overcome his tendencies to sin. He tells us that he finally and dramatically found the security he sought in the doctrine that man is saved by faith alone, a faith that, in a way contrary to what we have seen of Scripture and tradition, dispenses with works and is really a confidence in God more than a submission to an objectively revealed truth on the authority of God.

A cluster of doctrines was attached by Luther to his experience, which is the one unifying factor of his teaching. Man in the present order is completely corrupt and without freedom in the moral order for anything but sin. This is the result of original sin through which man has lost an essential element of his being, namely the Spirit, the source of his moral freedom and his original innocence. Hence, fallen man is enslaved to Satan and can do nothing in any way to approach justification. This justification, which has been merited by Christ, is imputed to those who believe (in Luther's sense) in Christ. Such a justification does not remove original sin itself nor infuse a created habit of grace into man. It is extrinsic justification in that God no longer imputes man's sins to him. Thus it does not restore to man free will. His will and the acts that come from it continue under the necessitating impact of his evil tendencies or, if it does good, is necessitated by that of God. If man's will before and after justification is not free to believe or not, do good or not, it is wholly passive in the process of justification. Thus the only determining element in his justification is God's eternal choice. Man's acts result inevitably from God's choice. All of this is proved by St. Paul, whose teachings in Romans only Augustine among the Fathers and Gregory of Rimini among the Scholastics understood.[71] The whole expression of his doctrine in the early period of his religious revolt was centered on the problem of justification, but it clearly implied as an immediate consequence the doctrine of predestinationism in an extreme form.

A somewhat different perspective appears in Luther's *De servo arbitrio*, written in response to Erasmus' *Diatribe* and published in December, 1525. In this work, which Luther later always considered with unique satisfaction as an excellent expression of his gospel,[72] he proclaimed that his teaching on this matter of the will

[71] See above, footnote 60.
[72] See Humbertclaude, *Erasme et Luther*, p. 273, footnote 1, where the

of man in its relation to God was the cardinal point of his doctrine.[73] Erasmus had evaded any developed treatment of the
philosophical bases for man's freedom in his first work against
Luther both because of his dislike for Scholasticism and because
of his policy of arguing the case for freedom on the grounds
Luther recognized; namely, Scriptures. But in his response Luther
departed from his frequently expressed contempt for philosophy;
and he stated that the philosophical question of man's freedom
was the critical test.[74] He proceeded to show that man's freedom
was completely incompatible with the eternal immutability of
God's foreknowledge of man's acts, God's sovereign will, and God's
omnipotence.[75] Hence to his previous denials drawn from Scrip-

---

author quotes from a letter written by Luther in July, 1537, indicating that
he had become disinterested in his other works. The writer has depended
upon this excellent work of Humbertclaude for the analysis of Luther's
De servo arbitrio and of Erasmus' works that follow. And his references to
these works are taken from Humbertclaude's very generous quotations, in
the editions he uses. Also see on this subject J. Paquier, "Luther. Le serf
arbitre et la prédestination.—Erasme et Luther," *DTC* 9.1 (1926), 1283–
95.

[73] See Luther, *De servo arbitrio* in *Opera latina varii argumenti* (Frank-
fort ad. M., 1873), 7.367, where he addresses Erasmus concerning his
attack upon Luther's denial of free will: ". . . Solus prae omnibus rem
ipsam es aggressus, hoc est summam causae. . . . Unus tu et solus cardinem
rerum vidisti et ipsum jugulum petisti. . . ." See also Pacquier, *art. cit.*,
col. 1285.

[74] See *ibid.*, where Luther chides Erasmus for neglecting the philosophical problem of free will.

[75] See *ibid.*, 267: "Cum autem tales nos ille ante praescierit futuros,
. . . quid potest fingi, quaeso, quod in nobis liberum sit, aliter et aliter fieri,
quam ille praescierit? and 133: ". . . Deus . . . omnia incommutabili et
aeterna, infallibilique voluntate . . . proponit. Hoc fulmine sternitur et
conteritur penitus liberum arbitrium." and 317: ". . . Deus . . . omnia in
omnibus . . . operatur, dum omnia quae condidit solus, solus quoque
movet, agit et rapit omnipotentiae suae motu, quem illa non possunt vitare
nec mutare, sed necessario sequuntur et parent, quodlibet pro modo suae
virtutis."

Luther has been interpreted as denying simply that man has a moral
freedom to do good without the help of grace, but holding that he has
freedom of self-determination in indifferent matters such as building a
house. See M. Adler, *The Idea of Freedom: A Dialectical Examination of
the Conceptions of Freedom* (New York, 1958), pp. 416–7. Actually the
lack of freedom in the moral order that is taught by Luther goes further
than this; for him, man after the fall necessarily does what is good if he
receives grace for this purpose, and he necessarily does evil if he does not
have it. Some of his writings favor freedom in indifferent matters, but his
philosophical arguments against freedom in *De servo arbitrio* deny even

tures, he added those drawn from philosophy. And the philosophy here is similar to that of Bradwardine which Luther would have known through Gregory of Rimini and, perhaps, Wyclif.[76] A second difference of perspective in this book by Luther is the fact that his doctrine of predestination seemed to take a more central position than it had earlier in his doctrine. In this book he distinguished within God his manifest will (that expressed by Scripture) and his hidden will. By his manifest will he wishes to save all men, but by his hidden will he brings about the life or death of each as he wills. And of this will there is no reason or cause, for to assert that there is one would be to deny its divine character. God loves or hates with a divine immutable will, and the lot of man accordingly is inevitably directed to heaven or hell.[77]

Erasmus, whose *Diatribe* elicited the *De servo arbitrio,* and whose *Hyperaspistes* answered it, is a representative of one trend among the sixteenth century, pretridentine, Catholic explanations of the mystery of predestination and grace.[78] The first of these works Erasmus wrote in a respectful, persuasive, humane style since he thought that the extreme teaching of Luther was in large part due to the bitterness of his adversaries. Here he confined himself to the problem of the freedom of the will in relation to God, which he rightly thought central to Luther's doctrine, and to the use of Scripture and common sense to prove such freedom. He defined

---

this. The modern interpretation of Luther to the effect that he simply stresses the necessity of grace for man to prepare for justification and do good seems to be one sign that many modern Protestants do not follow him in his real teaching on this matter. For Karl Barth's teaching on predestination, which differs from that of the early Protestants, see P. H. Bouillard, *Karl Barth. Parole de Dieu et existence humaine* (Paris, 1957), 1.125–64.

[76] See Humbertclaude, *op. cit.,* p. 101, footnote 1; Glorieux, *art. cit.,* col. 772; and Cristiani, "Wyclif," col. 3610–1. The last author denies that Luther was under any direct influence from Wyclif in the initial *elaboration* of his doctrine, though he holds that Luther probably knew of the *Trialogus,* published at Basle in 1525. Luther denied the freedom of the will on philosophical grounds earlier than 1525; see Pacquier, *art. cit.,* col. 1284–5.

[77] See Humbertclaude, *op. cit.,* pp. 123–6, and Luther, *op. cit.,* p. 276. See also Cristiani, "Réforme," col. 2054, for Luther's distinction between God's hidden and manifest will.

[78] For the analysis of these works, see Humbertclaude, *op. cit.,* pp. 45–91, 178–260.

free will as "the power of the human will, by which man can apply himself to the things that lead to eternal life, or turn himself away from them."[79] He found a great number of scriptural texts that proved the existence of free will, and he was convinced that the few that seemed opposed to it, such as the ninth chapter of Romans, could easily be explained by common sense in accord with free will.

After the violence of Luther's response to his first book, Erasmus wrote his more vigorous work, the *Hyperaspistes;* and it is only in this that he entered more thoroughly into the difficulties raised concerning freedom, now calling upon the help of philosophy for which he previously had little use. In the second part of this book he established the existence of free will in the moral field, and he showed what it could and could not do of itself in the state of fallen nature in the order of natural morality. Man cannot gain salvation without grace, nor can he, properly speaking (*de condigno*), merit justification. Can man prepare himself for justification so that there is a certain fittingness (merit *de congruo*) that it be given to him? To this Erasmus answered that, generally speaking, God prepares his grace for those who do all that they can. "These good deeds do not confer the justice of the gospel, I confess, but they invite the kindness of God to add on his part what is lacking to the powers of nature."[80] There is only a negative and indirect preparation on the part of man, though a positive and direct one would not harm the gratuity of grace, for such a preparation would come from free will and that itself is a gift of God.[81] When God helps the will, he does so at times by exterior help and at times by interior illumination and inspiration, but this help is generally indifferent and not determining. It is up to the will to accept or reject it. The will has enough natural power left in it after original sin to accept grace.[82]

As free will is in accord with grace, so too it is in accord with the divine attributes. God's foreknowledge is more properly knowl-

[79] Erasmus, *De libero arbitrio diatribe sive collatio* in *Opera omnia,* 9 (Lyons, 1706), 1220-1.

[80] Erasmus, *Hyperaspistes diatribae adversus Servum arbitrium Martini Lutheri libri duo, Opera omnia,* 10 (Lyons, 1706), 1499.

[81] *Ibid.,* p. 1528. See Humbertclaude, *op. cit.,* pp. 237 ff., and 224, footnote 2, where he shows Erasmus' doctrine of God's pact with man who prepares himself for justification.

[82] See *ibid.,* pp. 232 ff., and Erasmus, *op. cit.,* p. 1454.

edge, since in his eternity, he sees all things as present to him. Thus his knowledge does not change the natures of things. It is rather these things that change the manner of God's knowledge. If my sight of a free act does not remove its contingency, no more does God's.[83] In like manner, the divine will desires in a contingent way what depends on our free will in the matter of salvation. Thus God has good reasons for his predestination of one and his reprobation of another; both of these acts take place after God has foreseen the merits or sins of the men involved. He has loved Jacob because he foresaw he would be worthy of this, and he hated Esau because of his foreseen unworthiness.[84] Erasmus called upon the Greek Fathers as authority for his explanation; it was only Augustine in his later writings who taught differently among the Fathers, and Erasmus could never bring himself to agree with him on this matter.[85]

There were examples of Catholics at this time who adhered more to the Augustinian tradition, such as Cajetan, who in his commentary on St. Thomas' doctrine on predestination, defended antecedent predestination against Henry of Ghent and Peter Auriol.[86] There were, in fact, different expressions of both the theory of antecedent predestination and of consequent predestination, as one would expect from the previous history and from the systematization of the two views toward the end of the century by Banez and Molina. Among the early sixteenth-century explanations, that of Erasmus had special interest because it was the explanation of the foremost humanist of the age and because, in different ways, it anticipated the doctrine and tendencies of Molina.

3. The Council of Trent and the Modern Period

THE COUNCIL OF TRENT.—In the Council of Trent's decree on justification,[87] the Church reasserted the truth of God's saving

[83] See *ibid.*, p. 1427.
[84] See *ibid.*, pp. 1429–30. See also Humbertclaude, *op. cit.*, pp. 253 ff.
[85] See Erasmus, *op. cit.*, p. 1435.
[86] See Cajetan, In *ST*, 1.23.5.
[87] For the text see D 792a–843. For commentaries see Rondet, *Gratia Christi*, pp. 273–86; J. Rivière, "Justification," *DTC* 8.2 (1925), 2164–92; F. Cavallera, "La session VI du concile de Trente," *Bull. de littér. ecclés.*, articles distributed through volumes 44–50 (1943–49), that treat in detail the development of only the first seven chapters of the decree.

activity in man to guard Christians against the current Protestant errors on justification. In the exposition of this mystery, however, the Council took care to be as free from the errors of the humanists as it was from those of the Protestants. For the most part, it abstracted from deciding among the theologically different explanations held by orthodox Christians concerning different aspects of justification, such as the relation of the theological virtues to sanctifying grace. But in the explanation it did give, it struck such a balance between the activity of grace and the free response of the will that it has come to be regarded as one of the most remarkable documents in the history of the Church.

Our interest in this decree is restricted to its teaching on the efficacy of grace and of predestination, to see whether our interpretation of Scripture is in accord with it. In our understanding of Scripture generally and of St. Paul, all those united to Christ by justification are ordered to heaven by a predestination that is objectively efficacious, though frustrable by the resistance of the free will. Moreover, the Christian life and its acts are caused by graces to which must be attributed wholly the power and the actualization of man's meritorious acts, but graces which in the full sense of the word can be resisted by free will. Is this explanation in accord with the teaching of Trent?

Before showing in more detail the Council's doctrine, we can state that, since it treats directly justification and not predestination, its doctrine on the latter is more implicit than explicit in those aspects of it in which we are interested. But one cannot deny that its doctrine on God's justification of man and his completion of this justification to bring man to heaven does really imply a doctrine on predestination. We have seen that the scriptural doctrine on God's divine intention with reference to man's salvation is contained for the most part in the account it gives of how, in fact, God acts with man in the temporal order. Moreover, God's activity in justifying man and giving him aids to gain heaven is an exercise of the divine governance; but the divine governance is the exercise, in turn, of the divine providential plan, of which predestination and reprobation are parts. Hence, the Church's doctrine on God's governance in the temporal order is evidence of God's divine intention with reference to the salvation of men. To deny this would be to adopt with Luther a distinction between God's manifest will and his hidden will, and to project one's own conception of what God's hidden will is without taking into account, or even contrary to, the signs he has given of that will through his governance of the world, and the teaching contained in Scripture, and the Church's official statements concerning that governance. If we keep this in mind and also recognize that the decree is not deciding among various Catholic theologies on grace and free will, we cannot say that the decree explicitly or formally teaches a frustrable predestination and grace in the sense we have found in St. Paul. But it seems to us that a study of the decree in which the parts are interpreted in view of the whole will show that our understanding of St. Paul is in full accord with it. This will be evident from an examination of the general development of the doctrine in each part of the decree as well as from some particular passages. The decree comprises three main parts, treating initial justification (c. 1–9), the conservation and development of this justice (c. 10–13), and the recovery of justice after serious sin (c. 14, 15) respectively, all concluded by a chapter on merit or the fruit of justification (c. 16).

In describing initial justification, the decree first asserts the powerlessness of nature or the law to free man from the condition of injustice or sin that he shares as a result of Adam's fall, a condition in which free will remains, even though it is weakened and inclined to evil (c. 1). Man can be freed only by the redemption of Christ, which was a propitiation for our sins, *not for ours only but also for those of the whole world* (c. 2).[88] The liberating justification comes to those to whom Christ's redemption is communicated (c. 3). After sketching the process of justification (c. 4), the Council speaks of the necessity of a preparation for justification in the adult (c. 5). In this statement, remarkable for its expression of the relation of grace to free will, the Council declares:

> . . . that the beginning of justification in adults must arise from the prevenient grace of God through Jesus Christ. That is, it comes from his call by which they who have no merits are called, so that they who were through sin averted from God, may be disposed through his stimulating and helping grace to turn themselves to their own justification, by freely consenting to and cooperating with

[88] 1 John 2:2, quoted in D 794. See also Cavallera, *art. cit.*, 49 (1948), 25.

this same grace. This occurs in such a way that when God touches the heart of man through the inspiration of the Holy Spirit, man does not do nothing, for he receives that inspiration which he can also reject, but he cannot by his own free will without the grace of God move himself to justice before him.[89]

In the formulation of this chapter, the Fathers had no difficulty in agreeing on the perfect freedom of man to respond to or to reject prevenient grace. This is particularly noteworthy in view of the later opinions of theologians who, while teaching that the will *can* reject the grace that is, in fact, effective, teach also that effective grace antecedent to the will's choice is infallibly efficacious so that, given such a grace, it is infallibly certain man will cooperate and not resist. We have seen that such a view is common to Thomists and Molinists, though the former hold that the antecedent grace is intrinsically infrustrable, while the latter hold that it is extrinsically so since God's determination of circumstances is in accord with what he knows the will would do. One cannot affirm that the Council's statement condemns such a teaching of an infrustrable prevenient grace, since the theologians hold that the antecedent infallible grace (which an effective prevenient grace always is) is responded to freely, though with an infallibly certain consequence, given such grace. But the text seems to us to imply that the Council meant more by freedom than the theologians did. When the Council used the words "freely consenting" and "which he can also reject," it was not accepting a technical philosophical meaning of freedom (i.e., that implied in the Thomist's and Molinist's theories of the antecedent efficacy of grace) that would, in fact, be opposed to the popular meaning of the word. There is no indication in the proceedings that the Fathers were restricting the meaning of the freedom of the will in such a way. Hence the passage should be taken to mean that even the prevenient grace that will, in fact, gain man's consent is, in the normal providence of God, really frustrable. There is no infallible connection in principle (in either the Thomist or the Molinist's meaning) between such a grace as prevenient and the acceptance of the grace by the will.

To anticipate the Council's teaching in later chapters on the relation of grace to free will, we should note that it holds that not

---

[89] D 797. See also Canons 4 and 5, D 814, 815. See Cavallera, *art. cit.*, 49 (1948), 231–40.

only the power to act well but the actual good acts themselves are effected by God's grace. It quotes St. Paul's statement that God *works in you both the will and the performance.*[90] And it warns the Christian against taking glory in himself and not in the Lord when he performs good works, for these are God's gifts.[91] Hence it seems to us that our opinion that Scripture teaches both that grace is antecedently frustrable, and that it is completely due to the power of grace that man performs the salutary act, is in full accord with Trent.

This section on initial justification continues with a description of the acts preparatory for the justification of the adult (c. 6), the nature of justification itself through inhering grace and the gifts (c. 7), and the place of faith in man's justification (c. 8). It is concluded by a chapter (c. 9) against the absolute subjective confidence that one is justified which the Protestants held to be the essential condition of justification. In the face of this, the Council teaches that no one should doubt the promises and the mercy of God, the efficacy and merits of Christ's redemption, or the efficacy of the sacraments. But since men who look at their own weakness and defective dispositions have reason to fear, such absolute confidence is neither a condition for justification nor possible for man to have.[92] By this, the Council reflects Scriptures' doctrine on the objective certainty of God's intention to save and on the subjective dispositions of man as the only source of uncertainty. It is difficult for us to harmonize this with those theories that hold that the man who fails to reach heaven is reprobated antecedent to God's knowledge of his personal sin.

The second part of the decree treats the conservation and increase of justification. It begins with a general statement of this increase (c. 10) and then (c. 11) shows that it is both necessary and possible for the justified man to observe the commandments. "For God does not command impossibilities, but in commanding he warns you both to do what is in your power and to ask for what is beyond your power."[93] The next chapter (c. 12) denies that anyone, while he is in this life, can without a special revelation

[90] Phil. 2:13, quoted in c. 13.

[91] See c. 16, D 810.

[92] See c. 9, D 802, and can. 13 and 14, D 823, 824. See also Rivière, *art. cit.*, col. 2186–88, for a discussion of the development of this chapter.

[93] Augustine, *De natura et gratia*, 43.50 (ML 44.271) quoted in c. 11, D 804.

142

affirm with certainty that he is among the predestined in the sense that he cannot sin, or that, if he does, he will certainly be restored to grace. Our understanding of St. Paul's doctrine of a frustrable predestination is in accord with this, as it is with the following chapter in which the Council teaches that no one can have such a certainty that he has the gift of perseverance, that, it mentions, comes only from God (c. 13). Still all should have an unshakably firm confidence in God's help, "for God, unless men desert his grace, will complete the good work that he has begun."[94] The Council gives no grounds for fear in God's dispositions to the justified; the only grounds for fear is that one will be unfaithful to God's grace. And thus the Council insists that under the grace of God, man should obey God's commands and act against that love of the world that is the source of sin. We think that our interpretation of St. Paul is in accord with the Council's assurance that the justified can have perfect confidence in God's help and that God will complete the work he has begun unless they reject his grace.

An objection may be raised to this interpretation of the Council's teaching on perseverance and thus, implicitly, on predestination, from its condemnation of those who held "that the justified man can without the special help of God persevere in the justice he has received, or with it cannot persevere," and the way in which it speaks of final perseverance as "that great gift of final perseverance."[95] If the justified cannot without a special help (*speciale auxilium*) persevere, and if final perseverance is a great gift, then the Council seems to imply that some gift is added to that of justifying grace that distinguishes the one who perseveres from the one who does not. In fact, theologians generally teach that it is of faith from Trent that the justified can persevere, but many also hold that a special grace that is antecedently infallibly efficacious is given to some of the justified (namely, all who in fact persevere) that assures their actual final perseverance.[96]

It seems to us that such a view on final perseverance cannot be

[94] C. 13, D 806. See also Canon 26, D 836, which also shows the objective certainty of God's disposition toward the justified, conditioned by man's perseverance.

[95] Can. 22, D 832: "Si quis dixerit iustificatum vel sine speciali auxilio Dei in accepta iustitia perseverare posse, vel cum eo non posse: A.S." Can. 16, D. 826: "Si quis magnum illud usque in finem perseverantiae donum se certo habiturum absolute et infallibili certitudine dixerit, nisi hoc ex speciali revelatione didicerit: A.S."

[96] See A. Michel, "Persévérance," *DTC* 12.1 (1933), 1283, 1298.

attributed to the Council. It is justified neither by the final statements nor by the proceedings of the Council that led to them.
From the proceedings we know that the phrase *speciale auxilium*
in the twenty-second canon was the work of the Augustinian
Seripando. The Bishop of the Canaries tried to have the phrase
removed two times, but it was retained without an explanation of
its meaning. Seripando simply stated in response to the objection
that it did not refer to divine concurrence and that in consequence
no theologian could seem to be condemned by it.[97] If this is true,
it does not refer to an antecedently efficacious grace, since many
theologians did not accept that understanding of perseverance, as
we have seen. Moreover, the very phrasing of the canon asserts
that this special help gives the *power* to persevere. The canon says
nothing of a special help that gives *actual* perseverance either for
a time or until the end of life. Since all theologians think that it is
of faith from Trent that all the justified have the *power* to persevere, they must in consequence hold that all the justified are
given this special help that Trent states is necessary that one be
able to persevere. In short, the canon must be interpreted in terms
of the chapter to which it refers, that does assert the power of all
the justified to persevere even to the end. Why then does the canon
speak of a *special* help? Humanly speaking, one may say that the
understanding of the Fathers and the theologians at Trent of the
relation of perseverance to justification was not so clear or united
as to obviate any discrepancies in vocabulary in matters of detail.
Perhaps more correctly we can understand by the special help
something added to the grace of justification, the *right* to the
providential help of God and the interior grace that will actualize
what grace is as a seed, namely, eternal life. It would seem, then,
that the Council's use of the phrase "special help" in the canon
cannot be used to sustain the theory that final perseverance is an
antecedently infallibly effective grace.

And the same must be said with reference to the Council's assertion that final perseverance is a "great gift." If one of the justified has persevered to the end and another has not, it does not
necessarily mean, in the Council's doctrine, that the former received a greater prevenient grace than the latter; it does necessarily mean that the latter rejected the grace that was present to

[97] See *ibid.*, col. 1284.

144

complete the work of justification. It certainly does not mean that the former received an infrustrable prevenient grace while the latter received only a sufficient grace in the sense of the schools, for this would be contrary to the opinion of many medieval and sixteenth-century theologians. Final perseverance is truly a great gift, even though it is not effected by an antecedently infallibly efficacious grace, but by one that is frustrable. It is such a gift whether it involves the restoration of a man to the grace that he has lost or the unbroken fulfillment of the grace of justification in one who does not resist the objective efficacy of grace that, like a fountain of living water, raises him up to eternal life. It is this that the Council implies, not the addition of an infrustrable grace to the grace of justification for those who, in fact, do persevere to the end.

In the third part of the decree, the Council teaches that a man who has fallen from grace can be justified again, since Christ has established for him the sacrament of penance (c. 14), and that grace is lost, not only by infidelity, but by every serious sin (c. 15). In the chapter on merit (c. 16) that concludes the decree on justification, the Council affirms: "Therefore there should be proposed to those who work well to the end and hope in God eternal life both as a grace mercifully promised to the sons of God through Christ Jesus, and as a reward which due to the promise of God himself is to be faithfully returned for their good works and merits."[98] Here the Church teaches that eternal life is promised to the sons of God, that is, to the justified if they are faithful to God. What is this divine promise save a firm, deliberate, divine plan to bring to glory all the justified who are not finally unfaithful? And what is this but the predestination that St. Paul teaches? What, too, does it imply for the men once justified who do not reach heaven save that they did not reach it in spite of God's antecedent firm intention (or predestination) to bring them there? In other words, their reprobation is in no sense antecedent to their final infidelity and God's foreknowledge of it. In short, our interpretation of St. Paul is in full accord with the Council of Trent. And it is difficult for us to see that a theory that teaches the infallible efficacy of antecedent predestination or grace is in accord with Trent.

[98] C. 16, D 809. For commentary, see J. Rivière, "Mérite," *DTC* 10.1 (1928), 751–761.

SOME LATER DEVELOPMENTS.—Much of this doctrine of the
Council of Trent was, however, implicit in its teaching and not explicit. Moreover, the then current interpretations of some crucial
scriptural texts, the teaching of some Fathers and later theologians
in accord with such interpretations, the philosophical problems involved, and perhaps the circumstances of the sixteenth century
made it virtually impossible for the implications of Trent to be
fully realized at the time. This, in our opinion, makes it understandable how there was gradually developed after Trent that dichotomy of explanation of the mystery of predestination and grace
contained in the Banezian and the Molinist systems. This dichotomy reflected the division we have seen recur in each new
age of the Church, and it was made inevitable by presuppositions
frequently accepted, though, once more in our opinion, not sustained by the teaching of Scripture, the implications of Trent, or a
theologically significant tradition. We need not give once more an
explanation and a criticism of these systems from the teaching of
Scripture and tradition, since this is already contained in all we
have thus far seen. It remains for us here only to recall a few later
statements of the Church elicited by theories on grace that did not
remain within the limits set by Trent, and to see what the attitude
of the Church has been toward the Banezian and the Molinist
systems.

Michael Baius (1513–1589) was a Louvain theologian who
sought to pass over the centuries of Scholasticism to recover the
pure Augustinian doctrine on grace. His interpretation of the past
was influenced by Protestant and nominalist teaching, and the
doctrine at which he arrived was Pelagian with reference to the
condition of the angels and the state of original innocence, and
Protestant with reference to fallen man. A large number of propositions taken from his works were condemned by Saint Pius V in
1567.[99] For our purposes it is sufficient to indicate the condemned
elements of his doctrine that refer to the efficacy of predestination
and grace in the two states he analyzes. With reference to the first
state, which he thought natural, he taught that eternal life was to
be given to the angels and man because of their good works which

---

[99] For the condemned propositions, see D 1001–1080. Concerning
Baius see Rondet, *Gratia Christi*, pp. 287–93.

were natural and which merited the reward of eternal life in a strict order of natural justice. Because of the fall, the freedom of man's will was reduced to the condition of a necessary spontaneity; and all the acts of man without the grace of faith are sins, even mortal sins, the only kind of sin Baius recognized. Free will without the help of God's grace can only sin. Even for fallen man who has been renewed so that he acts under grace, there is not a real liberty from inner necessity; but this does not prevent such acts from being meritorious since they continue to be spontaneous.[100] It can easily be seen that this doctrine affirms an antecedently necessitating grace and hence holds an absolute predestinationism. So its condemnation by the Church is in accord with her doctrine at Trent and that of St. Paul.

Before the death of Baius there had already begun the famous controversy between the Dominican and Jesuit theologians on the relation between grace and free will.[101] In the years after the Council there gradually emerged the two quite opposed explanations of the relationship between grace and free will that we analyzed in the first chapter. The presupposition in the theological order common to both schools that posed the insoluble dilemma was above all the absolute infallible efficacy of predestination and, secondly, the antecedent infallible efficacy of the grace that actually effects a good act. The point of controversy was whether predestination was antecedent or consequent upon God's knowledge of man's merits and whether this infallible efficacy of grace was due to the intrinsic nature of the grace or to the eternal knowledge God had through *scientia media* of what use each man would make of all possible graces. And with these central points were associated a whole constellation of dependent controversies.

The dispute on this problem both in Louvain and in Spain became so violent that Pope Clement VIII called the matter to Rome. There the problem was discussed, usually under the form of de-

---

[100] See prop. 1–5, D 1001–5; 25–8; 37–40, D 1037–40; 41, D 1041; 66, D 1066.

[101] For the history of the sixteenth-century origins of this controversy and the "Congregationes de Auxiliis" established by Popes Clement VIII and Paul V in Rome between 1598–1607, see Vansteenberghe, "Molinisme," *DTC* 10.2 (1929), 2095–2101, 2141–5, 2154–66; and Rondet, *op. cit.*, pp. 294–308.

ciding what in Molina's book should be censured, under successive Congregations, the later ones presided over by Pope Clement VIII and then Paul V. After interminable discussions there was still lacking sufficient reason to censure one theory rather than the other. And so in his final judgment on the feast of St. Augustine, August 28, 1607, Paul V declared that, though a decision was desirable, it was not necessary. The Dominicans hold that grace does not destroy freedom, but perfects it, and moves it in accord with the nature of the will. The Jesuits hold that the whole initiative in salvation comes from God's grace. So the former are far from Calvinism, and the latter are far from Pelagianism. Hence he allowed the two schools to continue to hold their opinions, but forbade each to qualify the other position with a censure.[102] The controversy was quickly taken up once more by new defenders in each school; and while new acts of the Holy See attempted to keep the dispute within proper limits, it has never given a doctrinal decision on the issue controverted.

It was in the midst of these disputes on the relation of grace to free will that Cornelius Jansen (1585–1638) sought to bring about a reform of the Church in France through a restoration of the true theology of grace as found in Augustine.[103] The doctrine of his monumental work *Augustinus*, published two years after his death, was, with some differences, that of Baius argued with greater erudition. It taught, like Baius, that the state of original innocence was owed to man, that the fall left man's will with simply a freedom from violence but not from inner necessity, that all acts performed by those without the grace of faith are sins, and that grace (which he described as a *delectatio caelestis*) is necessitating. This clearly involves a predestinationism for fallen man.

Taking the opposite of the five propositions of Jansen condemned by the Church in 1653, we can see that on several points the doctrine implied by Trent is made more explicit. Jansen's main errors singled out for condemnation so emphasized the efficacy of grace that they restricted God's universal will to save, the extent of his grace, and the freedom of man. By condemning them, the

[102] See D 1090. For later acts, see *loc. cit.,* footnote 1, D 1097, and footnotes 1 and 2.

[103] On Jansen and the Jansenists, see Rondet, *op. cit.,* pp. 309-19.

148

Church taught that grace is never lacking to the justified man for the fulfillment of the commandments of God, that men in the fallen state do at times resist the grace of God, that for merit and demerit in this state liberty from external constraint is not enough; there is also needed the freedom from inner necessity that Jansen denied to fallen man. Correcting his interpretation of the Semipelagian heresy, the Church declared that they were not condemned for teaching that interior prevenient grace was such that man could resist or obey it. And finally it denied that it is Semipelagian to assert that Christ died for all men.[104]

As all know, the Jansenists by shifty casuistry sought to escape the Holy See's condemnation; and they continued to teach their errors. Hence, abstracting from other acts of the Church, in 1690 errors of the followers of Jansen were condemned by Alexander VIII. Here the Church condemned statements that Christ died only for the faithful, that pagans, Jews, heretics, and others in like conditions received no influence from Jesus Christ, and that sufficient grace was harmful (since it didn't really suffice to do good).[105] Still later many statements of Quesnel that were saturated with the doctrine of Jansen were also condemned. His doctrine included statements that stressed the efficacy of God's will and grace in such a way that he jeopardized the freedom of the will to resist and limited God's salvific will.[106] In its teaching against the Jansenists then, the Church made more explicit her doctrine of God's universal salvific will and of the freedom of the will to resist the prevenient grace of God.

During the period of the Jansenist heresy and down to the present, the Thomists and the Molinists have continued to defend the harmony of grace and free will in accord with their different theories.[107] The dispute has been carried on in the fields of biblical exegesis, interpretation of the Fathers and of St. Thomas, the history of papal statements, the evidence of tradition, and (last,

[104] See D 1092-5. Each of Jansen's propositions is condemned as heretical.

[105] See D 1291-1321, esp. 1294-6.

[106] See D 1351-1451 taken from the Bull *Unigenitus* issued by Clement X in 1713.

[107] For a survey of the history of these controversies see Vansteenberghe, *art. cit.*, col. 2172-84, and Rondet, *op. cit.*, pp. 319-28.

149

but far from least) philosophical principles. There has been a succession of great controversies from the beginning of the dispute to the present century, engaged in by constantly new champions who have arisen in successive generations for one side and the other. Despite the early emergence of some new systems such as the new Augustinian system and the Sorbonne school, and despite the occasional individual in one school or the other who has disavowed some basic principle of the system, a phenomenon particularly apparent in the twentieth century, the positions today of these schools remain essentially the same as in the beginning of their conflict.

Hence it is unnecessary to follow the fortunes of these theories through the modern period. We may conclude our study of Scripture and tradition by recalling what, in our opinion, these norms of revelation have taught. They testify to the doctrine that, while God wills all to be saved, he has predestined to eternal glory all of those whom he has united to Christ though justification by a predestination that is objectively efficacious, but frustrable by the will of the man involved. God's normal providence leads the justified to the goal of eternal life through graces that are likewise objectively efficacious, giving both the power to act and the actual use of the will in acts profitable for salvation, but frustrable by the will of the one who receives them. Reprobation of the moral adult, both the one who has been and the one who has not been justified, is only consequent to the sin of the person involved. Because of all the evidence presented so far, we think that this explanation is taught by Scripture and at least implied by the Council of Trent and other statements of the Church; Scripture and the teaching of the Church are certainly not opposed to this explanation. Consequently, we are of the opinion that the presuppositions concerning the content of revelation that are at the source of the theological controversy on this mystery are not sustained by the true sources of our knowledge of revelation. A great deal of value remains in these explanations of the mystery, but they still seem to us to be in these aspects inadequate theories of the mystery of the relation of predestination and of grace to man's free will.

It now remains for us to attempt to gain some further understanding of this revealed mystery through an analysis of the naturally knowable realities involved, the relation of God's knowledge, will, providence, and causality to the act of the will of the rational creature.

CHAPTER FIVE

Grace and Free Will

O UR STUDY of Scripture in the second chapter has shown us a concrete expression of the harmony between God's saving intention and activity on the one hand and man's free response to it or rejection of it on the other. According to our understanding of Scripture and particularly of St. Paul, while God wants all men to be saved, he has predestined all those whom he has justified through union with Christ. As a result of this predestination he works by grace the will and performance of their Christian lives, and he will complete the work of salvation that he has begun in them. While the Christian is still in this life, however, he may cease to believe or to act in accord with his belief; if he does, he will be rejected, as the Jews were rejected. Thus while predestination and the grace that is its effect are antecedent to man's saving acts and cause all that is good in these acts, as antecedent they can be frustrated by the resistance of man's will. If man continues till death to reject the merciful initiative of God, he will in turn be reprobated. The official teaching of the Church has seemed to us to confirm this interpretation of Scripture and especially of St. Paul.

Banez and Molina, on the other hand, thought that Scripture and tradition meant by predestination an absolute divine intention for those who were its objects. This is apparent throughout their explanation of the mystery, as is clear from the analysis of their theories we presented in the first chapter. Hence, from the outset of their explanation of the harmony between predestination and the freedom of the rational creature they had a problem that in our opinion is not posed by Scripture and the teaching of the

152

Church. Faced as they were with the problem of harmonizing an absolute predestination and man's freedom, Banez, Molina, and many others asked whether God's predestination was antecedent to his foreknowledge of man's acts or consequent upon it. Banez found evidence in Scripture that it was antecedent, while Molina found evidence that it was consequent. And the philosophical analysis which each made of the relation of God's will, knowledge, and causality to the acts of the free creature for the purpose of defending and explaining the harmony between God's predestination and grace and free will was in accord with the interpretation each gave to Scripture and tradition. Banez's philosophical analysis of the harmony between God's perfections and the created free will is similar on its own plane to his interpretation of Scripture and tradition and thus serves as an explanation and defense of the latter. And the same thing is true of Molina.

All are agreed that there is harmony between the natural order and the supernatural order, but the fact is that Banez and Molina presented different analyses of the natural order, each of which was similar to an interpretation of Scripture and tradition that differs from the one we presented. If either of these analyses of the natural order between God and the free created act is proved by the arguments adduced to support it, it would seem to cast serious doubts upon the interpretation we have given of Scripture and the teaching of the Church. Therefore we must make an examination of the natural relation between God and the free created act to see whether it is in accord with the doctrine we have found in Scripture and tradition. This necessitates a presentation of a tentative explanation of the natural realities involved and an investigation to see whether the philosophical opinions of Banez and Molina in those aspects which are opposed to what we have so far presented are proved by the evidence they advance.

Such a philosophical explanation would be necessary even though there were no difference of opinion in this matter. For God has made known his supernatural mysteries through the instrumentality of realities we naturally know. To explain God's mystery of redemptive intention and fulfillment, Paul taught that God *wills* all men to be saved, that he *predestines* some and *foreknows* them, that he *works* within Christians their *will* and *performance*

153

of saving acts, and that if Christians *do not abide* in God's goodness, they will be rejected.[1] Thus St. Paul is asserting that intrinsic to this supernatural mystery are acts and realities that are natural and thus open to man's natural knowledge to some extent. To take an analogy from another revealed mystery, as Christ's humanity is a constitutive element of the hypostatic union considered as a whole, so too God's will, knowledge, providence, and activity within the created will are constitutive elements of the mystery of the relation of grace to free will. To understand the supernatural mystery, then, we should not only examine the meaning of the words Paul uses, the biblical doctrine that molded his thought, or the passages in which he expresses himself; we should also analyze what these natural realities and acts are that are intrinsically constitutive of the mystery of predestination and grace, as we analyze human nature to gain deeper insight into the mystery of Christ. To understand these natural realities, one must do more than understand Paul's personal experience of them, since in attributing them to God he did not restrict their meaning to his personal understanding of them.[2] Moreover, the words Paul used did not primarily signify his concepts or ideas, but the reality extrinsic to him from which these concepts were drawn. That is, Paul knew these natural realities in creatures and analogically predicated of God the perfection he found there. Thus when he said that God *knows, wills, works* in Christians their will, the mystery he expressed cannot be understood adequately save through an understanding of these realities of knowledge and willing, and how they are present in God. These realities cannot be profoundly understood simply by descriptions accessible to common sense. To one who has a correct understanding of philosophy, it is not difficult to see that it is within its compass and proper function to understand these natural realities at least to some exent.

---

[1] See Rom. 8:28–30; 11:22; Phil. 2:13; I Tim. 2:4. We must note that the revealed mystery is most properly not the words by which it is expressed either in Scripture or in the Creeds. Rather, it is the actual objective divine redemptive intention and activity in its relation to man's free will, a relation or order of things that exists before man expresses it or believes it. It is this that is the object which Paul expresses and Christians believe. See St. Thomas, *ST*, 2-2, 1.2.c, and ad 2.

[2] See Rom. 11:33–5.

154

The use of philosophy for this purpose is not restricted to those cases where Scripture uses terms also employed by philosophers. For example, there are expressions in St. Paul that attribute *only implicitly* to God's redemptive activity natural acts that are open to philosophical investigation. He writes to the Philippians that *it is God who of his good pleasure works in you both the will and the performance.*[3] Though St. Paul does not use here the vocabulary of the philosopher, it is an easy step of philosophical induction (particularly in the light of other scriptural teaching on the subject) to say that he is in fact teaching that God *causes* the acts of will by which man interiorly and exteriorly performs saving acts. Another example of this is found in St. Paul's warning to the Christians of Rome. *See, then, the goodness and the severity of God: his severity towards those who have fallen, but the goodness of God towards thee if thou abidest in his goodness; otherwise thou also wilt be cut off.*[4] Paul had previously told these Christians that God has predestined them to glory and given them everything necessary to reach it. Now he tells them, if we are to use philosophical expressions, that they are *free* to accept or reject the antecedent saving intention and grace of God. As long as the interpretation of the passage is correct, the use of such words as fully state the objective mystery Paul is expressing as the words he himself uses.

Hence, the need of a philosophical analysis for an adequate understanding of the mystery of God's grace is evident. Such an approach has been practiced from the earliest centuries of the Church, and its results are found in the councils of the Church. Indeed, as the above account shows, it is present in Scripture itself. So both Scripture and tradition show its legitimacy and necessity. Contempt or neglect of philosophy in explaining the mystery expressed by Scripture has not infrequently led to erroneous interpretations of revelation.

[3] Phil. 2:13.
[4] Rom. 11:22. It seems that from expressions such as these we gain judgments which we express in more philosophical terms not so much by deduction but by induction. This induction seems analogous to that by which in the natural order one gains first principles. This latter is described by Aristotle in *Posterior Analytics*, 2.19. Whereas natural principles are gained from concrete natural experience, the recognition that these principles are true in the supernatural order derives from the concrete experience expressed in Scripture and tradition.

The fact that the use of philosophy in explaining the revealed message has at times led to error is therefore due not to its use but to its false use. It is a false use to the extent that the philosophical analysis of the natural reality such as freedom or causality is inadequate, for such defective philosophical analyses lead to a defective explanation of the revealed mystery. But even where the initial philosophical doctrine is correct, there will still be a defective explanation of the revealed mystery if the natural knowledge is the controlling factor in the explanation. Although the revealed mystery is expressed by natural realities, and these natural realities are intrinsic to the objective supernatural order (as the humanity of Christ is to the hypostatic union), the supernatural mystery transcends the natural objects of man's knowledge and his natural ability to know. Thus the natural realities that man knows are present in the revealed mystery in a way that transcends their state as the natural objects of his knowledge. For example, a human nature is present in Christ in a somewhat different manner than it is in other men. How it exists in the supernatural mystery is shown by Scripture and tradition; and hence in the application of a correct philosophical analysis of a natural reality to the supernatural mystery, Scripture and tradition are the controlling factor. That is, the theologian applies his natural philosophical knowledge to explain a supernatural mystery by a process of analogy determined by Scripture and tradition or the teaching of the Church, the norm of revelation.

It is this method that we shall adopt in the following part of this study, the purpose of which is to use the knowledge offered by philosophy to understand the harmony we have found expressed in Scripture between God's saving intention and activity and man's freedom, and to defend it against objections reason may raise. In our philosophical analyses we shall proceed in accord with the philosophical principles of St. Thomas because of our conviction of the basic validity of his philosophy. We shall take that basic validity for granted here, though we may note that the power his principles have to help toward an understanding of this supernatural mystery is itself a witness to their validity. We shall also take for granted a general understanding of his philosophical principles and shall restrict ourselves in the main to developing those principles that are more immediately relevant to our purpose.

In this way we shall study first God's causality of man's salutary acts and secondly the order of his providential intention that guides his activity in time. A study of the problems in this sequence seems appropriate from the philosophical viewpoint since in the natural order our understanding of God is gained from a knowledge of his effects, and from the theological viewpoint since the biblical reflections on the divine redemptive intention generally derive from knowledge of God's redemptive activity. In the present chapter, then, we are concerned with God's causality through grace of man's salutary acts, both the individual free act and the succession of acts which leads to the fulfillment of the Christian life. To understand how God causes through grace man's individual free act, we must understand how he causes the free act in the natural order. Since man's will is a created power, this problem involves two stages. In the first place, how does God cause the operation of a created power as such? And in the second place, how does God cause the operation specifically of the free created power?

1. *God's Causality of the Creature's Operation*

To understand how God causes the free created act, we must understand how he causes the created act, for the act of free will is the act of a created power. Hence, the manner of acting essentially consequent upon the nature of a power as created is found in the will's manner of acting. Moreover, partial reason for the divergence between Banez and Molina concerning God's causation of the free act is their difference in the explanation of his causality of the act of the creature. In the explanation that follows we shall adhere closely to the words themselves of St. Thomas to try to assure our analysis a fidelity to his teaching, a teaching that has been given various interpretations. We shall recall in their proper places the differences between Thomists and Molinists on the question. Texts and references to substantiate our interpretation of their opinions in this and the following chapter are given in chapter one.[5] We shall not try once more to justify these interpretations.

THE CAUSALITY OF THE CREATED OPERATION BY GOD AND THE CREATURE.—In the first place, Banez, Molina and their schools *agree with St. Thomas* on the fact that both God and the creature cause the operation of the latter. Some philosophers have held that the creature's operation is caused, not by itself, but by God who, upon the application of the creature to its object, acts without the mediation of its causality. Such a theory is both gratuitous and false, for it is contrary to the evidence of our senses and of our reason. In effect it implies that all our evidence is deceptive, since the objective evidence indicates that the act of burning is really an act of the fire, as other acts are the acts of their created cause. This theory also implies that the natures and powers of the creatures are purposeless and that there is no real reason why fire rather than some other creature has the specific effect of burning. Finally, it is contrary to the goodness of God, for it implies that he did not give to creatures that share in his own being that created causality is. Hence, the operation of the creature and its effect is really caused by it. Since to cause is to influence the being of another, this means that the existence of the effect really derives from the creature's act and power. Moreover, since "to act is nothing other than to communicate that by which the agent is in act,"[6] the specific nature of the act and effect of the created cause derive from the specific nature of its operation. Thus the determination and the existence of the effect really derive from the act of the creature since it is really a cause of its effect.

On the other hand, some philosophers have held that the creature's act is caused exclusively by it, and not by God. This, too, is false, for God does cause the creature's operation and that in various ways. In the first place, he causes it by *creating* the creature with its natures and powers. By creating it, God gives the creature its nature and powers in such a way that they remain

---

[5] For the teaching of Banezians and Molinists, see above pp. 5 ff. and 19 ff. The basic text of St. Thomas concerning God's causality of the act of the creature is *De pot.* 3:7, but he treats the same matter in other places, the main parallel texts being In 2 *Sent.*, 1.4; *CG*, 3. 65–70; *ST*, 1.105.5.

[6] *De pot.* 2.1. Also see, *De Anima* q. un., 12.

God's possession and in complete dependence upon him. Created being does exist as an act or perfection distinct from God; but since this created act is derived from God who alone is essentially act or existence, it exists as a participation of the being that God is of his essence. St. Thomas expresses this distinctness of the creature from God as follows: "All things are good to the extent that they exist; but all things are called being not through the divine existence but through their own existence; therefore all things are good not by the divine goodness but by their own goodness."[7] However, this created act by which the creature is formally existing, good, or enjoying any other perfection is that by which it participates the source of this perfection in God. As St. Thomas writes: "we are called good by the goodness which is God, and wise by the wisdom which is God because the goodness by which we are *formally* good is a certain participation of divine goodness, and the wisdom by which we are *formally* wise is a certain participation of divine wisdom."[8] At times he expresses this distinctness and this dependence of created perfection upon God by the image of the relation of the air suffused with light to the sun.

> Every creature is related to God as the air to the illuminating sun. For as the sun is luminous by its nature but the air becomes luminous by participating light from the sun, not however by participating the nature of the sun, so only God is being by his essence, because his essence is his existence, but every creature is being in a participated way, and not because its essence is its existence.[9]

Since the creature has its being and power in this way from God, when it acts it is using something that is God's possession. It is like a steward with whom a master deposits his money that the steward may gain more. As the master is said to do what the steward does with his money and at his command, so God is truly said to cause the good the creature performs with its participated being.

Secondly, God causes the act of the creature because he *conserves* in being its nature and powers. The reason why such conservation is ascribed to God is important for our purpose, since it shows the proper effect of God's causality and the proper effect

---

[7] *ST*, 1.6.4. sed contra.
[8] *Ibid.*, 2–2, 23.2. ad 1.
[9] *Ibid.*, 1.104.1.

of the creature's causality.[10] A caused subject is dependent upon its cause according to the effect that it receives from it. Thus, if the cause ceases to operate, the subject ceases to gain from its cause the effect it was receiving from it. For example, if the formal cause of a physical body is destroyed, that body ceases to be the particular kind of thing that it was. Indeed this particular thing also simply ceases to be, since being follows the form of the thing. The same is analogously true of the effect's dependence upon the other causes. It is to be noted that the cause of the coming to be of a thing's form and being is frequently not the cause of the form or being as such. For example, a building has as its form the nature of its materials and their coherence according to a definite pattern. If this form is destroyed, the house ceases to be a house and simply ceases to be, since its being depends on its form. The building depends for the coming to be of its form and thus of its being as a house upon the activity of its builder. So if he ceases to act while the house is still in the process of construction, the house ceases to come to be. But if he ceases to act after the house is completed, the house continues to exist, for it depends upon its builder properly not for its form and being, but for the coming to be of its form and being.

A similar thing occurs in the natural effect of the created cause. For example, when an animal generates another of the same species, it does not properly cause the form of the effect, for if it did, it would be the cause of itself, since it too is included under this form. The animal is the cause of the coming to be of the form (and thus of the being) in this particular matter. And this it causes by disposing the matter so that it be receptive of the form, and by educing the form from the potency of matter.[11] So if such an agent ceases to operate before its effect is fully gained, the coming to be of the effect ceases. But if it ceases when the effect has already come to be, the effect continues, since it does not depend upon this agent for its form or being as such. In a way similar to this, no creature can be the cause of *being* as such as its proper effect, for if it were it would be cause of itself. A creature can be the proper cause only of the *coming to be* of its effect or operation.[12]

[10] See *ibid.*, 1.104.1; *De pot.* 5.1.

[11] See *De pot.* 5.1.

[12] See *ST*, 1.45.5: "Inter omnes autem effectus universalissimum est ipsum esse. Unde oportet, quod sit proprius effectus primae, et universalis-

160

There is, of course, a proper cause of the form and the being of the creature, not only the intrinsic cause, which is found in the essence and existence of the creature, but an extrinsic cause. There must be an extrinsic cause since any perfection of the creature is a participated perfection, and so it depends upon the principle to which it belongs essentially and in an underived fashion. To explain the proper extrinsic cause of forms, St. Thomas did not make use of Plato's doctrine of subsistent ideas. So he did not reduce forms to a separated idea specifically the same as the corporeal form. Rather he held that the forms of all creatures were ultimately shares in the perfection of the divine essence, each determined in its specific nature by the exemplars of the divine mind. So, too, it is God who is the proper cause of the being of the creature, for only he has being as properly his own. He is essentially being, while all others participate being from him. He does not cause being to exist in the creature in the same way as it exists in himself, as one animal causes its nature to exist in another of the same species. For the created essence cannot possibly receive existence as it is in God, namely, as one with the essence. The essence of the creature is itself created and thus exists contingently and not of itself. Hence, the creature depends upon God not only for its coming to be, but for its continued existence itself. Hence, too, if after the creature begins to be, God withdraws his causality infusing existence within it, the creature immediately ceases to be. That is, all creatures, besides receiving their being from God, are conserved in their nature and in being by him. This conserva-

---

simae causae, quae est Deus." See also *ibid.*, ad 1: "Nullum igitur ens creatum potest producere aliquod ens absolute, nisi inquantum esse causat in hoc." In examining the causality of the creature in *ST*, 1.104.1, St. Thomas shows that whenever a creature causes, it causes the coming to be of its effect and the coming to be of the form of its effect. In this sense, the proper effect of the creature's causality is the *coming to be* of its effect. But he shows that in some cases where the created effect is not univocally the same as its created cause, it may receive from its created cause, not only the coming to be of its form and being, but its form and being. For this, St. Thomas gave examples from the physics of his day; perhaps we may see as an example of this the dependence external human acts have for their human form and being upon man's intellect and will. The being of these acts is, in a way, a coming to be, so their dependence upon the creature for their being does not diminish the truth that *the proper effect of the creature's causality is the coming to be of an effect, while that of God is the being simply speaking of the effect.*

161

tion is not an act distinct from initial creation but rather a continuation of the creative act by which the creature came to be.[13] God by this direct conservation, as well as by the indirect conservation through which he preserves creatures from corrupting influences, is said to cause the acts of the creature. If a doctor is said to cause the vision of a patient whose sight he has saved, God is much more properly said to cause the operations of the creature by conserving in being and form of being the powers and nature from which these operations flow.

Thomists and Molinists agree that God causes the creature's acts by the fact that he creates and conserves its nature and powers. Thirdly, they agree that his causality of the creature's acts extends *beyond this* creation and conservation, for there is something more in the act of the creature than simply in its nature and powers before the act. The act or operation of the creature is a participated perfection, as every created perfection is; and it is an act over and above the creature's being. As the creature then depends upon God for the coming to be and the existence of its being, it depends upon him for the coming to be and existence of its operation. And since the latter is in addition to the former, God's causality of the operation is a causality in addition to creation and conservation. It is impossible for the creature to gain this further act by a causality that is exclusive of the act of the first cause, since then the creature would be the first cause of being. God cannot create a being that can proceed to act without being actuated by himself, since it is essential to the creature to act in accord with the nature of its being and thus in dependence upon the first cause.[14]

Though several scholastics have asserted that God causes the operation of the creature by a causality that is properly a creative causality, such is not the opinion of Banez, Molina, or St. Thomas. If such were the manner of God's causality of the creature's opera-

[13] See *ibid.:* "Sicut igitur fieri rei non potest remanere, cessante actione agentis, quod est causa effectus secundum fieri: ita nec esse rei potest remanere, cessante actione agentis, quod est causa effectus non solum secundum fieri, sed etiam secundum esse." And see, ad 4: "conservatio rerum a Deo non est per aliquam novam actionem, sed per continuationem actionis, qua dat esse. . . ."

[14] See *ST*, 1–2, 109.9: ". . . nulla res creata potest in quemcumque actum prodire, nisi virtute motionis divinae." See, too, *ibid.*, 109.1; In 2 *Sent.*, 37.2.2, where this is applied to the created will.

tion, the creature would not cause the act. For no creature can share in creative activity. It cannot share in it as a principal cause, since the proper effect of creation is being, which is the proper effect of God alone. Nor can it be an instrumental cause of creation, since an instrumental cause contributes to the effect of the principal cause by conferring something proper to itself. For example, the brush in the hand of the artist brings beauty to the canvas by applying paint to it. But such an instrumental causality presupposes a subject upon which the instrument works before the achievement of the effect of the principal cause. Creation is the causation of being with no pre-existent subject, so it is impossible for God to use an instrument in such causality. Hence, God's causality of the creature's operation is not by way of creation.[15]

DOES GOD PREMOVE THE CREATED POTENCY THROUGH A CREATED ACT?—On these conclusions there is essential agreement between Thomists and Molinists, though we have defended these conclusions in accord with St. Thomas' metaphysical understanding of *esse*. *Their difference* in the matter that is our central concern here lies in the more specific explanation of the manner in which God causes the operation of the creature. The Thomists hold that God's causality of the act of the creature is through a created act which is distinct both from the uncreated divine action and, as the act is received by the creature, from the operation of the creature. By this created act, God actuates the creature through a physical, premoving, and predetermining motion acting upon the created potency. The Molinists hold that God causes the operation of the creature not through a created act distinct from the operation of the creature, but immediately by his own divine power, not exercised as previous to the creature's operation or as bearing upon the created potency, but as a simultaneous concurrence with the creature's operation. This concurrence is a general influence which receives its specific determination from the created cause.[16]

[15] See *ST*, 1.45.5.
[16] Besides our treatment of this in the first chapter, see Garrigou-Lagrange, "Prémotion physique," *DTC* 13.1 (1936), 31–51; and R. Moore, "Motion divine chez saint Thomas d'Aquin," *Studia Montis Regis*, 1 (1958), 93–137. For the Molinist position, see its expression in Suarez, *Opusculum primum de concursu, motione, et auxilio Dei*, lib. 1, cap. 4, n. 6. *Opera omnia* 11 (Paris, 1858), 20: "Atque ex his omnibus quoddam

163

In attempting to discover the truth of this matter, we must first recall that all causality is a causality of being, either of substantial being or of a modification of it.[17] Since the creature really causes, it exercises a causality of being. The being of the animal generated does come from the parents, and the modification of being present in all accidental changes that are the result of created operations does come from its created cause. However, a perfection is the *proper* effect of the cause to which it belongs essentially. But being belongs essentially to God and to God alone, since only his essence is existence. Hence, the being that is the effect of any created operation is properly the effect of God. The being, then, that is the effect of such an operation comes from the creature not as its proper and proportionate cause, but rather as an *instrumental* cause used by God in the operation, for the creature causes being not in virtue of its own nature and form, but in virtue of a participation in the causality proper to God. And this is to cause as an instrument. A brush with which an artist paints does not confer beauty and order upon the canvas in virtue of its own form, but through a participation in the artistic activity that comes from powers of the artist.[18] Since this is true because of the nature of created operation as such, every created cause performs its operation as an instrument of God who alone is the principal cause of being. Man's will, then, also operates as an instrument of God, for its act too is a modification of being,[19] though insofar as it is specifically different from necessary created causes, it operates in a way specifically different from the way they do.

Since the creature causes in virtue of power proper to God,

---

principium colligendum est, ad quod stabiliendum haec omnia diximus, nimirum, hunc generalem concursum Dei ad actionem voluntatis, seu causae secundae, quoad hunc proprium et immediatum influxum in ipsum effectum, non esse aliquid distinctum vel praevium ad actionem causae secundae, neque circa causam ipsam versari, ei aliquid conferendo quo ad agendum vel inclinetur amplius, vel confortetur, aut in vi agendi consummetur. Probatur, quia ostensum est hunc concursum esse eamdem causae secundae, ut est Dei agentis et concurrentis cum illa; . . ."

[17] See *CG*, 3.67. See also *Com. in meta.*, lib. 5, 1, 1, n. 751.

[18] See *ST*, 1.45.5. Cf. also *De pot.*, 3:7.

[19] St. Thomas denies that the will is an instrument as lower creatures are (*ST*, 2–2, 23.2), but asserts that it is in an analogous manner an instrumental cause under God (*De ver.*, 24.1. ad 5).

the creature possesses this power through participation. But the question is whether this participated power is in the creature immediately through the uncreated divine activity or through a created act. We must answer that the creature participates God's power through a created act, for, as St. Thomas teaches, all perfections formally within the creature are participated from God through created acts distinct from God. God himself cannot be the formal cause of a creature's perfection, since by this he would enter into the creature as a constitutive element of its being. He actuates the created potency by a created act. This act does not find in the creature the same form or perfection of being as it has in God's uncreated activity, and thus is, like existence, so dependent upon God's causality that immediately upon the cessation of this divine action the created act ceases to exist. To express the fact that the act by which God brings about the creature's operation has no fixed being in the creature, but is there in an impermanent and transitory way, St. Thomas calls it an *esse viale* or *esse incompletum;* and he compares it to an *intentio sola.* In a text justly famous he writes:

> But that which comes from God in the natural thing by which it acts is as it were only an *intentio* (i.e., an inclination or motion toward) having a certain incomplete being, in the manner in which colors are in the air and the power of art in the instrument of the artist . . . thus its proper power can be conferred upon a natural thing as a form remaining within it, but not the force by which it brings about being as an instrument of the first cause. . . .[20]

Granted, then, that that by which the created potency actually acts as an instrument of God is a created act and not immediately the uncreated divine power, this created act is the actuation of the potency. This act, or *esse viale,* is not the efficient cause of the operation of the creature. God is the first and principal cause of its operation as a causality of being, and he exercises this causality through the *esse* by which he actuates the potency. This *esse viale,* then, is that by which the created potency is formally and existentially in act.[21] The question remains whether the potency gains this actuation by God *moving* the potency itself or by his simply *concurring* with it in eliciting the act. The potency as it is

[20] *De pot.,* 3.7. ad 7.
[21] See *De ver.* 22.5. ad 8.

in potency is related passively to the act that actuates it, as that which receives the actuation or as that which is moved from potency to act by the actuation. Hence, the created act by which God operates in the creature as in an instrumental cause bears upon the potency itself as it is in potency; God actuates the potency by moving it to act through the *esse viale*. It is clear that such is the doctrine of St. Thomas who writes that "the power of the instrumental cause is acquired by the instrument by this very fact that it is *moved* by the principal agent."[22] And speaking of the creature as God's instrumental cause, he says that it is the cause of the effect of the principal cause "insofar as it participates something from the power of the principal cause through its *movement*."[23] Since God actuates the created potency by movement, the movement (and *esse viale* by which that movement is effected) is related to God somewhat differently than it is to the created potency. It comes from God as the agent (*actio*), and it is received by the potency as its actuation (*passio*). Thus, though it is the same created act by which God moves the creature and the creature is moved, there is a difference between it as the action of God and as the reception of actuation by the created potency.[24]

Finally, this movement which God exercises in his instrumental cause is prior at least in the order of nature to the reduction of the created potency to act and thus to the creature's operation. And so, too, the act by which God moves the created potency has a like priority to the operation of the creature. As St. Thomas says, "the movement of the mover precedes the change of the moveable according to nature and causality."[25] Hence the creature acts through being premoved to act by God. Thus God reduces the created potency from potency to act by a *physical or existential premovement,* and not simply by a simultaneous concurrence. Simultaneous concurrence is to this premovement as God's conservation is to his creation. That is, it is simply the continuation of God's action through the *esse viale* within the creature when the creature is actually acting.

To understand how the activity of the creature as instrumental

---

[22] *ST* 3.64.4. ad 3. See also *ibid.,* articles 1 and 4.
[23] *De pot.,* 3.7. See also *De ver.,* 27.7.
[24] See In *Phys. Aristotelis,* lib. 3, lect. 5, nn. 13 ff., and *ST,* 1.41. ad 2.
[25] *CG,* 3.150. Also see *ST,* 1-2, 113.8.

cause of a perfection proper to God, namely, being, is related to its own proper causality, we must recall that an instrument causes the effect of the principal cause through causing some effect proper to itself. For example, the brush causes beauty in the hand of the artist through applying paint to the canvas. The created will causes an increase or modification of the being of the agent by making some particular act or choice. In any case, the secondary cause achieves the effect proper to God through an act proper to itself which has a priority of nature to the achievement of what is proper to God. Since this is so, God causes the effect proper to himself through causing the effect proper to the creature. We saw above, when analyzing God's conservation of the creature, that the proper effect of the created cause is not the being of the effect, but the coming to be of this being. So God causes the *being* that is the effect of and intrinsic to the creature's operation through moving the creature by the created act to cause the *coming to be* of this being. For example, he causes the form and being of the offspring generated by an animal through moving the animal to generate this nature in this matter.[26] It is in this aspect of the creature's operation that it is more properly called second, principal cause as related to the first causality of God, whereas it is called instrumental cause with reference to God as principal cause in its causality of being. This causality is, of course, exercised by God in the created will as well as in all other creatures, for the will is not a first cause of its act, but a second, principal, and free cause. It does not exclude the causality of the first cause in its act, but on the contrary demands it since it is by this causality that it passes from potency to act.[27]

The Molinists, however, present various *objections* to this analysis of God's causality in the operation of the creature. In the first place, they seem to think it impossible for God to sustain in act the created operation by an *esse viale;* for if such an *esse* were needed, another would be needed to sustain this in act, and so on to an infinite series. Hence God sustains the creature in operation

---

[26] Since the created power is related to its proper operation as potency to act, God's movement of the creature to its proper operation is a movement of it from potency to act. St. Thomas refers to this manner of God's causality of the creature's operation as the third way in which he causes the created operation. See *De pot.*, 3.7.

[27] See *ST*, 1.83.1. ad 3;1–2, 109.1.; *CG*, 1. 67.

immediately through his uncreated action. Against this we have shown that the creature participates in the uncreated divine perfection through a created act formally within the creature. This does not demand an infinite series of created acts, for while the created act is that *by which* God causes and conserves, that properly receives such an act which is itself caused and conserved. God, for example, causes and conserves the being of the supposit by a created existence. Since he does not properly conserve or cause the existence, but the supposit, there need not be a formal act by which he conserves the existence; the existence itself is the principle of the conservation of the supposit. Also God properly causes the operation of the creature, and so there must be a created act by which he does this; but this created act does not demand another created act since it, properly speaking, is the created means and not the object of God's causality.[28]

In the second place, the Molinists state that God's actuation of the created potency is not, at least in every case, prior to the operation of the creature. In answer to this, we must say that no created potency is essentially operation, as no created being is essentially existing. If it were, it would always be in act and would never either begin to act or cease acting. Since the created potency is not essentially in act, it must receive act or actuation for it to act. In such reception the potency is essentially passive, and the principle that actuates it is active. So in the order of nature the actuation of the potency is prior to its operation. And since God is the first cause of every actuation, no potency proceeds to act without being premoved by him.

Finally, they say that if God moved the potency to act only through an *esse viale*, he would move it through an act intermediary between himself and the operation and effect of the creature. Thus he would not be immediately present to the creature's operation and effect, but only mediately present. Since this is false, there is no such movement of the potency through an *esse viale*. To this we answer that a created cause is present to something on which it is acting, particularly if it is not acting upon one subject through another subject. For example, a writer

[28] St. Thomas asserted the need of a created act by which God causes the operation of the creature in an answer to an objection like that which Molina raised. See *De pot.*, 3.7. ad 7.

is present to the pen he uses; and the fact that he gives a movement and direction to the pen is the means of his union with it,
and not an obstacle to his presence. God, however, acts within the
created cause by an *esse viale* through which he moves it, and
thus he is immediately present to the created *cause*.[29] The created
cause acts in virtue of its participation through the *esse viale* of
the divine power to cause being. But, as St. Thomas teaches, the
power of the more universal cause is more necessary and more
immediately present to the effect than the power of the more particular cause.[30] God's causality within the creature is more necessary for the causation of being than that of the creature, and it is
more in virtue of God's causality than that of the creature that
being is caused. Hence, the action of God bears more immediately and intrinsically upon the effect of the creature's operation and upon the operation itself than does that of the creature.
Thus there is a twofold presence of God to the creature in its
act. He is immediately present in his being (*immediatione suppositi*) to the creature because he operates upon it. And he is
immediately present to the creature and its effect because it is in
virtue of his universal power that the creature operates (*immediatione virtutis*). If God acts upon one creature through
several other creatures, it may be that he is not immediately
present to the operation of that creature in the first sense. However, no matter how long the series of intermediate causes is, God
is immediately present to the lowest cause in the series in the
second sense, since this cause causes being more immediately in
virtue of God's power than in virtue of its own. Hence, God continues to be present *immediatione virtutis*, and since God's power
is his divine being he is even in this case present *immediatione
suppositi*.[31]

Hence Molina's objections, in our judgment, are not valid. We
should also note that St. Thomas explicitly rejected the image
Molina used to explain God's causation of the creature's act
(namely, that of two men drawing a boat to shore) as a valid
representation to God's relation to the creature in its act.[32] And in

[29] See *CG*, 4.21.
[30] See *De pot.*, 3.7; In 1 *Sent.*, 37.1.1.c. and ad 4;12.1.3.c and ad 4;
CG, 3.70.
[31] See *De pot.* 3:7.
[32] See *Contra errores Graecorum*, 1.23.

the same place he pointed out the basic weakness of such an explanation. Such a theory implies that the operation and effect of the creature is gained by the addition of two imperfect powers, or that the whole of the power and of the use of that power evident in the act of the creature does not have God as its first cause. This implies that God is not the first cause of some being. For the creature, on this hypothesis, is first cause in *using* the power God gives it to enable it to act or in placing the condition necessary for this power of God to result in the act of the creature. In any case, it makes the creature first cause of being in some way, and such a consequence shows a radical weakness in the theory.

DOES GOD PREDETERMINE THE CREATED OPERATION?—Some Molinists, as we showed in the first chapter, agree that God does move the natural and free power to act by a physical premotion, but they add that this *premotion is indifferent* and general and that it is determined to one individual effect or act by a causality exclusively that of the created power. This seems, they say, to be the doctrine of St. Thomas who, when speaking of God causing the effects of creatures, states that "he gives being to things. But the other causes as it were determine that being."[33] When he speaks specifically of the free cause, he seems to teach the same doctrine. He writes that "the potency of the will considered in itself is indifferent to various acts. The fact that it proceeds determinately to this act or that is not from another determining it, but from the will itself."[34] The creature, and particularly the free will, they conclude, has no need that God determine its act, since it can determine itself by its own form and free choice; indeed, a divine determination seems superfluous. The fact that the creature, and not God, determines its act also seems to them to result from the nature of the dependence of the creature on God as an instrumental cause in the causality of being. An instrumental cause has a causality proper to itself, just as a saw has a definite manner of cutting from itself and not from the carpenter who uses it; and so it has an effect proper to itself. In the creature's causality under God, the being of the operation and effect seems to come from God, but the particular kind of being of the operation and effect

[33] In 2 *Sent.*, 1.1.4. See *CG*, 3.65. para. 5.
[34] In 2 *Sent.*, 39.1.1. See also *ST*, 1–2, 109, 6. ad 3.

seems to come from the created cause. Thus the premovement by which God brings about this causality seems to them to be a general premovement, and the determination of the operation seems to come, not from God's causality, but from that of the creature.

To this we must say that God is the first cause of the determination of the operation and the effect of the creature as well as of the existence of the operation and the effect. This is demanded by the nature of the creature's causality. The determination of the creature's operation comes from the term of its operation, as the architect's activity is determined by the building he is constructing and the animal's generating by the offspring it is bringing into existence. It is also determined by the intrinsic principle of determination, namely, by the form that determines the nature of the operation of the creature. The architect's activity is determined by his preconceived plan, and the animal's generative activity by its natural power of generation and its actuation. The operation is determined by a form of nature in operations of nature, and by a known form in other operations. Now the intrinsic form of the creature is caused and conserved in being by God as first cause. This is true of its natural form, as we have seen; and it is true of form possessed in knowledge as we shall see in the next section. Since it is in virtue of this form that the creature acts, it is acting in a determinate way as a second cause dependent upon God as the first cause of the determination of the act. The object toward which the creature tends in its operation determines the act. It does so by determining the power by which the creature acts through a form within it, such as the specification it gives to the plan of the architect. But St. Thomas writes that "both the action of the mover and the movement of the mobile thing tend toward something. But the fact that the movement of the mobile thing tends toward something comes from the action of the mover."[35] We have seen, however, that it is God who moves the creature to act. The movement of the creature, then, to particular term and thus the determination of its act comes from God as first cause.

This same conclusion results from a proper understanding of God as first cause. The whole of the operation and the effect of the creature must be attributed to God as first cause, as St. Thomas

[35] ST, 1-2, 12.1. See also ST, 1.105.5 c. and ad 3.

teaches.[36] God is not first cause in the sense that part of the activity comes from the creature and part from God, but in the sense that the whole activity comes from the creature and the whole from God. It comes from the creature as second cause and from God as first cause. Since one aspect of the operation and effect of the creature is its determination to one individual act, God is the first cause of this as well as of the existence of the act. He determines the creature, not by an act that is immediately attributed to the divine nature, since an act of nature has an effect of the same nature as the cause, but by an act that is immediately attributed to the divine intellect and will. God causes the determination of the creature through the idea or exemplar in his divine mind, as an architect causes the determination of a building through his preconceived plan. But while the architect's causality presupposes the nature of the material he has to work with, and thus he is not the complete source of the determination of the building, God's causality presupposes nothing since everything in the creature comes from him. He causes everything in the creature, not only the form by which it has its common nature, but the particular matter by which it is individuated. And so he determines the form of a creature's being or activity, not only according to the nature that it has in common with others, but according to its individual nature. As St. Thomas says, "there is nothing in the thing by which its common nature is determined of which God is not the cause."[37] We may add that if God were not the first cause of creatures and their acts according to their individual differences, he could not direct a creature to an individual end, and thus his providence would not be universal in its causality. To direct a being to a particular end demands that God cause within that being individual qualities that fit it for the end, and individual acts that lead to the end. Thus, if God did not cause the creature and its operation according to its individual nature, his providence would be severely limited. Since, as we have shown, he causes the individual character of the being and its activity through the individuated form within the being and

[36] See *CG*, 3.70.

[37] *De ver.*, 2.4. Also see *In Peri. herm.*, lib. 1, lect. 14, n. 197. See also *ST*, 1.15. 3.c. and ad 4; 44.3; *CG*, 3.24. para. 2; 52. para. 3; 69; 97; *passim*.

its powers of operation, and through moving the being to its individuated object in its activity, God determines the creature and its acts intrinsically and not simply by the determination of circumstances that surround the creature's act.

Perhaps some have found difficulty with the doctrine that God determines the nature of the creature's act because they have thought that if the determination of the operation and effect comes from the creature it does not come from God, and if the determination comes from God, it does not come from the creature. But the preceding explanation of God's causality of the creature's act argues very strongly against this. St. Thomas states that, "as the divine power, namely the first agent, does not exclude the action of the natural power, so neither does the first exemplary form, which is God, exclude the derivation of forms from other inferior forms, which cause forms similar to themselves."[38]

The fact that the creature is the instrumental cause of God in its causality is not contrary to our explanation. It is true that instrumental causes used by men have a causality proper to themselves that is exclusively their own, but this is due to the fact that not everything within the instrument comes from man. The whole of the creature derives from God, and hence the whole of its activity derives from God as first cause since it acts in accord with its nature. Therefore it does not have causality exclusive of that of God. Moreover, God's causality in the creature's act is not restricted to causing being in general. We have seen that what is proper to the creature is to cause the *coming to be* of the effect with its form and existence, while it is proper to God to cause the effect according to its *being and form*. Since the effect of the causality of the creature and of God is an individual effect, both the creature and God cause the individual character of the effect. The creature causes the coming to be of the individual, while God causes the being of the individual or its individual being. The same effect can be due to both God and the creature because they are not causes in the same order; God is first and principal cause, while the creature is second and instrumental cause.[39]

Our explanation is in harmony with St. Thomas's statements concerning the self-determination of the will. St. Thomas taught

[38] *De pot.*, 3.8. ad 17. See also *ST*, 1.23.5; 1.105.1. ad 3.
[39] See *De pot.*, 3.7. ad 3; 5.1.

that the will has dominion over its own self-determination in such
a way that it was not determined by another in a necessary way,
as lower beings are determined, but not in a way to exclude the
first causality of God in its self-determination. He writes:

> . . . the will is said to have dominion over its act not through the
> exclusion of the first cause, but because the first cause does not so
> act in the will that it determines it to one of necessity as it de-
> termines nature. And therefore the determination of the act re-
> mains in the power of reason and of will.[40]

The way in which the created will can preserve its own dominion
over itself when it acts under the first causality of God will be
examined in the next section. But from what has been said in this
analysis it seems evident that the will, like every other created
power, moves from potency to act only under the first causality of
God. This causality is exercised by God through a created act by
which he physically premoves the created potency to its act. God
not only moves the potency to act; he also determines the nature
of the act in the sense of moving the potency to an act of a specific
and individual nature. Since he does this through a created form
that actuates the potency and thus is prior to it insofar as it is in
potency, it can be said in this sense that God predetermines as he
premoves the created potency to act.

According to the explanation we have given in this section,
the created cause remains a true cause of its operation, though it
exercises its causality in dependence upon the first cause. And
God is first cause of every created operation. He is first efficient
cause since every creature acts in dependence upon him as first
agent. He is first exemplary cause since the creature determines a
being, effect, or operation in virtue of the first causality of the
divine mind. He is ultimate final cause since every creature in its
acts seeks some good, and created good attracts in virtue of the
uncreated good it participates.

2. *God's Causality of the Act of the Created Free Will*

THE PROBLEM.—To understand how God causes the act of the
creature's free will, one must know the nature of the free will and

[40] *Ibid.*, 3.7. ad 13. Also see *ibid.*, ad 12; ad 14; *CG*, 3.89; 90; 91; 68; *De
ver.*, 24.4.c. and ad 1; *ST*, 1.23.1. ad 1; 1–2, 10.4.

the manner in which it naturally proceeds to act, for, as all agree, God causes its act in accord with its nature. In their analysis of the nature of the free will and its act, there is *an area of agreement* between the Thomists and the Molinists which is fully established by philosophical principles and which we need only recall. There is in man, besides the appetitive powers he has in common with animals, a rational appetite, that is, a spiritual appetitive power that follows intellectual knowledge of the good and thus has the good as such as its object, as distinct from the sensible good of the sensitive appetites. Although it is necessary, if this power operate, that it seek good or the happiness of the one who wills, it is free in the choice of acts by which it seeks this happiness. This freedom is not the mere fact of the spontaneity present in man's choices, for spontaneity is also present in the acts of lower appetites, such as the natural appetite of the plant for growth. The natural appetite for such growth is spontaneous since it comes from within the plant itself and not from an outside agent acting contrary to its inner inclination. Nor is human freedom simply the fact that knowledge of the desired object precedes the choice, for the animal has such knowledge and its act of desire follows necessarily the knowledge of an object fitting for it. There is an essential difference between the animal's knowledge and that of man that allows man to be free in his choice. Man's knowledge of the good is intellectual. That is, he knows the good or end not simply in its material conditions but, at least in some general way, as such. He sees an act that attracts him, not only as this particular act, but in its relation to the perfection of man and the good as such. Thus he can reflect upon the act, compare it with a more general norm and with other possible acts by which he can gain his end, and then judge which will more fittingly bring him to his happiness or perfection. Moreover, in this life the things that man knows appear to him as an admixture of good and evil, so his choice is not necessitated by the objective good or his subjective knowledge of it. Of course, there are not infrequently obstacles in the individual man to the proper exercise of his freedom, such as a domination by habit or passion and a lack of knowledge or exterior freedom of action. Here, however, we are speaking of an interior power of freedom (or free power); moreover, the normal man has an actual freedom of choice in a large area of his decisions. He may act or not, may do one thing or another. That is, he has freedom of the exercise of his will act and freedom of the specification of his act. Thus he is said to determine his own choice, to be the cause of his own act, or to move himself to act.[41]

Concerning the causality of the good or object upon the will, we should note two matters on which the Thomists and Molinists agree. In the first place, they agree with each other and with St. Thomas that such causality upon the rational appetite is completely in accord with man's freedom, for it is natural for the appetite to act out of love and desire for the good. The attraction that the good exercises on the will in drawing it to act is not contrary to the will's inclination, since in drawing the will to act, it places an inclination in the will to desire it. Even if a good, such as the vision of God, were to draw the will necessarily to act in this way, such a causality would not be contrary to the will's freedom, but rather in accord with it.[42] There is another point on which they agree concerning the causality of the object, and it is this that we think open to question in itself and as an interpretation of St. Thomas' teaching. They hold that the influence that the good or end exercises upon the will to bring about the exercise of the act is a merely moral or metaphorical influence, as distinct from a physical or metaphysical one. That is, it does not have a physical causal influence in eliciting the act of the will or in causing the act of the will with reference to the simple exercise of the act. It does not have such a physical causality whether it is considered alone or in conjunction with the will.[43]

[41] St. Thomas explains and defends the freedom of the will in ST, 1.82 and 83; De ver., 22; 24.1 and 2; De malo, 6. art. un. He speaks of the will as cause of itself in ST, 1.21.1. ad 3; 83.1. ad 3; 3.65.5. ad 2. He states that the will determines itself in De ver., 22.4. ad 1. Every appetite in a sense moves itself to action that is in accord with its inclination, since its movement proceeds from an intrinsic principle. The will is said to determine and move itself insofar as it transcends the condition of lower appetites by having the fact and the direction of its movement in its own control and choice.

[42] See for example De ver., 22.5. ad 2. Suarez expresses this in accord with his explanation of grace in Opusculum primum, lib. 3, cap. 14, n. 12, p. 226.

[43] See above, ch. 1, footnotes 29, 45. Also see Garrigou-Lagrange, "Prémotion," col. 42–3. See J. de Finance, S. J. "La motion du bien," Gregorianum, 39 (1958), 5–42. This article is a somewhat phenomeno-

They explain this position by statements of Aristotle that the end is not active in causing except metaphorically, and the teaching of St. Thomas that while the principle of the specification of the will act is its object, the principle of the simple exercise of the act is the will.[44] Moreover some Thomists hold that the fact that man acts freely even during aridity, when he does not experience the attraction of the object, shows that the object does not physically cause the act. Also God brings about the will's act with intrinsic and infallible efficacy, while the influence of the object on the will in this life does not infallibly incline the will to act. Hence, God moves the will to act in some way other than through its object. Suarez holds that the will has a sufficient inclination to act of itself, so physical causality on the part of the object is superfluous. Also the act of the will is a vital act, and so it must come from the will and not from the object. Both the Thomists and the Molinists agree, then, that the will itself is the principle of the exercise of the act without a physical causality from the end. In consequence, they also agree that God physically causes the act of the will with reference to its exercise by a causality in the order of efficient causality as distinct from one through the object or in the order of final causality.

Having agreed thus far, the Thomists and Molinists disagree concerning the causality of the object in the order of the specification of the act, the nature of the will as free, and the way in which God causes the act in the order of efficiency. While the Thomists generally hold that the object known by the intellect and presented by the last practical judgment to the will does specify the act of the will, the Molinists, and in particular Suarez, deny to the object any essential causality of the specification of the will act. Suarez holds that the Thomists' position is contrary to the freedom of the will and that the will is active enough to specify itself.[45]

---

logical study of the will's act which, from the analysis it gives, one would expect to result in the attribution to the good as intentionally present to the will some physical causality. The author does not, however, draw this conclusion from his evidence. He refuses to attribute to the good a physical causality, and he essentially restricts himself to the traditional solution.

[44] See Aristotle, *On Generation and Corruption*, bk. 1, c. 7, 324 b 15; St. Thomas, *De malo*, 6. art. un.; In 2 *Sent.*, 39. 1. 1. ad 2.

[45] For Suarez's position, see *Disputationes metaphysicae*, 19. nn. 5 and 6.

Each school's doctrine on freedom is closely related to its explanation of how God causes the act of the will. The Thomists hold that "freedom is the dominating indifference of the will toward the good proposed by the intellect as not good from every aspect."[46] That is, the will has an active, dominating power in deciding which good the practical intellect will present to the will in the last practical judgment. When this judgment takes place, the will's act must follow; but the will is always able to prolong or influence the investigation by the intellect and thus to determine its last practical judgment. This active free act of the will is the act of a created potency. So, to proceed to this act, the will must be reduced to act by God as every other created potency is reduced to act. Hence God moves the will to this free act through a physical predetermining premovement in the order of efficient causality. The will receives this actuation passively in the same order of efficient causality, and so actuated it actively proceeds to its act of choice. Although it has been in this way premoved and predetermined prior, by a priority of nature, to its active choice, such an actuation is not contrary to its freedom. God is so powerful that he causes not only the will act, but also the free manner of its act. It is true that, once actuated, the will cannot not act (*in sensu composito*), but the will retains the power to act differently (though under such an actuation it will never in fact use it) and would act differently given another actuation (*in sensu diviso*). While a man is sitting, he cannot stand; he can only stand by relinquishing the sitting position. Such an incompatibility of two actuations at once is not contrary to freedom. Moreover, in its act the will has an active domination over its choice, and this choice is exercised about an object not in every way good. Since the will is not necessitated in choice of an object that is not in every way good, it acts freely under the power of God moving it to act.[47]

The definition of freedom and the explanation of God's causality of the free act given by the Molinists differs from this. Molina holds that "that agent is called free which, once everything necessary for acting has been granted, is able to act or not to act, or to do one thing in such a way that it could also do the

[46] Garrigou-Lagrange, "Prémotion," col. 69.
[47] See *ibid.*, 39–51; 67–71; also his "Prédestination," *DTC* 12.2 (1935), col. 2969–73; and above, ch. 1, footnotes 28, 29.

opposite."[48] Thus they deny that the will is reduced to its act by a physical premoving predetermination, for on this theory, once everything necessary for the act is given, the will can do nothing but act. They hold that the will is an active power in such a way that once it is proximately prepared for act it contains its act eminently within itself and can thus proceed to second act or its free operation without the need of a previous actuation by God. It proceeds to its act under the first causality of God which they explain as a simultaneous concurrence on the part of God with the will act. Or if some of them admit the need of an actuation of the will antecedent to its act, they say that this is a general actuation which is determined exclusively by the act of the will.

In attempting to understand how God moves the will to act, we must understand how the will naturally proceeds to act, since God causes its act in accord with its nature. We have already seen that the will is a created potency and as such its act is a reduction of potency to act. God then moves it by a created act (or *esse viale*) that is the means by which he physically premoves it and also predetermines it in the sense of giving to the potency the specification of its act. The central question here concerns the *manner* in which the created act or the *esse viale* reduces the will to its act. Does it do so in the order of efficiency or in the order of finality through a physical causal influence of the object? If it is by way of the object, does it simply specify the will act through the object, or does it also physically cause the exercise of the will act through the object? We must also ask how the will determines or moves itself to its deliberate free act. In our previous section we showed that in our judgment the Molinists were mistaken when they denied that the will as created potency needed to be premoved to its act according to the act and the specific determinateness of the act. Are the Thomists then correct when they hold that, once the will has been actuated, it cannot not act? To gain the answers to these two

[48] See above, ch. 1, footnote 24. Suarez holds that this indifference of the will antecedent to its act is ". . . verissima, et valde necessaria et fortasse est quasi cardo totius concordiae gratiae cum libero arbitrio . . ." *Tractatus de gratia Dei,* "Prolegomenum 1. De requisitis ad formalem libertatem et usum liberum," cap. 2, n. 13. *Opera omnia,* 7 (Paris, 1857), 9.

questions, we must investigate the specific nature of the will act as it is distinct from the acts of other created potencies.

THE NATURE AND CAUSALITY OF AN IMMANENT *Actus Perfecti.*—In discussing the operation of the creature, St. Thomas writes:

> There are two kinds of action. . . . One is that which passes into some exterior thing conferring upon it something which it receives, as to burn and to dry. But another is that which does not pass into an external thing but rather remains in the agent himself, *as to feel, to understand, and to will.* Through this sort of action a change is not conferred upon some external thing; the action remains wholly in the agent.[49]

There are, then, basically two kinds of operation, transitive action and immanent action. And the act of will, like the act of intellect, is an immanent act. We shall approach an understanding of the act of the will through understanding *the characteristics of an immanent act in an examination of the intellect's act.* Since both to know and to will are immanent acts, the nature of the acts and their production are to this extent the same, while they differ insofar as they are immanent acts of different powers.

In the first place, the act of knowledge is *immanent* because it is an act which remains within the agent of the act, namely, the one who knows, and indeed within the power of the intellect.[50] The transitive act, on the other hand, passes from an agent to something that receives the action, as the action by which a man moves an object external to him, or the action by which a man through the act of his will commanding his own powers of movement moves himself from one place to another. Here the act remains transitive, since it passes from one power of man to another.

In the second place, the immanent act is an act of a power that has already been perfected in act (*actus perfecti*), while the act of a thing which receives its action through transitive action

---

[49] *ST*, 1.54.2. This distinction occurs in Aristotle, *Metaphysics,* bk. 9, c. 8, 1050 a 25. See St. Thomas' commentary on this passage (lect. 8, n. 1862) and *ST*, 1.27.5; *De pot.,* 9.9.

[50] Some places where St. Thomas describes the intellectual act are *De ver.,* 8.6; *De pot.,* 8.1; *ST,* 1.18.3. ad 1; 34.1. ad 2; 56.1. The following treatment depends upon these texts and the others cited below.

180

(e.g., the movement of some object from one place to another) is an act of a being in so far as it is in potency. The thing acting under transitive movement is moving toward some term, the term of either accidental or substantial change, and it is in the process of change or movement until it reaches that term. It is susceptible of movement to such a term only insofar as it does not now have it, but is able to have it; for once it possesses the term, it can no longer be moved toward it; and if it were not able to possess it, it could not be moved toward it. Thus its act is an act of a being in potency insofar as it is in potency. The act ceases when the potency is fulfilled. Thus, too, an essential element intrinsic to this act is the actuation of the changing thing by an agent and the thing's passive reception of that actuation. It is this kind of act that is properly called movement. The act of intellect and will are not of this kind, and to show their difference from such an act they are called *actus perfecti,* and they are said to be movement only improperly or metaphorically speaking.[51]

If they were, properly speaking, movement, they would not be perfections simply speaking and thus would not be formally within God. By stating that the act of the intellect is an *actus perfecti,* St. Thomas is expressing the fact that the intellect knows, not insofar as it is in potency or is being reduced to act, but insofar as it has already been actuated or perfected in act. It knows insofar as it has already been determined by the object of knowledge. Once it has received its object and is one with it, it knows its object. It is then clearly different from movement properly so-called. One does not say that, once man has walked to the term toward which he was moving, he walks. No, he walks insofar as he has not yet gained his destination or term. But the intellect knows insofar as its term or object is present to it intentionally and has already fully actuated it; in fact, the more fully the object has actuated it, the more fully is the intellect in act. In the physical order, when a being has received its substantial form, it exercises that form or

---

[51] Aristotle indicated this difference between the operation of the powers of knowledge and physical movement in *On the Soul,* bk. 3, c. 7, 431 a 5 f. In his commentary on this passage (*In De anima,* lib. 3, lect. 12, n. 766), St. Thomas treats the act of the will like that of intellect and sense as an *actus perfecti.* See also *ST,* 1.59.1. ad 3; 1.27.5; *CG,* 1.13; 73; *De ver.,* 24.1. ad 14.

kind of being. In like manner, once it has been determined by its object, the intellect, as it were, is the object intentionally. And since it exercises its act insofar as it is already perfected, the intellectual act is called an *actus perfecti.*

It is the act of knowledge, then, that is the *actus perfecti,* but it is not simply the initial act of knowledge by which the intellect knows in general some object. It is also the process of reasoning. In this act the intellect progresses from a knowledge of principles to a knowledge of conclusions. Although for the progress of its knowledge the intellect needs to be determined or actuated anew by the external object in various ways, the immanent act itself by which it arrives at conclusions from premises is essentially still an *actus perfecti.* Since the knowledge of conclusions is implicitly present in the knowledge of premises, by an adequate knowledge of the premises the intellect in an eminent way already possesses the conclusion. At this stage it is in act with reference to the premises and in potency with reference to the conclusion; but since it possesses the latter eminently, St. Thomas teaches that "it is clear that the intellect through the fact that it knows the principle reduces itself from potency to act with reference to the knowledge of conclusions."[52] This is not a reduction of potency to act in the sense in which this is found in the movement of a being from one place to another. In this case, the being does not have the term eminently before it reaches it in fact, and so it cannot be said that it reduces itself to act. But the intellect's knowledge of conclusions is a participation in its knowledge of the premises, and thus, since it has the conclusions eminently, it reduces itself to act in the process of reasoning.

A consideration of the way in which the intellectual word results from the intellectual knowledge may help to clarify this matter. In one place St. Thomas states that the "conception [which in the context he identifies with the word] is considered as a term of action," but in another he teaches that it is not a term of movement.[53] The concept in the sense of the intellectual word is the effect or product of the act of understanding, but it differs from the product or term of a transitive act. It is, in the first place, immanent to the acting power and indeed to the act of under-

[52] *ST,* 1-2, 9.3.
[53] *De pot.,* 8.1. See *ST,* 1.45.2. ad 3.

standing itself. Also the intellectual word is the result of an *actus perfecti*, the intellect's knowledge of the object. But the term of an object being moved by transitive action is the result of an *actus imperfecti*. Because of this difference, St. Thomas teaches that the word is a term of action, but not of movement. The word seems to be a participation in the intellectual act as a property of an essence is a participation in the essence, and it seems to flow by a natural emanation from the intellectual act as the proper accidents flow from an essence in nature. St. Thomas distinguishes such an emanation from movement properly speaking. For example, he writes, "The emanation of proper accidents from the subject is not through some change but by a certain natural consequence, as from one there naturally results another, as color from light."[54]

A third difference between an immanent act and the action of a being moved by transitive act is the manner in which the thing acting gains its actuation. The thing moved by transitive act gains its actuation from an agent distinct from itself and by a movement of efficient causality properly speaking, as the house that is being built gains its construction from the builder and his activity. A power of immanent action such as the intellect does not have a reduction to act as essential to its proper act. But the created and, specifically, the human intellect, before it acts, is in potency with reference to the objects of its knowledge, and it is not always acting, so the act in which its knowledge properly consists must be preceded by an actuation of the intellect that is properly a reduction of it from potency to act. Since the intellect is a power whose act is immanent, *this actuation comes to it from its object* as it is intentionally present to the intellect and actuates it so that it may know. Thus the object intentionally present in an immanent act performs the function that in a being moved by transitive act is performed by the actuation of efficient causality received from its agent. In other words, the principle by which an immanent act receives its actuation is the object intentionally present to the power. St. Thomas expresses this as follows:

In the action which remains in the agent, it is necessary that the

[54] *Ibid.*, 1.77.6. ad 3; see also *ibid.*, corpus; 77.1. ad 4; ad 5; *De ver.*, 14.5; 22.11. ad 6.

object be united to the agent that it proceed to act, as it is necessary for the object of the sensitive power to be united to the power of sense that it actually know. And so the object united to the power is related to action of this kind as the form which is the principle of action is to other agents. For as heat is the formal principle of fire's warming activity, so too the object of vision as intentionally present to the power of sight is the formal principle of vision in the eye.[55]

As the warmth of the fire as received by an object is the formal principle through which it is warmed, so too the object intentionally present to the intellect is the formal principle through which it is actuated in its own order, that of knowledge.

As we have already indicated, there are two stages to the intellectual act in man. Since man's intellect is in potency before it is in act, it must be first reduced to act. This reduction from potency to act is brought about in the intellect through the object as it is intentionally present to the intellect as determining the intellect to know. We need not recall the process by which the object is made intentionally present through the activity of the abstractive intellect upon the phantasm and upon the knowing intellect itself. We simply wish to note that, since in this stage the intellect is properly speaking being reduced from potency to act through its object, it is being premoved and predetermined to act by its object. For, as we have seen, the reduction of a created potency to act is a physical premoving and predetermining causality. In the second stage of the intellect's act, which follows this first stage as effect follows cause, and which properly constitutes the act of knowledge, the intellect knows in virtue of the object intentionally within it as its intrinsic formal cause. So the whole of the actuation comes from the object, but in this act the intellect is the active principal agent of the act. A being that is moved by transitive act to a particular term is not the active principal agent of the act by which it approaches that term, for within its act it is essentially in potency and receptive of actuation from the agent. But the act of knowledge is an act of a power that has already been perfected in act and thus the intellect (or man by his intellect) is the active principal agent of the act. It elicits this act

[55] *ST*, 1.56.1. See also *De ver.*, 8.6. c. and ad 8.

as one principle with the object which is its intrinsic formal cause.[56]

Since this is the manner in which the intellect naturally proceeds to act, God as first cause causes its act in accord with it. So God, besides creating and conserving the intellect in being, moves it to act through its object by which it is actuated. St. Thomas writes: "Hence God moves the created intellect insofar as he gives it power to understand, either natural or supernatural, and insofar as he impresses upon it the intelligible species and holds and conserves both in being."[57] God does not cause the act of the intellect any less for causing it through natural created objects which intentionally impress themselves upon the intellect and thus determine its act. These creatures act upon the intellect through their form and essence and accidental modifications, but these are what they are through a participation in the divine essence and the first causality of God. Moreover, they act and the abstractive intellect acts under the first causality of God, so by causing the intellect's act through other creatures God causes its act no less than if he caused it without the mediation of such objects.

The Causality by God and Man of the Free Will Act.— Since this is the manner in which a power whose act is immanent is actuated and proceeds to act, it seems to us that *it is in this way that the will is actuated and proceeds to act*. And it is our opinion that such is the teaching of St. Thomas, for he mentioned that the will's act was an immanent act and an *actus perfecti* in the very places where he analyzed the nature of such an act.[58] The difference between the act of the will and that of the intellect occurs, not insofar as both are immanent acts, but insofar as they are specifically different immanent acts. The act of the intellect is an intentional becoming of the form of the thing known, and hence St. Thomas compares its act to rest or to being. But the act of the will is more like an inclination to the object, since its act is to love and desire. This inclination toward the good which properly

[56] See *ibid.*, 8.6.
[57] *ST*, 1.105.3.
[58] See above, footnotes 49 and 51.

constitutes the will's act is not that transitive movement which the will originates through commanding other powers of man to act for the acquisition of the loved object. It is most properly that immanent act of the will which is an affective inclination of love toward the good and, in man who has not yet reached complete possession of the good, the affective inclination of desire toward the good and the acts that gain it.[59] Now in the acts of the will, such as the love for a particular good or the desire to perform a particular act, there is a twofold element which we have already mentioned. There is the determinateness or specification of the act, and there is the simple exercise of the act. Since, then, the difference between the will and the intellect as immanent acts is that, while the intellect is a possession of the forms of things, the will is an inclination to the good in an act that has both specification and simple being, we can see that the object actuates the will differently from the way in which it actuates the intellect. It actuates the will to bring about this inclination according to its double quality of specification and exercise. This is what one seemingly must conclude from St. Thomas' analysis of an immanent act and of the nature of the will's immanent act. But since it is so generally denied that the will is reduced to act, particularly in the order of simple exercise of its act, by its object, we must examine St. Thomas' doctrine on this matter more closely.

It seems evident from our experience itself that the direction or *specification* of the will's act comes from its object. The object of love polarizes that love, and the goal of our activity determines the specification of the acts the will must take to reach it. We are also aware from our own experience that the object is presented to the will to love, and direction toward a desired goal is presented to the will to mold its act by the mediation of our intellectual acts. The phenomenon of unconscious motivation does not prove that the intellect does not present the object to the will. For unconscious motivation does not mean that the person acting does not know what he loves or what he is doing; it refers to the fact that he at times does not fully know why or for what value he loves this object or performs this activity. Such unconscious motivation is consistent with the presentation to the will by the intellect of the object to be loved and of the nature of the act to

[59] See *ST*, 1.27.5; 81.1; 1–2, 28.1; *De ver.*, 22.12.

be performed. So St. Thomas' doctrine is in accord with experience when he writes: "If therefore we consider the movement of the powers of the soul from the part of the object specifying the act, the first principle of movement is the intellect, for in this way the understood good moves even the will itself."[60] The act of the intellect as it directs the will in its activity is said to be an act of the practical intellect. While in the process of taking counsel concerning how to act in a particular case there may be various judgments on what must be done, it is the last of these judgments that the will follows in its activity. So the intellect is said to direct the will or specify its act through the last practical judgment. It is true that in this act the intellect *actively* directs the will and the will passively receives the direction from the intellect.[61] But this is not contrary to the freedom of the will in its act, since its *actus perfecti* is of such a nature that it can accept or reject the direction that comes from any specific intellectual act. We shall examine below the freedom of the will in the second stage of its act, namely, that which properly constitutes its *actus perfecti*.

Since it is by the object through the mediation of the intellectual act that the will's act is determined or specified, it is in this way that God naturally causes the determination of the will's act. He determines the will's act by determining the last practical judgment of the intellect, and he determines this in accord with the manner of its action analyzed above. For example, God gives to the will its determination for its good moral action through giving to man the external means that show him to some extent what the moral norm for his actions is, and through impressing this knowledge upon the intellect and causing it to make the correct moral judgments in accord with its nature. As we have seen previously, God is no less the source of the determination of a creature's nature or act because he exercises this determination through a secondary cause than if he exercised it without such a secondary cause.

Granted that the specification of the will's act comes from the object as presented to the will by the intellect, does the object as good have a physical or existential causality in bringing about

---

[60] *De malo*, 6. art. un. See also *ST*, 1-2, 9.1.c. and ad 3; 3 ad 3; 6 ad 3.
[61] See *De ver.*, 22.13. ad 10. See also ad 4; *ST*, 1.83. ad 2.

the will's act with reference to the simple *exercise* of the act? The evidence of our experience points to an affirmative answer to this question. For we find that we are impelled to love an object through the goodness of the object made present to us. It is present to us externally, for example, through a physical presence or through description of it or persuasion exercised upon us, and it is present to us interiorly or intentionally through the attractive influence such a good exercises upon our appetitive powers. If the good that a person greatly loves or the goal that he greatly desires to achieve is destroyed or made impossible of achievement, there seems to be no reason for acting, and the removal of the good seems to remove the physical stimulus to activity. So the fact that we act under the influence of the good upon us and cease to act when the good is removed in one way or another as a motive of action seems to indicate that our will and other appetites act under an existential causal influence that the good exercises upon them. The phenomenon of aridity does not disprove such a conclusion, since aridity is not the removal of the good according to its spiritual reality, but according to its sensible presence. Hence, if a person continues to seek a spiritual good in the midst of aridity, he is acting in virtue of the spiritual value of the good, and his loss of his previous experience is simply due to the fact that the spiritual good is not present to him under the sensible guise it previously had.

It is not only our experience, but also the principles and explicit statements of St. Thomas that seem to indicate that the end or good actuates the will in the order of the simple exercise of its act. In an immanent act the object of the power exercises the causality that in a transitive act comes from the agent, and the causality in the latter case is an existential causal influence that both determines and simply moves the subject that receives it. The burning of the wood that comes from the fire or the direction and impulse that a pen has in the hand of a writer are both interior actuating principles of the subject moved. In an analogous way the causality exercised by the proper object of a power whose act is immanent is the intrinsic principle of the actuation of that power. In both the transitive act of the thing moved and the immanent operation of the power, the effect is physical, and thus in both cases the causal influence that brings it about is physical.

The fact that the immanent act of the will differs in nature from that of the intellect does not prove that the will's act is not actuated by its proper object, but it proves that it is actuated in a different way by its object, namely, that way apt to elicit an act of the will rather than an act of the intellect. The will's act is an inclination or immanent movement, and so its proper object actuates or exercises a causal influence upon it to bring about its act as simple inclination as well as inclination toward a definite object or act. The will's proper object is the end or the good, and thus the good as end or final cause does, in our opinion, physically actuate the will in the order of exercise.

It is very difficult to escape the conclusion that such a doctrine is necessitated by St. Thomas' teaching on the will's act as an immanent act. Moreover, it is very difficult to attribute any other meaning to his direct statements on the matter. He states, for example, without qualification that "the will is reduced to act by the desirable thing which quiets the movement of its desire."[62] A principle that is said without qualification to reduce a power to act causes the act by an existential or physical (as distinct from what some call moral) causality because it is only such a causality that can reduce a power to act. Moreover, St. Thomas speaks of the good *efficaciously* moving the will to act when he writes that "no matter how efficaciously some good moves the will it still cannot force it, because from the fact that it desires something the will has an inclination toward it, and this is contrary to force."[63]

[62] *CG*, 3.88. Aristotle wrote that ". . . the object of appetite starts a movement and as a result of that thought gives rise to movement, the object of appetite being to it a source of stimulation." *On the Soul*, 3.10. 433 a 18, 19: *The Basic Works of Aristotle* (ed. by R. McKeon, New York, 1941), p. 598. So although Aristotle said that the good or end is not active in causing except metaphorically, this may mean that it does not act as the efficient cause acts. He may not be rejecting a metaphysical causality or physical reality in the final cause, as he was not rejecting a physical reality in the operation of the intellect when he said it was not movement properly speaking.

[63] *De ver.*, 22.5. ad 2: ". . . dicendum, quod quantumcumque aliquod bonum efficaciter moveat voluntatem, non tamen ipsam cogere potest; quia ex quo ponitur quod velit aliquid, ponitur inclinationem habere in id quod est contrarium coactioni." See also ad 8: "Et praeterea, sicut verum est proportionatum intellectui ita et bonum affectui. Unde verum propter hoc quod est in apprehensione, non est minus natum movere intellectum quam bonum affectum. Et praeterea, hoc quod voluntas non cogitur a bono, non est ex insufficientia boni ad movendum, sed ex ipsa ratione voluntatis, ut

It is difficult to interpret an efficacious movement of the will as a moral causality that has no causal influence in the real sense of the word upon the will. A causal influence is, properly speaking, an existential influence; to say that the end has no existential or physical influence in eliciting the will act is to say that it has no causal influence properly speaking. If it has no causal influence, why has the good as eliciting the act of an appetite always been called a final cause? St. Thomas also states that "by the fact that the will wants the end, it moves itself to will the means to the end."[64] As the intellect reduces itself to a knowledge of conclusions from its knowledge of premises, the will desires the means in virtue of its desire of the end. The intellect proceeds to this new knowledge from the actuation the premises give it. Thus, too, the will proceeds to a desire of the means through the actuatian given it by the end. Since its desire of the means is a physical act, the causal influence of the end in bringing about this desire is physical. Finally, in a treatment of this matter where St. Thomas distinguished the specification of the will's act from its exercise, he stated that, while the principle of the specification of the act is the object, the principle of the exercise of the act is the will or subject of the act. But then he added: "The one who moves, acts because of the end. Hence it remains that the first principle of motion with reference to the exercise of the act is from the end."[65] It is true, then, that St. Thomas teaches that the will is the principle of the act with reference to its exercise, but this presupposes (and does not exclude) that the prior principle that actuates the

---

ex dictis patet." See also art. 2; art. 9. ad 7. The teaching of some Thomists that the good can never infallibly move the will to act save in the beatific vision seems to us to be inconsistent with these passages of St. Thomas. From these passages we conclude that, since the good can move the will efficaciously to act at times, God acting within the will through the good can also with infallible efficacy induce the will to take in accord with its freedom a particular good act when he wishes. St. Thomas held that, though the common means of confirmation in grace was the vision of God, God could bring about such a confirmation without the beatific vision as a special privilege in some cases (see *ST*, 1.100.2). God can present to the will a good object or act in such a persuasive manner that the will will infallibly elicit the act to which God wishes to move it.

[64] *ST*, 1–2, 9.3: See also ad 3; *De malo*, 6 art. un. ad 20.

[65] *De malo*, 6. art. un. See also *ST*, 1–2, 9.1; *De ver.*, 22.12. For a more specific explanation of how the good seems to move the will in the order of exercise, see my article "Existence, the Intellect, and the Will," *The New Scholasticism*, 29 (1955), 145–74.

will with reference to its exercise is the end, since a power elicits an immanent act in virtue of the causal influence of its proper object. The act is an act of the will, and it is a vital act. Hence "it is not without the operation of the will that the will tends towards the desirable object."[66]

Since, then, the will is actuated with reference to the exercise of its act according to its nature by the end or good intentionally present to it, God as first cause moves the will to act through the causal influence of the end. And so St. Thomas explains God's causality of the act of the will as he does God's causality of the act of the intellect. He holds that "as the intellect . . . is moved by its object and by him who has given the power of understanding, so the will is moved by its object, which is the good, and by him who has caused the power of willing."[67] In this same passage he shows that only God can move the will sufficiently and efficaciously as an object, since only he and no created good fills the will's desire. Moreover, the power of willing is caused only by God, since it is an inclination to the universal good which is God. St. Thomas concludes his treatment on this subject by writing that "it is proper to God to move the will in both ways, but particularly by interiorly inclining it."[68] There is no contradiction between his statement that God interiorly inclines the will to its act and his teaching that the will is actuated by the good operating within it. God inclines the will to its act as first cause, but we have seen that he causes the operations of creatures through a created act of an *esse viale*. It is of the nature of the will to be inclined to its operation by the good. Hence the created act or *esse viale* by which God inclines it to act is the good as present to the will and attracting it to its act. Thus he moves the will to love the end, to desire the means to reach the end, and to avoid the things which deflect it from the end through presenting to it, by way of its proper object, the value or goodness of the object to be loved and act to be performed.

The fact that God moves the will to act through created goods does not lessen his causality of the act of the will. Among the created goods that the will seeks, the primary subjective value

[66] *De ver.*, 22.5. ad 10.
[67] *ST*, 1.105.4.
[68] *Ibid.* See also 1-2, 9.6.

that is its object is the actualization of the being of the one who wills, though such an actualization, is of its nature ordained to God as the ultimate, final cause of man's activity and to the perfection of other rational creatures. To see how God is the cause of the will's actualization of the subject, then, is to see how he is the cause of the acts of the will through the causality of created goods. God as first cause draws the will to actualize or perfect through its activity the person whose will it is, for it is God who, by creating the will, directs it to this end, places the impulse toward this end within it, and draws it to the acts that achieve it. God draws the will to elicit acts to gain this goal through the final causality that the perfection of the person as intentionally present to the will exercises upon it. The actualization of the person and the created act by which it is intentionally present to the will as attracting it are both participations in the divine goodness, and hence they exercise their causality upon the will in virtue of the first causality of God. Since the *esse viale* by which the will or any appetite is moved to act is its proper object, it is a good and, as present to the will or appetite, a created good. And since every such act is a participation in the goodness of God, every actuation of the will or any appetite insofar as its act is a tendency to the good has God as its first cause.

Granted, then, that the will is moved to act by its object, *how does it proceed to act?* As we have seen, the act of the will is essentially an *actus perfecti* like the proper act of the intellect. However, the proper act of the will in man must be preceded by a reduction of the will to act, since the human will is a potency that is not always in act and thus has to be reduced to act. The good has to be brought into the presence of the will and actually attract it before the will proceeds to a deliberate act. In this first stage of the human will's act there is, then, a movement properly speaking of the will or a reduction of it from potency to act. So in this stage the will is essentially passive. As St. Thomas expresses it, "the appetite potency is a passive power whose nature it is to be moved by the apprehended object."[69] This movement, as we have seen, is both a simple movement of the will in the order of exercise and a specification of the act of the will. And since this

[69] *ST*, 1.80.2.

192

stage takes place before the will's proper act of love, desire, or choice, it is a premovement of the will. It can be called a physical, premoving, and predetermining causality in the sense that, prior to the act of the will, it gives actuation and specification to it, not in the sense that once the will is so actuated it must proceed to its deliberate act. We will treat this latter point below, but here we should note that, since such an actuation is essential to the act of the human will and since God moves the will to act in accord with its act, he moves the will to act through a physical predetermining premotion exercised by the object of the will. The Molinists' denial of such an actuation is due most of all to their fear that it is inconsistent with the freedom of the will. In our opinion this objection loses its force when it is seen that the will is actuated by the good and that its proper act is an *actus perfecti*.

The act in which the will's act properly consists is the immanent act of affective inclination toward the object.[70] And this is an *actus perfecti*, so the proper act of the will is essentially different from the act of a thing that is moved by transitive movement, such as the act of the physical body that is moved by a man from one place to another. Such an act is essentially within the act itself a reduction of potency to act, while the will's act is essentially the act of a power already perfected in act. Thus the thing moved by this transitive act is essentially passive within the act and distinct from the agent of the act, while the will is essentially active within its proper act and hence the active agent of the act. The will within its proper act acts in virtue of the actuation of its object intentionally present to it. As there is one principle of the act of understanding, but this principle is composed of two elements, namely, the intellect itself and its object within it, so too there is one principle of the act of will, but this principle is composed of two elements, namely, the will itself and its object within it. And as the total actuation in virtue of which the intellect actively acts is conferred by the object, so too the total actuation of the will in virtue of which it acts is from its object. The will is related to its object that actualizes and determines it somewhat as the being is related to its existence and essence. As the being actively exists according to a certain form of being in virtue of its existence and essence, the will actively loves and chooses in virtue of its object

[70] See above, footnote 59.

193

within it. This is the way in which the will is actuated within its proper act. If it were moved as a physical body is moved, its act would not be voluntary, since it would simply be moved and would not move itself.[71] Since it is, then, an active agent in virtue of its object and is not passively moved by its object within the act itself, it is in this way that God moves it when it chooses or deliberately acts. Since it does this in virtue of its object as the formal and actualizing principle within its act, it performs the act in virtue of the concurring rather than the premoving actuation of its object. Thus God's causality of the act of choice through the object within the will is properly a simultaneous concurrence rather than a premotion, though this causality is preceded by a premotion and is exercised through the same *esse viale* by which God premoves the will, namely, the object.

What is true of the will's simple act is proportionately true of its complex act of willing the means as well as the end. The will may will the means in the same act as that in which it wills the end, particularly when there is only one means that can lead to the end. Or when it wills the end it may still be in potency with reference to the willing of the means. But such a state of potency is not the same as the state of a physical body that has been moved part way to its term in reference to what remains to be transversed. This physical body is essentially still in potency with reference to this term and has not yet been perfected in its act; thus it cannot move itself to what remains of the movement. The will has been perfected in act; and thus, when it wills the end, it possesses in an eminent way the will of the means. In virtue of its willing the end, therefore, it can will the means, or it can reduce itself from potency to act with reference to the means.[72] Thus in some cases the will may will the means after willing the end without further premovement from without. But in other cases it may proceed to the desire of the means after another act of desire for the end or in virtue of a desire for the means as such. Though there is a new external actuation of the will in such a case, the act itself of desire of the means is an *actus perfecti*, as every proper act of the will is.

There remain two questions for us to ask concerning this act of

---

[71] See *ST*, 2-2, 23.2.
[72] See above, footnote 64, and *ST*, 1-2, 10.2; 9.3. ad 1.

the will. In the first place, can the will refuse to act once it has been premoved and predetermined (or prespecified) by its object? It is the nature of the will in the condition of this life that the external objects presented to it and the way in which they are intentionally present to it are not and do not appear to the will as complete fulfillments of the will's love of the good. The external objects presented to the will in this life seem to be admixtures of good and evil, partially in accord with the inclination of the will and partially not in accord with it or against its inclination. The person to whom such an object is presented may reflect upon his own tendency, compare the proposed object or act to his tendency, and reject it as not fulfilling his impulse toward the good.[73] Thus, even though the object has been presented to the will and has thus premoved it and predetermined it toward a particular act, the will may reject it and not proceed to its proper deliberate act. Hence, according to the nature of the will in this life, its deliberate choice is not preceded by an antecedently infallible actuation that is infrustrable. Perhaps the primary reason for which Banez thought there was such an actuation is that the alternative to it seemed to be the teaching of Molina which seemed to him contrary to the created character of the will's act. In our opinion, what we have presented is both an alternative explanation and one in full accord with the will's creaturely status.

Our second question is whether, after the will in the first stage of its act has been reduced from potency to act, it still needs to be premoved to act for it to perform its deliberate will act. Our answer to this is that, once the will has been reduced from potency to act in the first stage of its act, it is a power that has been perfected in act. Thus its act of deliberate choice is not the act of a power in potency, but the act of a power that has been perfected in act. Once it has been perfected in act, therefore, it may perform its deliberate will act without further actuation in the sense of a premovement, but not without the actuation of its object within it in virtue of which it acts and not without the simultaneous concurrence of God.

An objection may be raised to this answer in that it seems to

[73] Note that St. Thomas held that the will as well as the intellect has the power to reflect upon itself. See *De ver.*, 22.12; *ST*, 1–2, 11.3. obj. 3; 16.4. ad 3; 17.6. ad 1.

imply that the deliberate act of the will is a new perfection of which the will, and not God, is the source. To this we say that, while the will is the second cause of the act, God is the first cause insofar as he premoves the will to perfect it in act and to perform the good act, since God's premovement tends, not only to perfect the will in act, but to bring about the deliberate act itself. It is this deliberate act that is the purpose of the premovement of God. Secondly, God is the first cause of the use of the act, or of the deliberate act itself, insofar as the total principle of actuation within the will in act is the object present within it. It is through the object that God causes the will's free choice, not as a transitive, but as an immanent act; not as an act of the will insofar as it is in potency, but as an *actus perfecti;* not as a necessary act, but as a free act of the rational creature. If the will acts, it is totally in virtue of this object within it that it acts; and since the object as formal and existential cause of the act itself is simultaneous with the act, God moves the will within the act itself by a simultaneous concurrence.

Another objection that may be raised is that, if the will is perfected in act before it makes its deliberate choice, there is no reason for the will to make the deliberate choice since there is no further perfection that the choice can give it. To this we answer that the will has been perfected in act so that it will elicit the deliberate choice of the good as an active agent, not that it may simply experience the attraction of the good. So it remains for the will under the actuation of the good to affectively respond to it and seek real union with it. By this it gains subjective personal participation of the good that is intentionally present to it through the object.

In conclusion of this study of the natural manner in which the created will acts, we can say that the Banezian teaching that the will is reduced to act by a physical predetermining premotion and the doctrine of the Molinists that antecedent to the act of the will when it has received everything necessary for its act it can still act or not act, are, in our opinion, opposed only if the will's reduction to act is explained in the order of efficiency. If its reduction to act is explained through the object of the will, then one can see that for it to act it needs to be premoved by God, and yet after it has received everything necessary for its act in the sense of a premovement or prespecification, it can still act or refuse to act.

THE CAUSALITY OF THE SINFUL ACT.—Now that we have proposed an explanation of how the will moves to act considered simply as act, we must ask *how the will moves to the sinful act*. We shall restrict ourselves here to one aspect of this problem. From the nature of the will and its act as we have analyzed it, we simply ask whether the first source of the sinful act is the will's rejection of God's premovement to the good or an antecedent divine permission of sin that is inevitably followed in an individual case by the creature's sin. In our study of revelation we saw that, while God allowed for unrepented sin the punishment of a moral blindness and hardness of heart that led to further sin, antecedent to man's sin he did not in any way want man to sin, but on the contrary wanted him and gave him the means fully adequate to do good. In the next chapter we shall examine from a natural consideration of the divine will whether God can antecedently permit an individual sin in the sense that the sin inevitably follows from his permission. Here we simply ask from the nature of the will whether it is the ultimate source of its sin, and we refer primarily to the first formal sin of rational creatures, whether angels or men. To answer this question, we must recall the nature of the sinful act and then examine the causality by which it comes about.

Concerning the nature of sin there is disagreement among the commentators of St. Thomas on the philosophical problem and on the doctrine of St. Thomas. Many explain sin or moral evil as composed of two elements that are always found in the sin of commission. One of these elements is positive, namely, the ordination of the act to an evil object, and this is the formal element of sin. The second element is a privation of rectitude in the act, though this is not so much of the essence of the moral evil as a necessary consequence of it. Other commentators understand sin to be an evil human act that has two elements, the human act itself and the privation of moral rectitude. While the former is the material, the latter is the formal element of sin. Texts such as the following seem to indicate that the second interpretation of St. Thomas is the correct one.

. . . sin is nothing other than a bad human act. It has its human

197

character from the fact that it is voluntary . . . but a human act is evil from the fact that it is out of accord with its measure . . . And so Augustine placed two elements in the definition of sin: one which pertains to the substance of the human act which is as it were the material element in sin, when he said "a statement, a deed, or a desire" but another, which pertains to the nature of evil, which is as it were the formal element in sin, when he says: "against the eternal law."[74]

Evil is not of its nature positive, though it necessarily has something positive as that in which it inheres. Of itself, evil is a privation of the perfection that ought to be in a being or an act. And the same is true of sin, which is an evil act in the moral order. Hence sin or moral evil has as its subject the human act and as its formal element the lack of the perfection that the human act should have, namely the lack of due moral perfection. This is the act's lack of ordination to God according to the norm of reason and the divine law.

Since sin is formally a privation of the will's ordination to God in accord with reason and the divine law, it appears from the nature of the will's act that the will itself is the first source of its sin. We have seen that, antecedent to the will's act, it is premoved and predetermined by a causality that has God as its first cause. Such an initial premovement that comes from the nature of man as second cause and from God as first cause can only be a movement toward the morally good, that is, to the actualization of man's being in accord with the norm of reason and God's law. For if it were not, nature would be intrinsically corrupt and God would induce man to sin. Moreover, we have seen that this premovement makes the will capable of performing an act in accord with it as an active agent of the act, and that it does so in the sense that, after the will has been so actuated, it needs no further premovement to perform its deliberate choice. However, we have also seen that the will, after being actuated by its object through this premotion, need not respond by making the free act to which the good inclines it, when the good appears to it as not completely

[74] ST, 1-2, 71.6. See also ad 1; 2-2, 118.5; CG, 3.6; De malo, 1.4. ad 7. For a study that seems to us to prove the second interpretation listed above to be the teaching of St. Thomas on the nature of moral evil, see Dermot Mulligan, C.SS.R., "Moral Evil: St. Thomas and the Thomists," Philosophical Studies, 9 (1959), 3-26. This article is a summary of a doctoral thesis presented at Louvain.

satisfying the will's desire of the good. Since, then, antecedent to its deliberate act the will of its nature has an inclination to the moral good and completely adequate actuation to act in accord with this inclination, the moral evil that follows in the case of sin is fully due to the will itself as its ultimate source. This is true in the case of the first sin of the rational creature. This is true also of later sins, though there may not be before each later sin an adequate proximate premovement to the moral good, because the lack of this premovement is due to the earlier sins.

When the will rejects the antecedent inclination to the moral good, and sins, there is still being in the physical act that it elicits, and insofar as there is being in the morally evil act it has God's causality as its first cause.[75] However, since the privation of the correct ordination in the human act is the formal element of the sin and the created will is the source of this, it is the first cause of the act of sin, even though God is the source of the being that remains in the act. It seems that the act comes about in the following way. The will has an antecedent movement to the good in accord with the moral order, that is, to the actualization of the person in a way that is explicitly or implicitly subordinated to God as the final end and norm of the act. However, since the will is not confirmed in good, the attraction of the perfection of its subject is not, in the influence it exercises on the will, necessarily subordinated to the influence of God as the ultimate moral norm and end. Thus the will, by a certain disproportionateness in its love for the secondary good and the forgetfulness of the moral norm this causes in the intellect, proceeds in its act with a privation of the correct ordination to God.[76] Thus in his deliberate sinful act man acts in virtue of the antecedent movement to the moral good or to the actualization of his being in accord with the moral norm, but he accepts this premovement only defectively or partially. He accepts the norm of his acts, namely, his human nature, as the norm even in the sinful act, but now considered not integrally but partially. And he accepts the premovement to the actualization of his being, but now not as this is subordinated to

---

[75] See *ST*, 1–2, 79.2. See also In 2 *Sent.*, 37.2.2.

[76] See *ST*, 1–2, 79.2. See also *ibid.*, 1. ad 3. For the psychological genesis of the sinful act, see *CG*, 3.10; *ST*, 1.49.1. ad 3; 1–2, 76.4. ad 1; 2. ad 5; *De malo*, 1.3.

God and not as this actualization is considered integrally. The privation in the human act is due to the fact that the sinner accepts his nature only partially as a norm of his acts and the actualization of his nature only partially as the end of the acts, not as considered integrally and subordinated to the ultimate norm and end of moral activity, namely, God. The actuation of the act that is sinful is due to the fact that the actualization of the subject and the nature of the subject are still to some degree the end and the norm of the act. Since the remaining act is secondary to the privation, and the will is the first source of the privation, the will's privation of due order in the act is antecedent to God's co-operation with the act contained in the sin. Moreover, it seems that God's actuation of the act that remains with the privation of the sinful act is not by way of premovement, but by way of simultaneous concurrence, since it is by such a causality that God causes the deliberate act itself.

It seems to us that the explanation of the will that we have given shows to some extent how God is the first source of being in the act of man, how the free creature is the first source of sin and only of sin, and how God moves the will to act both in accord with his own divine nature as first cause and in accord with the will's freedom. Moreover, it seems to us that the reasons advanced by the Molinists and the Thomists to sustain their theories do not invalidate the opinion we have presented. We say this both because of the evidence presented above for our opinion and because of certain weaknesses that seem to us inherent in the theories of the Molinists and the Thomists. The Molinist explanation may show that the will is intrinsically free and the source of its own sin, but to us it does not seem to explain the will's act adequately in accord with the first causality of God or the created nature of the will. And even their defense of the freedom of the will seems to be somewhat weakened by their doctrine of God's determination of the circumstances of man's acts in accord with *scientia media,* for this in a way substitutes an extrinsic determinism of the human act for an intrinsic determinism. The Thomists' explanation may adequately defend the first causality of God in all acts of the creature, but to us it does not seem to do this in a manner consistent with the nature of the free will's act. For their doctrine that holds that the created will must be preceded by an antecedently infallible movement to the good if it is to act, and an antecedently infallible divine permission that it sin in this particular act if it is to sin seems to us inconsistent with the freedom of the will. Their answer that God is so powerful that he causes not only the act of the free will, but the freedom of the act, does not seem adequate, since we do not think they explain God's causality of the free will's act in accord with the nature of the will as an immanent free power. Their teaching that, since the will is directed toward an object that is not in every sense good, it is free under the causality of God, as they explain it, is unconvincing; for if the will is moved to the deliberate act by a premovement in the order of *efficient* causality, its act does not seem voluntary, whether the object is partially good or wholly good. Their claim that the will under such causality is free *in sensu diviso* to perform another act, though not *in sensu composito,* does not seem to us to escape the difficulties we have just mentioned. Finally, their use of these distinctions employed by St. Thomas to defend his explanation of the freedom of the will under the causality of God seems inapplicable since his explanation in our opinion differed from that of Banez, and so the distinctions do not have the same meaning in both cases.

THE MOVEMENT OF THE WILL TO A SALUTARY ACT BY GRACE.— Finally, we must indicate the relevance our explanation of the natural relation of God's causality to the free will's act has to the *supernatural mystery of grace.* In the first place, let us recall once more the doctrine of St. Paul that we found in the second chapter. In our opinion St. Paul taught that God has predestined all those whom he has justified, and that he has a sincere desire that all others be saved and come to a knowledge of the truth. The word by which St. Paul expressed the divine intention for the salvation of those whom he justifies ($\pi\rho o\acute{\omega}\rho\iota\sigma\epsilon\nu$), we noted, is much stronger than that used by him to express the divine intention for the salvation of others ($\theta\acute{\epsilon}\lambda\epsilon\iota$); he has predestined the former and he wants the latter to be saved. As a result of this divine intention for the salvation of men, God gives external and interior helps to bring about man's cooperation with his saving intention and activity, and man's cooperation is thus God's work. St. Paul, for example, stated that those whom God has predestined he has

201

called, justified, and glorified; and he told the Christians of Philippi that God would complete the work he has begun in them and that he works the will and performance of their Christian lives. Although God has predestined to glory those whom he has united to Christ through justification, and in the temporal order will complete the work he has begun, and work their will by which they remain faithful to Christ, those whom God so treats are still able in this life to reject God's predestination and saving activity within them. If they do and continue to do so, God will reject them as he has rejected the Jews, and they will become reprobate. We have given the reasons for this interpretation of St. Paul in the second chapter, and hence there is no need to repeat them here.

What we have presented in this chapter has been an analysis of God's causality of the free created act for the purpose of explaining to some extent this mystery of predestination and grace or of God's saving intention and activity as it refers to the work of God within the will of man to bring about his designs. God's *working* man's will and performance of salutary acts is a case of God's *causing* man's free will act. Hence, the proper characteristics of God's causality of man's will acts are found in God's causality of man's salutary acts. Thus, when God causes man's salutary act, he does so through a created act (or *esse viale*) that physically premoves and prespecifies the will through the order of final causality for the purpose of bringing about the deliberate free act of the will.[77] God by this created act reduces the will from potency to act so that the will is perfected in act and thus capable of eliciting its free cooperation with God as an *actus perfecti* in dependence upon God's simultaneous concurrence. But before it so acts, it is also capable of rejecting God's initiative, since God's causality as antecedent to the will's free act is frustrable. Unless, then, the sources of revelation indicate something to the contrary, what is true of the natural order of God's causality of man's free

[77] Hence we agree with Augustine and the Augustinians in that we explain grace's causality of the salutary act through the physical influence of the good within the will. See above, chapter 3, f. 69; chapter 1, f. 56. We think that the nature of the will's act as immanent indicates this, but we think that Scripture and the freedom of the will's act indicate that this causality of the good is not antecedently efficacious in God's common providence.

acts is found in his causality of man's salutary acts. In our opinion Scripture and the teaching of the Church show, as is clear from our chapters on this matter, that God's causality of salutary acts is in accord with what we have found through philosophical analysis. And the philosophical analysis helps us to understand how God's causality of salutary acts is in accord both with God's perfections and with man's freedom and creaturely nature.

However, there is a difference between the order of salutary acts and that of man's natural acts. The former have as their norm, not only nature, but the order of faith; and they are directed to an end that is the vision of God himself and thus transcendent to what the natural powers of man can achieve of themselves under God's natural causality. The order of salutary acts is called the order of grace since it is a completely free gift from God to man. It is completely free because it transcends the rights and powers of nature and because it is given to man who has sinned in Adam and thus is made unworthy of God. And so also the interior created gift by which man shares or participates in this order is called a grace. Moreover, the created act that is given to elicit particular acts in this order is called an actual grace. An actual grace that tends to elicit an act of the intellect is called a grace of illumination and that which tends to elicit an act of the will is called a grace of inspiration.

Since there is this difference between God's causality of salutary acts and his causality of natural acts, what is true of the latter is only analogously true of the former. For our purposes here we need only note that the order of salutary acts is higher in the scale of values than that of man's natural acts. God's causality in the former case shows a greater gift as its origin, a greater purpose as its end, and a greater actuation by which it moves the will to act, namely, grace.

There is one specific application of our analysis of grace through revelation and reason that we should perhaps make explicitly, and that is to the question of *the difference between sufficient and efficacious grace*. It seems to us that from the evidence of revelation and reason this distinction can have two meanings, or there is a twofold distinction between sufficient and efficacious grace. In our philosophical analysis of the will we saw that the will was moved to act by God through a created act in the order of final causality. It is in virtue of this one act that the will is premoved to act or reduced from potency to act and that it actually elicits the free act as an *actus perfecti*. In the analysis of revelation (and of reason for its own order) we saw that the total initiative in the sinful act was man's rejection of God's prevenient help, and not the insufficiency of God's help. It is helpful, then, to make a distinction between sufficient and efficacious grace to show that God is not responsible for man's sin, and the analysis in the natural order helps us to understand the nature of this distinction. Actual grace is the created act by which God premoves the will to act and cooperates through simultaneous concurrence in the deliberate free act itself. In the former case it makes the will capable of eliciting the deliberate act, since it perfects the will in act, and so it can fittingly be called sufficient grace. In the latter case it actually causes the free act, and so it can fittingly be called efficacious grace. The division is not a division of grace as antecedent to the will's act, that is, of prevenient grace. Rather, sufficient grace is grace as prevenient, and efficacious grace is the same grace as aiding the will in the free act itself. The physical act of grace is numerically the same in both cases, though it has different functions in each case. The fact that sufficient grace makes the will truly able to elicit the salutary act without the need of any further prevenient grace shows clearly that God is not responsible for the failure of the will to perform the act to which he calls it. The fact that it is in virtue of efficacious grace (as the source of all the power or actuation manifested in the free act) that the will acts shows that it responds to prevenient grace, not through the addition of its natural power or by its own initiative, but simply through the power of grace itself, of the same grace that had been prevenient and now is simultaneously actuating the will within the free act itself.

A second division between sufficient and efficacious grace seems to be suggested by St. Paul's distinction between God's saving intention as it reaches those whom he justifies and as it reaches others. As it reaches the former, it is called predestination; as it reaches the latter, it is called a desire that they be saved and come to a knowledge of the truth. Since predestination is the divine intention ordaining a man to heaven in such a way that Paul could say that such a man is already glorified and since justification is a guarantee of eternal life unless man withdraws, the grace that is present to the justified seems to be in God's common providence much more powerful than that present to those who are not justified. To indicate this, one does well to distinguish the antecedent or prevenient grace present to the justified from that present to others by calling the former efficacious and the latter sufficient. Grace in the justified is like life in the living, while grace present to those not justified is like the preparation for the resurrection of a dead man to life. As life in a way tends of its nature to bring forth the acts that preserve, increase, and protect it, so does antecedent grace in the justified. So it can fittingly be called efficacious in this sense and not in the sense that man with such antecedent grace cannot refuse to cooperate with God's grace. Grace is present to others sufficient to bring them to justification, though it does not come from a permanent intrinsic principle within them; and thus the antecedent grace present to those who are not justified is fittingly called sufficient.

There does not seem to be a basis in revelation or reason as shown by the nature of the will for a division of antecedent or prevenient grace into an efficacious grace in the sense of a grace that is antecedently infallibly destined to elicit the deliberate act and a sufficient grace in the sense of a grace that is antecedently certain not to elicit the free response. There does not seem to be a basis for such a division whether one would base efficacious grace upon the intrinsic efficacy of grace or upon the extrinsic divine determination of circumstances in accord with *scientia media*. The evidence we have examined seems to us to be inconsistent with such a division. For revelation shows that the justified has received a grace that antecedently is destined to elicit meritorious acts since it comes from God's predestination. But it shows also that man can resist this grace. Reason shows that the premovement by which God perfects the will in act is so adequate for the deliberate act that there is needed no further premovement to act. Thus under the power of the object the will can act, but antecedent to its deliberate act it can also resist and refuse to act.

It is true that God, who is omnipotent, can when he wishes in either the natural or the supernatural order give the will a premovement to good that antecedent to the will's response is infallibly destined to elicit the act. But since this manner of causing the will's act transcends the order of nature as shown by the way in which the will naturally proceeds to acts of choice in this life and the order of grace as shown by the way in which the will is actuated by grace, when it occurs it partakes of the nature of the miraculous. God's power to cause the will's act in such a way does not prove that he commonly does so; and when it occurs, God still moves the will to act in accord with its nature, that is, through its object. So no matter how effectively God moves the will to act through its object, the movement is not contrary to its freedom (though it may transcend it) since it puts a desire in the will itself to move itself to act as active agent. Or, to speak more accurately, it puts a desire in the will so that man by his will moves himself to act as active principal agent.

3. God's Causality of Man's Final Perseverance in Grace

We have seen that man through grace is ordained to an end that transcends his nature and natural powers, and we have also seen how God moves man to move himself in a particular act to the acquisition of this end. It remains for us to investigate how God causes man to continue till death to move himself toward this end or how he causes man's actual perseverance in grace till death. In this question, as in our previous question, we are simply interested in showing the harmony that exists between God's grace and man's free will. We shall first briefly recall the doctrine of the Church on this matter; then we shall try to explain the harmony between God's causality of man's perseverance and the freedom of man's will; and finally we shall answer various objections to the explanation we forward.

THE CHURCH'S TEACHING AND THE PROBLEM.—Theologians generally hold, and it seems that they reflect the Church's teaching in this matter, that man's *actual* perseverance in grace till the end of his life is caused by God and that it is for the one who receives it a great gift that is not given to all of the justified. Paul asked the Corinthians, *what hast thou that thou hast not received?*[78] If everything in the Christian life is received as a gift from God,

[78] 1 Cor. 4:7.

206

surely this is true of man's perseverance in the Christian life till death. This final perseverance is not given to a man by the fact that he is justified, since it is something that must be prayed for even after one has been justified. This is indicated by Christ's warning to his disciples: *Watch and pray, that you may not enter into temptation.*[79] The doctrine of the Church expressed in its official acts continues this teaching of Scripture; for it too teaches that, even though man is justified, he needs the grace of God to persevere in the practice of virtue and he needs daily to petition God for the grace of perseverance.[80] In his explanation of this necessity St. Thomas distinguishes the virtue of perseverance from the actual perseverance of the Christian in grace. The former is given in a man's justification, and by this he has a firm intention to persevere. But that man actually persevere in the practice of the good Christian life till death demands a grace other than that which man has received in justification. This grace is not another habitual grace. Rather it is the providential protection of God and the actual grace that brings about the continuance in good and the protection against temptation that are essential to persever-ance. The justified need God's moving grace to persevere as they need his moving grace for any salutary act. And in the present order they have a special need for it because of the enduring effects of original sin in them. They continue to be burdened with an ignorance of what they really need in the moral order and with a disordered affection or inclination to the things of the world. Man's will is properly ordered to God by the grace of justifica-tion, but order is not immediately restored in the sensitive appe-tites. Thus man continues to feel rise within him impulses against the order of charity, and this very fact makes a perseverance in good more difficult than the performance of particular good acts. Hence the necessity of a special grace for a man's perseverance in the practice of the good Christian life. This grace is called the gift of final perseverance when it gains man's perseverance in grace till death.[81]

In their explanation of the nature of this gift of final persever-ance, the Thomists and the Molinists generally hold that the gift

[79] Matt. 26:41.
[80] See D 132, 183, 806, and above, pp. 191-3.
[81] See *ST*, 1-2, 109.9 and 10; *CG*, 3.156.

or grace is antecedently infallibly effective or efficacious. While the Thomists hold that it is intrinsically efficacious, the Molinists hold that it is effective through the knowledge God has of what man would do given any circumstances and his consequent determination of circumstances. Thus they hold that it is extrinsically efficacious. Those of the Molinists who hold that God predestines man to heaven antecedent to foreknowledge of his merits hold with the Thomists that God gives the gift of final perseverance antecedent to his knowledge of man's merits. Those who teach a predestination only after God's foreknowledge of man's merits hold that the gift of final perseverance is in a way the last of God's gifts to man working out his salvation, and a gift given consequent upon God's knowledge of the good acts leading up to the end of man's life.[82]

THE NATURE OF THE GIFT OF FINAL PERSEVERANCE.—The question for us here, as in the case of the grace that causes man's individual salutary act, is whether revelation shows the existence of an antecedently infrustrable gift of final perseverance as the normal means by which God gains the salvation of those who are saved. And here, as in the case of the individual grace, we must say that, in our opinion, neither revelation nor reason shows the existence of such a gift. Revelation seems to show the existence of what one may fittingly call a grace of final perseverance given to all the justified in the act of justification, but a gift of perseverance that is, antecedent to the free creature's cooperation with it, frustrable. This seems to result from the doctrine of St. Paul that we found in the second chapter, namely, that God has predestined all of the justified to the glory of heaven and that he has in some true sense already brought them to the completion of their earthly pilgrimage. If such is the intention of God in justifying man, the grace that is the effect of God's justification of man does not only or indeed primarily establish an individual as presently justified, but rather as eternally united to God in glory. It establishes him in this fulfillment, not as presently achieved, but as the end toward

[82] For the difference between Thomists and Molinists on this matter see A. Michel, "Persévérance," *DTC* 12.1 (1933), 1298–1300. Also for this and the difference between the Congruists and the other Molinists, see above, chapter 1, footnotes 52 and 61.

which grace naturally and successively lifts the justified unless it is resisted and frustrated by man. Paul seems to teach this in many passages. In one of these passages he compares the power God exercises within the Christians to that which he has exercised in Christ in raising him from the dead and setting him at his right hand in heaven. In like manner, *even when we were dead by reason of our sins, (God) brought us to life together with Christ (by grace you have been saved), and raised us up together, and seated us together in heaven in Christ Jesus . . .*[83] The created act by which the power of God is exercised in the supernatural order in creatures is called grace. So it seems that grace has already in some way brought the justified to the completion of his justification in heaven. In this same way Paul assures the Philippians, *that he who has begun a good work in you will bring it to perfection until the day of Christ Jesus.*[84] Since these texts are addressed to Christians generally, they show that the justified already have final perseverance in the intention of God and in the grace that is within them, though, as other texts of Paul make clear, Christians may by their own resistance frustrate the effect natural to the grace within them. We have seen that this interpretation of St. Paul seems to be in accord with the teaching of the Council of Trent.[85]

An understanding to some extent of the nature of this gift of perseverance is given by the following considerations. Actual perseverance is the continuance till death in the state of grace, and the gift of final perseverance is the grace that effects this or that *conserves* man in the state of grace. Thus, as different theologians have pointed out,[86] the gift of final perseverance is to man's actual perseverance as God's natural conservation is to man's endurance in life. Since this is true, what is true of natural conservation is analogously true of the gift of final perseverance. As we have seen previously, God conserves a man in being by an

---

[83] Eph. 2:5–6. Christians have in the Holy Spirit within them a pledge of their inheritance (Eph. 1:14), an inheritance that is theirs as sons of God and joint heirs with Christ (Rom. 8:17).

[84] Phil. 1:6.

[85] See above, 190 ff.

[86] See Cajetan In *ST*, 1–2, 114.9; F. C. -R. Billuart, *Summa Sancti Thomae hodiernis academiarum moribus accomodata*, "Tractatus de gratia," dis. 8, art. 5, n. 5.

uncreated act and by a created act. The uncreated act is not an act distinct from the divine act of creation of the human soul, but rather the continuation of that same act by the divine will. Nor is the created act by which man continues to exist really distinct from that which formally causes his initial existence. It is simply the endurance in being of his initial existence. We may add two more statements concerning this natural conservation. In the first place, as God initially gives an existence proportioned to the nature of the creature, so he conserves the creature in being in accord with that same nature. Since the human soul is naturally immortal, God's conservation of it is naturally unending. Secondly, the created act by which God conserves the creature in being is the principle of its actualization as well as of its conservation. Thus the natural existence of man is the actualization of his nature in the order of being as well as the intrinsic principle of the conservation of that nature. It is the actualization of that nature on the level of being, since it gives it existence. But the nature is not actualized perfectly on the level of being; it is only through operations and the perfection of the proper operations that the created nature is actualized. Since the existence of the creature is the actualization of the created nature, it seems that it is in some way the source of that actualization on the accidental level of operations. It seems that the existential act of the supposit is the source of the existence of the proper accidental powers of the nature and, in some way, partial intrinsic source of the exercise of these powers that leads to the actualization of the nature.

Sanctifying grace is the life of the soul in the order of grace. Hence God's intention that man be conserved in grace is exercised in the soul through sanctifying grace itself, not as simply the intrinsic principle of man's justification, but as the intrinsic principle of the continuance of that life of grace according to its nature. Since grace is a participation in the life of God, its nature is to endure forever; and so, when God initially gives being in this order and conserves it, he conserves it in such a way that it endures forever. That is, he gives in the act of justifying man a gift of final perseverance, and he gives this to all who are justified. The intrinsic created act through which God conserves man in grace, then, is sanctifying grace itself. But since sanctifying grace is the actualization of man's supernatural life and not simply

210

the principle of its conservation, it tends to actualize it, not simply in the order of habit, but in that of operation. It is in some way the source of the proper powers of man as elevated to the supernatural order and also of the exercise of those powers by which man's fulfillment of the order of grace is gained.

There is a great difference, however, between grace as the principle of man's perseverance and the natural existence as the principle by which God conserves the creature in being. The former, unlike the latter, is a modification of man's being that is essentially connected with the moral order, for sanctifying grace is essentially connected with charity that informs the will of man. Therefore, while man's natural conservation in being cannot be destroyed by man's acts at least as it concerns the existence of his soul, the gift of final perseverance or his conservation in the order of grace can be destroyed by man in this life. By the loss of charity man loses sanctifying grace; and since man does lose charity by a deliberate choice of a created value as his ultimate goal, or by a deliberate serious sin, he loses by such an act the gift of final perseverance. This analysis of God's conservation of man in the order of grace helps to explain the teaching of Scripture. The conclusion seems to be that God gives to all the justified in the act of justifying them a gift of final perseverance which, however, they may frustrate by their own deliberate seriously evil act. There does not seem to be evidence to prove the existence of an antecedently infrustrable gift of final perseverance as the means by which God conserves in grace those who reach heaven.

SOME DIFFICULTIES CONSIDERED.—Objections may be raised to this explanation of the gift of final perseverance. For example, it may be argued that God chooses means proportionate to the end he seeks. Those who reach heaven receive heaven as an absolute gift from God, and so in leading them to heaven God has used an absolute means. Since the gift of final perseverance is this means, it is an absolute and not a frustrable gift. To this we answer that the gift of heaven is absolute in the sense that it completely transcends man's natural powers and thus is in no way due to him; that the principle that ordains man to this end (grace) is not merited by man, but given to him as a gift from God; and that one who is established in this grace will inevitably gain its completion

211

in heaven unless by his own deliberate choice he frustrates God's intention and gift. But, as we have seen in Scripture and the teaching of the Church, it is not an absolute gift in the sense that man cannot frustrate God's intention to give it to him. So the gift of final perseverance that we describe is proportioned to the way in which God ordains man to heaven in the present order; for since it is given in justification itself, it is an unmerited gift which inevitably assures man's salvation unless he frustrates its natural result by his deliberate serious sin. But it is a gift that, as antecedent to the fulfillment of its purpose, can be frustrated by man.

One may say that final perseverance is a great gift, and it is a greater gift to receive a movement to heaven that is antecedently infrustrable than to receive one that is frustrable. Moreover, men are told to pray for perseverance; if they are given this in justification itself, there is no reason to pray for it since it is already given. To this we answer that the nature of the gift of perseverance is, of course, known to us from the doctrine of the sources of revelation and not from our conception of what attributes it must have to make it a real gift. And revelation seems to indicate that it is a gift that can be frustrated antecedent to the achievement of its purpose. The reason for prayer seems more evident on the premise that it is a frustrable gift than on that that it is infrustrable. In the latter case, it is thought to be given either antecedent to God's foreknowledge of man's merits or consequent upon such foreknowledge. If it is given consequent upon such foreknowledge, it seems that man's perseverance in the good is not the effect of the gift of perseverance; if it is given antecedent to such foreknowledge, then it seems that prayer is useless since one either has or will not have the gift, antecedent to any divine consideration of one's prayer. Since it is a frustrable gift given at justification, prayer seems to be necessary, not so much to gain the gift itself, but the fulfillment of the gift; for if man refuses to pray for its fulfillment and for his own fidelity to it, he is resisting the gift or prevenient grace of perseverance since it tends to elicit those acts that assure man's perseverance in grace.

Another objection may come from the fact that not all persevere. If all do not persevere, all have not been given the grace of final perseverance. In other words, since only some persevere, they have been given a special help superadded to justification that explains this greater goodness in them. To this we answer that, while all have received in justification the gift of final perseverance, this gift as antecedent to man's response is frustrable. Hence the reason why some persevere is not that they have received an infrustrable antecedent grace, and the reason why others do not persevere is not that they have not received such a grace. The reason why the latter do not persevere is their resistance to the antecedent grace of perseverance. The reason why the former persevere is the grace of perseverance which they have not resisted.

This itself seems to lead to a further objection, namely, that the gift of perseverance does not give merely the power to persevere, but actual perseverance; for if it gave merely the former, the use of the power would be due to man and not to God. To this we answer that we admit that the gift of perseverance gives actual perseverance as well as the power to persevere. It gives the actual perseverance as a grace concomitant with man's act and the power to persevere as an antecedent grace, analogous to the manner in which the grace destined to elicit a particular act does according to the explanation we have given above. When a man is justified, he is assured of the divine intention to bring him to heaven and thus of the effects of that divine intention, namely, an external providence that protects him from temptations he cannot overcome, the internal conservation in grace, and the internal actual graces necessary at the different stages of his life for his actual perseverance in grace. This grace, however, as antecedent can be resisted. Moreover, the greater goodness in the one who does persevere over the one who does not persevere is present in him through the fact that, in addition to antecedent grace which he has in common with the other, he has concomitant grace that elicits his acts of perseverance.

Another objection is found in the consideration that man's non-resistance to grace itself is the effect of the grace of perseverance. So the fact that one man does not resist the antecedent grace of perseverance is the effect of this antecedent grace. And if the non-resistance to grace is the effect of the gift of perseverance, it can only be because this gift is antecedently infrustrable. We answer this by saying that non-resistance to grace is related to acceptance of grace as withdrawal from one term in the movement of a physical object is related to its approach toward the other term. It is through the same actuation that the physical object withdraws from the one term and approaches the other, or that the will both does not resist and does accept grace. The will's acceptance of grace is caused by grace insofar as it is concomitant with the will's act and not as antecedent to it; thus the non-resistance to grace is also caused by grace as concomitant, and not as antecedent. So grace as antecedent can be frustrable, although grace causes the non-resistance of the will, since it causes this not as antecedent but as concomitant.

Again it may be argued that the reason that demands that there exist a grace of final perseverance demands also that it be antecedently infrustrable. Man cannot have control over the time of his own death and thus he cannot bring it about that there is a conjunction between his being in the state of grace and the time of death. Moreover, it is beyond the power of man to establish his will immovably in the good in this life. Thus he has need of the grace of final perseverance that assures the conjunction of the state of grace and of death whether this is through keeping the will immovably fixed in grace or through raising once more to the state of grace the man who has fallen into sin after his justification. But only an antecedently infrustrable grace can preserve a man immovably fixed in the practice of the good; if it were frustrable, man's changeableness in this world would not be overcome. Moreover, since it is only God who determines the time of man's death, the conjunction of death and the state of grace is a gift that depends only on him. Scripture indicates that God assures the final perseverance of man through assuring this conjunction of death and grace. It says of one whom God loved that he was *snatched away, lest wickedness pervert his mind or deceit beguile his soul*.[87]

To this we say, in the first place, that Scripture shows that man, under the movement of grace toward his eternal fulfillment, can still reject God's grace and thus not reach heaven. The grace of redemption in this life is normally such that it takes away from those who do not resist it the actual falling from grace, but not the ability to fall from grace. So the grace of final perseverance conserves man in grace in the midst of man's defectibility and even

[87] Wis. 4:11.

214

his proneness to sin due to the abiding results of original sin, and not by removing this possibility of man's failure through his rejection of grace. Secondly, neither revelation nor reason seems to prove the existence of a gift of final perseverance in the sense of a gift that abides in the justified after he has fallen from grace through serious sin and one that continues to assure his eternal salvation. Since the gift of final perseverance is the conservation of man in grace, it is lost when man loses grace. If man regains grace, it is not through the causality of the gift of final perseverance, but through grace gained from God's salvific will, a grace that may be more generously given to some than to others, but that is given to all in this life. In the third place, we are speaking here of the order of God's supernatural providence as shown in the grace God gives to men. According to our understanding of Scripture and reason, God gains the perseverance of man through a gift of final perseverance given to all in the act of justification, a gift that naturally conserves man in grace till its fulfillment in heaven, but a gift that can be frustrated by man's will. Thus it is not a gift in the sense of an antecedently infallible divine decree that death and the state of grace shall occur together in a particular case, whether this decree occurs before or after God's foreknowledge of man's merits, and whether the effect is gained through removing a man from the world before he has sinned or through restoring him to grace after he has sinned. God may act beyond the order that his grace indicates, and it seems from the statement quoted from Wisdom that at times he does. But this is a gift that transcends the order of grace that he has established and not the gift of final perseverance that is the explanation of the perseverance of all who persevere in grace till death. The statement from Wisdom is one that refers only to an individual person, so from it nothing can be deduced about the nature of the gift of final perseverance as such.

Finally, one may say that man in the present order still has an inclination to sin even after his justification because of the effect of original sin called concupiscence. A gift of perseverance that will effectively conserve man in grace in the midst of such an inclination must be one that gives a much more powerful impulse to the good than would be needed in another condition of the human race. So while it may be true that the gift of perseverance given to Adam and to the angels was frustrable, it seems that man in the present condition needs an infrustrable impulse to the good if he is to persevere. To this we say that the doctrine of Scripture from which we have drawn our explanation of the gift of final perseverance refers to the grace given to men in the present order. And while that doctrine clearly teaches the certainty and the firmness of the divine intention to bring the justified to heaven and the fullness of the objective power of grace to effect this, it also teaches the frightening ability men continue to have in this life to reject this grace and divine intention and to become reprobate.

CHAPTER SIX

God's Sovereignty and Man's Freedom

THE HARMONY taught by Scripture and tradition to exist between God and free will refers not only to the relation between grace and free will, but also to that between the divine plan and free will. In the first part of this study we presented what seems to us to be the teaching of Scripture and tradition on this harmony. In the preceding chapter we advanced a philosophical analysis of God's causality of the creature's free will act for the purpose of explaining to some extent and defending this harmony as it refers to grace and free will. In the present chapter we shall advance a philosophical analysis of God's providence, knowledge, and will in their relation to free will to help to explain and defend the harmony we found expressed in Scripture and tradition between God's plan for the salvation of the free creature and the acts of the free creature.

We shall not, then, in this chapter attempt to show once more what Scripture and tradition do teach on this matter. We have already seen that for exegetical reasons both Banez and Molina understood God's predestination to be an absolute divine intention for the salvation of the individual. In the dilemma this posed Banez held that predestination was the first of God's intentions for the one to be saved, while Molina held that it was the last. The former accordingly held that God predestined the individual antecedent to his foreknowledge of his merits, while the latter held that God predestined him only consequent upon foreknowledge of his merits. We have already shown in our analysis of Scripture and tradition that in our opinion the dilemma that is at the origin of this divergence between Thomists and Molinists

217

is not necessitated by the doctrine of revelation. For reasons previously advanced it seems to us that the predestination taught by St. Paul is one that is conditioned on man's fidelity to God in this life and thus one that can be frustrated by man's bad will. Hence, we can say both that God's predestination is antecedent to man's merits and that God does not have an absolute unconditioned intention for the salvation of the individual while he is still in this life. The reasons from Scripture and tradition on which our opinion is based have already been presented and will be taken as the basis for what follows in this chapter.

What we have already written, however, does not adequately explain or defend the harmony between God's will in the order of grace and man's free will. By the philosophical analyses they presented, Banez and Molina seem to call into question our interpretation of the harmony expressed by Scripture. They do this, not simply through their philosophical explanations of God's causality of the free will act, which have been examined in the preceding chapter, but also through their opinions on the relation between the uncreated source of God's created causality and the free will act of the creature. Their explanations of the infallibility of divine providence, the divine foreknowledge of the created free will act, and the efficacy of the divine will seem to present philosophical difficulties to our understanding of predestination as a conditioned divine intention. Thus, to defend our understanding of predestination, we must see whether, in fact, natural, philosophical considerations invalidate it. Moreover, predestination is included within God's providence for the rational creature; and so to understand the supernatural mystery to some extent, one must make an analysis of providence in the natural order and of God's will and knowledge that providence involves, all in their relation to the free act of the creature. We are restricting ourselves to the considerations about these matters that are necessary to show the nature of the harmony that exists between God and free will, and we in no way intend to give an exhaustive treatment of any one of them. With this intention we shall analyze successively the relation of God's will to the created free act, the relation of God's infallible knowledge to the created free act, and the relation of God's providence to the movement of man to his perfection. At appropriate places we shall show the relevance of these philosophical analyses to the supernatural mystery that is our central concern.

1. *The Divine Will and the Creature's Free Will Act*

TEACHING COMMONLY ACCEPTED AND THE PROBLEM.—As a basis for our analysis of the natural relation between God's will act and that of the free creature, we must recall the relevant truths that all theologians accept. In himself God is infinite, and thus he is a personal being[1] endowed with intellect and will of unmeasured perfection, and possessed of supreme happiness that is incapable of intrinsic addition or subtraction.[2] Whatever being exists outside of God is caused by his intellect and will[3] by the causality through created acts which we described in the preceding chapter, and exists as a participation in his being. Since God has need of nothing outside himself for his perfection and happiness, his will to create is wholly free.[4] And since this will to create is a will to communicate a share of his goodness and perfection to creatures, it is properly speaking an act of divine love. All creatures, then, have the perfection and the measure of perfection they do have as a result of God's love and the measure of His love for them. One creature is better than another because it is loved more than another.[5] The ultimate purpose of God's will in creating is neither a divine need to be fulfilled (since his inner perfection is infinite) nor the created good loved for its own sake (since this is infinitely below him). Rather the uncreated divine goodness is the ultimate purpose in creating,[6] as the object of the love of friendship is the purpose of action. God creates to express the value of his infinite goodness and his love of this goodness. So all

---

[1] See *ST*, 1.29.3.

[2] See *ibid.*, 1.26.1–4.

[3] See *ibid.*, 1.19.4.

[4] See *ibid.*, 1.19.3. God's creative act can be called necessary only in a meaning that detracts in no way from the freedom of the act. Because of divine immutability, granted that God has freely chosen to create, he cannot on that supposition now do otherwise.

[5] See *ibid.*, 1.20.1–4.

[6] See the Church's expression of the purpose of God's creative act in the First Vatican Council, Ses. 3, c. 1. See also *De pot.*, 3.15. ad 14; *ST*, 1.19.2; 44.4.

good intrinsic to creation and particularly that good that is the fulfillment of the creature is caused by divine goodness through the mediation of God's will, and is a sign of his goodness and his love of his goodness.[7] Hence the intrinsic actualization or good of creatures is his purpose in creating and acting in the world, but it is a purpose ordained to the ultimate one of his own uncreated goodness.

As the love of the divine will and the exemplary causality of the divine intellect is the first cause of the goodness and nature of every creature, it is the first cause, too, of the morally good free will act and every aspect of it. Since the created act by which God causes is causally antecedent to that of the free creature, God's intellect and will as first cause premove the creature to its particular good act; his act does not follow the initiative of the creature or simply concur with its act. Moreover, this divine causality and the intention of God's will and intellect that is its source is one that bears intrinsically upon the created free act; it is not limited to the extrinsic determination of circumstances or the conferral simply of power to act rather than the free act itself, for the intrinsic created act within the free will that actualizes and determines it is a participation in the act of the divine will and intellect. Since these attributes of God's causality and hence of his divine intention relating to the free act of the creature were examined in the last Chapter, we need not delay on them here.

Concerning the relation between the divine will and the sinful act of the rational creature, all theologians agree that God in no way wills the sins of the free creature, but simply permits them. St. Thomas shows that this follows from the nature of moral evil and the object of the divine will. Evil is the privation of the good that should exist in a being or in an act. Death is the privation of the life of the being, and sin is the privation of the right order in human acts. Since the proper object of any appetite—whether it be natural, animal, or intellectual—is the good, no appetite can desire evil for its own sake. While nothing can desire evil for its own sake, it may desire some good, the acquisition of which demands the sacrifice of another good. For example, when the lion wants food, it desires secondarily the death of the deer; the man who seeks the pleasure of an immoral act wants incidentally the priva-

[7] See De pot., 3.15. ad 5.

tion of the right order in his acts. A desire of evil in this way, the only possible way, is an incidental or accidental desire of evil rather than a desire of it for its own sake or an essential desire of evil. And even such a desire of evil is only possible when the agent wants the good he is directly seeking more than that which he sacrifices in the evil attached to his pursuit of the good. This is true of the divine will, since it is essentially ordained to divine goodness, and so St. Thomas concludes this analysis by writing:

> God wants no good more than his own goodness, although he wants some particular good more than another particular good. Hence God wills in no way the *evil of sin* which is a privation of the order to the divine good. But he wills the *evil of a natural defect* or *the evil of punishment* by willing some good with which such an evil is conjoined. Thus by willing justice he wills punishment, and by willing to preserve the order of nature he wills certain things to be corrupted in accord with their natures.[8]

Since, then, God loves no good more than his own goodness, he cannot will sin even accidentally, since this is a privation of the right order to his goodness. Some have thought that God does will sin to exist, since it results in a greater perfection of the universe; the Romans' persecutions of the Christians led to the patience of martyrs. But this does not show that God willed this sin of the Romans even accidentally; it simply shows that he is so powerful that he can make their sin serve his own purpose. God does not will the sin of man in any way. But as his governance of the world shows, he does not, as he could, prevent sin from taking place. Hence, he permits or tolerates sin in the world.[9]

The question central to the problem of the nature of the harmony between God's will and the free acts of the created will can now be posed. Granted that the particular good free act of the creature is due as to its first cause to an intention of the divine will which in its desire that the creature perform this particular act both precedes the act of the creature and intrinsically and causally affects the free power and act itself, is this divine intention as antecedent to the good free act of the creature frustrable? Is it in its condition as antecedent frustrable by the resistance of the created free will or is it infallibly effective of its result, the

---

[8] *ST*, 1.19.9. See also *De pot.*, 6.1. ad 8.
[9] See *ST*, 1.19.9, ad 1; ad 2; ad 3,

good act of the creature that follows? Note that when we ask whether God's antecedent intention is frustrable or not, we refer simply to its relation to the particular good free act of the creature, and not to its relation to the larger purpose to which God ordains that particular created act. A similar question can be asked of the morally evil act in the natural order. This is only permitted by God, as all theologians agree, and not willed by him. But what is the nature of this permission in its condition as antecedent to the sinful act that takes place in history? Is it such that, antecedent to its actual occurrence, the particular sinful act in history is absolutely certain to occur? Or is it such that, antecedent to the actual occurrence of the sinful act, there is no basis for certainty that it will occur? In this question we restrict ourselves to the nature of God's permission of the first formal sin of a particular rational creature. If the creature has already sinned seriously against God, God can in justice withdraw his sustaining power from the creature in punishment for the previous sin and thus allow him to fall into further sins; if he does not, it is simply due to his divine mercy. Theologians generally are agreed on this; the critical problem is the nature of God's permission of the first sin of the rational creature.

Before we present our own answer to these two critical questions, we shall recall the opinions of Banez and Molina. As we saw in the first chapter, they are in essential agreement in their answers to these questions, though for different reasons. Both held that the natural good free act is due to the divine will in such a way that, antecedent to the free choice of the creature in time, the divine will's intention that the act take place is infallibly efficacious.[10] Their difference was on the nature of this efficacy; their philosophies agree in holding the fact of this efficacy. We have shown in the first chapter the reasons that motivated such a conclusion, so here we need only recall the main ones. Banez thought that, since the choice of the created will was a movement from potency to act, it must be preceded by a physically predetermining premotion which by a priority of nature determined the act of the will. The first source of such a created causality is a divine intention that is also effective antecedent to the act of the

[10] See ch. 1, pp. 33 ff.

created will. Moreover, he thought that the whole goodness of the free created act could not be attributed to God as its first cause unless the act were due to an antecedently effective divine intention. Also the decree of the divine will was for Banez the medium by which God has eternal knowledge of the free act of the creature; he held, therefore, that it must be intrinsically effective of itself to give certain knowledge of the free created act.[11] Molina's explanation of God's causality and knowledge differed from this, but he arrived at this conclusion he held in common with Banez from different premises. Granted his interpretation of God's causality of the free act and his theory of *scientia media*, God has knowledge of what the free will would do given any circumstances in which it could be placed, and he has this knowledge before he actually determines the particular circumstances in which to place the individual. The intention of the divine will by which God places the free creature in the circumstances he knows will eventuate in its good act is in its condition as antecedent to the actual choice of the created will in time infallibly effective in bringing about the good act. It is extrinsically effective because of the fact that God's intention follows *scientia media*, but it is infallibly effective.[12] Other considerations have seemed to support this philosophical conclusion of Banez and Molina and have been adduced at various times. For example, God's omnipotence, his immutability, the eternal and causal antecedence of his will act to that of the creature, and the infallible efficacy of his providence—all have seemed to necessitate such a conclusion.

Banez and Molina explain God's permission of the first sin of a particular rational creature in an analogous manner. They hold that God's permission of the first sin of a rational creature is such that, antecedent to the actual free choice of the creature in time, it is certain he will sin. Before the actual sin that occurs, God's permission is such that the sin is certain to follow. Such a permission is necessary in Banez's opinion to explain how God has infallibly certain knowledge of the future free sinful act of the creature, and he is explicit in holding that the first sin of the rational creature is preceded by a divine permission in his sense.[13]

[11] See ch. 1, pp. 5 ff.
[12] See ch. 1, pp. 24 ff. and footnote 53.
[13] See ch. 1, footnotes 16–18, 32–33.

Moreover, this is implied as the converse of his doctrine that the good act of the rational creature must be preceded by an infallibly effective divine intention if it is to take place. Hence, the same or similar considerations motivated his explanation of the one and the other. He defended his explanation against attacks upon it by affirming that God has no obligation to prevent all sins or to sustain the free creature in the practice of the moral good. Moreover, he held that in the order of the execution of God's providence the bad will of the free creature preceded God's denial of the help to sustain it in good.[14] Molina's doctrine of God's intention following *scientia media* implies that the creature's sinful act is preceded by a divine permission in the sense of a choice of circumstances that give adequate helps to avoid the sin, but which in fact God knows will be followed by the sin. Molina held that God's permission of the first sin of the rational creature in this sense was not due to any previous sin on the part of the creature.[15] The responsibility for the sin is completely the creature's and not God's, since it is due to the self-determination of the creature foreseen in *scientia media*. God's part is simply the determination of the circumstances.

Our opinion is that the divine intention or desire that a particular good free act of the rational creature in the natural order take place is not infallibly effective of this particular act or infrustrable antecedent to the cooperation of the free will of the creature. It is conditioned, and thus can be rejected by the creature. We also think that God's permission of the first sin of a rational creature in the natural order is that contained within a frustrable intention that the creature do good, and is not such that it is certain to be followed by the sin of the creature. We shall present our reasons for this opinion and try to answer difficulties that may be raised against them. Later we shall use this philosophical analysis we give here to explain to some extent the message of revelation concerning God's will in its relation to the morally good act or sinful act in the order of grace. And we shall conclude by considering some arguments from fittingness that have been used in this matter.

[14] See ch. 1, footnote 33.
[15] See ch. 1, pp. 27–28.

GOD'S WILL AS ANTECEDENT TO THE GOOD FREE WILL ACT IN HISTORY.—How can we know whether the divine intention or desire by which the individual good free act of the creature in the natural order is anticipated is frustrable or infrustrable? We cannot know it by the fact that the good act follows at times and does not follow at other times, because we are asking this question specifically of the good act that does in fact take place. And we are asking, not whether the created causality, but whether the uncreated causality or intention of the divine will that is the first cause of the created free act is frustrable or not antecedent to the co-operation of the free will. It seems that our knowledge of the nature of this uncreated divine intention is gained as our knowledge of other divine attributes is gained, namely, through the created effects of God. Thus from the nature of the act of the free will and the created cause that brings it about, we can induce the nature of God's antecedent divine intention that it take place, unless such an induction would be incompatible with God's perfection. This is based on the fact that the divine will in its causality of creatures and their acts is guided by divine wisdom. In its desire of the act of a creature, the divine will is not autonomous, unrelated to, or opposed to the order of divine wisdom. It is specified by divine wisdom so that it desires that order of things that is determined by divine wisdom. And we know the order of things that divine wisdom has established in the world through the things of the world. The natures of creatures and thus the manner of acting proper to various creatures is the result of the first causality of the divine mind, and hence these natures show the order that is established by divine wisdom and imposed by it upon the world and upon the divine will to direct its causality of the things of the world. Hence the activity of creatures shows us, not only the nature of the created causality that brings it about, but the nature of the uncreated causality of the divine will that is its source.

In the last chapter, we examined the nature of the rational appetite or will of the creature, the manner of acting proper to it in this life, and the created causality by which God brings about its act. It is a power the proper object of which is the good presented to it by the intellect. Its act is an *actus perfecti* or a self-movement and self-determination in virtue of the causality exercised upon it by its object. And in this life the good presented to it does not and does not appear to satisfy its desire completely. So we found that under God's causality that is exercised through the object presented to it, the will is completely free to act or not to act. That is, antecedent to its act the premovement and predetermination that God exercises upon it through its object is frustrable, conditioned, and can be rejected. The good free act that takes place is anticipated by a causal influence of the good that is not antecedently infallibly effective in eliciting the act. From this it would seem that the desire or intention of the divine will that is the source of the good act of the creature through the causal influence of the good is also frustrable, conditioned, and subject to rejection by the will of the creature if it so desires. It seems, in other words, that it is not antecedently infallibly effective or infrustrable as it is related to the particular free good act of the rational creature.

It also seems to us that such is the philosophical teaching of St. Thomas. There are, it is true, some texts that seem opposed to such an opinion. For example, when we examined St. Thomas' doctrine in our study of tradition, we saw that he thought that predestination was an absolute divine intention for the salvation of the individual rational creature. But St. Thomas adopted such a position because of his interpretation of revelation, and not because of his philosophical principles. Moreover, he said at least once that the effect of such a predestination was gained "from the concurrence of many causes that are contingent and able to fail in gaining their effect."[16] It is difficult for us to see how he could say this if he thought that philosophical principles demanded that the divine intention antecedent to any particular good act of the free creature must be infallibly effective of that particular act. Another statement that may seem opposed to our opinion is his teaching that if God moves the free creature to act, it is impossible that the creature not act.[17] This, however, is a conditional statement and does not distinguish God's premovement from his simultaneous concurrence with the created free act, so it does not

[16] *De ver.*, 6.3. ad 3. See above, ch. 4, pp. 115 f.
[17] See *ST*, 1–2, 10.4. ad 3; 112.3; *De ver.*, 2.12. ad 1; ad 2.

prove or indicate that the good free act of the creature is, according to the order God has established, anticipated by an infrustrable divine intention. St. Thomas also writes that God wants some effects to occur necessarily and for these fits necessary causes, and he wants some to take place contingently and for these adapts contingent causes.[18] But this leaves unanswered the question whether God in his ordinary providence wants individual good free acts of the rational creature to exist by a will that is antecedently infallibly effective or not.

The following passage of St. Thomas is more difficult to explain.

> God indeed moves the will immutably because of the efficacy of his moving power which cannot fail. But because of the nature of the will that is moved, which is related indifferently to different objects, necessity is not induced but liberty remains. So also divine providence operates infallibly in all things; and yet effects proceed from contingent causes in a contingent way, since God moves all things proportionately, each according to its own manner.[19]

This is written in answer to the objection that since movement by an extrinsic principle results in the inner necessity of the appetitive acts of animals, God's movement of the rational appetite results in the inner necessity of its acts. In the first part of his answer, St. Thomas shows that, while the animal's appetitive act follows a particular form that necessitates it, man's rational appetite is related indifferently to different objects, so his act is not necessitated. But in the same answer St. Thomas asserts that God preserves his divine attributes when he moves man's will. God "moves the will immutably because of the efficacy of his moving power which cannot fail"; and "divine providence operates infallibly in all things." Does this mean for St. Thomas that the good acts of free creatures are anticipated by a divine will and causality that could not in fact be resisted by the will of the creature? If we had only this passage, it would appear that this is what he means by the efficacy of God's power that cannot fail and the infallibility of divine providence. But even so our interpretation to this effect would be a deduction from his teaching, and perhaps it would not be a necessary deduction, since these divine perfec-

---

[18] See *ST*, 1.19.8; 22.4.
[19] *De malo*, 6. art. un., ad 3.

tions can, it seems, be preserved, even though the human will rejects an antecedent divine movement to the good.

There are, in fact, other statements of St. Thomas that more explicitly treat the question we are studying and that seem to correct the impression one may receive from some of the texts indicated above. These statements are found particularly in his various treatments of the question of God's knowledge of the free acts of the creature. We will examine in the next section St. Thomas' explanation of this knowledge; here we restrict ourselves to what is immediately relevant to our present question. In his first treatment of God's knowledge of free created acts, St. Thomas recalled the objection forwarded by some that God, who causes man's acts, is a necessary cause, and as a result man's acts are also necessary and not contingent. His answer is that when an act is caused by a first cause that is necessary and by an immediate cause that is contingent, the act is contingent, since the immediate cause can defect from the movement of the first. Although the sun is a necessary cause, a tree exposed to its light may not flower owing to some defect within it. In applying this to God and free will, he states that it can be that the created contingent cause will not act under the antecedent influence of God who is the first and necessary cause, since the will can defect or fall short of God's causality. And so he concludes that "the knowledge of God cannot exist together with the defection of the second cause. For it cannot be that at the same time God knows this man will run and this man will fail to run. And this is because of the certainty of his knowledge and *not because of his causality.*"[20] St. Thomas teaches here that it is not the causality of God that accounts for the infallibility of his knowledge of a contingent or free created act, for the second free cause can fail to act even when the first and necessary cause has exerted its influence upon it. If St. Thomas had thought that the good act of the created free will was anticipated by a divine intention or causality that was antecedently infallibly effective of this particular act, it seems to us that he would have affirmed, and not denied, that God's causality was the reason for the infallibility of his knowledge of the free created act. For indeed, if the divine intention is infallibly effective of this particular created act causally

[20] 1 *Sent.,* 38.1.5.

228

antecedent to the free choice of the free created will, it is of itself a medium of infallible knowledge. It is very difficult to draw any other conclusion from St. Thomas' denial that it is such a medium than that he did not think the divine intention and causality were infallibly effective of the particular free act antecedent to the choice of the free will.

What, then, does he mean when he writes that the first cause cannot fail to achieve its effect? It seems to us that he means that it is some larger divine purpose such as the divine glory, and not the particular free good act of the creature that takes place in time, that God wants with an antecedent infallible efficacy. Whether the free creature cooperates with God's providence or not, his purpose will be gained; and if the particular good free act fails to take place, this failure is due, not to the failure of God's intention or causality, but to that of the creature. Thus there is a compatibility between the unfailing power of God and the failure of the free act that he antecedently wants to occur. St. Thomas writes:

> . . . although the first cause exerts a more powerful influence than the second, still the effect is not completed unless the operation of the second cause come about. And hence if there is a possibility of failing in the second cause, there is also the same possibility of failing in the effect, although the first cause cannot fail . . .[21]

Therefore it seems to us that the teaching of St. Thomas is in agreement with the opinion we have presented. We find it very difficult to harmonize the statements we have just quoted from St. Thomas and others like them with the teaching of either Banez or Molina on this matter. Moreover, since their explanations of the relation of the intention of the divine will to the free act of the creature are dependent upon their understanding of the nature of the free act and the way that it is caused, we find the same difficulties against the former as we did against the latter in the preceding chapter.

God's Permission of the First Formal Sin of a Rational Creature.—The second question that we have to answer concerns

[21] De ver., 2.14. ad 5. See also ibid., ad 3; 2.12.c. and ad 1; ad 2; CG, 1.67; ST, 1.14.13. ad 1.

the nature of God's permission of the first formal sin of the rational creature in the natural order. When such a sin occurs in time, it has been preceded by a divine permission; for unless God permitted it, it could not take place. But what is the nature of this permission as antecedent to the free act of the creature? Is it one that, as antecedent to the free choice of the creature in time, can be a basis for certain divine knowledge that the creature will sin in this particular act? Is it of such a nature because the divine permission involves either a determination of circumstances in which God knows by *scientia media* that the creature would sin or a lack of the intrinsic sustaining divine help necessary for the creature to do good? Or is it, on the other hand, simply the permission involved in the frustrable character of the antecedent divine intention that the creature act in accord with the moral good as we have described it above? In our opinion it is the latter. The reason for this opinion is the nature of sin. Sin, as we have seen, is the privation of the right order of human acts; and the right order of human acts is that to which God has ordained man through the nature that he has given him. It is of the nature of man to be ordained to God as his last end and to achieve that end through free acts in accord with the moral norm. To elicit the morally good act, man has an absolute need of God's premoving divine intention and causality, as we have seen; and without this premovement to the good it is absolutely impossible for man to elicit such an act. This condition of man is the effect of the divine wisdom which is the source of the nature of creatures and the manner of their activity. Thus it seems that God's will is to give to man what is necessary to achieve the end to which God ordains him, and hence the premovement to the good without which man cannot do what is morally good.

It seems, moreover, that God would never lack an intention to give this premovement to the good to the rational creature in the natural order antecedent to its first sin, and in such a way that formal sin would result. For divine wisdom has ordained man to act in accord with the moral norm, and "it is impossible for God to will save what is contained in the plan of his wisdom. This indeed is like the law of justice according to which his will is right and just."[22] Since divine wisdom has given to the rational

[22] *ST*, 1.21. ad 2.

creature the nature that demands a premovement to the good if it is to avoid formal sin, such a premovement and the divine intention that is its source is owed to the creature, for "this is owed to each thing, that is ordained to it according to the order of divine wisdom."[23] It is not improper for God to owe the creature such help since the creature does not by this have a claim upon him of which God himself is not the ultimate source and end. Such help is owed to the creature ultimately to achieve the end God has in creation, namely, the manifestation of his divine goodness; and God has freely taken this obligation upon himself by the fact of creation. Since God has, therefore, an obligation to the creature and more properly to himself to give the premovement necessary to avoid formal sin, for him, antecedent to the creature's rejection of his help, not to give this would be, it seems, to act contrary to his own wisdom and justice. And since such a lack of an intention to help the creature would be a privation of the order of his justice, the sin of the creature would be imputed to God. For these reasons we cannot think that in the natural order the divine intention that the creature perform the good act and the premovement to the good necessary for the creature to avoid formal sin are ever lacking before the creature's resistance to God's will. The first formal sin of the creature is permitted by God, in our opinion, only in the sense that the antecedent divine intention and premovement to the good free act can be frustrated by the free will of the creature and thus not achieve their purpose.

In our opinion this is the philosophical doctrine of St. Thomas. It is true, as we pointed out when showing St. Thomas' place in tradition,[24] that because of his interpretatiaon of revelation he understood predestination to be an absolute divine intention antecedent to God's foreknowledge of man's merits. As a result of this he taught that God's reprobation of man was not ultimately because of man's sins. And he did not always teach that man's personal sin was the reason for God's refusal of grace. But these views are due to his interpretation of Scripture and of St. Augustine, and not to his philosophical analysis of the relation of created free acts to God's will. Hence, it does not seem to us that

[23] *Ibid.*, ad 3.
[24] See ch. pp. 115–121.

they can be used against the opinion we have presented above. And for the same reasons it does not seem to us that Banez's understanding of God's permission of the first sin of the rational creature can be identified with that of St. Thomas. Banez's conception of the nature of this permission applies to the natural order as well as to the order of grace, since it is dependent upon his understanding of the antecedent efficacy of God's causality and intention with reference to the free will act of the rational creature, and it is the means whereby he explains God's certain knowledge of the sinful acts of the rational creature. We need not delay further in pointing out what appear to us to be weaknesses in Banez's and Molina's explanations of God's permission of the sinful act of the creature. Let us now turn to answer certain objections that may be posed to our explanation. Objections related to the consequences of this explanation for the infallible divine knowledge of free created acts and the infallible efficacy of divine providence for the world in general will be treated later.

SOME DIFFICULTIES CONSIDERED.—In the first place, the objection may be raised that God's will that a particular free act of the creature take place is eternal, and so his causality which is identified with the act of his will precedes that of the free created will. Hence, because of God's eternity, what the act of the creature will be is determined before the creature itself acts. To this we answer that time differs from eternity as the succession of the acts of material beings from the single infinite act of God.[25] Thus the fact that God's causality of the free created act is eternal, while that of the creature is temporal, does not mean that God's act takes place before that of the creature. The one act of God is of a different order from the acts of creatures and is present to all that he causes, as the soul is of a different nature from the body and is present throughout it. So the fact that God's act is eternal does not demand that his causality be infallibly effective and infrustrable antecedent to the act of the creature.

It may be said that God's divine intention that an act of the created will take place is the first cause of this act and hence has a causal antecedence to it. Moreover, God's intention and causality

[25] See *ST*, 1.10.1 and 2.

is omnipotent as well as antecedent; hence it seems that it is infrustrable in its condition as antecedent to the act of the creature. To this we answer that, of course, if God wishes his antecedent intention and causality to be infrustrable, it can be resisted by no created will. But the omnipotence of God does not mean that he is unable to present to the will of the creature an antecedent causality which the creature can frustrate or resist. God's omnipotence in his antecedent intention and causality is exercised in accord with the order established by his divine wisdom, which we have examined above. Hence God's intention that the rational creature act in accord with the moral norm can be resisted by the creature. If God, in a particular case, draws a particular rational creature to a good free act by an intention and causality that is antecedently infrustrable, he is acting beyond the order he has established, for a special good he wishes to gain in this particular case. Such an incident, however, does not prove that God's ordinary intention or causality of the free created act was antecedently infrustrable. It simply proves that this particular incident went beyond God's ordinary providence.

St. Thomas teaches, it may be argued, that God wants some events to take place contingently, and so he adapts contingent causes for them. His will is so effective that it causes, not only the free act, but the freedom of the act. And in the same passage he states that "no defect of the second cause can prevent the will of God from producing its effect."[26] To this we say that St. Thomas' interest in this passage is to give the *first* cause of the contingency of created free acts. The first cause is not the contingent character or the created cause since, if it were, the contingency of its acts would not be the result of the divine intention and will; it is God who is first cause of the very contingency or freedom of men's free acts. Man's freedom is a participation in God's love. Moreover, the defect of the contingent cause cannot prevent God from achieving what he wants. So the first cause is the efficacy of the divine will that wants some things to occur contingently and hence makes contingent created causes for these effects, and brings about these effects contingently. Does this mean that antecedent to the creature's act God wants it to come

[26] *ST*, 1.19.8.

about with infallible efficacy, but in accord with its freedom? It does not appear to us to mean this, for this is another question which St. Thomas does not treat here. He here gives the first cause of the contingency of created free acts. The question whether, in fact, God causes such acts by an antecedently infallibly effective divine decree and causality depends upon the order of wisdom established by God. This order, as we have shown, indicates that God leaves the rational creature in this life free to reject his antecedent intention or desire that it act in accord with the moral norm.

It would appear to some, however, that an antecedent conditioned divine intention that the free creature do well is incompatible with the divine omnipotence, because such a divine intention leaves the creature free to escape from the divine power. To this we say with St. Thomas that, while a thing can escape from a particular cause, it cannot escape from a universal cause that embraces all particular causes.

> Since therefore the will of God is the universal cause of all things, it is impossible that the divine will not achieve its effect. Hence what seems to withdraw from the divine will in one order falls back into it in another. For example, the sinner who withdraws from the divine will as far as it lies within him by sinning falls under the order of the divine will when he is punished by his justice.[27]

The sinner, then, does not escape the divine power or prevent the divine will from being fulfilled save in a particular order, and so God's will is always fulfilled either through his antecedent will that the free creature do well and thus participate in God's goodness or through his consequent will that the sinner be punished and so manifest God's holiness and justice.

But it seems, it may be said, that such an antecedent will that is conditioned upon that of the free creature is opposed to the immutability of God and his will, since it would mean that God changes his will upon a change of the creature's will. To this we answer that it is one thing for God to change his will and it is another for him to desire a change in creatures.[28] Only the former

27 ST, 1.19.6. See in the same sense ibid., ad 3; ST, 1.103.7 and 8.
28 See ST, 1.19.7.

is contrary to immutability, for God can desire with an immutable will that now one thing occur and later its contrary. In his desire of the manifestation of his perfection, he may antecedently want a man to do what is morally good and then, consequent upon the man's resistance to God's help, that he not have the aid necessary to do what is morally good. What is a fitting means to gain God's glory in the one case may not be in the second. Hence, the conditioned antecedent divine intention we speak of does not imply a change in the divine will, but a divine will that there be a change in the creature if it does not submit itself to the divine will's desire for its good.

God, an objector may continue, is the author of all good; and it is due to him that one man is better than another. Thus if two men face the same temptation and one overcomes it while the other does not, the conquest by the one can only be reduced to God's greater love for him than for the other if the divine intention that preceded the act was infallibly effective. For if in both cases the antecedent divine intention were the same, then God would not have loved one more than the other, and the conquest by the one would not be due to a greater divine love. To this we say that the antecedent love and help God gives to both may be of the same degree. But while the one loses this help through his resistance, the other through God's help overcomes the temptation. And so he overcomes through a greater divine help than that possessed by the other, for he has God's concomitant aid as well as his prevenient aid, and not because he had a greater prevenient aid than the one who failed.

GOD'S WILL AND MAN'S ACT IN THE ORDER OF GRACE.—The analysis we have presented of the relation between the divine will and the morally good or sinful act of the free creature has great relevance to the parallel relation in the order of grace. Concerning the supernatural mystery, we found in Scripture and tradition that man's salutary act was a free gift of God's love to him and in no way a basis for pride, since there was nothing in it that was not given to him by God. Moreover, in examples from the Old and New Testaments, such as God's will of Abraham's obedience and the Christian's fidelity, we found that God's antecedent will of the

235

salutary act was, according to his usual providence, not infallibly effective or infrustrable, but rather conditioned upon the cooperation of the free creature. And finally in the examples of God's permission of the sins of Adam, of Pharaoh in refusing to release the Jews from Egypt, of the Jews' rejection of Christ, and of the infidelity of Christians we saw that the total initiative in sin was man's and not God's, and that God did not desert man unless he had already been deserted by man. It seems to us that the natural analysis we have presented shows that no argument from the natural relation of God's will to the act of the free creature can be advanced to disprove our understanding of Scripture and tradition. In fact, it seems to us that the natural analysis we have presented helps to explain the revealed mystery of God's desire that man believe and perform the other acts of the order of grace. What is true in the natural order in this matter is true in the supernatural order unless the norms of revelation indicate otherwise, as what is true of human nature is true of the human nature of Christ, so the natural analysis we have presented helps us to understand how God's will is related to man's salutary act or omission of it.

What is true of man's dependence upon God for his naturally good act is true of his dependence for his salutary act. The latter, like the former, results from God's love freely given and is the measure of God's love upon which man wholly depends. In fact, because of its supernatural character, the salutary act manifests a greater freedom of the divine will, a greater love, and a greater dependence on the part of the creature. The freedom in God's will that the creature have such a good is over and beyond the freedom of God's creative act, since the supernatural is not owed to man's nature. The greater love that is the source of the salutary act is evident in the fact that by it God ordains man to an end that transcends what he can achieve by his nature, and it is even more evident when it is given to mankind turned away from God by original and personal sin. Also, since such an act transcends man's natural ability and the power of his nature wounded by original sin, man depends upon God's power in eliciting it even more than he does in eliciting a natural act.

What we have said of the antecedently frustrable character of

God's will of the naturally good act of the free creature explains to some extent the conditioned divine will of man's salutary acts expressed by Scripture and tradition. In the supernatural, as in the natural order, God may ordain a person to a more perfect act than another or he may ordain one more forcefully than another to a good act, but the order established by his wisdom is such that his antecedent will that the creature perform the act is frustrable. He acts beyond this economy at times in the order of grace, as is apparent in Christ, in the Blessed Virgin to the extent that she was confirmed in grace, in God's intention that Peter's faith not fail, and in those saints who have been confirmed in grace during part of their lives. But in these cases God acts beyond the order established by his wisdom as his normal providence. As miracles are divine acts beyond the order God has established in creation and do not establish or change God's normal providence, so too in the cases we have mentioned God acts beyond the order he has established for mankind generally for the purpose of achieving some special good.

Finally, the analysis we have given of God's permission of man's first formal sin in the natural order helps us to some extent to understand the nature of his permission of an individual's first formal sin in the order of grace. It does not seem that God's permission of the sin of the angels who fell and of Adam's was antecedently certain to be followed by the sins that took place. Of course, God did not have to ordain all of the angels to heaven as a supernatural goal; he could have ordained some to a supernatural and others to a natural end. Thus he would not have sustained the latter in a movement to a supernatural goal, but in that case the fact that they did not ordain themselves to God with a supernatural love would not have been a sin, since it would not have been a privation of an order willed by God. Nor would it seem that the first formal sins of men in the order of fallen and redeemed humanity are preceded by a divine permission that is a negation of the prevenient grace necessary (as we explained in the preceding chapter) to avoid formal sin. It is with reference to fallen humanity that God has revealed the universality of his salvific will, and such a permission does not seem to us consistent with this universal salvific will. Moreover, we have seen that the Church teaches that the punishment due to original sin is the pain

237

of the loss of the beatific vision, while that due to personal sin is the pain of sense.[29] If God's permission of fallen man's first formal sin antecedent to his foreknowledge of that sin were an absence of a divine intention that man have the grace necessary to avoid it, and if the motive for this were original sin, it would seem that the pain of sense also is the punishment for original sin. For on this theory the pain of sense inevitably results from original sin through the medium of the formal actual sin that is permitted in this manner. Other matters pertinent to God's universal salvific will shall be treated in a later section, but from what we have said here it seems to us that God's permission of the first formal sin in the order of grace is only that permission that is implicit in the frustrable character of God's antecedent intention and grace moving man to a salutary act. The sin of man in the order of grace, as in that of nature, is wholly due to man's initiative, and it is in no way the result of God's intention not to sustain him in the practice of the moral good. Some men are more guilty than others in rejecting grace and the act to which it moves them, but in no case does God do more than will to permit or tolerate man's rejection of his antecedent grace before man has actually rejected it.

THE QUESTION OF FITTINGNESS.—In conclusion of this study of the relation of God's will to the act of the free creature in the natural and supernatural orders, we shall consider certain reasons that have been advanced to show that some order other than the one we have presented is more fitting to man's free act or to God's attributes. For example, it has been argued that it is more fitting for man's freedom that his self-determination within the free act be due to him as to its exclusive cause since it is this that is most distinctive of him as a free being. But to us the very reason advanced to support this opinion seems to demand that the self-determination of the free act be due to man only as its second cause and to God as its first cause, as we explained in the preceding chapter, since what is noblest in the act, more than any other aspect, must be due to God's causality. Man's self-movement and

[29] See ch. 4, footnote 27. See also G. Dyer, "Limbo: A Theological Evaluation," *Theological Studies*, 19 (1958), 32–49 where it is shown that recent theologians are unanimous in denying that infants who die unbaptized experience the pain of sense.

self-determination in his free act is a participation in God's own love of himself.

Others have argued that because of the very weakness and dependence of the free creature upon God, it is fitting that its good acts be anticipated by an infrustrable divine intention and causality, for this presents to him a greater help to avoid evil and do good. But to us it seems that the explanation we have advanced concerning the frustrable character of God's antecedent intention and causality more fittingly accounts for freedom as it is actually experienced in the world. Our experience, as well as the philosophical analysis of the will, shows how liable we are to fail even when we are anticipated by helps powerfully inclining us to do good. The order we have described is one that gives to man everything that is due to him in virtue of the nature God has given him. And it is a much greater gift to have been given the possibility of the achievement of the perfection of human nature than not to have received it, even though there is attached to human freedom the possibility, too, that man will reject God's antecedent intention for his perfection. Moreover, it is a far greater thing to have received the gift of grace than not to have received it, even though grace leaves man free to reject its antecedent movement to eternal beatitude and the salutary acts that merit it.

Some have thought that it would be unfittting for the divine transcendence and dignity to call man to what is good through an antecedent divine intention and movement which man has it in his power to reject since this would make the divine dignity subject to man's choice. To this we answer that that is exactly what sin is, a dishonor and insult offered to God as far as it lies in the power of the creature to do so; but God has created the free creature and has tolerated this possibility and reality of sin. In fact, for his wisdom to have established an order in which the antecedent divine desire that the free creature submit to him is frustrable shows clearly that the ultimate intention of God in his activity with man is not to gain man's submission. God's ultimate purpose is simply to give man a share in his divine goodness out of his divine benevolence and love for his uncreated divine perfection. Whether man accepts or rejects God's antecedent desire, he cannot really add to or diminish the ultimate purpose of God in creation, since the ultimate glory which God's activity in creation gives to him is contained within that divine act itself and the love for the divine goodness and the benevolence to creatures it manifests. Hence, man's rejection of the divine benevolence does not really detract from the divine transcendence or dignity.

Some have thought that it was fitting to divine justice for God to permit some men to sin in the sense of not wanting for them their natural or supernatural perfection antecedent to his foreknowledge of their sins, for creation should manifest the justice of God as well as his mercy. To us it seems that such a permission in the natural order would manifest, not the justice of God, but his injustice, since in our opinion the antecedent divine help necessary to avoid formal sin is owed to the rational creature. And such a permission means that God does not want to give this antecedent help to some creatures. Moreover, it seems to us that such a permission of formal sin in the order of grace, once God has manifested the universality of his salvific will, is incompatible with the expressed divine intention. We think it fitting that, on the understanding of God's permission of sin as we have explained it, those who reject God's antecedent help and sin be punished and thus manifest divine justice. We know from Scripture that if men do not repent their sins they experience this punishment partially in this life through a growing blindness to what is for their welfare and a growing moral hardness, but also that this life is a period of God's patience that holds out to men till death the means of repentance. Only in the next life will unrepented sin merit its final reward, and it is fitting that those who deliberately refused to glorify God's mercy glorify his justice through punishment.

Some have thought that it was not fitting to God's power that men be able to frustrate his desire that they do good. We know that some early Christians were scandalized by the fact that the Jews rejected Christ, and in turn were rejected by God, for this seemed to indicate a weakness in God and an inability to bring his desires to completion. But, as St. John and St. Paul explained, God's toleration of this rejection of Christ by the Jews was not due to God's weakness and did not obstruct the fulfillment of his ultimate goal. God's toleration of their disbelief showed clearly that he was not in need of their cooperation to gain either his purpose in the world or his own glory. The fact that they did not believe did not mean that they escaped God's power, for the sufferings they merited as a result proved that they were still in God's power and that they glorified his justice now that they had rejected his mercy. Moreover, their rejection did not prevent the fulfillment of God's intention in making the Jews his chosen people, namely, the extension of his kingdom throughout the world, for this was fulfilled essentially in Christ, and other instruments were raised up to spread Christ's message throughout the world. In fact, as St. Paul showed, God used the very resistance of the Jews to spread Christ's message more effectively throughout the world. For God to achieve his purposes in the world, within those who cooperate with him and in spite of the opposition of those who resist him, by a divine intention and causality that can be resisted by the individual seems to manifest the divine power in a more striking way than the use in God's common providence of an infrustrable divine intention and causality.

It has seemed to some more in accord with divine mercy that God's antecedent desire that man do good, and his grace by which it is brought about, be infrustrable. But since such a view of God's common providence is associated with the interpretation of his permission of sin as a lack of help to do good, it seems to us that this view reduces man's good acts to God's mercy in such a way that it reduces his sins to God's lack of mercy. Moreover we think that the explanation we have given of God's antecedent intention and grace shows clearly that the motive of God's gifts is his mercy. It seems to be a decisive proof of God's mercy that his grace is extended to men within the uncertainty of their response and the possibility that they will reject it. This seems to show that God is liberal and merciful out of his own divine generosity, and not out of an expectation of man's return of his love.

Finally, it has seemed to many that it is not fitting for God to permit evil, and particularly the evil of sin, if he can avoid it. If he can't avoid it, he is not omnipotent, if he can and does not, he is not the supreme good. To this we answer that the problem of evil is a great mystery which we in no way intend to treat at length here, so we shall restrict ourselves to several considerations that indicate there is nothing unfitting to God in his permission of sin as we have explained it. By the very fact that, out of love for his divine goodness and his desire to communicate a share of it, God creates, beings that are limited and defectible come into existence. Created being is of metaphysical necessity limited, since it depends on another for its being; but this limitation is an indication of the measure of the creature and not of God's omnipotence; and it is not an evil, for it is not a privation of being the creature should have. Like limitation, defectibility, in the sense of an intrinsic ability to fall into evils in the physical and moral orders, and actual evils in the physical order follow the nature of created and material being. It is the nature of things lower than man to sacrifice their being for man; it is the nature of man to die; and it is his nature on this earth to be able to turn away from God by free choice. The *physical evils* man must endure involve the sacrifice of immeasurably lesser goods than the good for the sake of which he must sacrifice them, namely, the acquisition of God and God himself, so it is not unfitting for God to ordain man to himself in a condition where he must sacrifice such goods to attain him. In fact, such a condition is the result in history of original sin, but such a condition can be the occasion for an ultimately greater perfection than man would have otherwise reached. It is true that this does not seem to justify all physical evil, since some, such as infants, are not in a condition to gain this benefit from such evils. However, even here we can say that if the infant is baptized, the possession of God to which he is ordained makes it far better for it to have life, even one that involves suffering, than not to have it. We do not know adequately the condition of the unbaptized infant in the next life to assert that there is no value for it in the life and sufferings it received. Much mystery remains when this is said, but this much seems to be true, namely, that one cannot say that the physical evils an individual suffers involve the sacrifice of his essential personal good without culpability on his own part, or that the personal good does not more than compensate for the physical evils the individual endures. Moreover, there is a greater good than that of the individual, the good of creation as a whole and the uncreated divine good, that adds further light to this mystery of suffering. And by faith we know that God would not allow an evil from which he could not draw a greater good.

In creating a being morally defectible, God accepted the possibility that some would sin; and he gave permission for this, not in the sense of a lack of his divine intention to sustain man in the practice of the moral good, but in the sense of allowing him to reject the antecedent divine intention and inclination to this good. Is it unfitting for God, then, to communicate this goodness of created being, as he has done, because some men will reject his antecedent intention for their perfection? Should the good that is given to such a vast number of created beings and the glory that is given to God not be given because some free creatures, in culpable rejection of the limited nature of their goodness, sin? The fact that some men will make a sinful use of created goods is, of course, in no way a reason for God not to create; for if it were, evil would overcome good through preventing the existence of the great good realized in the creation of the free creature and the glory God thereby gains. In fact, it is an indication of the transcendence of God and his mercy that he has created the world in the midst of the possibility of this evil, as the measure of the evils a man is willing to suffer for love of God and service of him is a sign of the measure of his sanctity.

2. God's Eternal Knowledge and the Creature's Free Acts

Another philosophical problem that has contributed to the differences among the various explanations of the relation of God's predestination and grace to free will, and that calls into question our account of this, is the problem of God's eternal knowledge of man's free acts. In this section we shall recall the problem through stating the differences between Banez's and Molina's solution to it, present the explanation of the harmony between God's knowledge and man's free act that seems to us to be in accord with St. Thomas' principles and to escape the difficulties of later theories, and answer some objections to the explanation we forward.

THE PROBLEM.—Here, as in other matters, the difference between Banez and Molina is only understandable in the light of the doctrine common to both. They agree with all Catholic theologians and with many others in their basic description of God's knowledge. God is endowed with the perfection of knowledge; the knowledge that his creatures enjoy and the spirituality of his

243

own nature demand that. Since God's knowledge has a perfection proportioned to that of his own being, its proper object must be no less than the divine essence itself. That essence and all it contains is understood by an intuitive, eternal, comprehensive vision, and known, not by successive divine acts, but by one simple act. Since God knows his own essence perfectly, he knows all the ways in which it can be imitated outside of himself. That is, he knows everything that is contained in his own power or in the power of his effects. This is a knowledge of all things possible, and it is called by St. Thomas a knowledge of *simple understanding* to distinguish it from a knowledge of things that will actually occur at some time, as actually occurring in time.

Knowledge of all things that actually occur in time must also be attributed to God since its lack would be a limitation of the divine perfection. This is called by St. Thomas the knowledge of *vision* (for the objects of our vision are things that exist in the world), and it embraces everything that occurs in creation, whether good or evil, important or unimportant, necessary or free. God knows everything that he causes. And since, as we have seen previously, his causality extends not simply to the generic or specific being of his creatures and their acts, but also to the individuating qualities or determinate notes of each, he knows the singular as it is distinct from all other individual beings or acts in creation, and he knows it by a knowledge that is both eternal and infallibly certain. The infallible certainty of God's foreknowledge of all free acts of creatures does not, however, render them necessary, but leaves them free. On this all are agreed.[30]

The difference among Catholic theologians begins when they try to explain how there is perfect harmony between God's infallible eternal knowledge and the free future acts of his creatures. We have seen that even in the early period of the Church there were apparent two tendencies in the answers forwarded to meet this difficulty. Some tended to emphasize the speculative quality of God's knowledge of the free future acts of man, and others to emphasize its causative nature. The former had less diffi-

---

[30] See the statement of the First Vatican Council, Ses. 3, cap. 1. D 1784. Also see *ST*, 1.14.1–16; A. Michel "Science de Dieu," *DTC*, 14.2 (1941), 1598–1620, which shows the different explanations of God's knowledge of free created acts, as well as what theologians agree on.

culty in showing the reality of the creature's freedom under God's knowledge than in protecting the universal causal primacy of God, while the latter inevitably had more difficulty in showing how freedom remained in the creature's choice. The Molinist and the Banezian explanations reflected in their own age these two tendencies.[31] As we saw in the first chapter, Molina taught that God knew what the free creature would do, given all possible circumstances and helps, by a form of knowledge which he called *scientia media*. This knowledge has as its object neither the merely possible nor the free act as actually occurring in time. Its object is more real than the merely possible and less real than the historical actuality, for it is what would occur because of the free choice of the creature within each of the infinite number of possible circumstances in which it could be placed by God. The content of this knowledge is determined by what in fact the free will would choose in each given circumstance in accord with Molina's explanation of the way in which the created will causes its act under God's simultaneous concurrence. Given this knowledge, God actualizes one of the sets of circumstances by his divine decree or act of will, and in virtue of this he has infallibly certain knowledge of what the free act in time will be. Since this knowledge of the free act in time is in virtue of *scientia media* and the divine decree, it is causally antecedent to the act of the free creature in time. But the divine causality involved is one that causes the circumstances and helps that the free will determines by its own free choice, so it is in no way contrary to the freedom of the will. Banez rejected this analysis and taught in its place that God's knowledge of the act of the free will act is causative in accord with his understanding of God's causality of the created free act. The medium by which God has infallibly certain knowledge of what the free future act of the creature will be is the eternal decree of his own divine will that is intrinsically effective antecedent to the act of the free will. This shows the causal primacy of God; it accounts for the infallibility of God's providence; and it is not contrary to the freedom of the created act since the divine will is so powerful that it determines, not only the fact of the created act, but the free manner of its coming to be.

[31] For analyses of Banez's and Molina's opinions on this matter see above, chapter 1, pp. 8–9, 23–24, and Michel, *art. cit.*

GOD'S ETERNAL KNOWLEDGE AND THE FREE ACT IN TIME.—As the first step of our attempt to explain how there can be harmony between God's knowledge and the free act of the creature, we must point out what seem to us to be weaknesses in both of these accounts. These weaknesses, as they refer to God's causality and intention in their relation to the free will act, have already been mentioned. Molina's explanation depends upon a theory of God's causality of the free will act that leaves to the created will a self-determination exclusive of the first causality of God. Since we cannot accept this for reasons previously given, we cannot accept the explanation of God's knowledge that essentially depends upon it. Banez's explanation depends upon his theory of the antecedent, intrinsic, infallible efficacy of God's causality and will in their relation to the free will act of the creature. The same reasons that seem to us to make this theory untenable prevent us from accepting his explanation of God's knowledge based on it. The evidence we have advanced throughout our study would seem to show that the order of God's wisdom for natural and supernatural free created acts in this world is one in which his divine will that they take place and his causality as antecedent to the free choice of the creature are not infallibly effective of these particular acts, but rather frustrable. His will and causality in this matter do not seem to us to be infallibly effective of the free act, either extrinsically or intrinsically, antecedent to the free choice of the creature in time.

Their common acceptance of the antecedent efficacy of God's decree and causality led Banez and Molina directly to a difficulty in their explanation of God's infallible knowledge of the free act in time that is also common to both. Neither of them demands the presence of free acts to the eternal knowledge of God as a necessary condition for his infallible knowledge of them as they commonly occur in history. Banez's theory of the intrinsic, antecedent, infallible decree of God, and Molina's theory of the extrinsically though antecedently effective decree, both explain his knowledge of the free acts of time without calling upon the presence of these acts to God's vision.[32] They both add that God's knowledge is indeed coexistent with the created act, but this is not the condition

[32] See chapter 1, pp. 8–9, 23–24.

246

in their explanations for its infallible certainty. The immediate medium in both cases for such infallible certainty is the divine decree causally antecedent to the creature's act and infallibly effective antecedent to the act of the creature in time. It is true that Molina's decree depends upon *scientia media,* but this knowledge of what the creature would do given all possible circumstances is clearly not one that demands presence of an act occurring in time to the eternal vision of God. No more than one of the creature's choices seen in *scientia media* will occur in each case; an infinite number of them will never occur, and yet God has infallibly certain knowledge of them. So it is clear that neither of these systems explains God's infallibly certain knowledge of the free created act through the coexistence of an act in time to God because of the relation of eternity to time.

Contrary to this, whenever St. Thomas explains how God has infallibly certain knowledge of the contingent act of the creature in a way compatible with that contingency, he teaches that this is possible because all acts of time in their existence are present to the eternal vision of God. We could call upon any one of his treatments of this matter to substantiate this statement since there is remarkable unity between his earliest and latest expressions of his docrine, but we shall give only his statement in the *Summa Theologica.*

> . . . something that is contingent can be considered in two ways. In one way in itself according *as it now actually exists;* and in this way it is not considered as future but as present, nor as contingent with reference to different possibilities, but as determined to one. And *because of this* it can be infallibly subject to certain knowledge, namely the power of vision, as when I see Socrates sitting. In another way the contingent act can be considered *as it is in its cause.* And in this way it is considered as future, and as a contingent event not yet determined to one because a contingent cause is related to opposites . . . God however knows all contingent things, not only as they are in their causes but as each one *exists* in itself. . . . Hence it is clear that contingent events are known by God infallibly, *to the extent that* they are subject to the divine vision according to their presence . . .[33]

[33] *ST,* 1.14.13. See also In 1 *Sent.,* 38. art. 1 and 5; 40.3. ad 5; *De ver.,* 2.12; *CG,* 1.66;67; *De malo,* 16.7. See J. de Finance, "La Présence des

247

St. Thomas' expression of the reason why God's knowledge does not interfere with the contingency of the rational creature's act cannot be improved. It is clear that a contingent act is, when it is taking place, necessary, not in the sense that it is intrinsically necessary but in the sense that as long as it exists it cannot not exist. This is called a conditional necessity coexistent with and not antecedent to the act itself. Hence, one who knows this act when it is taking place can know it with infallible certitude without removing from the act any of its contingency. Any act of time is coexistent with God and thus with God's knowledge; hence it is subject to knowledge of vision on the part of God. And so his knowledge of the free created act is always infallibly certain, and yet the created act is contingent.

It is admittedly very difficult for us to understand how God can have such knowledge of a future event. It seems to us that an event that is future can be known now with certainty only if it is contained necessarily in its causes and thus is not contingent. If it is contingent, knowledge that we have of it can only be conjectural. It seems that if God knows something that is future, either that thing is necessary or God's knowledge is not infallibly certain. But this difficulty which we have is due to the fact that we tend to attribute conditions that are proper to our own knowledge to God's knowledge.

Boethius draws an analogy that shows how invalid this approach is.[34] If our powers of sense could carry on a dialogue with our intellectual power of knowledge, they might well say that the universals which the intellect claims to know refer to nothing in reality. For if the universals did refer to something in reality, the knowledge of the senses would be false, since they know reality as concrete, material, and singular. It is beyond doubt, however, that what the senses know is true; therefore, the knowledge of the intellect is false. Reason would answer that, while it knows both the senses and what is proper to itself, the senses are limited to a lower degree of knowledge and hence cannot judge the higher power of knowledge. In like manner, man cannot conclude from

choses a l'éternité d'après les scolastiques," *Archives de philosophie,* 19 (1956), 2, 24–62.

[34] See Boethius, *Philosophiae consolatio,* 5.5.5–7 (ed. L. Bieler, CCSL ser., 1957, n. 94), 99–100.

the fact that he cannot know contingent future events with infallible certitude that God cannot know them. Things that are future to our knowledge are not future to God and his knowledge, since the relation of past, present, and future is proper to things contained within the order of time. The relation between an event future to us and God is one of coexistence, because God who coexists with each event of time has no succession within his being or act, but possesses the whole of his being and act in one simple act. If we said that God as coexisting with an event future to us is future to God as coexisting with our own present act, we would be attributing to God the change that occurs only in creation. God, then, knows events in time in accord with the nature of his own knowledge which is eternal, and thus he has a total and perfect possession of all truth at once in the *now*, not of time, but of eternity. What occurs successively in creation is open to God's knowledge at once, because it is coexistent with his eternal knowledge. And since this is so, God can have infallibly certain knowledge of events that are contingent and future to us. Our knowledge of how God's understanding is related to contingent events is more negative than positive, more a conviction or realization that he does not know in the way that we know than a clear understanding of exactly how he knows. But our understanding, such as it is, is sufficient to show us that he knows things as present to him by reason of his eternity.

Banez, Molina, and their followers would object that this presence of the free created act to God's knowledge by reason of his eternity is not a condition necessary for God's infallible knowledge of created acts that are contingent in accord with the order established by his wisdom. And they offer alternative explanations. The Molinists hold that, while the creature cannot have infallibly certain knowledge of contingent acts without the actual presence of these acts, God can have such knowledge without their presence. They give different explanations of the medium of this infallible divine knowledge. Molina holds that God has certain knowledge of what the creature would do in all possible circumstances because his infinitely comprehensive understanding of his own nature and the created nature contained within his essence gives him such knowledge. To this we can answer that the contingent event, such as the free act of the created will, exists in its cause in an undetermined manner. Until the will determines itself to do this rather than that, to act rather than not, its free act may exist or not exist. That is the difference between a contingent act of a free cause and an act of a necessary cause. Hence, though it may be known conjecturally in its cause, it is not known with infallible certitude; for if it were known with certainty before the will's choice through knowledge of the created cause, it would be determined to one before the free choice and thus would not be a contingent act. Neither God nor the creature knows the contingent act through knowing merely the created cause, for this inability to know it is not due to any weakness or limitation of knowledge. It is due to the indeterminateness of the thing known, namely, the contingent act in its created cause antecedent to its act. St. Thomas implies this clearly enough in the passage we quoted above, but it is contained even more directly in his statement that the contingent act considered simply in its cause "is not subject to *any* knowledge with certainty. Hence *whoever* knows the contingent effect in its cause alone has no more than conjectural knowledge of it."[35]

Suarez, who rejects Molina's explanation as untenable, advances an explanation of the medium by which God has certain knowledge of what the free will would do in all possible circumstances, that had already been refuted by Molina as incompatible with the freedom of the creature. Suarez holds that, of two contradictory propositions, one is eternally true and the other is false. This is true of what the free will would do given any possible circumstances. Thus God knows what the free will would do through a knowledge of the objective truth of the eternally true part of this contradiction. Aristotle, ages before Suarez, held that such a teaching would result in all events being necessary.[36] And it seems

---

[35] *ST*, 1.14.13. See also *In 1 Sent.*, 38.5. ad 6; *De ver.*, 2.12. ad 6.

[36] See Aristotle, *On Interpretation*, c. 9, 18 b 5 in *The Basic Works of Aristotle* (ed. R. Mckeon, New York 1941), p. 46, where he says of the principle on which Suarez's theory is based: "Now if this be so, nothing is or takes place fortuitously, either in the present or in the future, and there are no real alternatives; everything takes place of necessity and is fixed." See also St. Thomas, *In libros Peri Hermeneias expositio*, c. 9, lect. 13, and *ST*, 2–2, 171.3 where St. Thomas states that the objects of prophecy that show most properly the knowledge of God are not

that we must agree that such would be the consequence of Suarez's theory. If, when the will is about to perform its act or makes its choice, it is already objectively true in the way Suarez explains antecedent to the will's act that it will make one choice rather than another, the act is already determined. And if it is determined before the will chooses, the possibility of the act's being or not being, being this or being that, no longer exists. It is not contingent when the will comes to make its choice, and thus it is not free.

Moreover, it seems to us that Suarez's understanding of the nature of truth and its relation to the created act is faulty. St. Thomas shows that truth is predicated in the first place of the intellectual judgment, which is true (in the case of the speculative judgment of the created intellect) if it conforms to reality. Truth is predicated secondarily of the object external to the intellect, and as such it refers to the relation of that thing to an intellect or that perfection within the thing in virtue of which it has this relation. Natural things and acts are called true with reference to the human intellect insofar as they have something within them by which they can cause a true estimation of themselves. They are called true with reference to the divine intellect by that within them through which they are conformed to God's intellect, that is the inner form which they receive from God.[37] Hence, there is no truth that is outside an intellect or a being that has a relation to an intellect. Therefore, Suarez's objective truth is either the contingent act itself or it is the divine being as the first cause of this contingent act. If it is the former, it only exists when and in the manner in which the contingent act exists. And if it is the latter, the truth of the contingent act is only there in the manner in which God is the first cause of the contingent created act. We saw previously that God does cause intrinsically in the creature the determination of the free act, but does not cause this save through the act of the free creature. So the attempt by Suarez to find some basis for God's knowledge of the free act of the creature that is in

---

determined before they exist, but they are known by God because of his eternity that coexists with every point in time.

[37] See *De ver.*, 1.2. For an analysis of Suarez's understanding of eternal truths, see T. J. Cronin, S.J., "Eternal Truths in the Thought of Suarez and Descartes," *The Modern Schoolman*, 38 (1961), 269–88.

accord with Molina's theory of the created will as the ultimate source of its own determination seems to be, like every other explanation based on that theory, without sufficient foundation.

But Banez's explanation of the medium by which God knows the free act of the created cause seems to us no more satisfactory than that advanced by the Molinists. As the Molinists sought a medium other than the divine causality, Banez sought one other than the causality of the created free will. He held that God knew with infallible certainty what the creature's free act in time was going to be through the decree of the divine will antecedent to any consideration of the act of the creature as such. We have seen that St. Thomas taught that the divine will and causality as antecedent to the contingent act of the creature were not infallibly effective of the particular free act or, in other words, were frustrable. If this is true not simply as an interpretation of St. Thomas but as an interpretation of reality, then God's decree cannot be a sufficient medium of God's knowledge of the free act of the creature. Moreover, when St. Thomas taught that contingent acts could not be known with certainty *in their causes,* he in no way restricted these causes to created causes while holding that they could be known in the first cause abstracting from the second cause.[38] For Banez, then, and his followers to restrict St. Thomas' more general statements to mean simply that the free will act cannot be known with certainty in its *created* causes is not justified on the grounds of St. Thomas' texts. Nor is such a restriction, in our opinion, compatible with St. Thomas' explanation of God's causality of the contingent act of the creature according to the order of wisdom he has established. Finally, we can say that if St. Thomas had thought that the divine decree were the adequate medium of God's knowledge of the created free act, he would have abstracted from the eternal presence of the free act to God, as Banez did. The fact that he insisted upon the presence of the contingent act to God shows that his explanation of the medium of God's knowledge was not that of Banez.

We hold that God knows the free act of the creature by causative knowledge and in accord with the nature of his causality of the act. The things that a man makes he knows in a manner dif-

[38] See texts cited in footnotes 20, 21, 33, 35.

ferent from those things which exist antecedent to his causality and not in virtue of his causal influence. A man's knowledge of a color of a flower in nature is dependent upon the flower that he sees. A man's knowledge of something that he makes is not receptive as it refers to the thing as caused by him. Rather, it is active and causal, for he determines the nature of his effect through the idea he possesses of it and the application of this idea by means of his hands and the instruments that he uses upon the subject or matter on which he is working. Now the being of all created things and acts is related to God's intellect as an artifact is related to the human artist. Therefore the determination of the created being and act is known by God by a causal knowledge.[39] This is true with reference to the free act of the creature as it is true with reference to all other acts; for, as we have previously seen, God is the first cause of the free act as well as of other acts.

Thus God knows the free will act by the fact that he causes it, and furthermore he knows it in accord with the manner in which he causes it. Since the free act is caused by the free created will as well as by the divine will, God is the first cause of the act without being the exclusive cause of it. Moreover, the free act is not determined to one by the divine cause prescinding from the second cause, nor by the second cause subject to the first cause antecedent to its actual free choice, but by the free choice itself of the second cause subordinate to the first causality of God. Since this is the medium of God's causality, this is the medium by which he has infallible knowledge of the act. That is, he knows it through the medium of his own intellect and will acting as *first cause*, the created free cause as *second cause*, and *the act itself*. As the primacy in this causality is in the divine intellect and will, the primary element in the medium of God's knowledge is the divine causality with the free created cause and its causality completely subordinated to it. But the divine causality is not the exclusive medium. As St. Thomas writes: "Those things which are present, past, and future to us God knows according as they are in his power, and in their proper causes, and in themselves, and the knowledge of them is called the knowledge of vision."[40] It seems to us that this is the only adequate explanation of the medium of

[39] See *ST*, 1.14.8; *De ver.*, 2.14.
[40] *CG*, 1.66.

God's knowledge of the free acts of the creature as well as the only one consistent with the principles of St. Thomas on God's causality and knowledge of the free acts of creatures. This, of course, does not render God dependent in his knowledge on perfection received from the creature, since all the being in the created cause and its act is from God as its first cause.

When we say that the created will (and we may add the created influences upon it) and its act are the medium under the first causality of God by which he knows the free created act, we mean that they are such a medium, not insofar as they are outside the divine essence, but as they are contained in the divine essence and causality. This follows from the very nature of God's knowledge as causative. God causes the creature and created act as first cause through the exemplar of the divine mind and the act of the divine will, and thus he knows the created effect, not by receiving a form from the creature, but by the form and act which is within him and which the creature receives from him. In like manner, the human artist knows what he is making through the idea of his intellect by which he is causing his effect, and not through a form which he receives from his effect. God, of course, is the source of all the being in the created act, whereas the human artist is simply partial source of his effect, so God's knowledge of his effect is completely through the form and act within himself. The form and act within God is that in virtue of which he causes as first cause and the second free cause exists and acts. For the second cause and its act is a participation in the being of God through his first causality, as we explained in the preceding chapter. Thus, since it is contained in God as in the uncreated act that is its source, God knows the act of the free creature through the creature and its act as it is in God. St. Thomas writes: "God knows nothing outside himself if the *outside* refers to that *by which* he knows; however he knows something outside himself if this refers to that *which* he knows."[41]

In our view, then, neither the creature's causality of its own free act exclusive of God's causality nor God's causality exclusive of the creature's causality of its own free act is the adequate medium of God's knowledge of the free act of the creature. Both

[41] *De ver.*, 2.12. ad 11. See also *ibid.*, 6. c. and ad 1; *ST*, 1.14.11; and 5.

the divine causality and the creature's causality together (as explained in the preceding chapter) are the medium of God's knowledge. And in the divine causality, as it is the medium of this knowledge, the act of the divine intellect and that of the divine will are included for, as St. Thomas writes, "his knowledge is the cause of things, according as it has the will conjoined to it."[42]

As a further question about the nature of the divine causality as medium of God's knowledge, we may ask how the divine intellect and will are related within the medium of God's knowledge of the free act. They are related as a medium of God's knowledge as they are related as a medium of God's causality, since God knows as he causes. And they are related within their causality of the free created act as they are related within their causality of other created being. The form of created acts we reduce to the divine intellect as the ultimate source more properly than to the divine will, for it is the exemplary causality of the idea of the divine mind that is the first cause of the determination or formal act within creatures. We do not reduce this aspect of creatures to the divine will most properly since it is the nature of the divine will to receive the specification of its causal act from the divine intellect, as it is the nature of the created will to be directed or specified by the created intellect.[43] It is the function of the divine will not to add another formal specification to the divine exemplars, but to cause the existence of the created beings or acts of which the divine ideas are the exemplars. The divine will gives existence or "to be" to the created form that receives its ultimate determination from the exemplars of the divine intellect. What is true of the creature's causality is analogously true of God's causality, and St. Thomas writes of the former:

> Of one and the same effect even in us the cause is knowledge as directing, by which the form of the work is conceived, and the will as commanding, because the form as it is in the intellect alone is not determined to this whether it exist or not in the effect except through the will.[44]

Since the created will act, as every created being or action, is both act and determined act, God is cause of it by his intellect

---

[42] *ST*, 1.14.8.
[43] See above, chapter 5, p. 187.
[44] *ST*, 1.19.4. ad 4.

and will; and he knows it through the conjoined causality of his intellect and will, of his intellect as the source, as first cause, of the determination of the created act and of his will as source, as first cause, of its existence. So within the context of the explanation we have given of the way in which God's causality is the medium of his knowledge of the free created act, his divine intellect and will conjoined are the medium, the former as source of the determination (in the sense of the specification) of the created act, and the latter as source of its existence.

From what we have already said, we can understand in some degree how God knows the sinful act of the free creature. All agree that God knows it as he permits it. In our opinion, God's permission is that implied in the frustrable character of his antecedent intention and inclination of the created will to what is morally good. And hence we do not think that it is such that in virtue of his permission of a particular sinful act God knows with certainty that the sin will take place antecedent to the free choice of the creature in time. The presence of the sinful free choice in time to God by reason of his eternity is the condition for God's certain knowledge of it, as it is in the case of the free choice in accord with the moral norm. He knows the sinful act through his knowledge of the created will's rejection of his inclination of it to the moral good, an inclination that remotely or proximately precedes the sinful free choice. The evil act as such is not being, but the privation of the being that should exist, and in this case the privation of the moral order that should exist; and so it is knowable, not of itself, but through the good of which it is a privation. Since the good of which the sinful act is a privation is that to which God antecedently inclined the will, we can say with St. Thomas that God knows the moral evil through the good of which it is the privation,[45] or we can say that he knows it through the good to which he antecedently inclined the will. The physical good remaining in the sinful act God knows since he causes it, as we explained, through his simultaneous concurrence with the act.

It does not seem that we need to make a special application of this natural explanation of God's knowledge of the individual free act of the creature to the order of grace, since what is valid in the natural order is valid in this matter in the order of grace. We have

[45] See *ST*, 1.14.10; *De ver.*, 2.15; In 1 *Sent.*, 36.12; *CG*, 1.71.

seen that God's intention and causality in the order of grace for a particular free act is frustrable antecedent to the response of the will. Hence, God's knowledge of a free act in the order of grace is analogously the same as his knowledge of a free act in the order of nature, the difference being that the exemplar in the divine mind and the good that comes from the divine will in the order of grace are such that they incline the created will to an act of a higher order than simply the natural one. We shall see in the next section the relation of God's knowledge and will to the order of God's supernatural providence directing the rational creature to its goal. We must now examine some objections that may be advanced against the explanation we have given of God's knowledge of the free act of the creature.

SOME DIFFICULTIES CONSIDERED.—In the first place, one may object that, when God wishes, he can move the created will to act by a divine decree and created causality that is antecedently infallibly efficacious. If this is so, God does not depend upon the presence of the creature's act to him by reason of his eternity for his knowledge of what the creature's act will be. He knows it by reason of his own divine decree, his antecedent causality, and his knowledge of how the creature would react to his causality antecedent to its actual response. To this we answer that, of course, God can, if he wishes, move the will with antecedent efficacy to a good act, but this is not the order that his wisdom has established for the free creature, and our analysis is an explanation of how God knows the free act he causes in accord with this order. When God acts beyond the order he has established and causes the act with infallible antecedent efficacy, he still moves the will to act through the causality of the good upon it and not in an order of efficiency that is distinct from that of finality. Hence, the will is moved in such an act in accord with its nature, though the act cannot be said to be wholly contingent since it is determined in its first cause to occur antecedent (causally) to the free choice. The will may well subjectively proceed in the act as it does in acts that are simply contingent, namely, by being attracted to the act and its object, reflecting upon itself, comparing itself to the act and object, and moving itself to the act because of the greater value contained in the object of this act over that which it may lose through performing the act. The movement to the good in this way perfects and does not detract from the perfection of the will as it is clear in the will's response to the beatific vision. But since this act is not, strictly speaking or without qualification, a *contingent* act of the free creature, it can be known with certainty antecedent (causally) to its actual occurrence. Such is not the case with the wholly contingent acts of the free creature.

Also from God's power to move the will in this manner, it is apparent that he knows in some cases what the will would do antecedent to its act and he knows that certain objects will in fact draw the will to act antecedent to his vision (if one can speak this way) of the will's act. For example, he knows that if he gave to a created will the vision of himself, that will would inevitably perform an act of love of God. Without giving to the will such an infinite good, God can, as we saw previously, still effectively persuade the will to perform a particular good act in such a way that, antecedent to the act of the will, it is certain that it will perform it. He can do this, for example, by interiorly showing the intellect and will so effectively that a particular act is necessary for happiness that the will act shall without fail occur. Or he can dissuade it from a particular act by showing interiorly and very persuasively the immense suffering that would follow such an act, so that even before the will acts it is certain what it will do. But the fact that God knows how the will would or will act when it receives such an antecedently infallible inclination to act does not at all prove that he knows how the will would or will act with an antecedent help in accord with the order of wisdom he has established for the rational creature in both the natural and the supernatural order. So it is not contrary to what we have shown above; there is necessary the presence of the free will act to God by reason of his eternity for him to know it with certainty, when he causes it in accord with the order of wisdom he has established.

The objection may be raised that this explanation of God's knowledge of the future contingent event does not show that God knows now what will happen in the future. For the event does not exist until a particular point in time; and so if God knows it by reason of its presence alone, he doesn't know it until it exists, and his knowledge of it is not eternal. In answer to this, it is helpful to recall that a material thing as known by our intellect is immaterial since our intellect is spiritual and what is known by it must be adapted to its nature, but the fact that the thing as known is immaterial does not change its condition within itself. So, too, what is known by God's knowledge is eternal as known, since God's knowledge is eternal, but in itself it takes place at a particular point of time.

But, the objector may continue, this still does not explain how God knows the contingent act before it exists. That God has this knowledge is shown by the fact of prophecy. But if God knows the event in the sense that when it takes place he knows it by a knowledge that abstracts from time and thus is eternal, he still has to wait until the event takes place. God is not now present with something that will take place in the future since the other term of the relation, the contingent event, is not, and that which is not cannot be present to God always by reason of his eternity. This objection shows the difficulty we have in transcending our own manner of knowing to make an adequate judgment of God's. For us to say that God cannot know now the future event is the same as for the foot to say to our soul that, if it is present in the foot, it cannot be present in the arm. The foot identifies presence with its own manner of presence, and so it says that presence in the foot excludes presence in the arm. But the soul's manner of presence is different from that of the foot. It is where it acts, and since it gives life to the foot and the arm, it is present in both. We identify now with the *nunc temporis* in which we are and know, and we say that God cannot now know the future act or now be present to a future act. But God's now is the *nunc aeternitatis* which is not bound down to a particular point of time as we are. He is where he acts, but he acts in what is future to us as well as within us with one divine act, and so he is present to both at once (i.e. in the same *nunc aeternitatis*, not the same *nunc temporis*). We are present in different times by different acts, so we do not know the contingent future now. As the soul acts in different parts of the body and hence is present to different parts, God acts in the present and the future by one act, and hence he is present to both and knows both by one act and not by successive acts.

Still one can object that the act in time is not coterminous with God, and hence God's knowledge of it is not coterminous with his being if it depends upon his presence to the thing in act. To this we say that the arm is not coterminous with the activity of the soul, but the soul is present to the arm and foot at once. Thus it is not necessary that an effect be coterminous with the influence of the cause for the cause to be present to it when it is present to another; it is simply necessary that the cause influence the one and the other in the one act. The act of time is not coterminous with God's causal knowledge, for he causes many other things; but God causes all the acts of time in one act and hence is present to all and knows all in one act.

Still another objection can be presented to this position, and that is the fact that, while God begins to be creator at the time of creation, he does not begin to have knowledge of a free act of the creature. His knowledge is completely invariable since the relation of the thing known to God's intellect is in accord with the nature of God's intellect.[46] In the first place, we answer this objection by a consideration applicable as well to the preceding objections. If the invariability of God's knowledge made it impossible for God to have a truly conditioned intention that man respond to grace which man is completely able to reject, then it would seem that God's reprobation is antecedent to his foreknowledge of the individual's sins. And in our understanding of Scripture, reprobation is only consequent upon man's sins. Hence, insofar as our interpretation of revelation is valid, it would seem that it must be possible for God to present to the free will grace which, antecedent to the creature's response, is not certain to gain man's response or to be followed by his rejection. It must be possible for God to have an intention that the creature reach heaven which gives way to repobation only because of the creatures's sins beyond the measure God has determined to endure. It must be possible for God to have an intention which is not certain to achieve the good acts of the free creature antecedent to the free response of this creature. In the second place, we answer this objection as we answered that based on the immutability of the divine will. As God by one immutable will wants a creature to perform a good act antecedent to its response and does not want him to when he rejects prevenient grace, so God knows by invariable knowledge the changes in free will, such as the fact that

[46] See *ST*, 1.14.15. ad 1.

antecedent grace is presented to the created will and that the created will does not perform the act to which grace attracted it. This is possible because of the eternal character of God's knowledge as explained above.

Again an objection may be raised that, if God's knowledge is causal knowledge, he knows a thing when and only when he causes it, and thus he knows it when and only when it is. In answer to this we first admit that it is true that God knows it when it is, but this knowledge as it is in God is eternal, as is God's causality. This does not mean that the free created act is itself eternal, but that it is eternal in its condition of being known by God. Secondly, when we refer to God's causal act here, we mean his uncreated causal act, not the created actuation by which he causes; and since all created actuation and acts are participations in the same uncreated act that is both one and eternal, it is the same uncreated act by which God caused the first created act in time and causes created acts now. Hence, God knows in one eternal act all the free acts that succeed each other in time. This answer does not remove the mystery from God's knowledge, but it does show that it is completely false to limit the act of his knowledge to a particular *nunc temporis* and thus to ascribe to it the relation our judgments have to a future event.

Another objection that may be raised is that, if the created free act is partially the medium of God's knowledge, it seems that God's knowledge is specified by the act of the creature, either the good act or the sinful act. To this we say, in the first place, that God's knowledge of the created act is a causal knowledge, and so we judge it in this matter as we do his causality. God's causality of the creature and its act is a real relation only on the part of the creature and not on the part of God, as the relation between an object that causes us to know is real on the part of our intellect and one of reason on the part of the thing. All the being, moreover, in the contingent act specifies the divine intellect only insofar as it is in its first cause, the divine essence, as a rock specifies or perfects our intellect only as it is the species in the intellect and not as it is in the world outside. Hence, the fact that the created contingent choice is partial medium of God's knowledge in no way implies that the divine intellect draws specification or perfection from the created act. Since God's knowledge of an act as sinful is through the good of which it is the privation, in this respect God's knowledge of the sinful act is similar to his knowledge of the good act. Moreover, only being can specify an intelligence; a privation of being is known by the being it is opposed to as darkness by light and by the intellect's construction, in a way, of an *ens rationis* that signifies the lack of this being. So, since it can be said that the good act of the creature does not specify the divine intellect, this can be said with all the more truth of the sinful act.

One may object to our analysis of God's knowledge of the contingent act of the creature that it does not account for God's knowledge of what the free creature would do in conditions other than those that actually take place. The Molinists and the Thomists both hold that God has such knowledge, and it seems to them that Scripture, tradition, and reason support their position.[47] The Molinists explain how God has such knowledge through their *scientia media*, while the Thomists explain it by infallibly effective but conditioned divine decrees. There are other differences, too, between the two schools on this matter. The attribution of such knowledge to God is the foundation that is essential for the Molinist explanation of God's relation to free will, while for the Thomists it is simply a consequence of their doctrine of God's divine decrees. The Molinists hold necessarily that God has knowledge of what all actual or possible free creatures would do given all possible circumstances. While some Thomists extend God's knowledge of conditioned futures to the same limits, most assert that God has a limited number of decrees determining what free creatures would do given other circumstances, and thus his knowledge in this order need not be and is not as universal as the Molinists hold. In any case, their explanations agree in attributing to God an infallibly certain knowledge of contingent created acts without the necessity of their presence to God by reason of his eternity. So from the fact that God knows what the contingent created act would be (or, as they are called, futurables), it seems to follow that God can know the free created act without its presence to him by reason of his eternity.

[47] For the arguments advanced to sustain this thesis see, for example, J. B. Franzelin, *Tractatus de deo uno* (Rome, 1883), pp. 476–89.

In answer to this we say that in our opinion the perfection of God's knowledge does not demand that he have this certain knowledge of what the free creature would do in circumstances other than those that actually occur, beyond what we have conceded in the answers to the preceding objections.[48] This is suggested, in the first place, by the serious difficulties that are attendant upon any explanation that has been given of God's knowledge of these conditioned free future acts that are called futurables. In Molina the doctrine that God has such knowledge is dependent upon his explanation of God's causality of the free created act and his theory of *scientia media*, neither of which seems to us tenable. In Banez the doctrine that God has such knowledge depends upon his opinion that for the free acts of the creature God's antecedent intention or permission is always infallibly effective of the free act. And we do not think this corresponds with the order of wisdom God has established. In both Molina and Banez the doctrine that God has knowledge of what the creature would do in other circumstances depends upon an explanation of divine knowledge of the free created act without the necessity of the act's presence to God by reason of his eternity. This leads one to ask whether this problem, the solution of which always involves such difficulties, is a real problem. That is, does the perfection of God's knowledge demand that he have such certain knowledge of what the free will would do in other circumstances than those that actually exist?

The answer to this, it seems to us, must be negative. Everything is knowable insofar as it is being. Free acts that occur in time are knowable as existing. Those things that are not, but can exist, since they are in the power of God or his creatures, are possible; and thus they are knowable as possible or able to be. But, in our opinion for reasons previously explained, contingent acts of the free creature do not have a determined being antecedent to the acts themselves in time; antecedent to the contingent choice of the creature, they are determined neither in their causes (created or uncreated) nor in some objective truth independent from the acts of their causes. The contingent act antecedent to the free

---

[48] For a development of arguments against the existence of infallible divine knowledge of futurables or conditioned futures, see L. Janssens, *Tractatus de Deo uno,* 2 (Freiburg i Br., 1900), 43–63.

choice of the creature in time exists in its cause in such a way that, considering the dispositions of the free cause and the circumstances that surround it, there are differing degrees of probability that the act will take place. And so the probability of the contingent act taking place is knowable within its cause to the extent that the circumstances and dispositions of the cause indicate it. Therefore, since God knows all that is knowable and to the extent that it is knowable, he knows, antecedent to the free creature's contingent act, the degree of probability there is that the act will take place. And in the same way he knows how the free creature would probably act in differing circumstances. His knowledge in this matter is far surer than man's, since he understands so much more perfectly man's dispositions and the influence of circumstances upon these dispositions. But since the determination of the contingent act within the free creature antecedent to its choice is only probable and not certain, it is known as probable and not as certain. Since this is the measure of the being that the contingent act has in its cause, it is not a limitation of divine knowledge to assert that God knows it as probable and not as certain to exist. It would seem that men are led to attribute to God knowledge of contingent acts in their cause as certain to exist or knowledge of what free will would certainly do in other circumstances through a fallacy of their imagination. As they tend to extend time beyond the point when creation began to exist, they tend to extend the attribute of being determined to one, and thus knowability as such, beyond those things that are determined or knowable in such a way.

We may note here that, of course, if God in a particular case gives an infallibly effective antecedent movement to a good act, then he knows the act in the free will as certain to exist before the will elicits it, but this is not the antecedent movement God normally gives. Moreover, in his normal economy, God knows, antecedent to that act of the free creature, that *if it responds* to his premovement to the good, it will perform the definite acts to which God does premove it, and that *if it rejects* this premovement, it will fall into sin and the punishment that follows sin. But since the result of the creature's act depends upon the act itself of the creature, antecedent to the creature's act, God knows what will result by the same knowledge that he has of what the

264

created free act *will be*. And this knowledge is infallibly certain in virtue of the presence of the act to God's eternal knowledge, but it is not infallibly certain if it is considered causally antecedent to the act of the creature.

The arguments that have been advanced from Scripture and tradition do not seem to prove the existence of such an infallible divine knowledge of futurables or what the free acts of the rational creatures would be, given other circumstances than those that actually occur. There are three main texts in Scripture advanced to defend the existence of God's infallible knowledge of futurables. In the first case, David had heard that Saul was collecting his men and preparing to besiege him in the town of Keilah. So David asked God through the priest Abiathar whether Saul would come to Keilah and the townspeople would deliver him into his hands. Upon an affirmative answer to both of these questions, David left Keilah, and Saul gave up his intentions.[49] God's answers to these questions prove no more than his knowledge of the dispositions of Saul and the people of Keilah at the time and a judgment based on these. Since such an explanation accounts for the knowledge here ascribed to God, one can hardly claim on the basis of this text that God has infallibly certain knowledge of what men would freely do in circumstances other than those that actually take place. In the second text, the prophet Elisaeus told Joas, the king of Israel, to strike a group of arrows on the ground. And when Joas stopped after striking them three times, Elisaeus in anger told him that he should have continued till five or six times. If he had done that, God would have given him complete victory over Aram; but as it was, he would only have three victories.[50] Hence, the argument goes, God knew what Joas would have done in other circumstances than those that actually took place. The explanation seems to be that, antecedently, God ordained Joas to have a complete victory over Aram, but, because of the lack of persistence shown symbolically in the case of the arrows, he would only gain a partial victory. We readily admit that God has knowledge of what would have happened if Joas had fully cooperated with God, but this is due to the antecedent objective efficacy of God's

[49] See 1 Sam. 23:7-13 and, for a similar text, Acts 22:17-21. For a study of these biblical texts, see Ceuppens, *Theologia biblica*, 1.162-4.
[50] See 2 Kings 18:13-20. Also see Jer. 38:14-20.

premovement to good that can, however, be frustrated by man. It does not prove God's foreknowledge of futurables as understood by many theologians. The third incident is Christ's lament over the towns of Galilee where he had preached and performed his miracles. *For if in Tyre and Sidon had been worked the miracles that have been worked in you, they would have repented long ago in sackcloth and ashes.*[51] Christ brought forth this parallel to express graphically the ingratitude, the culpable blindness, and the punishment due to these towns of Galilee that rejected his message. And so he tells them what pagan and corrupt towns would have done if his miracles had been performed in them. Considering this text within the context of the purpose of Christ's words and the popular manner of his expression, it can scarcely be claimed that they prove the existence of an infallible divine knowledge of futurables. A knowledge of the dispositions of the people of Tyre and Sidon and of the effect his miracles would have upon them, in which it was seen that their acceptance of Christ's message was the probable or morally certain effect in the contingency Christ supposes, fully accounts for his statement here. Even if we admit that this statement by Christ indicates infallibly certain knowledge of a futurable, it proves only that God knows what miraculous antecedent helps he can use to gain infallibly man's response. It does not prove that God has infallible knowledge of the effect antecedent helps within the order of his common providence would have upon man's free will. Therefore, the scriptural doctrine is not opposed to what, in our opinion, the natural evidence shows, namely, that God does not have the infallible knowledge of futurables that is attributed to him by some theologians.

Neither do the statements of tradition, which are also forwarded as theological reasons supporting God's infallible knowledge of futurables, seem to establish its existence. For when the Fathers seem to grant that God has such a knowledge, they are really interested in another matter and are not studying for its own sake God's knowledge of what would have happened. For example, from the fact of the fall of Adam and others, the Manicheans argued that either God's knowledge was limited in that he did not know that Adam would fall, or he was not good in that

[51] Matt. 11:21. See also Luke 10:13.

he created Adam knowing that he would fall.[52] The Fathers
generally conceded that God had the knowledge that Adam would
fall, but was completely free from blame and responsibility for his
fall, since he gave him all the help he needed to remain faithful.
Their point here was that God was blameless even though he may
have known that Adam would fall; it was not a defense of God's
knowledge causally antecedent to Adam's act. Secondly, at times
the Fathers seem to suppose that God knows what a man would
have done had he continued to live longer than he did. To the
Pelagian teaching that God counts for a man's merits or demerits
what he would have done had he continued to live longer, Augustine answers, in the first place, that it is absurd to think God
counts this for merit. Then, as another rebuttal, he asks why God
did not withdraw those from the world who lived a good life for
a while then when they were living a good life rather than later
when they fell from God's favor. He says that one cannot say either
that to act in that way was not in God's power or that he did not
know their *future evils.* Here we may note that Augustine's answer
to the Pelagians was that even supposing God to know what man
would do had he lived longer, it is foolish to suppose that God
would judge man by what he would have done; it was not an
affirmation that God actually has such knowledge. Also in his
second reflection given above, he ascribes to God knowledge of
future evils and not precisely of evils that are *futurables.* Moreover, in commenting upon the text of Wisdom that one whom God
loved was *snatched away, lest wickedness pervert his mind or
deceit beguile his soul,*[53] Augustine shows that the text implies,
not that God knows that the man would have sinned, but rather
that he withdraws him from the uncertainty of temptations.[54] To

---

[52] For texts of the Fathers, see Franzelin, *op. cit.*, pp. 484 ff., and
Janssens, *op. cit.*, pp. 45 ff.

[53] Wis. 4:11.

[54] See Augustine, *De praedest. sanct.*, 14.26 (ML 44.979): "Dictum
est secundum pericula vitae huius, non secundum praescientiam Dei, qui
hoc praescivit, quod futurum erat, non quod futurum non erat, id est, quod
ei mortem immaturam fuerat largiturus, ut tentationum subtraheretur
incerto, non quod peccaturus esset, qui mansurus in tentatione non esset."
Franzelin adduces other texts of Augustine where he does seem to teach a
divine knowledge of futurables, and Franzelin interprets the text cited
above as a denial by Augustine that God knows futurables as things that
will actually occur. The grammatical structure however seems to indicate

say the least, this statement of Augustine and a like one of Fulgentius make it difficult to say that early tradition was unanimously in favor of God's infallible knowledge of futurables.

In a work that lists various reasons that are a source of comfort for those whose children die while yet young, Gregory of Nyssa used the text of Wisdom quoted above to show that, out of mercy, God brings them from this life before they perform the evil he foresees they would commit if they grew up.[55] Gregory's purpose here is to show that God does not permit the death of the young without some good purpose that is achieved by that evil. We may say that this text indicates that Gregory accepts in an unreflective way knowledge of what would happen as an element of God's knowledge, but we think that probable or morally certain knowledge is sufficient to explain Gregory's text. In any case, one need not advance Gregory's reason to show that God's permission of evil is for man's good, since the death of a child can be a means of spiritual growth for the parents who accept it with trust in God's providence. Moreover, the fact that the child has been given life and with it the future share in some degree in happiness in the next life is itself a great gift. If God allows natural causes to run their course and take the life of the child while yet young, the child has more than it would have had if it had never had life. Gregory's reason would not explain all premature deaths and would make it more difficult to explain the growth of those who were good only for a while.

Finally, it is said that the practice of Christian prayer supports the existence of God's knowledge of futurables, for Christians at times pray that some gift may be given to them only if it will not lead to their spiritual harm. And this supposes that God knows what would happen to them in various circumstances. We answer that such prayer rightly supposes in God a knowledge of how men would probably react to different circumstances, and it also supposes the divine intention to give them the help to remain faithful to him if he gives them the gift they ask of him. But it cannot

---

Augustine is denying God knew (with infallible certainty at least) that the man *would have* sinned, and this indicates the object as a conditioned and not an absolute future. For a text like this one in the writings of Fulgentius, see Janssens, *op. cit.*, p. 46.

[55] See Gregory, *De infantibus qui praemature abripiuntur* (MG 46: 184).

suppose that God's gift of what they ask is a guarantee that they will not use it for their spiritual harm. So it does not suppose an infallible knowledge of futurables in God. What is true of this particular case is true of God's antecedent will that the free creature do well, namely, that it does not suppose an antecedently infallible knowledge of what the creature would do in all possible cases or of what it would do antecedent to its actual free response to God. God knows from his knowledge of the nature of man and of the individual what is a completely adequate help to premove him to a good act, and God wills the creature to do good by an intention and causality that is frustrable antecedent to the response of the free creature. When God wishes with an absolute will to gain a particular act of the free creature, he can cause the act with an antecedently infallible efficacy; but usually in such circumstances he seems to gain it, not so much through use of one individual antecedent movement, as through a succession of adequate but not compelling persuasions which, if resisted, are succeeded by others until the effect is gained. The question of God's providence with reference to God's ordination of the individual and the group of free creatures to their goal will be examined in the next section, but from what we have seen so far of God's providence with free creatures it is apparent that it does not rest upon God's infallible knowledge of what man would do in his free acts antecedent (causally) to their actual occurrence.

It seems, then, that a study of Scripture, early tradition, and theological reasoning are not contrary to the conclusions we have drawn by reason concerning this matter. That is, they are not contrary to the assertion that God's knowledge of what man would freely choose is not infallibly certain if one abstracts from the presence of this created act to God by reason of his eternity. We may add that tradition after the period of the Fathers is divided on this question. The philosophical doctrine of St. Thomas does not support the thesis of God's infallible knowledge of futurables, for he demands the presence of the free act in history to God through God's eternal knowledge, and he holds that God's antecedent movement of the creature to good in the free act is frustrable. Though the doctrine that God had such knowledge has been held by many theologians since the time of Banez and Molina, it has been held with such different interpretation (for example, some holding that God knows all futurables, and others holding that he knew only a limited number) that it does not constitute a real theological tradition. Moreover, as we have shown in the course of this study, there are many who have rejected it or the suppositions on which it is based. Hence it seems that there is no valid theological tradition contrary to the explanation that we have given of God's knowledge of the creature's free acts.

3. *God's Providence and the Freedom of the Rational Creature*

GOD'S PROVIDENCE AND THE PROBLEM.—Having examined the nature of the harmony that relates God's eternal will and knowledge to a particular free act of the rational creature, we are in a position to analyze the nature of the harmony that relates divine providence to the series of acts of the rational creature whereby it freely approaches its ultimate goal or withdraws from it. As an introduction to our study of this mystery, we must show what theologians agree on, the main differences among their explanations of this harmony as seen in the teachings of Banez and Molina, and the particular aspect of the problem that we shall treat here.

At the beginning of the first chapter of this study we showed that predestination is a revealed mystery, that it was necessary for one to be predestined to eternal glory to be saved, and that God's predestination is an aspect of his providence. Here we wish simply to recall those truths relevant to our purpose concerning the fact of God's providence, several of its attributes, and its application to the supernatural order. The *fact* that God has a providence over the things of the world is expressed by Vatican Council I: "All things that he has created God protects and governs by his providence, *reaching from end to end mightily and governing all things well.*"[56] Scripture frequently expresses this truth through teaching that God takes care to provide for all things what they need, and that the events in Jewish history and in the lives of individuals took place because of the antecedent

[56] Ses. 3, c. 1, D 1784. The text is from Wis. 8:1.

270

divine determination and plan that they come about. It is constantly expressed in Christian tradition, in statements, for example, that God governs all things, that all things are subject to the divine economy, that men are guided and directed to their fulfillment by a divine pedagody, and that there is a plan existing in the divine mind ordering all things to their end.[57] The argument of reason which St. Thomas presents to show the existence of this providence manifests to some extent its *nature*. Every good in creatures is the effect of God's causality, and hence not only the substance or powers of creatures, but their ordination to their end is caused by God. The ordination of creatures to their end, then, must pre-exist in the divine intellect and will. That is, there must be a divine will that they reach their end and a plan in the divine intellect ordaining them to their end. And "the plan of things being ordained to their end is properly speaking providence."[58] The *purpose* of providence, it can be seen, corresponds to that of creation, and thus it is ultimately the uncreated divine goodness and its manifestation or participation by creatures.[59] The participation of the divine goodness to which divine providence ordains creatures is made known to us by the natures of creatures and the purpose their natures manifest, as, for example, by the nature of man. The *universality* of providence is implicit, it seems, in St. Thomas' proof of the existence of providence. For since providence is the plan in the divine mind ordering creatures to their end, it exists in the divine mind for all creatures since all are caused by him; and it exists for all creatures not simply in general but as each differs from others since each is caused by God, not only in what it has in common with others, but in what is distinctive of it. Hence God's providence extends to necessary and contingent creatures, important and unimportant, and things seemingly fortuitous. Moreover, evils themselves fall under the

[57] For Scripture, see P. Van Imschoot, *Théol. de l'Ancien Test.*, 1.107–12, and A. Lemonnyer, "Providence," *DTC* 13.1 (1936), 935–41. For Greek Fathers see H. -D. Simonin, *DTC* 13.1 (1936), 941–60, and for Augustine see A. Rascol, *DTC* 13.1 (1936), 961–84.

[58] *ST*, 1.22.1. Also see R. Garrigou-Lagrange, "La providence selon la théologie," *DTC* 13.1 (1936), 985–1023, particularly 998–1008, where he establishes the existence of divine providence from the fact of finality in the world and the attributes of God.

[59] See *ST*, 1.22.4. See *ibid.*, 1.44.4, where St. Thomas shows that God is the final cause of the world.

providence of God, for they could not exist save through God's permission; and they are permitted "lest the perfect good of the whole be prevented from coming about."[60] Providence is not only universal; it is *immediately* related to each creature, although God governs some creatures through others.[61] And there is an *infallibility* about it that can be seen in God's providence whereby he freed the Jews from Egypt, brought them into the land he had promised, cared for individuals such as Joseph, and brought about events previously planned and prophesied. Man's providence for himself or others is not infallible, for there are many other causes which man does not control and that may frustrate the achievement of his purpose. But God is a universal cause; there is no other cause that escapes his control since all other causality is ultimately reduced to him as first cause. Hence nothing can prevent the achievement of his providential intention or the end of his governance.[62] This, however, does not mean that God imposes necessity upon free creatures. He acts with each creature in accord with its nature, and hence the effects he wants to come about through contingent causes he brings about in accord with the contingent nature of these causes.[63] There is harmony between God's providence and man's freedom.

In the present order, the end of God's providence is one that is supernatural, for he ordains the rational creature (and thus other creatures insofar as they serve the rational creature) to an end that transcends its nature, namely, that of a participation in the life of God as it is exercised by God himself or, in other words, the beatific vision. We should note carefully, however, that God does not by this cease to ordain man to the end that is natural to him. In fact, the perfection that is proper to man is contained eminently in his supernatural perfection, as the beatific vision contains the value of natural knowledge of God though in a higher way. And man continues to be ordained toward what formally or properly perfects him as man; for example, natural knowledge and natural love of God as they are distinct from supernatural knowl-

---

[60] *ST*, 1.22.2. ad 2. There is some question at least about St. Thomas' earlier opinion concerning the ability of reason to prove the universality of divine providence. See also *De ver.*, 14.9. ad 8, and *ST*, 2-2. 1.8. ad 1.

[61] See *ibid.*, 1.22.3.

[62] See *ibid.*, 1.103.7 and 8, *De malo*, 6. art. un., ad 3; *ST*, 1.23.6.

[63] See *ibid.*, 1.22.4.

edge and love will continue to exist when man possesses the beatific vision.[64] In the present order, God's providence ordains creatures to manifest his uncreated good through a created participation that is both supernatural and natural. The supernatural end to which creatures are ordained is, in a way, formal, since it is the determinative measure of their end; and the natural end is, in a way, material in the present order since it is subordinated to the supernatural and is, in a way appropriate to its distinctness, ordained to it. Now, concerning providence in the present order, all theologians agree that God wants all men to be saved or that God's salvific will is universal, for reasons we advanced in the study of Scripture and tradition. They are also agreed that the moral adult must fulfill certain conditions to be saved, namely, believe with supernatural faith in God and his providence, hope in him and love him in a similarly supernatural way, and fulfill his will. What means are necessary for man's fulfillment of these conditions are, they teach, made available to all moral adults. How this is done in all cases is of course difficult to discern; perhaps in the case of many, what is necessary is contained in primitive tradition handed down from one generation to another.[65] In any case God wants the salvation of all, and he does not *positively* reprobate any man antecedent to his sins that merit such reprobation.[66] Not all men are saved however; some among those whom he wishes to save God predestines to eternal life and others he reprobates. But his providence with man in this matter is wholly in accord with his divine attributes and with man's freedom.

It is difficult to see how any theologian can doubt what we have stated so far, but it is within this context that the differences in explaining the harmony between God's providence in the orders of grace and nature and man's freedom arise. Concerning

---

[64] See *ibid.*, 1.56.3; 60.1; 5; 62.7.

[65] On this subject see A. Michel, "Volonté de Dieu. Appendice: La volonté salvifique universelle," *DTC* 15.2 (1950), 3356–74, and Riccardo Lombardi, *The Salvation of the Unbeliever* (Westminster, Md., 1960). St. Thomas in one place holds that God would send an angel to one if this were necessary to give him an opportunity to be saved (*De ver.*, 14.11. ad 1), but later, in accord with his understanding of reprobation, he seems to imply that such aid may be denied because of original sin. See above, ch. 4, p. 119.

[66] See D 200, 316.

the order of grace, Thomists and Molinists agree, as we have seen previously,[67] in considering predestination to be an absolute divine intention for the salvation of the individual, so that one who is predestined is infallibly certain to reach heaven. To show that man's merits which gain the term of predestination come wholly from God, the Thomists hold that this predestination is antecedent to man's merits; and to show that predestination is in accord with man's freedom, the Molinists hold that this predestination is consequent upon God's foreknowledge of man's merits. As a result, the Thomists hold that God in a negative way reprobates, antecedent to his foreknowledge of their sins, those who do not reach heaven; and the Molinists hold that God reprobates man only consequent upon such knowledge. We have previously shown that, in our opinion, for reasons advanced in our analysis of Scripture and tradition, the predestination taught by revelation is the firm and objectively effective divine intention that the justified reach eternal life. Since this intention is one that is conditioned and frustrable by the bad will of the free creature while he is in this life, in our opinion predestination is both antecedent and conditioned or frustrable. Thus for the same reasons we do not think that the dilemma faced by Thomists and Molinists is imposed upon us by revelation.

But Banez, Molina, and their schools find in their philosophical analysis of God's providence conclusions that seem to render our interpretation of Scripture and tradition open to question and to suggest that the natural order is in accord either with an antecedent absolute predestination or a consequent one. Banez holds that, since the desire of the end precedes the desire of the means in the order of intention, God's providence presupposes his intention of the end. And if God's providence is considered without qualification, it involves means, not only apt for gaining the end, but those that are effective in bringing about the end. Otherwise the providence of God would be ineffective and the means he uses would be used in vain.[68] A modern Thomist presents an analysis of the relation of providence to (virtually distinct) other divine acts that seems to sustain this explanation by Banez.[69]

[67] See above, ch. 1, p. 33.
[68] See above, ch. 1, p. 10.
[69] See Garrigou—Lagrange, *art. cit.*, col. 1009–1111. Also see his explanation of the infallibility of divine providence, col. 1014–17.

274

Prudence in man, he shows, presupposes the firm intention to gain the end, for otherwise a man would not effectively and wisely guide his conduct to gain the end. In God, providence concerns ordaining a creature to its end and thus planning for the means whereby it will achieve the end. It properly consists, as St. Thomas says,[70] in a command on the part of the divine intellect of the means that ordain a thing to its end. Thus it presupposes, according to man's understanding, that God knows the end, wills that the creature achieve it, judges the means that are apt to bring it about, and freely chooses them. So it is a divine command of the particular means in view of the particular circumstances. Hence, it presupposes not only God's antecedent will by which he wants all created goods to come to their fulfillment, but God's consequent will that allows, in view of a greater good, some creatures to defect from their end, and that commands the means in view of the circumstances. This Thomist concludes that, since divine providence, properly speaking, presupposes this, it is infallibly effective in the sense of achieving the particular end toward which it ordains the creature. Applying this to the order of grace to explain what they find taught by revelation, the Thomists state that God's predestination is his providence in this infallible sense, while his universal salvific will is his antecedent will. When particular considerations are presupposed, such as the greater good of the universe and the manifestation of divine justice and of the measure of mercy salvation entails (but antecedent to a consideration of the individuals' sins), God by his consequent will allows some men not to reach their salvation and predestines others. Their understanding of the divine decrees and God's causal knowledge is, of course, in accord with this understanding of God's providence. The harmony between this providence and man's freedom depends on the power of God to cause the very freedom of the will in bringing the creature to its end and the fact that salvation is not owed to the creature.

In Molina's opinion, it is anthropomorphic to say that God's providence, like man's, presupposes the will of the end; for him, God's providence, like God's governance, reaches the means first and then the end. Moreover, he explains it in view of his understanding of freedom, God's causality of the act of the free crea-

[70] See ST, 1.22.1. ad 1.

ture, and *scientia media*. God first knows by *scientia media* what the free will would do given all possible circumstances, and he then chooses a particular set of these circumstances that give adequate means ordaining the free creature to its end, even though God knows in which creature this order of means will result in the achievement of the end and in which it will not. Then, finally, for those whom God sees in such an order moving toward the end freely and perseveringly, he wills that they achieve the end. The infallibility of God's providence is preserved here, since God by *scientia media* knows what the creature would do in any circumstances before he determines them; it is not necessary that it be infallible in the sense of efficaciously gaining the end to which it ordains the creature. It is in accord with freedom, since God determines the circumstances and not the free will in the sense of Banez, and the evil men do is from their own self-determination foreseen through *scientia media*. Applying this to the order of grace, the Molinists teach that the universality of God's salvific will is seen in the fact that he gives to all adequate means to get to heaven, predestination is the last of God's acts in the order of intention for the predestined, and reprobation is the last of his acts for the reprobate.[71]

In our analysis of the harmony between God's providence and man's free will, we presuppose our understanding of revelation's teaching concerning God's predestination as antecedent and conditioned, his reprobation as consequent upon man's sins and because of them, and his universal salvific will as excluding no one. Here we shall examine the relation between God's providential ordination of man to his natural fulfillment and man's free movement of himself to this end, and we shall then apply this natural order analogically to the order of grace to help us understand to some extent the relation between God's ordination of man to the beatific vision and man's freedom. The possibility of examining God's natural providence for man in the present order rests on the fact that man is still being directed by God to his natural fulfillment, although he has now been raised to a fulfillment or perfection that transcends his nature. Moreover, by original sin man's nature has not been corrupted, though he has been weakened in

[71] See above, ch. 1, pp. 25 f.

the understanding of and pursuit of his natural perfection. Hence, the nature of man in history, particularly when we abstract from aspects or influences we know derive from his elevation to a supernatural purpose, does show us something of the natural end to which God directs him and the manner in which his providence ordains him to this goal. In both the natural and the supernatural orders we are interested in God's ordination of mankind as a whole to its fulfillment more than his ordination of an individual to his fulfillment, since the common good takes precedence over the good of the individual and since treatment of the individual within mankind as a whole is a help in understanding such problems as predestination. Finally, it is with God's providence as it refers to Adam and Eve and their progeny that we are concerned.

God's Providential Ordination of Man to His Natural Perfection, and the Freedom of Man.—In the first place, in the natural order does God want first the creature's ordination to its end and secondly its ordination to the means proportioned to this end, or does he ordain the creature to the means first of all and only then to the end? Of course, in God's governance of the world he first gives the creature its being and powers, then its acts by which it moves toward its fulfillment, and only then its actual fulfillment. But the present question refers to the order of God's providential intention and plan ordaining the creature to its end. And in this order it seems that we must say that God's providence presupposes his will of the end or that his will of the means presupposes his will of the end. For it is of the nature of the will as will to desire the means in virtue of the end to which the means lead. It is not anthropomorphic to attribute this to God if it is done so analogically, that is, without the supposition of distinct acts of the divine will whereby he wills the end and the means. God does not want the means because he wants the end; rather he wants the means to come about because of the end. And this is the doctrine of St. Thomas.[72]

Since God wills the means for the end, his providence directing man in the natural order is specified by the end he wills for man, and the efficacy of his providence is dependent upon the efficacy with which he wills this end for man. As we have already

[72] See *ST*, 1.22.1. ad 1; 23.4; 19.5.

seen, the ultimate end of providence is the uncreated goodness of God himself, for love and the manifestation of which God creates and acts in creation; but subordinate to this is the created order of participated goods by which God manifests his divine being.[73] Specifically for man, the end of providence is the perfection that is in accord with the nature of man, since it is the function of God's providence to perfect his creatures in accord with their natures. We need not show here how we can know that the perfection of man's nature consists, not in the possession of any created good, but in the final and stable possession of God through a union of knowledge and love to be held perfectly only after the trial of this life is completed. We simply note that since this is the perfection of man's nature, it is to this that God's providence ordains him as to his ultimate goal. Since this is the perfection of human nature, by the fact of giving each man his nature God ordains him to this end. But since God's causality extends to all that individuates one man's nature from that of the rest of men, he ordains men singly within the potentialities of human nature to as vast a variety of representation or participation of the perfection of the divine being as there are individuals within the species, for the divine perfection so transcends created being that it cannot be fittingly represented save through a multiplicity of species and of individuals within the species of material being.[74]

Is the divine will in ordaining man to this natural end infallibly effective for all or for some particular men antecedent to God's consideration of their free response in time? We do not think that this is necessitated by the manner in which God causes man's acts, since, in our opinion, neither the first causality of God nor the potential character of man necessitates a causality of man's acts that is antecedently infallibly effective. Nor do we think that such an efficacy is demanded by the perfections of the divine will and the divine intellect, since God can antecedently ordain man to the performance of a particular free act in a way that is frustrable by man; and hence he can ordain him to the fulfillment of his

---

[73] See above, footnote 59 and *ST*, 103.2. ad 3: ". . . finis quidem universi est aliquod bonum in ipso existens, scilicet ordo ipsius universi: hoc autem bonum non est ultimus finis, sed ordinatur ad bonum extrinsecum, ut ad ultimum finem: sicut etiam ordo exercitus ordinatur ad ducem. See also *ibid.*, art. 4; *CG*, 3.17.

[74] See *CG*, 2.45; *ST*, 1.47.1 and 2.

nature by an antecedent causality that is also frustrable. Nor is it demanded by the divine glory or happiness, for if creation itself is not necessary to God, neither is the fulfillment of creation. In fact, since the divine will is guided by divine wisdom in its ordination of creatures to the end that is proper to them, and divine wisdom has assigned to rational creatures a freedom of activity in moving themselves to their fulfillment as well as in moving themselves to particular acts, it seems that in God's ordinary providence in the natural order he does not ordain men to their end in a way that is antecedently infrustrable. This is what the nature of the creature suggests, and there seems to be no divine attribute that demands otherwise, so it seems to us that we must conclude that God's ordination of the free creature to its end is not antecedently infallibly effective, but frustrable. That is, it is conditioned upon the fulfillment by the creature of the moral law and its love of God above all things, a condition which the rational creature is free to reject. If he rejects it, however, and resists more than the patience of God has determined to endure, he will lose the possession of God that perfects human nature and suffer punishment partially in this life and finally in the next life.[75]

Thus the infallibility of God's ordinary providence in the natural order is not to be understood in the sense that he infallibly fulfills the created end, to which he ordains a particular rational creature antecedent to a consideration of its free acts. Of course, God's providence is infallibly effective in gaining the *uncreated* good that is the end of his every act in creation, for every divine act is a manifestation of the goodness of God and God's love of this goodness. But in reference to the *created* end, providence is normally infallible in the sense that, if the particular rational creature withdraws itself from the fulfillment to which God antecedently ordains it, it falls under the punishment which, consequent upon unrepented sin, God wants for it. This seems to be the doctrine of St. Thomas. In comparing the certainty of predestination, in his understanding, with that of providence, he writes:

> The order of predestination is not certain in the same manner as the order of providence, for the order in providence is *not certain with reference to a particular end* except when the proximate cause necessarily produces its effect. In predestination however there is

[75] For St. Thomas' doctrine on eternal sanctions, see *CG*, 3.140–46.

found a certainty with reference to the particular end, and still the proximate cause, namely free will, does not produce its effect save in a contingent manner.[76]

And he shows that nothing can occur outside of divine governance or against it through showing that, if the creature escapes divine governance in one aspect, it falls under it in another.[77] Divine providence, then, in its normal ordering of the individual rational creature to its natural end is infallibly effective in the sense of absolutely determining its particular end only consequent upon God's foreknowledge of the creature's free acts in time.

More central to the divine intention than the fulfillment of the end of the individual man is the created end to which his providence ordains mankind as a whole, for as St. Thomas writes: "The particular good is ordained to the common good as to its end since the being of the part is for the being of the whole. Hence, also, the good of the people is more divine than the good of one man."[78] This good of mankind as a whole, within which God seeks the good of the individual man, is an order within mankind that is fitting, in a way, to the uncreated end to which it is ordained, namely, the divine perfection which it manifests. The end intrinsic to creation or mankind taken as a whole is not such a manifestation that would be proportionate to the divine perfection, but rather one ordered by the divine intelligence as a fitting expression of God's perfection. It consists in a certain fitting measure, variety, and order of men who achieve their personal perfection, an order determined, not by the individuals who will compose it, since we have seen that God's antecedent desire for their personal perfection is frustrable, but by the manifestation of the divine perfection to which God's intelligence directs it.[79] We ask now whether God's will that mankind as a whole achieve this created end is infallibly efficacious antecedent to his consideration of mankind's response. Concerning this, we can say that neither any need on the part of God nor any divine attribute makes it necessary that his ordination of humanity as a whole to this created end

[76] *De ver.,* 6.3.
[77] See *ST,* 1.103.7 and 8, and above, p. 234.
[78] *CG* 3.17.
[79] See above, footnote 73, and *De pot.,* 3.16.

280

be antecedently infallibly effective in gaining it. And no divine attribute or human resistance makes it necessary that God's antecedent ordination of mankind to this end be frustrable. For he is omnipotent and fully capable of effecting this end with antecedent infallible efficacy; and man's freedom is neither an obstacle nor an indication that God does not act in this way, since he can ordain mankind to this end through a succession of contingent causes each of which man can resist, but which are multiplied until the end is achieved.[80] From the evidence of reason we may see that it is fitting to the divine goodness to achieve the created end of mankind as a whole in this manner, for it is more important and closely related to the ultimate divine purpose in creation than the end of the individual; such a divine will and its achievement would be an extraordinary indication of divine wisdom and power; and it is fitting that God not allow man's evils to obstruct the fulfillment of the created end of his providence. But from reason we cannot know with certainty, it seems to us, whether in fact God's antecedent will ordaining mankind to this end is infallibly effective in this sense since it is not due to the creature or needed by God. We shall see later that there may be indications in revelation that God's antecedent will for this natural fulfillment of mankind as a whole is infrustrable in this sense; but now, whether that ordination comes from a frustrable or infrustrable divine will to achieve this common created end, we will briefly examine the manner in which God's providence ordains mankind to it.

In general, God ordains man to this end in accord with his nature, so by understanding his nature we can know something of the way God's providence directs him to his natural end. An objection may be raised that man's nature in the present order is elevated to the supernatural end through grace, and it is wounded by original sin; hence, a study of this nature will not show us specifically the characteristics of God's providence with man in relation to his natural end. This objection, however, does not seem convincing, since, as we have seen, man continues to be ordained to his natural perfection while he is raised to one that is higher; grace is not an intrinsic change of nature, but a new nature given

[80] See *De ver.*, 6.3.

to man which perfects him and leaves his human nature intact; and original sin was the loss of grace and the preternatural gifts, but not a corruption of man's nature. Hence, man's acts in time do manifest his nature and thus something of the manner in which God's providence ordains mankind to reach its purpose; and they show what is distinctive of God's providence in this regard, particularly to one who knows the change wrought in man through grace and original sin and who thus can to some extent distinguish in man's ordination to his historical purpose and activity for that purpose what is due to his ordination to a supernatural end and what to his ordination to one that is natural. Therefore, it seems to us that from man's nature in history, and thus from man's individual and social acts in history that manifest that nature, we can know something of the manner in which God's providence ordains mankind to its natural end. We shall briefly examine three aspects of this providence that can be induced from three characteristics that qualify man's approach toward his end, namely, his material and spiritual nature, his personal and social nature, and his freedom, all of which are relevant to our central interest in God's ordination of mankind as a whole to a supernatural end. It seems to us that (besides the importance of this for its own sake) this perspective casts light on God's predestination and salvific will as it reaches the individual.

In the first place, the *composite nature* of man as a rational animal composed of body and spiritual soul makes known to us something of the manner in which God ordains him to mankind's fulfillment by his providence and governance of the world. Facts of history that reflect this aspect of man's nature and this nature itself seem to show how God's providence and governance working in time brought man to his initial existence and direct him toward the fulfillment of mankind's purpose. There is a vast amount of evidence that before the appearance of man in the world there was, through long ages, a progressive improvement in the conditions sustaining life and a succession of organisms that in similarity and function gradually approached the organism of primitive man.[81] Moreover, a consideration of the nature of man as he

[81] For an excellent presentation of the scientific evidence for evolution and a study of its relevance to philosophical and revealed truths, see M. Grison, *Problèmes d'origines, l'universe—les vivants—l'homme* (Paris, 1954).

now is in its relation to lower creation shows that man is the perfection or fulfillment of lower material beings, for he is the highest
manifestation of material life; he emerges from lower creation in
virtue of the spirituality of his soul and his higher activities; it is
he whom lower creation serves; and it is by his knowledge and
love that it shares God's perfection more immediately. It would
seem, then, that both the evidence of science and the nature of
man indicate that God has providentially ordained man to come
into existence through an evolutionary process that is in accord
with man's material and spiritual composite nature.

It also suggests that God ordains mankind, once it exists, to
approach its natural fulfillment by a gradual evolutionary process
through which it approaches this goal only by intermediate stages
that in a progressively greater way participate the perfection in
which this natural purpose consists. The evidence of paleontology
and pre-history, for example, support this by showing the gradual
growth of man's cranial capacity and the gradual development of
tools toward greater variety for many specific tasks, greater
beauty, greater complexity.[82] History, too, presents much evidence
for the same conclusion. Man's expansion over the world, his sub-
jugation of lower creation through knowledge and inventions that
serve his physical needs and allow him greater freedom from the
limitations of matter, and his achievement of cultural and social
goals befitting the dignity of man as benefits more generally ac-
cruing to men have all normally been gradual processes that have
built upon previous achievements. This is not simply the way that,
in fact, mankind has developed; such a manner of development is
due to the very nature of man. For since man is a material being,
he initially possesses his ultimate perfection only potentially,
with the potentiality that is fulfilled only by a multiplicity of acts in
kind and number and by a process that is very gradual. And hence
it seems that this is the manner in which God's providence and
governance ordains men to their fulfillment, not only as individuals,
but as a group. History is meant by God's providence to be the
medium by which he gains his purpose with man.

By this we do not mean that successive generations are meant
by God's providence in the natural order to share knowledge and
love of God in ever greater intensity, for these acts of man are

[82] See *ibid.*, pp. 193–245.

more spiritual and hence more independent from the condition of man's body and circumstances. Nor do we mean that intermediate stages of history do not have a meaning and value of their own. For each stage is in its own right a unique participation of divine perfection and manifestation of that perfection; and it is proper to mankind because of its potential character to manifest the divine perfection through a succession of stages in history. What we mean is that God intends to gain in this way with men as a group his purpose in the sense of both an increasing number of men who participate in his perfection and a greater manifestation or participation in that perfection through secondary human values that are progressively more in accord with the dignity of man. And we may add that this manner of man's development seems to have been God's intention even antecedent to the fact of original sin, for in the first chapter of Genesis, God is said to have blessed the first man and woman from whom all men take their origin and to have told them: *Be fruitful and multiply; fill the earth and subdue it. Have dominion over the fish of the sea, the birds of the air, the cattle and all the animals that crawl on the earth.*[83] This expansion over the earth and the conquest of it consequent upon this expansion is inevitably a gradual process and all the more so since mankind took its origin from one couple. Genesis' teaching on the later origins of those who dwell in tents and have flocks, of those who play the harp and flute, and of those who forge vessels of bronze and iron[84] shows that the gradual growth of human culture is also in accord with scriptural teaching.

The second aspect of human nature that shows us something of the nature of the providence and governance by which God directs and moves man to his goal is the *personal and social character* of man. Since man is a person, God does not seek the achievement of his divine uncreated goal or created goal in any way that involves the sacrifice of the individual's essential fulfillment as the means by which it comes about, either in the sense that God positively wants this sacrifice or that he does not have an intention for the fulfillment of the individual. He may, of course, allow cer-

---

[83] Gen. 1:28.
[84] See Gen. 4:20–22, and A.M. Dubarle, *Le péché originel dans l'écriture 60.* Genesis shows too that in fact this development of men was frequently due to irreligious motives.

tain evils to befall individuals lest, by preventing them, the good he seeks from mankind as a whole be impeded; but one cannot say that in his natural providence he allows, antecedent to the individual's sin, the sacrifice of man's essential good of a union of knowledge and love with God in the next life, a good that far more than outweighs those which man suffers the loss of in this life. Not only does God not sacrifice the individual's good to that of mankind as a whole; in his providential intention, the work man is to do for society is to be a means of his growth to his personal fulfillment. This is so, in the first place, since by fulfilling his function in society man is to cooperate willingly in God's purpose and in the process grow in participation in God's perfections in a way unique to himself. It is so, in the second place, since one man differs from other men by that which individuates his nature, namely, matter; and it is God himself who as first cause is the source of this individuation[85] through causing his being within a determined society and stage of its history, and for a particular function within this context. It is the end or purpose of the individual within society in virtue of which God's providence, which reaches all individuals in their individual differences, determines the individual's being.

Since man is of his nature a social being, God's providence ordains him to gain the means of his fulfillment through society; and he ordains mankind as a whole toward its end through the means of social institutions that provide those things necessary for life in accord with the dignity of man. Among these institutions the family, the state, and the world-wide organization of states necessary to ensure a just peace generally among mankind hold prime place. Since these are demands of human nature itself, though not all are demanded at all times, it is the divine intention that is their ultimate source; and man's activity in promotion of these institutions is, insofar as it is such a promotion, the effect of God's first causality and direction, as all good in creation is the effect of God's first causality. Also due to this social nature of man, God's providence antecedently provides the resources, men, and particularly leaders that are needed for the fulfillment of man's social purpose at each stage of history. These men whom he provides, and particularly those individuals or groups he specially endows

[85] See *ST*, 1.14.11.

for leadership in all spheres of human needs, receive the benefits they do from him from a special choice of God, but from a choice that is within the context of God's intention in history, and not simply for their particular welfare. God's intention so endowing them reaches them in his intention to provide the things necessary for mankind generally to achieve the purpose appropriate for that particular stage of history. And the welfare of society at each stage depends upon the fulfillment of their function on the part of those so provided and, once more, particularly on that of those endowed as leaders in society.[86]

And this brings us to the third aspect of human nature that shows us something of the manner in which God's providence ordains mankind to reach the end he antecedently wants for it, namely, man's *freedom*. It is proper to man to move toward his perfection through freely choosing the values that perfect him and through freely determining his own activity and moving himself in virtue of these values. And since this is the nature that God has given man, it indicates that divine providence ordains mankind to reach its goal through men's free self-movement and self-governance, and not through means that would be either opposed to this or irrelevant to it. Hence, too, God in his governance moves men to this goal through a causality that works upon their minds and wills, through giving them understanding of the end that will perfect them as a group and the moral norms that will guide them to this perfection, and through stirring up in them the desire of this perfection and an aversion from what threatens or destroys it. Because the freedom of men in no way prevents the goodness of their acts from being caused by God as first cause, the progress toward the perfection of mankind's purpose as toward that of the individual is wholly due to God as first cause and to man simply as a participant in the causality of God to the extent that he cooperates with this causality. This causality is one that is for each particular stage or group of mankind antecedently frustrable, as in the case of God's causality of the acts of the individual man. Man can act in accord with it; but if he does, he does so freely. He can

---

[86] Scripture shows that God's providence extends to peoples as well as individuals; in fact, the Old Testament doctrine insists more on the former than on the latter. See Is. 5:26–30; Dan. 2:31–45; Amos 9:7; *Van Imschoot, Théol.*, 1.108.

also reject it. That is, mankind at any particular stage or in any particular group can, as in the case of the individual, reject God's antecedent intention for its fulfillment of what is for its welfare at that particular time. It may, for example, by a disordered desire on the part of society or its leaders for secondary and immediate goods neglect to seek the understanding of what is for its more ultimate welfare and to act in accord with it. By this defective activity it may, as in the case of the individual who sins, gain some secondary good or preserve that which it has for some time. But to the extent that physical reality remains in its activity and effect, this defective activity still has God as its first cause and source through the cooperation that he continues to give to men even after they reject that to which he antecedently impels them. So even those secondary goods men may gain through this means —such as greater wealth, greater power, greater prestige, and some elements of human culture—are due to God as their first cause.

This explanation of God's providence in relation to man's freedom, one may say, is opposed to divine sovereignty, for it allows men to escape God's providential plan and to frustrate its fulfillment. But we answer that, correctly understood, it seems no more contrary to this sovereignty than sins of the individual free creature are. In the first place, the stage or portion of humanity that so reject God's antecedent will escapes from one aspect of God's providence only to fall under another, namely, his punishment. Unrepented sin in the individual results in proportionate punishment in the next life and partial punishment in this life through at least a diminishing understanding of what is for his welfare and a growing moral hardness. History shows that those groups of mankind that reject the divine law as it is appropriate for their particular condition and that continue to do so suffer a corruption of the common good sooner or later as a result of this very rejection. Societies as well as individuals progressively lose in such circumstances the understanding of what is for their good and the will to perform it. And they inevitably suffer an inner corruption that may take various forms. It may be increasing interior social disorder between classes, increasing despotism, cultural stagnation, opposition, and ultimately defeat by external enemies; but whatever form it takes, it is experienced by that society. And since it does result from their rejection of God's law, for it is his law that guides men to their fulfillment, it is experienced by that society as God's judgment and punishment in history. We do not say that that society will not for a time achieve some secondary goods through its rejection of God's law or that the corruption immediately follows upon its social offenses, but in our opinion history does witness that such a corruption of the common good does take place. On the other hand, we are not saying that whenever a society does suffer grave social evils of this kind, this proves the fact of grave social disorders within that society. Sufferings of this kind may in God's providential purpose be simply permitted by him to avoid impeding a greater good; they may, in addition to this or primarily, be a means of purification of that society; or they may be the means by which that society fulfills a great historical mission, such as civilizing its oppressors. We simply say that those groups of mankind that do persistently reject God's law suffer eventually an inner corruption as a result.

An objection may be advanced that this punishment of a society is unfitting, since it embraces the individual who may in no way be responsible for the failure of that society to respond to God's will. To this we answer that the individual also benefits from advantages possessed by the society in which he lives, even though he in no way is responsible for those advantages. Moreover, the evils he may suffer because of the society in which he lives do not deprive him of his essential personal fulfillment, and this is of such a value that it more than compensates for those things that he loses by involvement in his particular society. Also these sufferings can be for man an occasion of personal growth if he submits himself to God and raises his desires from transitory things to those that are more enduring.

Hence, it does seem fitting that a society that so sins be so punished, both for the reasons that show the fittingness of punishment in the case of sin by an individual and for the added reason that it does not seem that a society as such can be punished in the next life. Hence, if it went without punishment for its unrepented sins, it would flout God and the order he has established without redressing its faults; it would escape the divine providential intention; there would be one order of justice for the individual and a completely different one for men socially; and there would be less motivation inducing societies to conform to God's law. Moreover, besides these natural reasons that indicate such is the manner of God's governance of the world, Scripture frequently teaches that peoples are punished for the evils they do by God's judgments in history.[87]

A second consideration that shows such societies do not frustrate the divine purpose in history or the intention of divine providence that is its source is shown in the fact that the ultimate created good God seeks from mankind as a whole is not the cooperation with his purpose by mankind at any particular stage of history, but, as we have seen, the ultimate order among mankind that represents in a fitting way the divine perfections. Thus, if society at some particular stage rejects God's will, it is not frustrating a purpose that is antecedently directed toward its cooperation in an infallibly effective manner. And if it rejects the fulfillment of the mission God has given to it, God can raise up later causes to bring this about, and multiply such contingent causes until the contingent effect he antecedently wills comes about.

Thirdly, the rejection of God's will by such a society can be turned by God to gain his purpose in history more fully than if the society had initially cooperated with him. The created goods such a society has left God's law to amass God can use to further his purpose with mankind, and the later society he raises up to fulfill the purpose the prior society rejected can be one that will fulfill it more effectively. Hence, God's toleration of society's rejection of his law does not permit it to escape or frustrate his providence or governance of the world toward the end he antecedently wills to achieve.

These, then, are, in our opinion, some aspects of the manner in which God by his providence and governance in the world directs and moves mankind toward its natural purpose.

God's Ordination of Mankind to a Supernatural End in Christ.—Now that we have considered God's guidance of man to his natural goal, we can relate this to his providential ordination

[87] See Amos. 1-2, and the warnings of many of the prophets against the nations. An interesting article relevant to this teaching in the New Testament is A. Feuillet, "Les origines et la signification de Mt 10, 23 b," *Catholic Biblical Quarterly*, 22 (1961), 182-98.

of man to his supernatural goal in the present order. In the first place, from what we have seen in the natural order, it would seem that philosophical evidence concerning God's providence is not contrary to our understanding of Scripture and tradition on this matter. For example, since, in our opinion, God's natural ordination of an individual man to his end is both antecedent to his acts and frustrable so that the one who reaches his end was not antecedently certain to do so and the one who fails was not antecedently certain to fail, the natural evidence is not opposed to our understanding of predestination as a divine intention ordaining the individual to his supernatural end in a way that is both antecedent and frustrable. In fact, it seems on its own level to be in accord with what we found in Scripture and tradition. In the second place, then, we can use what we have seen in the natural order of God's providence to help us understand God's direction of man to his supernatural end as we have found it expressed in Scripture and tradition. We shall not in this treatment establish once more what these founts of revelation seem to teach; we shall simply try to explain to some extent through the natural order of providence what we have found earlier in this study. We shall analyze successively how God's ordination of man in the present disposition to a supernatural end is found in Christ, in each individual man, and in mankind as a whole. Since the present dispensation is that of fallen and redeemed humanity, what we say has direct relation only to Adam and Eve and their progeny after original sin. Moreover, since in the present economy of redeemed humanity man reaches his natural fulfillment in the next life only if he reaches his supernatural fulfillment, and he can live in this life for a long time without serious sin only if he has grace, God's ordination of man to the supernatural end in the present order is also the supreme means by which he ordains him to his natural end. Thus what we say below is a necessary supplement to what we have already said, even as this refers simply to man's ordination in the present economy to a natural goal.

St. Paul writes of Jesus Christ that *all things have been created through and unto him, and he is before all creatures, and in him all things hold together.*[88] St. Paul here is writing of Jesus Christ and

[88] Col. 1:16–17. See the whole passage 1:15–20; Eph. 1:10; 1 Cor. 3:22–23.

not simply of the Word of God, as the whole context of the passage shows clearly, for the one of whom he speaks in the sentence just quoted he says in the next sentence is the head of the Church. He teaches here that Jesus Christ is the one for whom (*unto him*) all things are created and thus that he is the final cause of creation and, we may add, of God's providence and governance of the world since the end of this is the same as that of creation. The reason St. Paul gives to show that Christ holds the first place among all creatures and thus is the purpose of all is that *it has pleased God the Father that in him all his fullness should dwell.*[89] Part of Paul's thought in this passage is that Christ holds the first place in creation in virtue of his humanity through which he saved mankind, for, as all creation is involved in man's fall, it is also in his restoration.[90] But this does not fully explain the primacy in creation that St. Paul attributes to Christ in this whole passage, since this primacy extends to Christ being the final cause of the creation of all material and spiritual beings, and, as the passages we quoted show, he attributes this to Christ in virtue of his divine attributes and nature. What we have written concerning the end of God's creation and providence helps us to understand this. For this goal is ultimately the good of God himself and subordinately the good of the creature that manifests the goodness of God. Since in Christ dwells the fullness of the Godhead through hypostatic union with his human nature, the man Christ gives glory to God and manifests the perfection of God in a way that is both interior to creation and is proportioned or equal to the divine perfection itself. Moreover, the participated goodness of no other creature adds in intensity to the glory given to God by Christ or is independent of Christ, since the supernatural perfection of man and the healing of his nature is participated from Christ the Redeemer, and all created perfection is participated from him who is God incarnate. Thus Christ is the end of God's creation and providence in the orders of nature and grace. And since in the material world the higher orders of perfection in the natural order have come about, it seems to us, by an evolutionary process, Christ is the goal of evolution, the one in whom evolution's development reaches its fulfillment intrinsic to the world.

[89] Col. 1:19.
[90] See *Bible . . . de Jerusalem* note on Col. 1:19.

291

Because Christ is said to be the final cause of creation by St. Paul, some have thought that the Incarnation was absolutely decreed by God antecedent to his foreknowledge of man's sin. This does not seem to be a necessary conclusion; for whether the Incarnation is decreed before or after such knowledge of man's sin, it is the end of creation and God's providence, since God's purpose intrinsic to creation is the glorification or manifestation of God's perfection through a communication of this perfection to creatures. And granted the Incarnation, the fulfillment of God's purpose is found in it, whether it was decreed before or after the knowledge of Adam's sin. In the former case it is the final cause of creation from God's initial absolute intention; and in the latter it is the final cause that assumes creation to an end that transcends the purpose initially intrinsic to it. Since revelation constantly teaches that the reason for the Incarnation is the redemption, it seems that we should say that, antecedent to God's foreknowledge of man's sin, it was only hypothetically decreed on the condition of man's sin.[91] Thus God became man to give to God the glory denied to him by man's sin, first of all that glory given to him in God incarnate and then that given by those for whose redemption he came. In this is seen how powerless man is by sin to frustrate the ultimate created end of God's creation; for in Christ, God fulfilled what man resisted, fulfilled it in an infinitely more perfect way, and so turned man's sin itself to promote his glory. Finally we can see in this that God permits sin (in the sense in which we explained that permission) not simply not to impede the greater good that he seeks, but for his divine glory which is gained more perfectly by such permission.

GOD'S SALVIFIC WILL, PREDESTINATION, AND REPROBATION IN RELATION TO THE INDIVIDUAL FREE CREATURE.—In the present economy God wants this perfection of the supernatural order to be possessed, not only by Christ, but by all men; for he has willed that all men gain the end of the supernatural order and has providentially ordained them to that end. This we have seen in the teaching of Scripture and tradition concerning the universality of God's salvific will, the providential means he took to achieve this through Christ, and his predestination of some to eternal

[91] See *ST*, 3.1.3.

glory. The question before us now concerns the relation between this will and providence of God on the one hand, and the free will of man on the other. What is the relation of God's universal salvific will and predestination to free will?

The universality of God's salvific will is such that, as the Church has progressively clarified and all theologians agree, it excludes no man in the present order. Our question is whether it is such that it is incompatible with reprobation of a man antecedent to God's knowledge of his sins in time. It would seem that God wants all men to be saved and reprobates none antecedent to his personal sins or his resistance to God's antecedent will beyond the measure God has determined to endure. The scriptural evidence for this will not be repeated here. We simply note that it consists in its unrestricted expressions of God's salvific will, the fact that the passages adduced to support a reprobation antecedent to man's personal sins (such as the ninth chapter of Romans) do not mean this, and its teaching that God's wrath is only consequent upon and because of man's sins. The development of tradition in the teaching of the Church and of theologians was, we saw, in the direction of more unreserved expressions of this teaching of Scripture. Moreover, Scripture teaches that God's wrath is poured out on man only after man's protracted and unrepented sin, and not simply after man's initial sin. This is contained in the scriptural doctrine that this life is the period of God's patience, and the length of this life is the measure of God's patience and of his attempt to win the sinful man from his sinful ways. For example, St. Paul asks of the sinner:

> Dost thou despise the riches of his [God's] goodness and patience and longsuffering? Dost thou not know that the goodness of God is meant to lead thee to repentance? But according to thy hardness and unrepentant heart, thou dost treasure up to thyself wrath on the day of wrath and of the revelation of the just judgment of God, who will render to every man according to his works.[92]

Since such is the teaching of Scripture, it seems to us that in the present order God's antecedent salvific will is such that he reprobates no man save for his unrepented personal sins.

Objections can be raised against this conclusion. In the first place, there are the objections that derive from a natural analysis

[92] Rom. 2:4–6. See Peter 1.3:20; 2.3:9; Wis. 11:23 ff.

of the infallible efficacy of the divine will and providence. Since the divine will is infallible, God's permission of a particular individual to fail to gain his eternal goal must precede that individual's sins, for if he did not permit man to fail he would not fail, and if he sustained man in the practice of the good he would overcome his tendency to fail. Reprobation, then, in the sense of a permission for man to fail to gain eternal happiness must precede God's foreknowledge of the creature's sins. To this we answer that God's will of the fulfillment of a particular rational creature in the natural order, or his providence ordaining the creature to that end, is not antecedently infallibly effective in gaining that particular created effect. It is infallible in the sense that, if the free creature does not glorify God by achieving its fulfillment, it does so by suffering punishment and manifesting the divine justice, and it may be called infallible in that, if the creature does not resist, God's antecedent intention will certainly carry him to his fulfillment. Thus, since God's antecedent desire of the natural fulfillment of the rational creature can be frustrated by its free will, God's permission of its failure is not an antecedent intention not to sustain the creature in the good, but simply a toleration of its rejection of God's antecedent intention for its fulfillment. And this is not reprobation. So it would not seem that objections from the natural order of God's will and providence invalidate our understanding of Scripture and tradition.

Another objection is that the supernatural order is not owed to the free creature, and so it is no defect in justice in God if he raises some to this order and does not raise others, antecedently desires that some gain the supernatural end and that others do not. Our answer is that, as such, the statement is true. God could raise some angels to a supernatural end and not others, but in this case the fact that the latter did not ordain themselves to God with a supernatural love would not be sinful, since it would not be a privation of an order God desired for them. Moreover, if the objection is that God could raise some of the descendants of Adam and Eve to a supernatural end and not others, still it seems that if he had done this he would have given the latter the natural means necessary to overcome the weakness induced by original sin that makes it morally impossible for man to observe for long the natural law. Otherwise such individuals would, with antecedent infallibility, sin seriously at some time, and thus, because of original sin, they would be subject to the pain of sense as well as the loss of the beatific vision; but this seems to us difficult to harmonize with the teaching of the Church. In any case, even though God could will the supernatural end for some and not for others, this is not the case in the present order, since he has expressed his universal salvific will for fallen humanity and hence does not antecedently reprobate men because of original sin. As for the angels, theologians commonly teach that all were given sanctifying grace, and this is an ordination to a supernatural end.

But a final objection may be raised from the condition of the infant who dies unbaptized. Antecedent to his personal sin he is excluded from the beatific vision, so there seems to be an antecedent reprobation. To this we answer that such exclusion from the beatific vision seems to be reprobation in only a qualified way, for the infant does not suffer the pain of sense; then, too, we cannot say that it does not share a degree of personal, natural fulfillment that more than compensates for physical sufferings it may have endured. Thus the fact that God allows infants to lose the beatific vision antecedent to their personal sin does not show that his reprobation of moral adults is antecedent to their personal sin. And it does not disprove the universality of God's salvific will; it, at most, proves that God does not will the salvation of the infant to such an extent that he would prevent the action of the secondary causes, according to their normal laws, that brings about its death in its unbaptized state.

This brings us to the mystery of *predestination* in its relation to man's free will. We have seen that St. Paul and the Gospels taught that all who have been justified through their incorporation into Christ in the Church are predestined to eternal glory by God. For all these there is a firm divine intention that they reach heaven, an intention that is unconquerable by any created power and one so effective in bringing them to heaven that it can be said God has already established them in heaven. But the Christian can withdraw his own fidelity to God while he is in this life and through this be finally reprobated in spite of the fact that he has been predestined to glory. It is not necessary for us once more to give the evidence on which we based our judgment that this is, in fact, the teaching of St. Paul and that tradition, particularly as it is expressed in the Council of Trent, at least implies it. Nor is it necessary now to show that the evidence of philosophy is not opposed to this interpretation, for the whole treatment of philosophy which we have so far engaged in has, in our opinion, done so. It simply remains for us to give an explanation (which in view of all we have written so far can be very brief) of the frustrable character of predestination and its relation to God's foreknowledge.

Justification through incorporation into Christ of its very nature is the destruction of man's sins and the infusion through sanctifying grace and the theological virtues of a created share in God's uncreated justice and life. Hence, of its very nature it is not simply the acquisition of present justice, but the preservation and growth to eternal life of this initial justice which as a seed contains its eternal fulfillment. This is so since sanctifying grace is a participation in God's life and is consequently of its nature enduring to eternity, since God's own life is eternal. And charity is a love of God above all created things, so no created good has the power to make the man endowed with the power of charity place his final goal in a created good and thus lose sanctifying grace.[93] Thus, as we explained in the preceding chapter, justification endows man with a gift of final perseverance.

It is the divine causality that is the first and proper source of this immense created gift. Such a gift, then, shows in the divine will a love for the justified greater than his love for men who have not received this gift, since every created gift is the effect of God's love and one has a greater gift than another because of the fact that God loves him more than another. This gift also shows in the divine will a free choice or election that separates this man from those not justified through incorporation into Christ and prefers him to these others. Since the gift of sanctifying grace is eternal life in seed, the love and election that it manifests in the divine will is a divine choice of the individual for eternal life. This divine election or choice differs from God's salvific will in that the former has already given eternal life, while the latter is a desire to give it; the former is God's intention for those he justifies, while the latter is his intention as it reaches those not justified, but whom God wants to justify. St. Paul seems to be speaking of God's

[93] See ST, 2.2, 24.11.

will for those who do not have saving faith when he mentions his universal salvific will, for he presents this truth as a motive for Christians to pray for all men. *This is good and agreeable in the sight of God our Savior, who wishes all men to be saved and to come to a knowledge of the truth.*[94] Hence, while God's election is the gift of eternal life on the part of the divine will to those whom he justifies, his salvific will, it seems, refers to his divine will offering divine life to those not justified through calling them to justification.

As justification shows in the divine will a choice of man for eternal life, it also shows in God a divine plan and will ordaining man to eternal life that is other than his providence ordaining one not yet justified to this end, and this we call predestination. Thus it is a special part of God's providence ordaining man to a supernatural goal, namely, that providence that reaches the justified. It is most properly and immediately God's providence with those whom he has justified through incorporation into the Church or Christ as his members, and it is in this sense that St. Paul uses it. But since those who are justified by Christ's merits without actual membership in the Church also receive eternal life in seed through inhering sanctifying grace, God has predestined them too. It seems, however, that as these participate in Christ in only a secondary way since they are not actual members of Christ, so, too, they are predestined in only a secondary way, for the means by which God ordains them to heaven are not as powerful or complete as those by which he ordains actual members of Christ to heaven. The latter, through being members of Christ, have the helps of the Church's teaching of Christ's message in its integrity and without error, the sacraments, the sacramentals, the authorized guides to heaven in the successors of the apostles, and many other helps or means ordaining them to eternal life that those outside the Church do not have. They enjoy God's governance, then, in a special way and hence, too, his providence and that part of providence that is predestination. Hence, predestination is more properly said of those justified within the Church, but it is said properly of all the justified. For it is justification that shows the existence in God of a plan and will ordaining a man to heaven

---

[94] 1 Tim. 2:3-4.

that is infallibly effective antecedent to man's acts, in the sense that, already, before man has finished his course in this life, God has established him in heaven and has a plan and intention objectively and infallibly effective in moving him to this end.

But the effect of predestination, namely, the seed of eternal life in the grace of justification, makes known to us not only this intention and plan to God, but also the fact that the free will of the justified whom it concerns can in this life frustrate it. For the effect of this divine intention in the justified is a grace that is essentially connected with charity and that has not yet introduced the justified to the beatific vision. Charity does place within man's will a tendency to love God above all things; but in this life man does not see God, and therefore the quest of God in this life does not appear to the will to be the total good. So man's will under charity remains free to choose a created good as its final goal and thus reject God as the end of his life. When this is done, charity and sanctifying grace are lost by the soul, since a deliberate choice of a created good as one's ultimate purpose is contrary to charity. And since the created grace or justification in this life is of such a nature, the divine providential intention or predestination that is its source is of its nature frustrable or subject to rejection by the free will of the justified man.

From this the relation of God's predestination to God's foreknowledge appears. According to our interpretation of Scripture, predestination is the divine providential intention that is the cause of man's justification. And so it is antecedent to God's knowledge (causally) of man's merits, since acts properly speaking meritorious only begin with justification, and it is not absolutely certain to gain its effect save consequent upon God's knowledge of man's continued fidelity to God in this life, since man is free to reject predestination in this life. The acts preparatory for justification are, of course, caused by God as first cause in his desire to justify man; and when they take place and actually end in justification, they are said to be caused by God's predestination because of their relation to justification and because of the fact that it is by one will that God prepares a man for justification and justifies him. So, since for St. Paul, God's call meant an effective call not resisted by man, he taught that it was an effect of God's predestination.[95] If these acts do not terminate in justification because of man's resistance, they cannot be said to be the effect of God's predestination since the term in virtue of which they are called such, namely justification, is not gained. They are, then, the effects of God's universal salvific will. Since man can resist God's preparation of him for justification, predestination is properly speaking consequent (causally) upon God's foreknowledge of such acts. St. Paul's teaching seems to be this, for he writes: *those whom he has foreknown he has also predestined* . . .[96] Finally, since God extends his grace to all men during the time they are in this life, which is the period of God's patience, those who are not justified are, while in this life, subject to God's universal salvific will and are not reprobated until they have completed this life in a state of final impenitence. Reprobation is only consequent upon God's knowledge of their death in final impenitence.

One may object that this explanation does not seem to be consistent with St. Paul's doctrine that *he [God] chose us in him [Christ] before the foundation of the world.*[97] According to the explanation given above, God's choice is not antecedent to his foreknowledge of a man's cooperation with the grace leading him to justification, whereas Paul asserts that it preceded the whole order of time. To this we answer that this text does not affirm an infrustrable or absolute divine choice of individual men, as an element of God's common providence, antecedent to his foreknowledge of their free response; in fact, such an interpretation would be inconsistent, as we have previously seen, with other elements of Paul's teaching.

GOD'S ORDINATION OF MANKIND TO A SUPERNATURAL END, AND MAN'S FREEDOM.—Now that we have examined to some extent God's ordination of mankind to a supernatural end as it is seen in Christ and the individual man, we can ask how it is found in mankind considered as a whole. In his ordination of mankind as a whole to the supernatural end of the present economy, how are

[95] See Rom. 8:30, and above, ch. 2, p. 56.
[96] See Rom. 8:29.
[97] Eph. 1:4.

God's will and providence related to the free acts of men? This question includes that of God's ordination of the individual to this purpose, since he wills the salvation of the individual within his will of that of mankind as a whole. It includes his ordination of mankind in the present economy to its natural end, since this is not gained without the achievement of man's supernatural end; and the rejection of God's providence ordaining man to the latter entails a rejection of that providence ordaining him to the former. And all of these questions are included in a way in that of Christ, since he is the final cause intrinsic to the world in the present order, or the goal of the supernatural and the natural orders of God's providence concerning society and the individual, for all things are directed to a manifestation of his perfection and thus of God's. Here we shall treat first the nature of God's will that mankind as a whole reach its supernatural goal and then the nature of his providential ordination of mankind as a whole to this end. This treatment can be very brief, for what we say is based on everything we have treated till now, and it is with only some few aspects of this inexhaustible mystery that we are concerned.

That God wills mankind as a whole to reach the end of eternal life is contained in the Old Testament teaching on the universal extension of the kingdom of God and the New Testament doctrine that the Church was commissioned by Christ to expand his mission to all nations[98] as well as in the affirmation of the universality of God's salvific will that we have already examined. What concerns us here is *whether there is an antecedent efficacy* in this divine intention to bring mankind to its supernatural end and what the nature of this efficacy is. The fact that God determined that this end would be achieved, and determined this antecedent to a consideration of the free response of mankind is implied (at least in the fuller sense) by Genesis 3:15, where God said to Satan in the guise of the serpent: *I will put enmity between you and the woman, between your seed and her seed; He shall crush your*

---

[98] See for example Is. 2:1–4; 60:11 ff.; Zach. 8:20 ff.; 14:16 ff.; Matt. 28:19–20; 16:18–19; Mark 16:15. Also see A. Feuillet, "L'universalisme et l'élection d'Israel," *Bible et vie chrétienne*, no. 15 (1956, Sept.–Nov.), 7–25, and by the same author, "Le Règne de Dieu et la personne de Jésus d'après les Evangiles synoptiques," in *Introduction à la Bible*, 2 (ed. A Robert and A. Feuillet, Tournai, 1959), 771–84, 800–18.

head, and you shall lie in wait for his heel.[99] Since Satan's efforts
were to destroy mankind's achievement of the goal to which God
ordained it, this promise of enmity and the crushing defeat of
Satan is basically a promise that the human race shall achieve
the union with God to which God antecedently directed it, in
spite of the opposition of Satan. This is much more than a simple
prophecy of the future event; it is a divine determination that it
shall be so. Many other Old Testament prophesies concerning
Messianic times seem to express the same absolute determination
of God that his will that mankind gain its eternal destiny shall
prevail. For example, in a definitely Messianic psalm, the Lord
speaks to the king set up by him in Sion: *Ask of me and I will give
you the nations for an inheritance and the ends of the earth for
your possession. You shall rule them with an iron rod; you shall
shatter them like an earthen dish.*[100] And in the New Testament,
Christ does not only direct his disciples to teach his word to all
nations; he has decreed that this shall in fact come about and no
power shall obstruct it. He has said that *this gospel of the kingdom shall be preached in the whole world, for a witness to all
nations; and then will come the end.*[101] St. Paul shows the decree
of God when he writes *that a partial blindness only has befallen
Israel, until the full number of the Gentiles should be saved.*[102]
And St. John's vision of Christ in the Apocalypse as the invincible
king who shall overcome all opposition of Satan and his agents in
the world teaches the same truth. *These will fight with the Lamb,
and the Lamb will overcome them, for he is the Lord of Lords,
and the King of kings, and they who are with him, called, and
chosen, and faithful.*[103]

It is clear that God has determined antecedent to his consideration of how men would respond that he will gain his purpose with mankind and that no resistance will frustrate his
purpose, but what does this mean? Those who understand by predestination an antecedently, absolute divine decree hold also that
God has antecedently predestined a multitude of men definite in

---

[99] Gen. 3:15.
[100] Ps. 2:8–9; see Ps. 71; Gen. 49:10.
[101] Matt. 24:14.
[102] Rom. 11:25.
[103] Apoc. 17:14; see also 19:16.

number and the individuals who will compose it.[104] According to our understanding, this is not the case. The antecedent efficacy of God's will for mankind as a whole does not primarily concern the individual or a group of mankind at any particular stage in history, and thus it is consistent with this efficacy that an individual who had been predestined not reach heaven and a nation that had been chosen for some purpose in God's plan be rejected. What this efficacy means, in our opinion, is that the divine glory will be manifested by all mankind, by those who accept the divine will, but also by those who reject it; for they too shall show in their own lot the power and holiness of God and his mercy toward his chosen ones. It means more than this, however, for though God leaves individuals and groups free to reject his will that they achieve their supernatural goal, he has determined that a fitting number of men in fact reach eternal life. This is shown in the Old Testament doctrine of the remnant of Israel and of the nations that will be saved,[105] and it is taught by the New Testament. For example, St. Paul writes that Christ assigns men to different functions in the Church *for building up the body of Christ, until we all attain to the unity of the faith and of the deep knowledge of the Son of God, to perfect manhood, to the mature measure of the fullness of Christ.*[106] St. Paul means by this, not only or primarily the development of the individuals within the Mystical Body, but the development to its fulfillment of the body of Christ as a whole. He writes in this same passage that *from him [Christ] the whole body . . . derives its increase to the building up of itself in love.*[107] This fulfillment of the body of Christ which is achieved in a final state only in the next life is the object of God's governance on earth and thus of his will in such a way that he will seek it *until* it comes about. And the measure that determines the term of the building of this body is the fullness of its head, Christ, so it consists in the order within the body and the number and perfection of its members that manifests in a fitting way the perfection of Christ and thus of God. Thus God wills in an antecedently infallibly effective manner the achievement of that

[104] See *ST*, 1.23.6.

[105] See Amos. 5:15; Is. 4:3 ff.

[106] Eph. 4.13. See the whole passage, Eph. 4:12–16, and its parallel, Col. 2:18–19.

[107] Eph. 4:16.

created good which is constituted by this perfection of the Mystical Body of Christ or the Whole Christ. This term does not, of course, refer to only a portion of the men who reach beatitude, as though other men will reach it as well. The Whole Christ in heaven embraces all who gain eternal salvation, a fact that is shown in St. John's vision of the heavenly Jerusalem of perfect proportions in the Apocalypse.[108] This heavenly Jerusalem includes all who are in heaven and is the Church of Christ in its fulfillment; its perfect proportions show it to be the perfect fulfillment of an antecedent divine plan and purpose with mankind considered as a whole.

This means, then, that the created good in the *supernatural* order that, in creating the world, God antecedently wanted to come about to manifest his perfection will with absolute certainty be achieved because of the antecedent efficacy of the divine will that desires it. But does it mean that the perfection in the *natural* order that God antecedently willed to come about will occur with the same certainty and efficacy? It seems that it does mean this, since the good that is the end or divine goal intrinsic to the created order is a unitary goal that embraces in an ordered way both the supernatural and the natural perfection. Moreover, Christ, who is both the end of creation and the head of the Mystical Body, and thus the determinant of the fitting measure of created perfection God seeks, is the perfection of the universe in both the supernatural and the natural orders. And so it seems that the perfection of the body that is fitting to such a head includes the perfection of the natural order as it does that of the supernatural order. The latter does not supplant the former, but perfects or completes it. Since it completes it in a way that transcends the limits of nature's powers, it seems, too, that God's will seeks efficaciously that completion of nature that is within its limit or proper to it.

This, then, is the unitary end toward which humanity and lower creation that serves mankind is directed; and God, who wills this goal with antecedent efficacy, will bring it about with the same supreme power. Since this is so, he governs mankind in view of this end, and his eternal providential plan directs it to this end. Development toward this end in time is what is meant

---

[108] See Apoc. 21:9 ff.

by progress in the world, and of this and of each stage and act, whether social or individual, that promote it God is the antecedent mover and director as first cause. He causes it, however, through the acts of man as second cause, and so his governance and providence direct man to bring about this end in accord with his nature. Man's nature in the present order is fashioned for this goal by the natural and supernatural powers given it, and God's providence and governance provide mankind with means to fulfill its purpose that are proportionate to it under both these aspects. But by original sin humanity lost its supernatural powers, became weakened in its natural powers in their ordination of mankind to its ultimate natural goal, and became subject to Satan; and thus God's providence and governance are proportioned also to man's fallen condition. We shall indicate below more particularly several aspects of the way God's providence guides mankind to its goal in accord with man's being in the present order.

Since mankind has fallen by original and personal sins, God's fulfillment of his purpose (and mankind's cooperation with him in that) is not simply a positive development always expanding toward the end that will be achieved, but also an opposition to and conquest of forces actively obstructing the progress of humanity toward this end willed for it by God. These forces are in the service, consciously or not, of Satan who continues to exercise his opposition to the divine will for humanity, who seeks the destruction, not only of the individual but of society, and who uses means that attack, not only the individual, but society as a whole. For this larger purpose he uses such agents as governments that ascribe to themselves divine honors and promoters of false teachings, both of which tend to turn man from God.[109] God's achievement, then, of his goal takes on the character of a redemption that is extended throughout the world as a liberation from the powers of Satan and sin. Man's progress toward his goal as natural is also at the expense of the rejection of forces opposed to its achievement, and he stands in need of the help of grace for its achievement. So the progress to the goal God assigned to humanity is in the midst of

[109] See Apoc. 13:1–18 and commentaries, e.g., L. Cerfaux and J. Cambier, *L'Apocalypse de saint Jean lue aux crétiens* (Paris, 1955), pp. 116–23; H. M. Feret, *The Apocalypse of St. John* (Westminster, Md., 1958), c. 5, "The Activity of Satan in History," pp. 111–36.

conflict and the suffering that that entails, a conflict, however, in which Christ will inevitably triumph and the powers on earth opposed to the fulfillment of his goal be either converted or destroyed.

What we have previously seen of God's providence guiding man toward his natural fulfillment—namely that it is in accord with his nature as potential, as personal and social, and as free—helps us to understand Scripture's teaching concerning God's providence ordaining mankind to the end of the present order that is centrally supernatural. In the first place, Scripture teaches that Christ, through whom mankind achieves its end, was born in *the fullness of time*,[110] and Christ directs his ministers to extend his mission, under the power of his grace and his Spirit, to all the world in a gradual way. He told his apostles that *you shall be witnesses for me in Jerusalem and in all Judea and Samaria and even to the very ends of the earth.*[111] This shows that God ordains mankind to bring about its supernatural goal and its conquest of Satan in accord with the potential character of man. Thus, its goal will be achieved only through a succession of stages, of agents, and of acts or, in other words, through history, each stage of which is ordained to promote the final purpose of history through gaining the particular stage of growth immediately proper to it. Since Christ is the goal of God's purpose with mankind, he is the end of history; and history after him is directed to the achievement of the fitting perfection of his body, the completion of the number of the blessed in their proper order and their supernatural and natural perfection. History will continue *until the full number of the Gentiles should enter* [the Church] *and thus all Israel should be saved*,[112] the full number being determined by what is fitting to manifest the perfection of Christ. We may also note that, since this is the purpose of history or of time, time for each segment of humanity is in a way relative to the degree in which it approaches this goal.

It is the message of revelation that man was initially destined to gain the means of his supernatural perfection through birth from Adam and later, upon Adam's sin, through Christ and, in

---

[110] Gal. 4:4; Eph. 1:10.
[111] Acts 1:8.
[112] Rom. 11:25.

New Testament times, union with him in the Church. The man, however, to whom such membership in the Church is not available is given at least the essential requisites for his salvation. And this shows us that God's providence ordains mankind to its supernatural goal in accord with the personal and social character of man, for it is natural to man to receive the things that he needs for his perfection through the society to which he belongs. In this and many other ways revelation shows that God ordains mankind to its supernatural goal in accord with man's social character. A chosen segment of humanity is made the instrument through which God's saving word is extended to other parts of humanity. God's choice of the Jews in the Old Testament and definite segments of Gentiles in the period of the New Testament is not simply for their own benefit, but that they may be agents for the extension of his kingdom, and the extension of that kingdom is gained through the cooperation of those chosen by God with his divine purpose in history. Moreover, as God elevates certain groups of men to fulfill his purpose, he appoints individual religious leaders for men and makes them and their cooperation with him the means of his extension of his kingdom. Thus, too, man's personal fulfillment demands his cooperation with God's purpose in history, and his activity in history is meant to promote his personal fulfillment and not to destroy it.

Finally, Scripture teaches that on the failure of Adam to fulfill God's will, Christ was sent into the world. On the failure of the earlier plagues to move Pharaoh to allow the Jews to leave Egypt, later plagues were sent. On the failure of the Jews to believe in Christ, Gentiles were chosen in their place. And this is a process that seems, in a way, to continue in the history of the Church. By this we see that God's ordination of humanity as a whole to its supernatural end in the present order is in accord with the freedom of human nature, for he achieves his purpose through a succession of contingent causes or agents, each of which may fail (according to his ordinary providence), but the one that fails in cooperation with the religious mission given it by God is itself rejected at least partially and for a while, and it gives way to later agents until the purpose of God in history is achieved. The resistance offered by society and especially by its leaders at a particular stage of history to God's intention is not contrary to the antecedent infallible efficacy of God's will and providence, since God desires with such efficacy not the fulfillment of its mission by a particular part or stage of humanity, but only the ultimate achievement of mankind's goal. Nor does such a society escape from the sovereignty of God, since, by so resisting, it merits its own rejection and loss of this mission in history as well as a consequent loss of its more immediate natural good the preservation of which depends upon a certain degree of fidelity to God's law on the part of society. Moreover, God can turn the very resistance offered to him by such a society to serve the more perfect fulfillment of his purpose with mankind in accord with the mysterious ways of his divine providence, that will remain largely hidden from us until its manifestation at the end of history.

Conclusion

IN THIS study we have attempted to defend and explain to some extent the harmony that exists between God's initiative and man's freedom in the order of grace and nature. The problem was posed through a comparison of the explanation given by Banez with that given by Molina. The former took as its basic principle the primacy of God, while the latter began with the fact of man's freedom. After seeing the marked differences between these interpretations, we tried to show their relation to the opinions held in common by both sides that seemed to be the origin of the dispute. And it was the teaching of Scripture, tradition, and reason on these points that we primarily studied.

In our attempt to express the mystery in a way that was free from the weaknesses of both these explanations, we first studied the way it was expressed in Scripture and tradition. In the former we saw the essential unity and development that bound together the teaching in the Old Testament, the Gospels, and the epistles of St. Paul. We saw, too, that this scriptural expression of the mystery affirmed even more vigorously (though more concretely) than Banez and Molina the distinctive character of God's primacy and of man's freedom, while at the same time it preserved the harmony of their mutual relation in a way achieved by neither Banez nor Molina.

Tradition, we saw, was a gradual growth in the understanding of the mystery expressed by Scripture, though this growth was by no means always a placid and uninterrupted development. In the patristic period the differing explanations given of this mystery by the Greek Fathers and by Augustine showed the first example (and perhaps the determining first instance) of what later tradition was so frequently to repeat, namely, the phenomenon of somewhat opposed theories tending to explain the harmony of God's providence and man's freedom. Viewed more deeply, of course, these were mutually complementary theories that owed the opposition that did exist between them to the limitations of the explanation they gave of the mystery. We saw that the Church's expression of the doctrine of grace and free will in the fifth and sixth century Councils in the West canonized, as it were, a great part of Augustine's contribution to the subject, but refrained from accepting all of his teachings relevant to it. In later tradition we saw the continuing appearance of partially opposed theories that witness to the Church's teaching by the way they complement each other. We saw this in the ninth century controversy, the thirteenth century theologians, and the late medieval explanation. The Council of Trent, on the other hand, transcended the opposed explanations of the mystery, and in its doctrine on grace and free will it seems to be tradition's most perfect expression of the mystery. It seems also, by its explicit teaching and by the implications of this teaching, to support the interpretation we advanced for the scriptural doctrine. The later expressions of the mystery are in continuity with earlier theories, though they are different, too; this difference is due in part to the philosophical developments that molded them, in part to the greater clarification of the Church's teaching given by Trent, and in part to the controversies of the age in which they arose.

In the second section of our study we sought to offer some explanation of the mystery as we found it expressed in Scripture and tradition, through an examination of the naturally knowable realities involved and their analogical application to the supernatural mystery. At each stage of this study we presented the problem and our answer in relation to the explanations given by the Banezians and Molinists, and our own explanation in each case was developed in accord with the philosophical principles of St. Thomas. We analyzed the created and divine causality involved in free created acts, first as created operations, then as free immanent acts of the will, and finally as a series of acts through which the actualization of man's being was gained. And we found that the natural order of God's relation to the free act is in accord with the relation we found expressed by Scripture and the teaching of the Church, and that it helps toward a better understanding of the mystery of grace and free will. Then we examined the same free human acts in their relation to the divine uncreated acts, God's will, God's infallible knowledge, and God's providence directing the individual man and mankind as a whole to a supernatural last end. In this last part we saw the manner in which the natural relation of God's will and knowledge to the free created act helps to explain to some extent the scriptural doctrine of predestination, God's universal salvific will, and reprobation, all treated as they refer to the individual free creature within the context of God's universal providence for man.

Throughout this study we have tried to see that there is, in fact, harmony between God's act and man's freedom in the order of grace and of nature. We should conclude by asserting what is, of course, apparent throughout the study. This harmony is not one that exists between opposed principles or one that is preserved only with difficulty. Rather, God's controlling providence and his causality by grace within man's will is the source and condition of man's achievement of true freedom.

The purpose of man's freedom is the purpose of the will, of which freedom is a characteristic perfection. Hence, its purpose is the actualization of what is initially only potential within man, the completion and perfection of his humanity. Its object is the achievement of this in a manner proper to man, namely, through man's self-determination and self-movement toward it through his personal free choice of what perfects him. It is of the nature of man that this choice be motivated by the greater value this goal has when compared with those secondary goods man must sacrifice to gain it, and that man's actions be guided and energized through his understanding of and willing attraction to this value. What is true in this matter as it concerns the individual man is true, too, of mankind as a whole.

Of man's natural and supernatural being that specifies for him his goal and is the interior root of his desire to achieve it, of the exterior means and the interior powers that make man capable of gaining his perfection, and of the acts by which he moves himself toward it, God is the first cause through his divine wisdom and love. This being and these powers and acts of man are but participations of God's being, given to man by an act of divine love that has as its created goal man's sharing in God's perfection and happiness. God's governance and causality in time is, therefore, directed to the gradual realization of man's fulfillment through the cooperative acts of man it seeks to elicit. These acts God seeks to gain by aids adapted to man's being and specifically by the interior illumination of man's mind concerning what is for his welfare and the attraction exercised by grace upon man's will to draw him to love and desire effectively what is for his welfare. Man is completely dependent upon this initiative of God's providence and causality to guide and move himself toward his true completion. This is true in the order of nature and far more true of the order of grace. Even more it is true in the present order of fallen and redeemed nature. In this order there are many obstacles that stand in the way of man's true achievement of perfection and of individual and social freedom. The root of these obstacles is that ignorance of what is for his true welfare and that captivity to lower values, and lower impulses that flow from original sin, man's past personal sins, and the social disorder they have established. Man can never of himself overcome these obstacles to achieve a persistent exercise of freedom in accord with his dignity as man and, what is far greater, his dignity and destiny as a child of God through grace. It is only God's providential designs and his grace that give man the understanding and the effective love that will bring about his true self-determination of his life, one that is freed from the domination of alien forces and is freely directed to man's perfection. The harmony between man's free will and God is achieved finally in practice rather than in theory or explanation. It is achieved when man, recognizing the personal love of God as the source of all he is, freely gives himself out of love for God and his glory to be the limited perfection God has made him. It is such love that enables man to obey from a completely interior principle rather than from constraint, and so enables him in his obedience to be fully self-moving and self-determining.

The completion of man's freedom will be found only in the happiness of the next life. It is only there that man will possess perfectly that freedom which St. Thomas describes as self-determination and self-movement, since it is only there that man will have perfectly the supreme power to move himself to act, the power of God himself within his will and intellect. He will enjoy this freedom in the greatest degree in his love of God, since by the beatific vision he will be fully aware of how perfect God is and how he perfects man. And he will unwaveringly prefer God to all creatures, since he will see that all creatures are nothing save what they share of God's perfection.

Index

313

A NOTE ON THE TYPE

IN WHICH THIS BOOK WAS SET

This book is set in Caledonia, a Linotype face created in 1939 by W. A. Dwiggins, which is by far one of the best book types created in the last 50 years. It has a simple, hard-working, feet-on-the-ground quality and can be classed as a modern type face with excellent color and good readability. The designer claims Caledonia was created by putting a little of each of Scotch Roman, Bulmer, Baskerville and Bodoni together and producing a lively, crisp book type. This book was composed and printed by the York Composition Company, Inc., of York, Pa., and bound by Moore and Company of Baltimore. The typography and design of this book are by Howard N. King.